A COMMUNITY OF CHARACTER

A Community of Character

Toward a Constructive Christian Social Ethic

Stanley Hauerwas

UNIVERSITY OF NOTRE DAME PRESS

NOTRE DAME   LONDON

The author and publisher are grateful to the following for permission to reprint:

Theology Digest for "Jesus: The Story of the Kingdom"

Journal of Religious Ethics for "The Church in a Divided World: The Interpretative Power of the Christian Story"

Silver Burdett Company for "Character, Narrative, and Growth in the Christian Life" from their *Toward Moral and Religious Maturity*

Second Printing 1982
Third Printing 1983
Fourth Printing 1986

Library of Congress Cataloging in Publication Data

Hauerwas, Stanley, 1940–
    A community of character.

    1. Christian ethics. 2. Social ethics. I. Title.
BJ1251.H325   241   80-53072
ISBN 0-268-00733-0

To
DAVID BURRELL
AND
ROWAN GREER

*for the constancy of
their friendship and ministry*

Contents

Contents

Preface

It is common testimony that writing is a lonely enterprise, but I have found it also requires and engenders community. I literally cannot write, and more importantly, cannot think without friends. Moreover through writing I discover friends I did not even know I had. This is not simply because writing puts me in contact with people I would not otherwise have met, but I discover others who have also thought about these matters and thus are able to teach me to understand better what I think. I know that sounds odd, since people who write supposedly know what they think, but I find my own thought illumined by the community that writing creates. If that were not the case it would indeed be hard to sustain the task, as I find thinking and writing, which may be the same thing, never gets any easier.

Therefore, I depend and place heavy demands on my friends. Some may think that I write too quickly and too much without letting my work mature, but most of what you find here has gone through many drafts that my friends have had to read and reread. For I depend on them for criticism in the hope that I will not only know what I think but be able to say what I think well.

All this is but to say I have many people to thank for helping me finish this book. I am particularly grateful to the University of Notre Dame and the Association of Theological Schools for grants that enabled me to have the time to finish writing the book. I appreciate the opportunity to deliver some of these essays as lectures at the College Theology Society, Gettysburg College, Wake Forest, Duke, University of Illinois Medical School, St. Louis University, St. Michael College, and Valparaiso. They provided me with fresh ears and criticism that often forced me to rethink and rewrite. In that respect, I also owe a debt of gratitude to my students at Notre Dame and the University of Chicago, who always seem ready to tell me where I am wrong.

As in my past work I have unashamedly made use of my colleagues at Notre Dame. But then what are friends for if you cannot use them? Rev. David Burrell has continued to bear the brunt of this burden. I have been thinking with him so long I am no longer sure where his ideas begin and mine end. Moreover, he has served as chairman of the Department of Theology at

Notre Dame for nine years, making possible a rich intellectual context for me and my colleagues. In spite of considerable administrative burdens, he has never failed to find the time to help me think and write better. I am deeply in his debt.

Thomas Shaffer, now professor at Washington and Lee Law School, has continually provided valuable criticism and insights. I am particularly grateful to Dr. David Solomon of the Notre Dame Philosophy Department, as he has saved me from many egregious philosophical errors. Even though he never fails to respect the primacy of my theological agenda, my disinterest in pursuing certain philosophical problems must pain him. I particularly appreciate, therefore, his continued willingness to make me a better philosopher. Others to whom I owe much are Dr. Peri Arnold, Dr. Robert Wilken, Rev. James Burtchaell, Rev. Enda McDonagh, and, of course, Dr. John Howard Yoder.

My debts, however, reach far beyond Notre Dame. Dr. James Childress has been my good friend and critic for almost eighteen years. That he has been so is a testimony to his patience and kindness. James Gustafson, Paul Ramsey, James McClendon, Charles Reynolds, David Smith, Richard Bondi, Fred Carney, William May, and Rev. Richard Neuhaus continue to be crucial conversation partners. Thomas Ogletree and Gene Outka have helped me immensely, not only by their taking the time to write critiques of my work, but through long conversations about the nature and task of Christian ethics. The debt I owe Alasdair MacIntyre is apparent on almost every page of this book, but I cannot let this opportunity pass without indicating my gratitude for his criticism and encouragement. Dr. Mary Jo Weaver has been a constant friend and critic whose Catholic sensibilities have often helped me appreciate what I would otherwise not see at all.

I have the good fortune to have a publisher and editor, James Langford, who not only provides invaluable suggestions about the form and style of my work, but also about the substance. I deeply appreciate his encouragement and support. I am also indebted to Ann Rice, of the Notre Dame Press, for her patience and skill in making this text read better than I can write.

In that respect, the reader also owes a large debt of gratitude to my wife. One of the unhappy effects of the women's movement has been the hesitancy of men to thank their wives for help with their work as well as the general assistance we each need for sustaining a family. I thank God that neither Anne nor I feel the need to apologize for our love and dependence on one another. Finally, I wish to thank my son Adam for his relish for life and his unflagging enthusiasm to get on with the adventure.

Introduction

1. The Central Contention

Though this book touches on many issues it is dominated by one concern: to reassert the social significance of the church as a distinct society with an integrity peculiar to itself. My wish is that this book might help Christians rediscover that their most important social task is nothing less than to be a community capable of hearing the story of God we find in the scripture and living in a manner that is faithful to that story. The church is too often justified by believers, and tolerated by nonbelievers, as a potential agent for justice or some other good effect. In contrast, I contend that the only reason for being Christian (which may well have results that in a society's terms seem less than "good") is because Christian convictions are true; and the only reason for participation in the church is that it is the community that pledges to form its life by that truth.

The subtitle used here, "Toward a Constructive Christian Social Ethic," denotes no new emphasis or direction in my work, but indicates my continuing interest in examining what it means to claim that Christian convictions are true. Indeed, I have been uneasy with the description of my work as "ethics," especially if ethics denotes a discipline separate from theology. I understand myself as a theologian and my work as theology proper. I have accepted the current academic designation of "ethics" only because as a theologian I am convinced that the intelligibility and truthfulness of Christian convictions reside in their practical force. Thus this book ranges from rather abstruse issues in christology to a discussion about why we should have children. I am convinced that such matters are interrelated and that the truthfulness of Christian convictions resides in understanding how they are related.

The justification for calling this book "social ethics" is that I wish to show why any consideration of the truth of Christian convictions cannot be divorced from the kind of community the church is and should be. Though much of the book involves a running critique of liberal political and ethical theory, my primary interest is to challenge the church to regain a sense of the significance of the polity that derives from convictions peculiar to Christians. In particular I have tried to show why, if the church is to serve our liberal society or any society, it is crucial for Christians to regain an appropriate sense of separateness from that society. I have tried to suggest that such a "separateness" may involve nothing more nor less than the Christian community's willingness to provide hospitality for the stranger—particularly when that stranger so often comes in the form of our own children.

Because I contend that Christian ethics is distinctive, I make no pretense to be doing ethics for everyone. However this does not mean I think my arguments can be judged only from within Christianity. Arguments are arguments, and I assume that my appeal to Christian convictions does not render my position immune from challenges by those who do not share those convictions. Moreover, it is my hope, and even my prayer, that something in all this may be of use to those who do not share the convictions of the Christian community. My insistence on the distinctiveness of Christian ethics is not meant to be defensive or exclusionary, but derives from a frank, and I hope honest, recognition that, methodologically, ethics and theology can only be carried out relative to a particular community's convictions.

That is what this book is all about. As theology it implicitly involves a critique of a great deal of contemporary theology that seeks to uncover the meaning of Christian "symbols" or "myths," as if those symbols had no social function. Though seldom noticed, the reductionistic tendencies of modern theology are as much due to the loss of a sense of the political significance of the Gospel as to the more strictly "intellectual" challenges engendered by the Enlightenment. The proponents of "political theology" are therefore right to claim that the meaning and truth of Christian convictions cannot be separated from their political implications. They are wrong, however, to associate "politics" only with questions of social change. Rather the "political" question crucial to the church is what kind of community the church must be to be faithful to the narratives central to Christian convictions.

Any community and polity is known and should be judged by the kind of people it develops. The truest politics, therefore, is that concerned with the development of virtue. Thus it is not without reason that Christians claim that the polity of the church is the truest possible for human community. It is from the life of the church, past, present, and future, that we even come to understand the nature of politics and have a norm by which all other politics can be judged. That the church has often failed to be such a polity is without question, but the fact that we have often been less than we were meant to be should never be used as an excuse for shirking the task of being the people of God.

If my suggestion that a polity should be about forming virtuous people has a dangerous ring, it is because we value our "freedom." But it is the burden of this book to show that "freedom" comes only by participation in a truthful polity capable of forming virtuous people. Such a people, contrary to our liberal presuppositions, are not characterized by an oppressive uniformity. Rather the mark of a truthful community is partly seen in how it enables the diversity of gifts and virtues to flourish. Therefore the church is not only a community of character but also a community of characters, since we are convinced that God rejoices in the diversity of spirits who inhabit his church.

Many are convinced that "social ethics" should be primarily concerned with policies and strategies to insure just distribution of resources, or the theories of justice presupposed by such policies. It is certainly not my intention to deny the importance of such issues, but when they are treated as the fundamental questions of social ethics, the contribution of the church is easily lost. For Christians no theory of justice can substitute for their experience and their discussion of what implications their convictions have regarding how they should care for and treat others within and without their community. Thus many who write as Christian social ethicists do so as if the nature and existence of the church as a separated community is irrelevant to the "real" issues of social change involved in trying to make a society more just. But if, as I contend, the church is a truthful polity, the most important social task of Christians is to be nothing less than a community capable of forming people with virtues sufficient to witness to God's truth in the world. Put as directly as I can, it is not the task of the church to try to develop social theories or strategies to make America work; rather the task of the church in this country is to become a polity that has the character necessary to survive as a truthful society. That task carried out would represent a distinctive contribution to the body politic we call America.

2. The Argument in Outline

It is unnecessary to repeat here all the arguments I develop in this work. The thesis at the beginning of the first chapter, as well as that chapter itself, is meant to introduce the reader to many major themes in the book. Indeed, if the reader, on finishing the book, were to reread the first chapter, I suspect it would take on new meaning. I shall refrain from trying to spell out in any precise way the relation between the various chapters, for it would add little and it seems wiser to let each reader make those connections.

The arguments I employ to present and defend my position are complex and interdependent in a manner that makes it difficult to separate out their various elements. Claims about the meaning and importance of narrative and its relation to character and the virtues, questions about the foundation of ethics and moral rationality, issues in christology and political theory, the significance of the virtues of hope and patience for the Christian life, judgments about the nature of contemporary American life, the meaning of marriage and the value of the family for the church are just some of the themes I develop and intertwine in what I hope adds up to a compelling argument. I do not apologize for its complexity, for I cannot now see how the contentions of the book could otherwise be adequately presented. It might be useful to indicate briefly the rationale for and relation between the three major parts of the book, however, for in doing so I can provide a broad outline of the argument.

Part I introduces the basic methodological claim that every community and polity involves and requires a narrative. The distinctive character of the church's social ethics does not follow from the fact that it is a narrative-formed community, but rather from the *kind* of narrative that determines its life. I try to suggest the content and nature of that narrative by discussions of christology and the authority of scripture. These issues are normally considered the domain of theology rather than social ethics, but my aim is to demonstrate that they involve questions about what kind of community the church must be to rightly tell the stories of God. I attempt to spell out further the nature and political relevance of a community formed by the story witnessed to by scripture by contrasting that story and community with the more limited meaning of "politics" as understood by American liberalism. In particular I challenge the dominant assumption of contemporary Christian social ethics that there is a special relation between Christianity and some form of liberal democratic social system.

Part II is primarily concerned with working out and defending the philosophical implications of my claims concerning the significance of narrative and virtue for social ethics. In particular I argue that the desire to provide a foundation for ethics abstracted from any community's history and tradition in fact produces an ethic that makes sense only on the basis of a particular political tradition—i.e., liberalism. What is even more destructive, the separation of ethics and politics results in the loss of any sense, either theoretical or practical, of the significance of virtue for political community. Concretely, I try to show how theories of moral development, such as Lawrence Kohlberg's, which are inspired by liberal political presuppositions, distort the nature of our moral existence. Such accounts of moral growth are antithetical to the Christian insistence that moral progress comes only as we learn to acknowledge our life as a gift.

Moreover I argue that the close connection between virtue and politics required by the Christian narrative enables the church to understand and face truthfully the divided character of the world. The "ethical problem" is not one just of decision, but of description and interpretation as well. The virtues required by the Christian story and community, therefore, are statements about the kind of world we live in and the kind of persons we must be to live morally in such a world.

Though Part II involves a critique of current moral theory my primary purpose is not polemical, but constructive. I am trying to suggest the recognition of the historic character of human existence demands an appreciation of narrative which shapes an ethics of virtue. As a means to develop this claim I discuss Aristotle's and Aquinas' still unsurpassed analysis of how the virtues are acquired and form the self. By criticizing Aristotle's and Aquinas' assumption concerning the unity of the virtues, I try to suggest how their analysis presupposed as well as required a narrative.

Theologically in this section I argue that the virtues of hope and patience are central for the story that forms the church. For the adventure in which the church plays a part is sustained only through hope, a hope disciplined by patience, since we recognize that our hope is eschatological—that is, that we live in a time when that for which we hope is not soon to become a full reality. This situation underwrites the political significance of the church as that institution which is able to create the time and space necessary for us to be faithful to the story of God.

Part III concerns the family, sex, and abortion. Some may wonder how this section is relevant to the book's central argument, for it is currently assumed that such issues are purely private. Nothing, however, could be further from the truth, and it is my belief that the more theoretical argument in the first two sections stands or falls with the perspective I develop about these more practical issues.

The family is a crucial focus for Christian social ethics, not in the hackneyed sense of being the ''bedrock'' of society, but because the kind and form of family created by the church is one of the most telling marks of the church's social significance. I think this is particularly clear when the church's understanding of the family as an intergenerational institution is contrasted with the current understanding of the family as an interpersonal association between individuals.

Given the position I am trying to develop, the family becomes the decisive indicator of a society's polity. In particular, the narrative nature of the family is crucial if the moral traditions and habits of a society are to be preserved and to grow. From this perspective questions of justice are secondary to questions of the nature and significance of the family. We must be able to encourage the virtues of patience and hope if we are to be capable of sustaining the Christian understanding of the significance of having and rearing children. The essays on sex and abortion continue to develop the theme of the political significance of the family. In these essays I have tried in particular to demonstrate how an appreciation of the political nature of an ethics of sex and abortion is necessary if we are to understand the distinctive light Christian convictions provide about these matters.

3.   A Personal Word

This is my third collection of essays. Some have suggested that it is time I cease writing essays and try to pull my position together in one book. I plan to write a short book in the near future attempting just that. But I think such a book cannot replace the kind of work I have tried to do in these and my past essays. For the essays make clear to the reader that my project is anything but finished and I am anything but certain how it is all to be ''put together.'' If the essays do what they are supposed to do, they invite the reader to enter into the project and to think through the issues, perhaps better than I have been able to do. Without presuming that my work has anything like the power of Wittgenstein's, it remains my intention that the essays, like his aphorisms, should make the reader think at least as hard, if not harder, than the author has about the issues raised.

Some may feel, however, that the unfinished character of my work derives from a more profound problem than my preference for the essay. For it is not clear from which church or tradition I write or for what church or group I write. I am, after all, a (Southern) Methodist of doubtful theological background (when you are a Methodist it goes without saying you have a doubtful theological background); who teaches and worships with and is sustained morally and financially by Roman Catholics; who believes that the most nearly faithful form of Christian witness is best exemplified by the often unjustly ignored people called anabaptists or Mennonites. In short my ecclesial preference is to be a high-church Mennonite. It is no wonder that some find it hard to pin down my position.

I have no intention of trying to justify my ambiguous ecclesial position. Perhaps the reason I stress so strongly the significance of the church for social ethics is that I am currently not disciplined by, nor do I feel the ambiguity of, any concrete church. Such a position could be deeply irresponsible, as it invites intellectual dishonesty. If I have written honestly it is only because I find the church so profoundly exists in the lives of my friends and others whom I hardly know but who hold me accountable. Because of them I understand myself to occupy the office of theology—and thus to be in service— rather than simply being another ''thinker.'' And because I wish to be faithful to that office, I find I must think and write not only for the church that does exist but for the church that should exist if we were more courageous and faithful.

PART ONE

The Narrative Character of Christian Social Ethics

1. A Story-Formed Community: Reflections on *Watership Down*

1. Ten Theses Toward the Reform of Christian Social Ethics

Luther began the Reformation by posting ninety-five theses which were meant to reform the church. I will begin with ten theses, but I can hardly claim to have such a grand project in view. While my theses are meant to be reforming, I propose only to challenge some of the conventional wisdom about the nature of Christian social ethics. Primarily I choose this manner for a mundane reason—I have more to say than I can defend here, but I intend to say it anyhow.[1] In this way, I can at least expose the central presuppositions of my position in spite of my inability to defend it.

1.1   The social significance of the Gospel requires the recognition of the narrative structure of Christian convictions for the life of the church.

Christian social ethics too often takes the form of principles and policies that are not clearly based on or warranted by the central convictions of the faith. Yet the basis of any Christian social ethic should be the affirmation that God has decisively called and formed a people to serve him through Israel and the work of Christ. The appropriation of the critical significance of the latter depends on the recognition of narrative as a basic category for social ethics.

1.2   Every social ethic involves a narrative, whether it is concerned with the formulation of basic principles of social organization and/or concrete policy alternatives.

The loss of narrative as a central category for social ethics has resulted in a failure to see that the ways the issues of social ethics are identified—i.e., the relation of personal and social ethics, the meaning and status of the individual in relation to the community, freedom versus equality, the interrelation of love and justice—are more a reflection of a political philosophy than they are crucial categories for the analysis of a community's social ethic. The form and substance of a community is narrative dependent and therefore what counts as "social ethics" is a correlative of the content of that narrative.

1.3   The ability to provide an adequate account of our existence is the primary test of the truthfulness of a social ethic.

No society can be just or good that is built on falsehood. The first task of Christian social ethics, therefore, is not to make the "world" better or more just, but to help Christian people form their community consistent with their conviction that the story of Christ is a truthful account of our existence. For as H. R. Niebuhr argued, only when we know "what is going on," do we know "what we should do," and Christians believe that we learn most decisively "what is going on" in the cross and resurrection of Christ.

1.4   Communities formed by a truthful narrative must provide the skills to transform fate into destiny so that the unexpected, especially as it comes in the form of strangers, can be welcomed as gift.

We live in a world of powers that are not our creation and we become determined by them when we lack the ability to recognize and name them. The Christian story teaches us to regard truthfulness more as a gift than a possession and thus requires that we be willing to face both the possibilities and threats a stranger represents. Such a commitment is the necessary condition for preventing our history from becoming our fate.

1.5   The primary social task of the church is to be itself—that is, a people who have been formed by a story that provides them with the skills for negotiating the danger of this existence, trusting in God's promise of redemption.

The church is a people on a journey who insist on living consistent with the conviction that God is the lord of history. They thus refuse to resort to violence in order to secure their survival. The fact that the first task of the church is to be itself is not a rejection of the world or a withdrawal ethic, but a reminder that Christians must serve the world on their own terms; otherwise the world would have no means to know itself as the world.

1.6 Christian social ethics can only be done from the perspective of those who do not seek to control national or world history but who are content to live "out of control."

To do ethics from the perspective of those "out of control" means Christians must find the means to make clear to both the oppressed and oppressor that the cross determines the meaning of history.[2] Christians should thus provide imaginative alternatives for social policy as they are released from the "necessities" of those that would control the world in the name of security. For to be out of control means Christians can risk trusting in gifts, as they have no reason to deny the contingent character of our existence.

1.7 Christian social ethics depends on the development of leadership in the church that can trust and depend on the diversity of gifts in the community.

The authority necessary for leadership in the church should derive from the willingness of Christians to risk speaking the truth to and hearing the truth from those in charge. In societies that fear the truth, leadership depends on the ability to provide security rather than the ability to let the diversity of the community serve as the means to live truthfully. Only the latter form of community can afford to have their leaders' mistakes acknowledged without their ceasing to exercise authority.

1.8 For the church to be, rather than to have, a social ethic means we must recapture the social significance of common behavior, such as acts of kindness, friendship, and the formation of families.

Trust is impossible in communities that always regard the other as a challenge and threat to their existence. One of the profoundest commitments of a community, therefore, is providing a context that encourages us to trust and depend on one another. Particularly significant is a community's determination to be open to new life that is destined to challenge as well as carry on the story.

1.9 In our attempt to control our society Christians in America have too readily accepted liberalism as a social strategy appropriate to the Christian story.

Liberalism, in its many forms and versions, presupposes that society can be organized without any narrative that is commonly held to be true. As a result it tempts us to believe that freedom and rationality are independent of narrative—i.e., we are free to the extent that we have no story. Liberalism is, therefore, particularly pernicious to the extent it prevents us from understanding how deeply we are captured by its account of existence.

1.10   The church does not exist to provide an ethos for democracy or any other form of social organization, but stands as a political alternative to every nation, witnessing to the kind of social life possible for those that have been formed by the story of Christ.

Too often the church's call for justice unwittingly reinforces liberal assumptions about freedom in the name of the Gospel. The church's first task is to help us gain a critical perspective on those narratives that have captivated our vision and lives. By doing so, the church may well help provide a paradigm of social relations otherwise thought impossible.

Each of these theses obviously involves highly controversial claims that require disciplined philosophical and theological argument.[3] However, I do not intend to supply that kind of discursive argument here, as I am more interested in trying to illuminate what the theses mean and how they are interrelated. In order to do that I am going to tell a story about some very special rabbits that inhabit the world of Richard Adams' book *Watership Down*.[4] I cannot hope to convince you of the correctness of my theses by proceeding in this way, but I do hope at least to help you understand what they might mean. Moreover it seems appropriate for someone who is arguing for the significance of narrative to use a story to make his point.

2.   The Narrative Context of Social Ethics

It would be misleading if I were to give the impression that I am using *Watership Down* only because it offers an entertaining way to explain my theses. The very structure of the book provides an account of the narrative nature of social ethics that is seldom noticed or accounted for by most political and social theory. Adams' depiction of the various communities in *Watership Down* suggests that they are to be judged primarily by their ability to sustain the narratives that define the very nature of man, or in this case rabbits. Thus *Watership Down* is meant to teach us the importance of stories for social and political life. But even more important, by paying close attention to

Watership Down we will see that the best way to learn the significance of stories is by having our attention drawn to stories through a story.

Watership Down is at once a first-class political novel and a marvelous adventure story. It is extremely important for my theses that neither aspect of the novel can be separated from the other. Too often politics is treated solely as a matter of power, interests, or technique. We thus forget that the most basic task of any polity is to offer its people a sense of participation in an adventure. For finally what we seek is not power, or security, or equality, or even dignity, but a sense of worth gained from participation and contribution to a common adventure. Indeed, our "dignity" derives exactly from our sense of having played a part in such a story.

The essential tie between politics and adventure not only requires a recognition of the narrative nature of politics, but it also reminds us that good politics requires the development of courage and hope as central virtues for its citizens. As we will see, *Watership Down* is primarily a novel about the various forms of courage and hope necessary for the formation of a good community. Adventure requires courage to keep us faithful to the struggle, since by its very nature adventure means that the future is always in doubt. And just to the extent that the future is in doubt, hope is required, as there can be no adventure if we despair of our goal. Such hope does not necessarily take the form of excessive confidence; rather it involves the simple willingness to take the next step.

Watership Down begins with the exodus of a group of rabbits from a well-established warren on the slim basis that one rabbit with the gifts of a seer thinks that warren is threatened with destruction. As a result the group is forced to undergo a hazardous journey in search of a new home, ultimately Watership Down, as well as the dangerous undertaking of securing does from the militaristic warren of Efrafa. It is important to note that the rabbits of *Watership Down* do not leave their old warren as a people (or a rabbithood). They leave only as a group of individuals joined together by their separate reasons for leaving the warren. All they share in common is the stories of the prince of the rabbits, El-ahrairah. They become a people only as they acquire a history through the adventures they share as interpreted through the traditions of El-ahrairah.

For this reason *Watership Down* is fundamentally a political novel. It is concerned with exploring what conditions are necessary for a community to be a viable polity. Thus much of the novel depicts contrasting political communities which bear striking similarities to past and present polities. Sandleford, the warren they must leave, is a traditional class society whose government is determined by loyalty to a strong and competent leader. On their journey they later encounter a warren that has no name but bears a striking resemblance to the modern welfare state in which the freedom of the individual is primary. And the third warren, Efrafa, from which they try to secure some does, is a highly organized and regimented totalitarian society. Each of these societies is characterized by a virtue that embodies its ideal form—i.e., loyalty, tolerance, and obedience.[5]

Even though none of these communities perfectly represent actual societies, they provide imaginative paradigms for tendencies in every polity, whether it be a state, a corporation, or a church. Basic issues of political theory, such as the relation of individual to community, the primacy of freedom and its relation to justice, and the legitimation of power, are obviously present in each of the communities described. It is extremely tempting, therefore, to interpret *Watership Down* as a commentary on current actual and theoretical political options. Only Watership Down, itself, seems to be an exception, as it is presented as an ideal society for which there is no ready analogue.

Without denying that *Watership Down* is a ready source of standard forms of political reflection, the book has a deeper insight to offer for social ethics. Although each society can be characterized by traditional political opinions and theory, Adams' intention is to show how such discussions are subordinate to the ability of a community to live and tell its stories. As we shall see, the crux of the viability of any society in *Watership Down* is whether it is organized so as to provide for authentic retelling of the stories of the founder and prince of rabbit history, El-ahrairah.

Adams is trying to help us understand politics not only as it organizes people for particular ends, but also as it forms them to be inheritors and exemplifications of a tradition. In other words, Adams suggests that society can best be understood as an extended argument, since living traditions presuppose rival interpretations. Good societies enable the argument to continue so that the possibilities and limits of the tradition can be exposed. The great danger, however, is that the success of a tradition will stop its growth and in reaction some may deny the necessity of tradition for their lives. The truthfulness of a tradition is tested in its ability to form people who are ready to put the tradition into question, or at least to recognize when it is being put into question by a rival tradition. Of course, as we shall see, some traditions lapse into complete incoherence and can be recovered only by revolutionary reconstitution.[6]

2.1   *The Story-Shaped World of Rabbits*

This is all very abstract, but I can make it concrete by calling your attention to the way stories function for the rabbits of *Watership Down*. First, there are several things about rabbits that we need to know. A rabbit is constantly in danger. Mr. Lockley, a famous expert on rabbits, suggests that rabbits are as strong as the grass (p. 167). That is certainly not very strong, for the strength of grass consists primarily in being able to grow back after it has been stepped on, cut, or burned. And just as grass grows back, so rabbits depend on their stubborn will to survive against all odds. And they are able to survive because they are fast, constantly vigilant, and have the wit to cooperate with one another.

Another thing we need to know about rabbits, at least the rabbits of *Watership Down*, is that they are lovers of stories. There is a saying among them that a rabbit "can no more refuse to tell a story than an Irishman can refuse to fight" (99). Rabbits are, to be sure, creatures of nature, but their "nature" is the result of the interaction of their biology with their stories. Their stories serve to define who they are and to give them skills to survive the dangers of their world in a manner appropriate to being a rabbit.

The first story told in *Watership Down* is the story of the "Blessing of El-ahrairah." I suspect it is not accidental that this is the first story told by the rabbits who left Sandleford, as all new communities must remind themselves of their origin. A people are formed by a story which places their history in the texture of the world. Such stories make the world our home by providing us with the skills to negotiate the dangers in our environment in a manner appropriate to our nature.

The "Blessing of El-ahrairah" is the account of Frith, the god of the rabbits, allocating gifts to each of the species. In the beginning all animals were friends and El-ahrairah was among the happiest of animals, as he had more wives than he could count and his children covered the earth. They became so numerous that Frith told El-ahrairah he must control his people, since there was not enough grass for everyone. Rabbits, however, are intent on living day by day, so El-ahrairah refused to heed Frith's warning.

Frith, therefore, called a meeting at which he gave a gift to all animals and birds. El-ahrairah, busy dancing, eating, and mating was late to the meeting. As a result he heard too late that Frith had given the fox and the weasel cunning hearts and sharp teeth, the cat silent feet and eyes to see in the dark. El-ahrairah, realizing that Frith was too clever for him, tried to hide by digging a hole. But he had only dug half way when Frith came by, finding El-ahrairah with only his back legs and tail above ground. El-ahrairah responded to Frith's greeting by denying he was El-ahrairah, but Frith, feeling a kinship with this mischievous creature, blessed El-ahrairah's bottom and legs, giving them strength and speed. El-ahrairah's tail grew shining and his legs long and powerful, and he came running out of his hole. And Frith called after him, "El-ahrairah, your people cannot rule the world, for I will not have it so. All the world will be your enemy, Prince with a Thousand Enemies, and whenever they catch you they will kill you. But first they must catch you, digger, listener, runner, prince with the swift warning. Be cunning and full of tricks and your people shall never be destroyed'' (37).

It is tempting to reduce this story to its obvious etiological elements—why rabbits have white tails and strong legs. But this would distort the importance of the story as the source of skills for rabbits to negotiate their world. The rabbit's task is not to try to make the world safe, but rather to learn to live in a dangerous world by trusting in stories, speed, wit, and each other's gifts. Rabbit existence in the world is contingent upon the utilization of the lessons learned from the story of their origin and the gifts provided by Frith. These gifts determine their very character as wild creatures of the world. When they try to exist without relying on their gifts they pervert their nature and become tame, subject to even more tyrannical powers.

2.2   The Substitution of Security for Narrative

Only against this background can we understand the events at Sandleford which resulted in the escape of some of the rabbits. Not that Sandleford was an extraordinarily unjust society, but it was no longer sensitive to the dangers which always threaten. In effect the destruction of Sandleford was the result of its success.

In many ways Sandleford was a typical rabbit community. At the top of the social order was the chief rabbit, named Threarah but usually referred to as "*the* Threarah." "He had won his position not only by strength in his prime, but also by level-headedness and a certain self-contained detachment, quite unlike the impulsive behavior of most rabbits. It was well known that he never let himself become excited by rumor or danger. He had coolly—some even said coldly—stood firm during the terrible onslaught of the myxomatosis, ruthlessly driving out every rabbit who seemed to be sickening. He had resisted all ideas of mass emigration and enforced complete isolation in the warren, thereby almost certainly saving it from extinction" (19). As a result the rabbits at Sandleford assumed that their security rested in their loyalty to the Threarah.

Directly under the chief rabbit were the owsla—"a group of strong or clever rabbits—second year or older—surrounding the chief rabbit and his doe and exercising authority" (14). The character of the owsla vary from one warren to another, but at Sandleford the owsla had a rather military character; their chief duties were seeing that no one tried to leave the warren and protecting the Threarah. The rest of the warren were rank and file ordinary rabbits or "outskirters." Basically, at Sandleford Warren the higher the status, the more favorable share in the distribution of goods. A member of the owsla, for instance, had the advantage over the outskirter in silflay (feeding), mating, and choice of burrows. The primary occupation of the rabbits at Sandleford had become competition for the higher status positions. The rule of the warren thus became "These are my claws, so this is my cowslip [a particular delicacy among rabbits]. These are my teeth, so this is my burrow" (14).

Stories of El-ahrairah still seem to have been told at Sandleford, but primarily as a means of entertainment, for it was assumed that the warren had weathered the worst. Into this warren were born Hazel, destined to become the chief rabbit of Watership Down, and Fiver, his strange brother who had the ability to sense the future. It was because Hazel had learned to trust his brother's gift that he paid attention to Fiver's premonition that Sandleford must be abandoned because it was soon to be destroyed. The basis for Fiver's concern was nothing but a piece of wood nailed to a post with the unintelligible script: "THIS IDEALLY SITUATED ESTATE, COMPRISING SIX ACRES OF EX- CELLENT BUILDING LAND, IS TO BE DEVELOPED WITH HIGH CLASS MODERN RESIDENCES BY SUTCH AND MARTIN, LIMITED, OF NEWBURY, BERKS" (16).

Hazel convinced one of the lesser members of the owsla, Bigwig, to obtain an audience with the Threarah so Fiver might deliver his prediction of destruction of Sandleford and the recommendation that they leave the warren. The Threarah, however, said in an extremely understanding voice:

> "Well, I never did! That's rather a tall order, isn't it? What do you think yourself?"
>
> "Well, sir," said Hazel, "my brother doesn't really think about these feelings he gets. He just has the feelings, if you see what I mean. I'm sure you're the right person to decide what we ought to do."
>
> "Well, that's very nice of you to say that. I hope I am. But now, my dear fellows, let's just think about this a moment, shall we? It's May, isn't it? Everyone's busy and most of the rabbits are enjoying themselves. No elil [enemies] for miles, or so they tell me. No illness, good weather. And you want me to tell the warren that young—er— young—er—your brother here has got a hunch and we must all go traipsing across country to goodness knows where and risk the conse- quences, eh? What do you think they'll say? All delighted, eh!"
>
> "They'd take it from you," said Fiver suddenly.
>
> "That's very nice of you," said the Threarah again. "Well, perhaps they would, perhaps they would. But I should have to consider it very carefully indeed. A most serious step, of course. And then—" (20–21)

Suddenly Fiver went into a trance, which gave the Threarah the excuse to dismiss them and to reprimand Bigwig for letting such unstable characters into his presence. That very stability provided by the Threarah for his warren made it impossible to be open to the seer. The stories of El-ahrairah had been domesticated in the interest of security and Sandleford thus became victimized by its own history. In fact its history had become its fate; it was no longer able to use tradition to remain open to the gifts and dangers of rabbit existence.

2.3   The Loss of Narrative as the Loss of Community

It might be expected that this would have happened at Sandleford; the purpose of most societies is to provide a sense of security. For example, though we are constantly reminded of the violent and accidental deaths occurring around us every day, most of us live as if we assume our social order is secure and we are safe. We can do this because we assume death happens only to other people. We are even sometimes vaguely comforted by reports of others' deaths, as such reports confirm our own presumption that we are protected by a magical invulnerability. Absorption into most societies is training in self-deception as we conspire with one another to keep death at bay. Ironically, the more our societies confirm this self-deception, the more dangerous our life becomes. We lose the skill of recognizing what danger is and where it lies. Deception becomes the breeding ground for injustice, since the necessity to hide the dangers of our world make it impossible to confront those aspects of our social order which impose unequal burdens on others.[7] Our conspiracy for safety forces us to see our neighbor as a stranger.

Good and just societies require a narrative, therefore, which helps them know the truth about existence and fight the constant temptation to self-deception. Lack of such a narrative is most vividly depicted in *Watership Down* by the encounter of Hazel and his friends with a warren which, because it lacks a name, I call Cowslip's warren, after the rabbit who invited them to rest there. The primary characteristic of this warren was that it allowed each rabbit to do as he pleased. The story that formed them was that they were no longer dependent on tradition. They assumed the way to stop history from becoming their fate, as it had for Sandleford, was to have no history at all.[8]

Before I can describe Hazel and his friends' encounter with Cowslip's warren I need to introduce two other characters crucial to the story. In addition to Fiver and Bigwig (who had left with them because he obviously had no future at Sandleford), there was Pipkin and Blackberry. Pipkin, like Fiver, was small; unlike Fiver, he had no gift or skill. Though weak and constantly in need of help, in some ways he is the most crucial rabbit for the determination of the character of Watership Down warren. By endangering themselves in order to care for Pipkin, the ability was developed to be open to the stranger.[9]

Blackberry, who was as rational as Fiver was insightful, also joined the band. It was he who helped them escape from Sandleford without having to leave the completely exhausted Pipkin behind by suggesting the extraordinary idea of floating Pipkin across a stream on a board. It should be noted that Blackberry's gift, like all the other rabbits, is a manifestation of the virtue of courage. For Blackberry's intelligence is more than brightness; it stems from his willingness to consider all aspects and alternatives of a problem, even when they are extremely threatening or unpleasant.

It is therefore to Blackberry that Hazel turns for advice on whether they should accept Cowslip's invitation to rest at his warren. It is a very tempting invitation, since they are tired after their escape from Sandleford, they are out in the open, and a storm is soon to break. Blackberry argues,

> There's no way of finding out whether he's to be trusted except to try it. He seemed friendly. But then, if a lot of rabbits were afraid of some newcomers and wanted to deceive them—get them down a hole and attack them—they'd start—wouldn't they?—by sending someone who was plausible. They might want to kill us. But then again, as he said, there's plenty of grass and as for turning them out or taking their does, if they're all up to his size and weight they've nothing to fear from a crowd like us. They must have seen us come. We were tired. Surely that was the time to attack us? Or while we were separated, before we began digging? But they didn't. I reckon they're more likely to be friendly than otherwise. There's only one thing that beats me. What do they stand to get from asking us to join their warren? (75)

Blackberry's logic is perfect, of course, but we shall see it leads to exactly the wrong conclusion. Fiver is convinced that they should not enter the warren, but as usual he is unable to give any reason and thus Hazel decides to follow Blackberry's advice. On entering they discover that there are some very "unnatural" aspects to the warren. It is roomy and well made with a large central room, but very few rabbits inhabit it. Those that do live there are big, but they are not, as Bigwig observes, very strong—nor do they have any fighting skill.

Even stranger is the absence of a chief rabbit, as everyone is allowed to do as he pleases.[10] Cowslip's invitation to them, for example, was made on his own initiative. They need no chief rabbit, because there is no need to worry about foxes or other enemies (elil). It seems that there is a man who kills all the rabbits' enemies and provides the rabbits with the best kind of food. They no longer need to hunt for their food, and they have even begun the unheard-of practice of storing food underground.

Stranger yet is that stories are no longer told. To repay them for their hospitality, Hazel suggests that Dandelion, a fellow escapee from Sandleford who has a gift for telling stories, entertain everyone by telling the story of the King's lettuce.[11] It is a story of how El-ahrairah bet Prince Rainbow not only that he could steal King Darzin's lettuce, which was guarded night and day, but that he could even get the king to deliver the lettuce to Rainbow's warren. If he won the bet Prince Rainbow must let the rabbits out of the marshes to breed and make homes everywhere.

El-ahrairah's plan was to have Rabscuttle, his close friend and commander of his owsla, gain entrance to the palace by playing with some children and then being taken inside with them. Once admitted to the palace, Rabscuttle found his way to the royal storeroom and made some of the lettuce bad, so that King Darzin would fall ill after eating it. At that moment El-ahrairah arrived disguised as a physician and examined the king. He told the king that the lettuce was infected by the dreaded virus Lusepedoodle, and because the infected lettuce is particularly deadly to rabbits he advised the king to send the lettuce to his worst enemy, El-ahrairah. The king thought this was a splendid idea, so El-ahrairah had the lettuce delivered and thus freed his people from the marshes.

Now this is obviously a story to delight any rabbit, for it is a story of wit, cunning, and humor that reinforces the point that the rabbits must survive using the gifts provided to El-ahrairah by Frith. After hearing the story, however, the rabbits of the warren of freedom were less than enthusiastic.

> "Very nice," said Cowslip. He seemed to be searching for something more to say, but then repeated, "Yes, very nice. An unusual tale."
>
> "But he must know it, surely?" muttered Blackberry to Hazel.
>
> "I always think these traditional stories retain a lot of charm," said another of the rabbits, "especially when they're told in the real old-fashioned spirit."
>
> "Yes," said Strawberry [another rabbit of the warren of freedom]. "Conviction, that's what it needs. You really have to *believe* in El-ahrairah and Prince Rainbow, don't you? Then all the rest follows."
>
> "Don't say anything, Bigwig," whispered Hazel: for Bigwig was scuffling his paws indignantly. "You can't force them to like it if they don't. Let's wait and see what they can do themselves." Aloud, he said, "Our stories haven't changed in generations, you know. After all, we haven't changed ourselves. Our lives have been the same as our fathers' and their fathers' before them. Things are different here. We realize that, and we think your new ideas and ways are very exciting. We're all wondering what kind of things *you* tell stories about."
>
> "Well, we don't tell the old stories very much," said Cowslip. "Our stories and poems are mostly about our own lives here. . . . El-

ahrairah doesn't really mean much to us. Not that your friend's story wasn't very charming," he added hastily.

"El-ahrairah is a trickster," said Buckthorn, "and rabbits will always need tricks."

"No," said a new voice from the further end of the hall, beyond Cowslip. "Rabbits need dignity and, above all, the will to accept their fate." (108)

The speaker was Silverweed, the poet of this strange warren, who recited a poem that ended, as follows:

I am here, Lord Frith, I am running through the long grass.
O take me with you, dropping behind the woods,
Far away, to the heart of light, and the silence.
For I am ready to give you my breath, my life,
The shining circle of the sun, the sun and the rabbit. (110)

As Silverweed recited his poem, Fiver became increasingly nervous and finally caused a stir by bolting out of the warren. Hazel joined him and Fiver again emphasized that they must leave because Silverweed spoke the truth for this warren—that rabbits in such a warren must learn to accept death. Hazel and Bigwig ignored this warning, however, since they continued to think that the warren might make a good permanent home.

Their hopes were quickly dashed when the next morning Bigwig was caught in a snare prepared by the farmer who protected the rabbits. Only by an extraordinary effort were they able to chew through the stake holding the snare and free Bigwig. Even that would not have been possible if Pipkin's small size had not allowed him to get down to where the peg was narrower. Though in bad shape, Bigwig immediately wanted to turn on Cowslip and the others for leading them into such a warren. Fiver restrained him, however, by constructing the story of this strange warren.

He suggested that the warren was the result of the farmer's realization that he did not have to keep rabbits in hutches if he fed and looked after some wild ones. He would snare a few from time to time, but not enough to frighten them away. As a result of the farmer's plan, the rabbits grew big and forgot the ways of wild rabbits. They also forgot El-ahrairah, for they had no use for tricks and cunning. Moreover, they had no need for a chief rabbit,

for a Chief Rabbit must be El-ahrairah to his warren and keep them from death: and here there was no death but one, and what Chief Rabbit could have an answer to that? Instead, Frith sent them strange singers, beautiful and sick like oak apples, like robins' pincushions on the wild rose. And since they could not bear the truth, these singers, who might in some other place have been wise, were squeezed under the terrible weight of the warren's secret until they gulped out fine folly—about dignity and acquiescence, and anything else that could make believe that the rabbit loved the shining wire. But one strict rule they had; oh, yes, the strictest. No one must ever ask where another rabbit was and anyone who asked "Where?"—except in song or a poem—must be silenced. To say "Where?" was bad enough, but to speak openly of the wires—that was intolerable. For that they would scratch and kill. (123–124)

Because they could not ask where anyone was, they also lost the most precious skill rabbits needed to survive—cooperation and friendship. One could not risk getting too close to another rabbit, for that one might be the next to die. Friendship implies mutual giving of aid, but these rabbits had accepted a social system that required them to look after themselves first.[12] Cowslip had extended invitations to strangers only because that increased the odds that they themselves would not be caught in the wire. Deception, thus, became the rule for this society, since the truth would require a concern for and trust in one another which these "free" rabbits were no longer able to give. It was no wonder that such rabbits were not interested in hearing about the adventures of Hazel and his friends or even those of El-ahrairah, for who "wants to hear about brave deeds when he's ashamed of his own, and who likes an open, honest tale from some one he's deceiving" (124).

Finally taking Fiver's advice, Hazel and the others decided to leave immediately. However just as they were leaving, Strawberry, whose doe had recently been snared, asked to be allowed to join their company. Just as the others were about to say "no," Hazel simply said, "You can come with us" (126). Thus, still homeless but in the beginnings of community, they accept a stranger even though he was a former enemy. As we shall see, their willingness to take the stranger into their midst becomes the very means of their survival.

3.   Gifts, Strangers, and Community

By attending to the stories in *Watership Down* I have tried to illuminate the relation between narrative and social ethics. For whatever else can be said about Sandleford and Cowslip's warren, their inability to maintain the traditions of El-ahrairah resulted in the corruption of rabbit community and nature.[13] There is, in addition, a close connection between the ability to tell the stories of El-ahrairah and the capacity to recognize and use gifts that often come in the form of friends. In order to better appreciate this connection we need to pay closer attention to the character of Hazel's warren, Watership Down.

The scraggly band of rabbits who escaped from Sandleford changed through their journey. The demands of their journey gave them not only renewed appreciation of the significance of El-ahrairah for their lives, but they learned to trust and depend on one another. They had become tenacious in their struggle for survival, and now understood one another and worked together:

> The truth about the warren had been a grim shock. They had come closer together, relying on and valuing each other's capacities. They knew now that it was on these and nothing else that their lives depended, and they were not going to waste anything they possessed between them. In spite of Hazel's efforts beside the snare, there was not one of them who had not turned sick at heart to think that Bigwig was dead and wondered, like Blackberry, what would become of them now. Without Hazel, without Blackberry, Buckthorn and Pipkin—Bigwig would have died. Without himself he would have died, for which else, of them all, would not have stopped running after such punishment? There was no more questioning of Bigwig's strength, Fiver's insight, Blackberry's wits or Hazel's authority. (129)

Such a community depends on the ability to trust in the gifts each brings to the group's shared existence. They must in a certain sense "be out of control," often dependent on luck to help them over their difficulties. "Luck" can be a very misleading term; more properly, it is fate put to good use by the imaginative skills acquired through a truthful tradition.[14] This is perhaps best exemplified in the story of the "Black Rabbit of Inlé."

3.1 How Gifts Make Us Safe

The story of the Black Rabbit of Inlé is told at the most dangerous moment in the lives of the rabbits who constitute the Watership warren. It is a time when their lives hang in the balance, a time when they will be called upon to take chances that few rabbits are willing to take. For they must secure does from Efrafa if their warren is to have a future. Bigwig insists that the story of the Black Rabbit be told, even though he will soon enter Efrafa itself in hopes of convincing some does to escape.

The story begins with King Darzin, tired of being constantly tricked and outwitted by El-ahrairah, finding an effective way to stop the rabbits from leaving their warrens. The rabbits are beginning to die of starvation and disease because they can silflay only with the greatest difficulty. El-ahrairah concludes that his only hope is to journey far away to the cold and lifeless world of the Black Rabbit of Inlé. It is his plan to bargain with the Black Rabbit to free his people.

We cannot take the time to speculate about the ontological status of the Black Rabbit, but we should know that he is fear and everlasting darkness. Though a rabbit himself, the Black Rabbit hates the rabbits and wants their destruction. Even in his darkness he serves Lord Frith by doing his appointed task, which is "to bring about what must be" (274). As it is said,

> We come into the world and we have to go: but we do not go merely to serve the turn of one enemy or another. If that were so, we would all be destroyed in a day. We go by the will of Black Rabbit of Inlé and only by his will. And though that will seems hard and bitter to us all, yet in his way he is our protector, for he knows Frith's promise to the rabbits and he will avenge any rabbit who may chance to be destroyed without the consent of himself. Anyone who has seen a gamekeeper's gibbet knows what the Black Rabbit can bring down on elil [fox] who think they will do what they will. (274–275)

El-ahrairah, with Rabscuttle, undertakes the arduous journey to the warren of the Black Rabbit so that he can offer his life in return for the lives of the rabbits. But the Black Rabbit points out that El-ahrairah's life is his already so he has nothing with which to bargain. El-ahrairah tries to trick the Black Rabbit into taking his life by enticing him into several contests, but El-ahrairah only succeeds in losing his whiskers, tail, and ears; finally he even tries to contract the dreaded white blindness. The Black Rabbit, although still completely unmoved by El-ahrairah's suffering, suddenly declares that "this is a cold warren: a bad place for the living and no place at all for warm hearts and brave spirits. You are a nuisance to me. Go home. I myself will save your people. Do not have the impertinence to ask me when. There is no time here. They are already saved" (283).

Because of El-ahrairah's weakened condition it took many months for him and Rabscuttle to find their way home. Their wits were confused, and they survived only by other animals giving them direction and shelter. After finding their way back to the warren at last, they discover that all their old companions have been replaced by their children. Rabscuttle, inquiring about the whereabouts of Loosestrife, one of the captains of owsla during the fighting, was asked

> "What fighting?"
> "The fighting against King Darzin," replied Rabscuttle.
> "Here, do me a favor, old fellow, will you?" said the buck. "That fighting—I wasn't born when it finished."
> "But surely you know the owsla captains who were?" said Rabscuttle.
> "I wouldn't be seen dead with them," said the buck. "What, that white-whiskered old bunch? What do we want to know about them?"
> "What they did," said Rabscuttle.

"That war lark, old fellow?'' said the first buck. "That's all finished now. That's got nothing to do with us.''

"If this Loosestrife fought King What's-His-Name, that's his business,'' said one of the does. "It's not our business, is it?''

"It was all a very wicked thing,'' said another doe. "Shameful, really. If nobody fought in wars, there wouldn't be any, would there? But you can't get old rabbits to see that.'' (284–285)

El-ahrairah did not try to respond to this conversation, but rather found a place under a nut bush to watch the sun sink into the horizon. In the failing light he suddenly realized that Lord Frith was close beside him.

"Are you angry, El-ahrairah?'' asked Lord Frith.

"No, my lord,'' replied El-ahrairah, "I am not angry. But I have learned that with creatures one loves, suffering is not the only thing for which one may pity them. A rabbit who does not know when a gift has made him safe is poorer than a slug, even though he may think otherwise himself.'' (285)

Lord Frith then gave El-ahrairah a new tail and whiskers, and some new ears that had a little starlight in them, but not enough to give away a clever thief like El-ahrairah.

Hazel's warren is Adams' attempt to show what kind of community might result in a group of rabbits that have learned that a gift has made them safe. But the recognition that their lives depend on luck causes them to work all the harder to make the necessities of their lives their destiny. Thus after a long journey they come to a particularly lonely and well-protected down that Fiver feels is the right place for their home. " 'O Frith on the hills!' cried Dandelion. 'He must have made it, for us!' 'He may have made it, but Fiver thought of it for us,' answered Hazel.'' (133)

Any community that has a story such as "The Black Rabbit of Inlé'' in its tradition can never assume that it "has control'' of its existence.[15] As much as Hazel and his companions desire a warren they can call home, they know also that they can never cease being on a journey. When rabbits yearn for and try to secure complete safety, their nature is perverted. They can only continue to rely on their wit and their courage and each other. Bigwig is particularly interesting in this respect, since we see him learn to trust not only in his strength and bravery but wit and the aid of others—particularly those who seem to have little to contribute.

3.2 Tradition, Nature, and Strangers

Often, claims that tradition is central for political and social theory are meant to have a primarily conservative effect. We are supposed to be convinced that we must do as our fathers did if we are to preserve those values we hold dear, or that society is too complex for planned change because such change always has effects which we have not anticipated. Those who would change society too often feel the only alternative to the conservative option is to find a rational basis for social organization which is tradition-free. As a result they become captured by a tradition which is more tyrannical because it has the pretense of absolute rationality. In contrast, I am suggesting that substantive traditions are not at odds with reason but are the bearers of rationality and innovation. The establishment of the warren at Watership Down is particularly interesting in this regard, because here we see tradition opening up new ways to distinguish the ''natural from the unnatural'' and to turn the stranger into a friend.

For example, among rabbits it has always been assumed that digging warrens is does' work. The rabbits which established Watership Down, however, were all bucks. Hazel argued that in the warren of ''freedom'' many things the rabbits did were ''unnatural,'' but ''they'd altered what rabbits do naturally because they thought they could do better. And if they altered their ways, so can we if we like'' (138). Blackberry, following the example of how the warren of the snares was dug around tree roots to allow for the large common room, began to dig amid some birch trees. Soon all the bucks followed his example.

It is important to note, however, that Hazel does not assume that rabbit nature is infinitely malleable. As we will see later, Efrafa is condemned because it is an ''unnatural society'' led by a fierce leader, General Woundwort, who is so unrabbitlike he will even fight a dog. In Efrafa, Woundwort has attempted to organize his rabbits so that they will feed at a certain time, rest at a certain time, breed at a certain time, and so on. Nature has its revenge, and rabbits in this strange warren actually die of old age, and overpopulation causes does to reabsorb their litters. For long ago El-ahrairah made a bargain with Frith that rabbits should not be born dead or unwanted; thus if there was little chance of a decent life it was a doe's privilege to take them back into her body unborn.[16]

The other crucial aspect of Watership Down is that this community continues to remain open to the stranger. Soon after finishing some of the runs they find a bloodied rabbit near death. As they tend to him they realize that it is Captain Holly of the Sandleford owsla. He tells them that Sandleford has indeed been razed by men and that only a few, like himself, were able to escape. Such a destruction is almost impossible for rabbits to comprehend, ''for all other elil do what they have to do and Frith moves them as he moves us. They live on the earth and they need food. Men will never rest till they've spoiled the earth and destroyed the animals'' (157). Holly, even though he is a sign of this terrible and incomprehensible evil, is allowed to join Watership Down. In doing so he apologizes to Bigwig for attacking him as he tried to leave Sandleford: "It wasn't I who tried to arrest you—that was another rabbit, long, long ago" (166). He has been changed through his suffering, and as such becomes a crucial member of Hazel's warren.

It is one thing to accept an enemy who is like yourself, but it is quite another to help those with whom you share no kinship at all. But that is what Hazel does, for just as El-ahrairah had been helped by other animals, so he helps a mouse escape a kestrel by letting him hide in one of the warren's runs. Hazel's friends are offended by this, but Hazel explains that in their situation they cannot "afford to waste anything that might do us good. We're in a strange place we don't know much about and we need friends. Now, elil can't do us good, obviously, but there are many creatures that aren't elil—birds, mice, yonil [hedgehogs] and so on. Rabbits don't usually have much to do with them, but their enemies are our enemies, for the most part. I think we ought to do all we can to make these creatures friendly. It might turn out to be well worth the trouble" (169). And soon another mouse tells them where to find the grass rabbits favor most.

Even more astounding is Hazel's rescue of Kehaar, a gull which had been injured by a cat so it could not fly. Condemned to the ground, he faced a certain death, but Hazel offers him hospitality in the warren. The rabbits even undertake an activity degrading to rabbits to insure his survival—digging for worms so that Kehaar might eat. Soon, however, Kehaar and Bigwig become fast friends, because it is apparent they share the same aggressive spirit toward life. Moreover, as we shall see, Kehaar proves invaluable in helping them secure the does from Efrafa.

For Hazel knew that as soon as they became reasonably safe the bucks would become lonely for does. While rabbits tend not to be romantic in matters of love, they have a strong will to perpetuate their own kind. Without does, no matter how good a life they established for themselves at Watership Down, nothing would matter. Rabbits survive by their dogged refusal to let the dangers of their life stop them from carrying on—which is nowhere more centrally embodied than in their insistence on having and rearing children. For it is only through their children that the tradition can be carried on. To fail to have children would be tantamount to rejecting the tradition and would symbolize a loss of confidence in their ability to live out that tradition.

As soon as Kehaar is well Hazel asks him to act as their air force and search the countryside for does. He finds two groups of does: some hutch rabbits at the nearby Nuthanger Farm and at the huge warren of Efrafa some distance away. Hazel chooses Holly to lead a group to Efrafa to see if they might be willing, because of overcrowding, to allow some does to leave. However they find that not only is that not possible, but that Efrafa represents an even more frightening political alternative than either Sandleford or the warren of freedom.

4.   Leadership, Community, and the Unexpected

Though the differences between the communities in Watership Down are pronounced, the most dramatic contrast is certainly between Efrafa and Cowslip's warren, the former being completely organized with each rabbit belonging to a "Mark" with a captain who controlled every movement, and the latter being characterized by almost complete freedom. The former was led by a fierce and dominant rabbit, and the latter has no chief rabbit at all. But in spite of their difference, in neither were the stories of El-ahrairah told. In Efrafa, Bigwig discovers that does recite poetry such as:

> Long ago
> The Yellowhammer sang, high on the thorn.
> He sang near a litter that the doe brought out to play,
> He sang in the wind and the kittens played below.
> Their time slipped by all under the elder bloom.
> But the bird flew away and now my heart is dark
> And time will never play in the fields again. . . .
>
> The frost is falling, the frost falls into my body.
> My nostrils, my ears are torpid under the frost.
> The swift will come in the spring, crying "News! News!
> Does, dig new holes and flow with milk for your litters."
> I shall not hear. The embryos return
> Into my dulled body. Across my sleep
> There runs a wire fence to imprison the wind
> I shall never feel the wind blowing again. (323)

The loss of the narratives of El-ahrairah at Efrafa has also resulted in a transformation of the position of chief rabbit. For General Woundwort is unlike any rabbit ever seen. As Holly described him, "He was a fighting animal—fierce as a rat or a dog. He fought because he actually felt safer fighting than running. He was brave, all right. But it wasn't natural; and that's why it was bound to finish him in the end. He was trying to do something that Frith never meant any rabbit to do" (467).

As a kitten Woundwort had seen his father killed by a man and his mother wounded and as a result eaten by a fox. He was rescued by a man who fed him so well he grew huge and strong. At the first opportunity he escaped, took over a small warren by killing any that would challenge his rule, and then united by force his warren with others close by to form Efrafa. In order to secure Efrafa he would not allow any further runs to be dug or the warren extended in any way—to do so might attract elil.

Though Woundwort had immense personal power, his only object seems to have been to create a warren that would be free from the tragedy of his parents. He not only organized the warren into Marks, but he gathered around him the bravest and most ferocious rabbits and made each of them live only to gain his special favor. These rabbits were sent out on periodic patrols so that any elil in the area could be reported and that strange rabbits, who might unwittingly attract elil, could be killed or captured. For Efrafa's safety depended on seeing that the unexpected did not upset their defenses. The primary rule for the owsla had become "Anything out of the ordinary is a possible source of danger" and must thus be reported immediately (338).

It would be a mistake, therefore, to think Woundwort an evil tyrant, for he was more like Dostoyevski's Grand Inquisitor. Nor is there any doubt that his leadership produced results, for Efrafa was remarkably safe. The only difficulty was that his followers lost the ability to think and make decisions for themselves. As a result, they increasingly had to bring every matter for judgment to Woundwort himself.

The kind of leadership that Hazel provides is obviously in marked contrast to Woundwort. Although he cares no less than Woundwort for his warren, he is prepared to take the risk of depending on others for the governance of the warren. In fact Hazel was never actually made chief rabbit, he just became chief rabbit because he seemed to know how to make the decisions that made best use of everyone's talents and he made everyone face up to the necessities of their situation. As they left Sandleford, for example, they became hopelessly lost and some wanted to simply quit or go back. It was Hazel, as lost as the rest, who said,

> "Look, I know there's been some trouble, but the best thing will be to try to forget it. This is a bad place, but we'll soon get out of it."
> "Do you really think we will?" asked Dandelion.
> "If you'll follow me now," replied Hazel desperately, "I'll have you out of it by sunrise." (62)

Note that Hazel's primary gift is his willingness to accept responsibility for making the decision when it is not clear what it is that should be done. Moreover he is willing to pay the price for such decisions; thus it is he who refuses to leave Pipkin behind at the stream on the grounds that "I got Pipkin into this and I'm going to get him out" (44). Other than this he lacks any characteristic that should make him the chief rabbit: He is not as strong as Bigwig, lacks Fiver's insight, and is not as clever as Blackberry. All he is able to do is say "Let's do this," and then live with the consequences. After finally making it through the night they reach some hills and Blackberry says, "Oh, Hazel, I was so tired and confused, I actually began to wonder whether you knew where you were going. I could hear you in the heather, saying 'Not far now' and it was annoying me . . . . I should know better. Frithrah, you're what I call a chief rabbit" (64).

Of course as a leader Hazel does have one advantage as he is the rare leader who has the courage to listen to the seer. Listening to seers is tricky business and is safely done only in a community on which the seer's insight depends. At one point, when Hazel decides against Fiver's advice, to be as heroic as Bigwig and raid the Nuthanger Farm for the hutch does, the whole affair almost ends in disaster. He was simply not cut out to be a hero. His leadership and his use of Fiver's insight depends on his willingness to rely on the other's strength. A leader like Woundwort simply cannot understand this kind of leadership. Thus in the final confrontation between Efrafa and Watership Down he is shocked to discover that Bigwig is not the chief rabbit.

Note that Hazel is not only an exceptional chief rabbit, but that it takes an exceptional community to have a chief rabbit like Hazel. This is nowhere better exemplified than in the decision to raid Efrafa to get the does. After Holly's attempt to secure the does peacefully from Efrafa it was clear to Hazel that their only hope was in trying to get the does by a raid. His plan was to have Bigwig join Efrafa as a stray rabbit and then with the help of Kehaar to escape with some willing does during a silflay. Hazel's problem was that he did not know how to get the group back to Watership Down without Woundwort's patrols overtaking them. But the incompleteness of the plan did not prevent them from following Hazel; they would simply have to trust in luck.

To make a very complicated story short, Bigwig was able to successfully join Efrafa and secure the cooperation of some does in an escape attempt. However the escape was complicated by an unexpected thunderstorm, which they were nonetheless able to turn to their advantage, and they were aided by an attack by Kehaar. Their escape, however, was successful only because Blackberry discovered a boat and saw how to use it.

During their march back to Watership Down an event occurred which graphically highlights the difference between Efrafa and Watership Down. In spite of the difficulty that escape from Efrafa involved, Bigwig took the time to also rescue Blackavar, a rabbit who had been severely beaten by Woundwort's guards for trying to escape earlier. As they proceeded home Blackavar warned them that they needed to be particularly careful of fox in a certain area, since he had learned that fox were often there through his patrols with General Woundwort. However Hazel decided that, because of the risk of General Woundwort catching them, they needed to go through the area, and as a result a fox got one of the does that had come with them from Efrafa. Later when Bigwig suggested to Blackavar that they should have taken his advice, he was shocked to discover that Blackavar had forgotten he had ever given the warning. Hyzenthlay, a doe from Efrafa, was able to explain why,

"In Efrafa if a rabbit gave advice and the advice wasn't accepted, he immediately forgot it and so did everyone else. Blackavar thought what Hazel decided; and whether it turned out later to be right or wrong was all the same. His own advice had never been given."

"I can't believe that," said Bigwig. "Efrafa! Ants led by a dog! But we're not in Efrafa now. Has he really forgotten that he warned us?"

"Probably he really has. But whether or not, you'd never get him to admit that he warned you or to listen while you told him he'd been right. He could no more do that than pass hraka underground."

"But you're an Efrafan. Do you think like that, too?"

"I'm a doe," said Hyzenthlay. (390)[17]

It was thus that the rabbits of Watership Down learned how extraordinary the form of leadership was they had evolved. Hazel was remarkable for his willingness to learn from all the others and for his ability to see that Watership Down depended on all their gifts. But even more remarkable was the character of their community manifested in their ability to sustain a leader who could make mistakes and yet remain chief rabbit. Security could not be bought by placing absolute faith in any chief rabbit, no matter how talented or brave, but their security depended on their willingness to trust one another with their lives. For only then could their various talents be coordinated in service for the community.

4.1   The Insufficiency of Power as Coercion

It is well known that Stalin responded to Pius XII's condemnation with the taunting question about how many divisions had the pope. Most assume that Stalin's point is well taken, for without divisions the power of the church counts for nothing. Yet in spite of all appearances to the contrary, Stalin's response masks the fundamental weakness of his position. A leadership which cannot stand the force of truth must always rely on armies. But a leadership so constituted must always respond to the slightest provocation that might reveal its essential weakness.

So Woundwort could not afford to let the successful escape of the does go unnoticed. His power depended on never being embarrassed, and the rabbits of Watership Down had done just that.

"And fools we look now," said Woundwort. "Make no mistake about that. Vervain will tell you what the Marks are saying—that Campion was chased into the ditch by the white bird and Thlayli [Bigwig's alias while in Efrafa] called down lightening from the sky and Frith knows what besides."

"The best thing," said old Snowdrop, "will be to say as little about it as possible. Let it blow over. They've got short memories." (416)

But Woundwort could not settle for that, and he made plans to send out patrols to find Watership Down. As he said, "I told Thlayli I'd kill him myself. He may have forgotten that but I haven't."

Hazel, confronting Woundwort on such a patrol, tried to make peace.

"You're General Woundwort, aren't you? I've come to talk to you."

"Did Thlayli send you?" asked Woundwort.

"I'm a friend of Thlayli," replied the rabbit. "I've come to ask why you're here and what it is you want."

"Were you on the riverbank in the rain?" said Woundwort.

"Yes, I was."

"What was left unfinished there will be finished now," said Woundwort. "We are going to destroy you."

"You won't find it easy," replied the other. "You'll take fewer rabbits home than you brought. We should both do better to come to terms."

"Very well," said Woundwort. "These are the terms. You will give back all the does who ran from Efrafa and you will hand over the deserters Thlayli and Blackavar to my owsla."

"No, we can't agree to that. I've come to suggest something altogether different and better for us both. A rabbit has two ears; a rabbit has two eyes, two nostrils. Our two warrens ought to be like that. They ought to be together—not fighting. We ought to make other warrens between us—start one between here and Efrafa, with rabbits from both sides. You wouldn't lose by that, you'd gain. We both would. A lot of your rabbits are unhappy now and it's all you can do to control them, but with this plan you'd soon see a difference. Rabbits have enough enemies as it is. They ought not to make more among themselves. A mating between free, independent warrens—what do you say?"

At that moment, in the sunset on Watership Down, there was offered to General Woundwort the opportunity to show whether he was really the leader of vision and genius which he believed himself to be, or whether he was no more than a tyrant with the courage and cunning of a pirate. For one beat of his pulse the lame rabbit's idea shone clearly before him. He grasped it and realized what it meant. The next, he had pushed it away from him. . . .

"I haven't time to sit here talking nonsense," said Woundwort. "You're in no position to bargain with us. There's nothing more to be said. Thistle, go back and tell Captain Vervain I want everyone up here at once."

"And this rabbit, sir," asked Campion. "Shall I kill him?"

"No," replied Woundwort. "Since they've sent him to ask our terms, he'd better take them back.—Go and tell Thlayli that if the does aren't waiting outside your warren, with him and Blackavar, by the time I get down there, I'll tear the throat out of every buck in the place by ni-Frith tomorrow." (421–422)

I cannot take the time to provide the details of Woundwort's attack, but Hazel and the rabbits of Watership Down were able to defeat him. They were able to do it because Bigwig used cunning as well as his strength and was able to fight Woundwort in a place where he could not make full use of his bulk; Hazel, taking a cue from Dandelion's telling of "Rowsby Woof and the Fairy Wogdog" (a story of El-ahrairah's tricking a dog into letting him steal the cabbage he was supposed to guard for his master), unleashed a dog from Nuthanger Farm that drove off Woundwort for the last time. (We are later told, however, that his body was never found. As a result he was said to live alone as a killer of elil. To this day does threaten their kittens by saying that if they do not behave the General will get them.)

4.2 *Peace*

Peace, as has often been pointed out, is not the absence of disorder and cannot be built on injustice. Rather peace is built on truth, for ultimately order which is built on lies must resort to coercion. It is, therefore, remarkable that peace seems to have come to Watership Down. Campion, one of Woundwort's former Mark captains, has now become chief rabbit of Efrafa. Hazel's original peace proposal is put into effect and a new warren made up of Efrafans and Downers is established between the two warrens. Hazel, never one to overlook a good thing, even incorporates some of the advantages of Efrafa, such as hiding run openings.

Perhaps even more significant is a suggestion that someday there might be peace between humans and rabbits. In the process of releasing the dog, Hazel was attacked by a cat and saved by a little girl at the farm. She saw that his wounds were cared for by a veterinarian, who released Hazel not far from Watership Down. It is not much, but it is something.

A yet more profound peace awaits Hazel, because a few springs later, as Hazel is dozing in his burrow, a stranger with ears shining with strange silver light comes and invites Hazel to join his owsla. Thus Hazel's part in the story ends, but his life has contributed to the further telling of the story. One lovely spring day shortly before his death, he and Silver come across one of the does of the warren telling her litter a story:

> "So after they had swum the river, El-ahrairah led his people on in the dark, through a wild, lonely place. Some of them were afraid, but he knew the way and in the morning he brought them safely to some green fields, very beautiful, with good, sweet grass. And here they found a warren; a warren that was bewitched. All the rabbits in this warren were in the power of a wicked spell. They wore shining collars round their necks and sang like the birds and some of them could fly. But for all they looked so fine, their hearts were dark and tharn [forlorn]. So then El-ahrairah's people said, 'Ah, see, these are the wonderful rabbits of Prince Rainbow. They are like princes themselves. We will live with them and become princes, too.'
>
> "But Frith came to Rabscuttle in a dream and warned him that the warren was enchanted. And he dug into the ground to find where the spell was buried. Deep he dug, and hard was the search, but at last he found that wicked spell and dragged it out. So they all fled from it, but it turned into a great rat and flew at El-ahrairah. Then El-ahrairah fought the rat, up and down, and at last he held it, pinned under his claws, and it turned into a great white bird which spoke to him and blessed him."
>
> "I seem to know this story," whispered Hazel, "But I can't remember where I've heard it." (470–471)

But at least as long as the story was told, his children would know that a gift had made them safe.

5.   Are Rabbits Relevant to Christian Social Ethics?

I have reached the end of my tale (no pun intended) and some may feel that I have failed to make my case. But remember I have only told the story of the rabbits to illustrate and illuminate my theses. The story was not meant to demonstrate that the theses must be accepted. That must await more direct theological and philosophical arguments.

Even allowing such a qualification, you may feel that the story is less than illuminating, because the life of rabbits is so discontinuous with our life. After all, rabbits, even the extraordinary rabbits of *Watership Down,* have no complex economic interaction, they do not form political parties, they do not invent complex forms of technology or machinery. They are simply too unlike us to even illustrate my case.

Without trying to claim a strong continuity between rabbits and us, I think at least the suggestion that we, no less than rabbits, depend on narratives to guide us has been made. And this is particularly important to Christians, because they also claim that their lives are formed by the story of a prince. Like El-ahrairah, our prince was defenseless against those who would rule the world with violence. He had a power, however, which the world knew not. For he insisted that we could form our lives together by trusting in truth and love to banish the fears that create enmity and discord. To be sure, we have often been unfaithful to his story, but that is no reason for us to think it is an unrealistic demand. Rather it means we must challenge ourselves to be the kind of community where such a story can be told and manifested by a people formed in accordance with it—for if you believe that Jesus is the messiah of Israel, then "everything else follows, doesn't it?"

2. Jesus: The Story
of the Kingdom

To anyone who wishes to argue with one about religion one can then only take the argument in cogent, logical terms as far back as his own first principles will allow. But because there comes a point at which such argument must cease, it does not follow that there is nothing more to say. It is no accident that the religious autobiography is a classic form of theological writing for this shows us how a man comes by the premises from which he argues. It goes behind the argument to the arguer. St. Augustine's *Confessions* are the classic document here. Thus it is not mere pious moralizing which connects the rise of unbelief with a lowering of the quality of Christian life. Where the Christian community is incapable of producing lives such as those of the saints, the premises from which it argues will appear rootless and arbitrary.

Alasdair MacIntyre[1]

For the searching and right understanding of the Scriptures there is need of a good life and a pure soul, and for Christian virtue to guide the mind to grasp, so far as human nature can, the truth concerning God the Word. One cannot possibly understand the teaching of the saints unless one has a pure mind and is trying to imitate their life. Anyone who wants to look at sunlight naturally wipes his eye clear first, in order to make at any rate some approximation to the purity of that on which he looks; and a person wishing to see a city or country goes to the place in order to do so. Similarly, anyone who wishes to understand the mind of the sacred writers must first cleanse his own life, and approach the saints by copying their deeds.

St. Athanasius[2]

1. Christology and Social Ethics

Even though neither of these quotes seems immediately relevant to questions concerning christology or social ethics, I hope to show that they raise central issues for both subjects. Though my topic is Christian social ethics I have a larger agenda in view. To be a Christian implies substantive and profound convictions about the person and work of Jesus of Nazareth. Christians have often disagreed about how to understand the significance of Jesus, but the centrality of Jesus for Christian identity has never been questioned. Yet when Christians turn from avowals about "being Christian" to social ethics, the substantive claims they make about Jesus no longer seem operative. Or their appeals to Jesus to support various social strategies appear accidental in that the social strategy has been or can be better justified on different grounds.

The separation between Jesus and social ethics is exhibited by the very way we have learned to formulate the problem—i.e., "What is the relation between christology and social ethics?" That we can ask such a question indicates that something is wrong. The question presupposes that the meaning and truth of commitment to Jesus can be determined apart from his social significance. In contrast I will argue that what it means for Jesus to be worthy of our worship is explicable only in terms of his social significance. In so arguing I am not only suggesting that a christology which does not properly treat Jesus' social significance is incomplete; I offer the more radical argument that a christology which is not a social ethic is deficient. From this perspective the most "orthodox" christologies are inadequate when they fail to suggest how being a believer in Jesus provides and requires that we have the skills to describe and negotiate our social existence.

We often forget that social questions were at the heart of the controversies from which the great classical christological formulas emerged.[3] Instead we reduce faith in Jesus to formulas which are assumed to be self-explanatory but which fail to direct our attention to how it is we are required to make Jesus' life our own. To try to recover the social meaning of discipleship I will suggest that the most significant christological formulation is still the most primitive—namely that the Gospel is the story of a man who had the authority to preach that the Kingdom of God is present. By recovering the narrative dimension of christology we will be able to see that Jesus did not have a social ethic, but that his story is a social ethic. For the social and political validity of a community results from its being formed by a truthful story, a story that gives us the means to live without fear of one another. Therefore there can be no separation of christology from ecclesiology, that is, Jesus from the church. The truthfulness of Jesus creates and is known by the kind of community his story should form.

1.1   *Jesus at the Mercy of Social Ethics*

Before developing my constructive thesis I need to document some of the reasons for the separation of Jesus and social ethics and explain why it is a christological problem.[4] As John Howard Yoder has observed, mainstream Christianity has assumed that Jesus is not relevant to questions of social ethics.[5] For example, Ernst Troeltsch claims "it is a great mistake to treat all the ideas which underlie the preaching of Jesus as though they were primarily connected with the 'Social' problem. The message of Jesus is obviously purely religious; it issues directly from a very definite idea of God, and of the Divine Will in relation to man. To Jesus the whole meaning of life is religious; His life and His teaching are wholly determined by His thought of God."[6] Therefore according to Troeltsch the central problems of the New Testament are

> always purely religious, dealing with such questions as the salvation of the soul, monotheism, life after death, purity of worship, the right kind of congregational organization, the application of Christian ideals to daily life, and the need for severe self-discipline in the interest of personal holiness; further, we must admit that from the beginning no class distinctions were recognized; rather they were lost sight of in the supreme question of eternal salvation and the appropriation of a spiritual inheritance. It is worthy of special note that Early Christian apologetic contains no arguments dealing either with hopes of improving the exist-ing social situation, or with any attempt to heal social ills. Jesus began His public ministry, it is true, by proclaiming the Kingdom of God as the great hope of Redemption; this "Kingdom," however... was primarily the vision of an ideal ethical and religious situation, of a world entirely controlled by God, in which all the values of pure spirituality would be recognized and appreciated at their true worth.[7]

We have learned to state Troeltsch's position in more nuanced ways, but the structure of his position remains dominant. Thus Jesus' irrelevancy for "social questions" is because: (1) he had an "interim" ethic, or (2) he was a simple rural figure caring little about problems of complex organizations, or (3) he had no power or control over the political and social fortunes of his society, or (4) he did not deal with social change but offered new possibility for self-understanding, or (5) he was a radical monotheist who relativized all temporal values, or finally (6) Jesus came to provide forgiveness, not an ethic.[8] Such claims of Jesus' social irrelevancy presuppose an account of "social ethics" that cannot be justified by Jesus' own life. The problem is not that Jesus had no social ethic, but that the one he had does not match up with the social ethic these positions want or require.

In fact, the "social ethic" most often required is one that provides the means to rule and control society. It is interesting that Troeltsch lists as "purely religious" questions those concerning "the right kind of congrega-tional organization, the application of Christian ideals to daily life, self-discipline in the interest of personal holiness, and appropriation of spiritual inheritance." Such issues are not issues of a social ethic because Troeltsch assumes that a social ethic must be relevant to the needs of an empire, not of parishes or families. Thus most assume that in Troeltsch's description of the three types of social strategies consistent with the Gospel—church, sect, and mystical—only the church type provides a social ethic that is consistent with the Christian's "responsibility" for the world. Some "natural law" account is thus assumed to be unavoidable. But what we must recognize is that Troeltsch's extremely useful account of the three types is done from the perspective of the "church type."[9]

Even allowing for the more sophisticated accounts of "social ethics" developed since Troeltsch, the main thrust of his view still dominates the perspective of Catholicism as well as mainline Protestantism. For Richard McCormick the question of whether Christian faith adds material content to what is known by reason has tremendous implication for public policy. For "if Christian faith adds new material content to morality, then public policy is even more complex than it seems. For example, if Christians precisely as Christians know something about abortion that others cannot know unless they believe it as Christians, then in a pluralistic society there will be problems with discussion in the public forum."[10] But McCormick then concludes that Christians do not come to the public forum with any special insight. Jesus is regarded "as normative because He is believed to have experienced what it is to be *human* in the fullest way and at the deepest level. Christian ethics does not and cannot add to human ethical self-understanding as such any material content that is, in principle, strange or foreign to man as he exists and experiences himself."[11] McCormick's concern seems to be that Christians should articulate a social ethic sufficient to guide, and perhaps even produce, those who would rule society. And that has to be an ethic acceptable to non-Christians, an ethic in which, at least in matters of content, Jesus is irrelevant.

Philip Wogaman argues that "we cannot concede that this is a 'post-Constantinian age' or a 'post-Christian era' if we mean by these terms that the Church should now relinquish attempts to organize the world on the basis of Christian presumptions."[12] For "the problem really is *not* whether or not Christian faith can tolerate attempts to direct the course of social history. Such attempts are inevitable. Nor is it whether or not Christian faith should countenance the use of extrinsic forms of motivation. This, too, is inevitable, even when we seek to avoid it within the life of the church itself. Rather, it is the faithfulness with which we do this planning."[13]

Unlike McCormick, Wogaman appeals to the "Gospel" in support of his position. If we wonder how he can find a charter for rulers in the Gospel, we discover that he looks not to the story of Jesus to determine what is "Christian" about his ethic, but to a series of propositions: (1) the goodness of created existence, (2) the value of individual life, (3) the unity of the human family in God, and (4) the equality of persons in God.[14] Wogaman claims that these are drawn from the "core" of the Christian faith, but it can be pointed out that these "presumptions" require little reference to who Jesus was or what he did for their meaning or intelligibility.

It is not my purpose to try to document on a case-by-case basis how one's understanding of "social ethics" determines whether or how Jesus is understood.[15] Rather I am content to make the conceptual point that our "christologies" are determined by our social ethical presupposition. To answer Jesus' question "Who do men say that I am?" we must be formed by the kind of community he calls into existence. Therefore any adequate christology must be political in its beginning, not just in the end.[16]

Yoder notes that recent christology has suggested that we must choose between the Jesus of history and the Christ of dogma,[17] between the Jesus who can be reconstructed by historical methods and the Christ who is the son of God.[18] Such a choice is usually assumed to result from historical research, yet if I am correct, it reflects a social ethic which has lost sight of the fact that Jesus is, in his person and in his work, a social ethic. In Yoder's words "The Jesus of history is the Christ of faith. It is in hearing the revolutionary rabbi that we understand the existential freedom which is asked of the church. As we look closer at the Jesus whom Albert Schweitzer discovered, in all his eschatological realism, we find an utterly precise and practicable ethical instruction, practicable because in him the kingdom has actually come within reach. In him the sovereignty of Yahweh has become human history."[19]

1.2   *The Story of Jesus Is a Social Ethic*

If Jesus cannot be said to have a social ethic or have implications for a social ethic but his story *is* a social ethic, then the form of the church must exemplify that ethic. How one settles straightforward christological issues will determine whether it is possible to give an account of how Jesus functions as the social ethic of the church. My own position would generally be associated with so-called "high christologies," but it also has many parallels with the christology of liberal protestantism, especially as found in the social gospel. Even though I do not share the liberal rejection of the classical christological formulas, the liberal concern to recover the centrality of Jesus' life strikes me as right.

The liberal attempt to return to the "Jesus of history" was motivated by an attempt to reformulate Christianity without being bound to the classic Christian dogmas associated with Chalcedon.[20] The tendency of logos or "high christologies" toward forms of subordinationism was not the liberals' primary concern, but they did see that in the classical christological formulation there was a "precarious loosening of the connection of the Son's divinity with Jesus of Nazareth, God's historical revelation."[21] Therefore, the search for the historical Jesus, in spite of its methodological shortcomings, at least helped to keep the church honest "through the constant pressure of having to do with a real human, historic figure. The controversy over the historical Jesus in theology is simply the modern form of the old question of Docetism, that ancient (and perennial) theological tendency so to absorb Jesus into current theological understanding that he becomes its construct. The concrete historical reality of the whole fabric called 'Jesus' cannot be inferred from the Christian conviction that the ever-living Lord is known in faith and is present in the heart of the believer, just as the character of that Jesus is not to be inferred from the believer's heart or theology."[22]

Walter Kasper made much the same point when he observed that Chalcedon, within the language and context of the problem at that time, provided an extremely precise version of what the New Testament understands to be involved in Jesus' history: "namely in Jesus Christ, God himself has entered into a human history, and meets us there in a fully and completely human way." But compared with the witness of scripture, "The christological dogma of Chalcedon represents a contraction. The dogma is exclusively concerned with the inner constitution of the divine and human subject. It separates this question from the total context of Jesus' history and fate, from the relation in which Jesus stands not only to the *Logos* but to 'his Father,' and we miss the total eschatological perspective of biblical theology."[23] I have no wish to suggest that the language of incarnation is inherently defective, but only that it can provide a warrant for the assumption that one can know who Jesus is or "what" he was in terms of essences, substances, and natures, without the necessity of in some way knowing Jesus himself—without, that is, being his disciple.[24]

To be sure, any christology must deal with how this particular individual is also affirmed as the savior of all people. But the appropriate form of his universality is lost if metaphysical and anthropological theories are made to substitute for the necessary witnessing of Christian lives and communities to the significance of his story. Witness presupposes and claims universality, but in a manner that makes clear that the universal can be claimed only through learning the particular form of discipleship required by this particular man.

For example it has been emphasized in modern theology that we know Jesus only from the perspective of the resurrection—that is, the only Jesus we know is already the Jesus of faith, the Jesus created by the church. Some think this is a decisive problem because it seems that the "real" Jesus is forever lost. But there is no "real Jesus" except as he is known through the kind of life he demanded of his disciples; that the Gospels display the grammar of such a life should not therefore surprise us. It only makes clear that the demand for "historical accuracy" is ahistorical insofar as the Gospels exhibit why the story of this man is inseparable from how that story teaches us to follow him.[25] As the Gospels show, only because the disciples had first followed Jesus to Jerusalem were they able to understand the significance of the resurrection.

I want to be especially careful how this is understood. For to emphasize the inseparability of knowing Jesus from how we must follow him may suggest too complete an identification of christology with soteriology. Even though a separation of christology and soteriology is not possible or desirable, too often soteriological concerns have determined what Jesus should be. When the soteriological issues become primary, one must ask, with Pannenberg, whether we have dealt with Jesus at all: "Does it not perhaps involve projections onto Jesus' figure of the human desire for salvation and deification, of human striving after similarity to God, of the human duty to bring satisfaction for sins committed, of the human experience of bondage in failure, in the knowledge of one's own guilt, and most clearly in neo-Protestantism, projections of the idea of perfect religiosity, of perfect morality, of pure personality, of radical trust?"[26]

Ironically the liberal concern to find the Jesus behind the dogmas foundered on its own awareness that the "historical Jesus" too often turned out to look like our prior ideal of what a good man should be. The humanistic assumptions of liberalism turned out to be the functional equivalent of logos christology, for Jesus, now stripped of metaphysical pretensions, became simply the best example of the kind of moral life that could be known and achieved. And this example stood independent of any personal knowledge of, or relationship with, Jesus.[27] Thus for Walter Rauschenbusch the significance of Jesus is that through his personality he initiated the Kingdom by democratizing the concept of God and by teaching the infinite worth of each personality.[28]

As James Gustafson points out, this is a danger for all christologies in which Jesus is understood primarily as the proponent of an ethic rather than how his ethic might be integral to his life. Whenever Jesus becomes a pattern for a universally valid moral way of life, his meaning is distorted. "Christ is a means of life which in turn has moral expression. Thus the Christian ethic is in its fullest sense a way and pattern of life for those whose faith in God has Jesus Christ as it center. It is not first of all a universally valid objective model of morality. This it may provide, but only as an expression of God's way to man in Jesus Christ."[29]

Therefore the claim that the story of Jesus is a social ethic means that there is no moral point or message that is separable from the story of Jesus as we find it in the Gospels. There can be no Christ figure because Jesus is the

Christic.[30] Jesus' identity is prior to the "meaning" of the story. There is no meaning that is separable from the story itself. And that is why there can be no easy parallels drawn between the story of Jesus and other redeemer-redemption accounts. The difference

> lies neither in the difference between the saving qualities and action nor in the difference between redemptive needs. It is simply the unsubstitutable person about whom the story is told—his unsubstitutable deeds, words, and sufferings—that makes the real difference. Such exclusive reference to the person of Jesus as is found in the Gospel story is characteristic of neither Gnostic nor mystery religions. The Gospel story's indissoluble connection with an unsubstitutable identity in effect divests the savior story of its mythical quality. The Gospel story is a demythologization of the savior myth because the savior figure in the Gospel story is fully identified with Jesus of Nazareth. The early Christians would substitute no other names.[31]

The Christian savior story and ethic is that of Jesus himself. Jesus determines the story as the crucial person in the story. Thus his identity is grasped not through other savior stories, but by learning to follow him, which is the necessary condition for citizenship in his Kingdom.

Put in more traditional categories, I am contending that Jesus' person cannot be separated from his work, the incarnation from the atonement. The severance between incarnation and atonement, as George Hendry says, "is the result of a failure to grasp the link that connects them, viz., the historical life of the incarnate Christ which is attested in the Evangelical records, or, in other words . . . if one party [Eastern] has sought to find the essence of the gospel at Bethlehem, and another [Western] at Calvary, and each of them thereby presented a distorted picture of the gospel, it is because neither of them took sufficient account of what lay between, in Galilee and Judea.''[32]

But to emphasize the particularity of Jesus' story makes another question unavoidable: How can this man also be God and consequently lay claim to universal, absolute, and insurpassable significance?[33] As I indicated above, the temptation is to anchor Jesus' universality in a metaphysical or anthropological account, free from the vicissitudes of history.[34] But to do so separates Jesus from social ethics by freeing those who claim to be his disciples from facing the fact that his universality rests on their faithfulness to the demands of his Kingdom. For faith has no

> timeless platform that lifts it outside the vulnerabilities of the historical realm. It boasts no certainty other than what accrues to a contingent event from the past, with its promise of claiming the present in the name of a purposive future. The person-event of Christ precedes a purposive

future. The person-event of Christ precedes particular responses of faith. Yet it is precisely by means of such responses—those of the original witnesses no less than their successors—that revelation has its on-going content and power. So completely is the truth of faith tied in with what is transmitted historically. Christological language is meaningful in relation to the actual life and impact of the man Jesus. And this relationship is made accessible to the present generation through the contribution of those who have already responded to that alteration of social-personal existence which roots in this Jesus.[35]

It may be, as Pannenberg argues, that Jesus' universal relevance is determined by the fulfillment of the hopes and deep longings of humanity.[36] But such fulfillment comes only as it is manifested by a particular community who have been trained by a particular man to surface and articulate a particular set of needs and longings. For Jesus' universality is manifested only by a people who are willing to take his cross as their story, as the necessary condition for living truthfully in this life.[37] As his cross was a social ethic, so they become the continuation of that ethic in the world, until all are brought within his Kingdom.

2.   Jesus: the Autobasileia

The claim that the story of Jesus is a social ethic can be made clearer if we attend to the obvious: The only way we learn of Jesus is through his story as we find it in the Gospel and as we see it lived in the lives of others. This fact has often been overlooked or thought to be accidental to the real meaning of the "Incarnation," but I argue that the narrative character of the Gospels is integral to the affirmation of Jesus' redemptive significance. This does not mean that the Gospels are biographies in the usual sense. They are proclamation; but the proclamation takes the form of a story of a man's life.[38] When this is recognized we can understand how Jesus provided a story to determine the polity of the church.

It has become a commonplace that one of the great contributions of critical scholarship has been a renewed sense of the significance of the Kingdom of God in Jesus' preaching and ministry. Ethicists have found this useful because the notion of the Kingdom sounds like it involves normative guidelines to inform a social ethic. The scriptures can be scavenged for individual sayings that seem to determine the character of such a Kingdom— love, justice, righteousness. But this strategy is doomed to failure because such norms fail to do justice to the eschatological character of the Kingdom.

Though there is no agreement how the various passages on the Kingdom as present, future, or even as growing are to be reconciled, there is a general agreement that the Kingdom first and foremost is the claim of God's lordship, his rule over all creation and history. Thus the Kingdom is "totally and exclusively God's doing. It cannot be earned by religious or moral effort, imposed by political struggle, or projected in calculations. We cannot plan for it, organize it, make it, or build it, we cannot invent it or imagine it. It is given (Mt 21:43; Lk 12:32), 'appointed' (Lk 22:29). We can only inherit it (Mt 25:34).''[39]

But the ambiguity surrounding the timing of the Kingdom and our inability to "make" it happen are not the primary reasons why the Kingdom should not invite speculation about what constitutes a just or ideal society considered in itself. Rather the reason the Kingdom cannot be made an ethical ideal is that the scripture refuses to separate the Kingdom from the one who is the proclaimer of the Kingdom. "Jesus is Himself the established Kingdom of God.''[40] Or in Origen's classical phrase, Jesus is the *autobasileia*—the Kingdom in person.[41]

In the New Testament the proclamation of the Kingdom of God and the acknowledgment of the Lordship of Jesus come together. The fact Jesus pointed to and preached the Kingdom without calling attention to himself is but an indication of the kind of rule he brings. His identity is revealed through his relation to God and the authority that relationship gives him to proclaim the Kingdom. "His vocation comes from the depths of his being. In the New Testament representation of Jesus Christ his authority and identity are absolutely inseparable from each other. The Church cannot in good faith try to separate what the Holy Spirit has joined. Jesus Christ is its only valid warrant for preaching the Kingdom of God.''[42] Put differently, Jesus refused to accept the role of Messiah as if it constituted a "part" that he was playing. Rather, his whole self is an act of participation in God's purpose for man. "He is the supreme agent of the Kingdom, agent both in the sense of one who acts, and in the sense of one who represents the interests of another. He holds nothing in reserve for some other role. His spirit does not recoil upon itself but leads him straightway into the most solid and massive relationship with the actual world. The religious term for this massive relationship is Lordship.''[43]

There is no way to know the Kingdom except by learning of the story of this man Jesus. For his story defines the nature of how God rules and how such a rule creates a corresponding "world" and society.[44] There is no way to talk about the social ethics of Christianity except as they are determined by the form of Jesus' life as we find it told by the general narratives.

The whole Jesus was permeated by the kingdom of God, and since that kingdom is the effectuation of God's reign, it is Jesus as a whole who points to the kingdom in a new way. Just as the parable does not illustrate ideas better stated non-parabolically, and so become dispensable, so Jesus is not merely an illustration for the kingdom which can be more adequately grasped apart from him—say in mystic encounters or in abstract formulation. His task was not to impart correct concepts about the kingdom but to make it possible for men to respond to it; as a parable of the kingly God, he invited men to look through him into the kingdom, with the result that his hearers could not respond to the kingdom without responding to him.[45]

But what could it possibly mean to claim that Jesus determines the character of the Kingdom in terms of actual sociological and political alternatives? At the very least it means that we are required to rethink our everyday sense of the "political." For to know the Kingdom through the story of Jesus requires us to believe that the polity into which we are called can only be based on that power which comes from trusting in the truth. Rauschenbusch rightly sees that Jesus requires a polity that goes beyond the bounds of conventional social ethics. As he points out, Jesus wielded

no sword but the truth. But mark well, that truth was a sword in his hands and not a yard-stick. It cut into the very marrow of his generation. It was mighty to the casting down of strongholds. So it has proved itself wherever it has been in dead earnest. It reveals lies and their true nature, as when Satan was touched by the spear of Ithuriel. It makes injustice quail on its throne, chafe, sneer, abuse, hurl its spear, tender its goal, and finally offer to serve as truth's vassal. But the truth that can do such things is not an old woman wrapped in the spangled robes of earthly authority, bedizened with golden ornaments, the marks of honor given by injustice in turn for services rendered, and muttering dead formulas of the past. The truth that can serve God as the mightiest of his archangels is robed only in love, her weighty limbs unfettered by needless weight, calm-browed, her eyes terrible with beholding God. . . . Jesus deliberately rejected force and chose truth. Truth asks no odds. She will not ask that her antagonist's feet be put in shackles before she will cross swords with him. Christ's Kingdom needs not the spears of Roman legionaries to prop it, not even the clubs of Galilean peasants. Whenever Christianity shows an inclination to use constraint in its own defense or support, it thereby furnishes presumptive evidence that it has become a thing of this world, for it finds the means of this world adapted to its end.[46]

2.1 Discipleship and Kingdom

I cannot hope to provide the scriptural basis to defend the view that Jesus is best understood as the story that authorizes the preaching of the

Kingdom. But I hope at least to suggest that this way of putting the matter is appropriate to the form and content of the Gospels by calling attention to the pericope containing Peter's confession in Mark. Peter's failure to understand his confession is an indication that it is necessary to know Jesus' story and why the Gospels appear as a story. The brief encounter between Peter and Jesus makes clear that the story of Jesus, like most good stories, changes the hearer. A story that claims to be the truth of our existence requires that our lives, like the lives of the disciples, be changed by following him. The interrelationship between this demand and the character of Jesus' messiahship is made clear as Jesus here asks what no man should ask from another—his life.[47] The "messianic secret" in Mark, whatever other purpose it was meant to serve, makes clear that to be a disciple of Jesus requires a training beyond what any of them had imagined. This is the lesson Peter had yet to learn.

> And Jesus went on with his disciples, to the villages of Caesarea Philippi; and on the way he asked his disciples, "Who do men say that I am?" And they told him, "John the Baptist; and others say, Elijah; and others one of the prophets." And he asked them, "But who do you say that I am?" Peter answered him, "You are the Christ." And he charged them to tell no one about him.
>
> And he began to teach them that the Son of Man must suffer many things, and be rejected by the elders and the chief priests and the scribes, and be killed, and after three days rise again. And he said this plainly. And Peter took him, and began to rebuke him. But turning and seeing his disciples, he rebuked Peter, and said, "Get behind me, Satan! For you are not on the side of God, but of men."
>
> And he called to him the multitude with his disciples, and said to them, "If any man would come after me let him deny himself and take up his cross and follow me. For whoever would save his life will lose it; and whoever loses his life *for my sake* and the gospel's will save it. For what does it profit a man, to gain the whole world and forfeit his life? For what can a man give in return for his life? For whoever is ashamed of me and of my words in this adulterous and sinful generation, of him will the Son of Man also be ashamed, when he comes in the glory of his Father with the holy angels." And he said to them, "Truly, I say to you, there are some standing here who will not taste death before they see the kingdom of God come with power." (Mark 8:27-9:1)

This is obviously not only an important passage for Mark but for the whole New Testament, as it asks the central question, "Who do men say that I am?" Each answer represents different religious and political options of the day. Peter at first seems to get it right, this is the messiah whom we have long awaited. This is the one who will restore us to power and glory, who will provide the power to return Israel to her preeminence among the nations. Peter has indeed learned the name.

But Jesus then begins to tell them that he is not going to be recognized as having such power, but indeed will be rejected and killed. And Peter, still imbued with the old order, suggests this is no way for a savior to talk; saviors are people with power to affect the world. To save means to be "in control," or to seek to be "in control," and Jesus seeks neither. His power is of a different order and the powers of this world will necessarily put him to death because they recognize, better than Peter, what a threat to power looks like. For here is one who invites others to participate in a kingdom of God's love, a kingdom which releases the power of giving and service. The powers of this world cannot comprehend such a kingdom. Here is a man who insists it is possible, if God's rule is acknowledged and trusted, to serve without power.

Jesus thus rebukes Peter, who had learned the name but not the story that determines the meaning of the name. For to say the name rightly is to know how to narrate the history of Israel to describe Israel; "to identify that people with the identity of Jesus Christ is to narrate that history of Jesus in such a way that it is seen as the individual and climactic summing up, incorporation, and identification of the whole people, by which people receive their identification."[48] But Peter had not learned what that kind of identification entailed.

So Jesus tells him. But he first calls not only his disciples, but the multitudes. This is not a word for the few. And the "truth" turns out to be that if we are to follow him we must learn to lose our lives, not as an end in itself but for "his sake." We can understand, perhaps, how we might need to lose our lives for family, homeland, or some noble cause—but he says you must lose your life for him, Jesus. Nor does he mean that self-sacrifice is a good in itself. Just as truth is not freeing unless it is his truth, so sacrifice will not help us unless it is the sacrifice that is done in the name and form of the Kingdom as we find it in his life. There is no truth beyond him: His story is the truth of the Kingdom. And that truth turns out to be the cross.

The cross was not something accidental in Jesus' life, but the necessary outcome of his life and of his mission. His death is of decisive significance, not because it alone wrought salvation for us, but because it was the end and fulfillment of his life. In his death he finished the work that it was his mission to perform. In this sense the cross is not a detour or a hurdle on the way to the Kingdom, "nor is it even the way to the kingdom; it is the kingdom come."[49]

And it is such because the cross more than any other event reveals the social character of Jesus' mission. Jesus was the bearer of a new possibility of human and social relationships. That is why the incarnation is not the affirmation of God's approval of the human (as previously defined on other grounds), but God's breaking through the borders of man's definition of what is human to give a new and formative definition of the human in Jesus.[50] The cross of Christ ''was not an inexplicable or chance event, which happened to strike him, like illness or accident. The cross of Calvary was not a difficult family situation, not a frustration of visions of personal fulfillment, a crushing debt or a nagging in-law; it was the political, legally to be expected result of a moral clash with the powers ruling his society.''[51]

It is in this way that Christian discipleship creates a polity; it is in this way it *is* a polity: Being a Christian is an expression of our obedience to, and in, a community based on Jesus' messiahship. And it was this that Peter had not learned; he assumed that this Kingdom would look like the kingdoms of the world. But he was wrong: the kingdoms of the world derive their being from our fear of one another; the rule of God means that a community can exist where trust rules, trust made possible by the knowledge that our existence is bounded by the truth. Like Peter, few of us are ready for such ''knowledge,'' but insofar as we are able to make it part of our lives we in fact become citizens of his Kingdom.

2.2 Discipleship and Community

To be a disciple is to be part of a new community, a new polity, which is formed on Jesus' obedience to the cross. The constitutions of this new polity are the Gospels. The Gospels are not just the depiction of a man, but they are manuals for the training necessary to be part of the new community. To be a disciple means to share Christ's story, to participate in the reality of God's rule.

I have tried to suggest that such a rule is more than the claim that God is Lord of this world. It is the creation of a ''world'' through a story that teaches us how such a rule is constituted.[52] Christians learn the power of this rule by loving as God has loved through Jesus' life. That is, they love their ''enemies, and do good and lend without expecting return'' for, if they do, their ''reward will be great, and you will be sons of the Most High; for he is kind to the ungrateful and the selfish. Be merciful, even as your Father is merciful'' (Luke 6:35-36).[53]

It is through such love that Christians learn that they are to serve as he served. Such service is not an end in itself, but reflects the Kingdom into which Christians have been drawn. This means that Christians insist on service which may appear ineffective to the world.[54] For the service that Christians are called upon to provide does not have as its aim to make the world better, but to demonstrate that Jesus has made possible a new world, a new social order.

It is a new world because no longer does the threat of death force us into desperate measures to insure our safety or significance.[55] A people freed from the threat of death must form a polity, because they can afford to face the truth of their existence without fear and defensiveness. They can even take the risk of having the story of a crucified Lord as their central reality. He is a strange Lord, appears powerless, but his powerlessness turns out to be the power of truth against the violence of falsehood.

The power that comes from trusting in truth is but a correlative of our learning through Jesus to accept our life as a gift. In Jesus we have met the one who has the authority and power to forgive our fevered search to gain security through deception, coercion, and violence. To learn to follow Jesus means we must learn to accept such forgiveness, and it is no easy thing to accept, as acceptance requires recognition of our sin as well as vulnerability. But by learning to be forgiven we are enabled to view other lives not as threats but as gifts. Thus in contrast to all societies built on shared resentments and fears, Christian community is formed by a story that enables its members to trust the otherness of the other as the very sign of the forgiving character of God's Kingdom.

By making the story of such a Lord central to their lives, Christians are enabled to see the world accurately and without illusion. Because they have the confidence that Jesus' cross and resurrection are the final words concerning God's rule, they have the courage to see the world for what it is: The world is ruled by powers and forces that we hardly know how to name, much less defend against.[56] These powers derive their strength from our fear of destruction, cloaking their falsehood with the appearance of convention, offering us security in exchange for truth. By being trained through Jesus' story we have the means to name and prevent these powers from claiming our lives as their own.[57]

From this perspective the church is the organized form of Jesus' story. The church provides the conditions we need to describe what is going on in our lives. That does not mean that all other descriptions are rendered irrelevant, but rather that we learn how to negotiate the limits and possibilities of those descriptions. We test them against the cross. It is in his cross that we learn we live in a world that is based on the presupposition that man, not God, rules.

Jesus is the story that forms the church. This means that the church first serves the world by helping the world to know what it means to be the world. For without a "contrast model" the world has no way to know or feel the oddness of its dependence on power for survival. Because of the church the world can feel the strangeness of trying to build a politics that is inherently untruthful; the world lacks the basis to demand truth from its people. Because of a community formed by the story of Christ the world can know what it means to be a society committed to the growth of individual gifts and differences. In a community that has no fear of the truth, the otherness of the other can be welcomed as a gift rather than a threat.

All politics should be judged by the character of the people it produces. The depth and variety of character which a polity sustains is a correlative of the narrative that provides its identity and purpose. The contention and witness of the church is that the story of Jesus provides a flourishing of gifts which other politics cannot know. It does so because Christians have been nourished on the story of a savior who insisted on being nothing else than what he was. By being the son of God he provided us with the confidence that insofar as we become his disciples our particularity and our regard for the particularity of our brothers and sisters in Christ contribute to his Kingdom. Our stories become part of the story of the Kingdom.

The most striking social ethical fact about the church is that the story of Jesus provides the basis to break down arbitrary and false boundaries between people. The church is an international society only because we have a story that teaches us to regard the other as a fellow member of God's Kingdom. Such regard is not based on facile doctrines of tolerance or equality, but is forged from our common experience of being trained to be disciples of Jesus. The universality of the church is based on the particularity of Jesus' story and on the fact that his story trains us to see one another as God's people. Because we have been so trained we can see and condemn the narrow loyalties that create "the world."

3. Jesus: The Story That Forms the Church

The account I have tried to provide, to illuminate how the story of Jesus is a social ethic, is often dismissed by those who are impressed by the fact that the Gospels do not give us the "historical Jesus" but only Jesus as the early Christians understood him.[58] We know that Peter could not have called Jesus the Christ because he did not speak Greek. Therefore it is alleged to be incorrect to speak of Jesus as a social ethic. The best we can do is speak of the Gospels as a social ethic.

I have tried to show that if we pay attention to the narrative and self-involving character of the Gospels, as the early disciples did, there is no way to speak of Jesus' story without its forming our own. The story it forms creates a community which corresponds to the form of his life. As Nils Dahl maintains,

> In all New Testament writings there is a close relationship between the church and Jesus, but within this relationship Jesus retains priority and sovereignty. Without doubt, it has always been possible to use the

sovereignty of the Lord to conceal his servants' will to power and to enforce conformity upon lax and dissident members of the church. But at least in the major writings of the New Testament, the memory of Jesus transcends ecclesiastical expediency and collective needs. For this reason, both loyal Christians and outside critics have been able to use the Jesus tradition to rebuke the state and the practices of the church at any given time and place. Some of the New Testament authors themselves have done this. In doing so, they did not follow any uniform pattern but drew upon various aspects of the tradition, using it for their own purposes. Just this diversity within the New Testament canon makes it impossible for a conservative or critical orthodoxy to resolve the problem of the relations between church and Jesus once and for all times. It rather calls for spiritual discernment, and the answer depends upon the ability to distinguish between the spirits.[59]

The social ethical task of the church, therefore, is to be the kind of community that tells and tells rightly the story of Jesus. But it can never forget that Jesus' story is a many-sided tale. We do not have just one story of Jesus, but four. To learn to tell and live the story truthfully does not mean that we must be able to reconstruct "what really happened" from the four. Rather it means that we, like the early Christians, must learn that understanding Jesus' life is inseparable from learning how to live our own. And that there are various ways to do this is clear by the diversity of the Gospels.

A truthful telling of the story cannot be guaranteed by historical investigation (though that investigation certainly can be in service to the truth), but by being the kind of people who can bear the burden of that story with joy. We, no less than the first Christians, are the continuation of the truth made possible by God's rule. We continue this truth when we see that the struggle of each to be faithful to the Gospel is essential to our own lives. I understand my own story through seeing the different ways in which others are called to be his disciples. If we so help one another, perhaps, like the early Christians when challenged about the viability of their faith, we can say, "But see how we love one another."

3. The Moral Authority of Scripture: The Politics and Ethics of Remembering

1. A Proposal for Understanding the Moral Authority of Scripture

> The canon does not contain its own self-justification but rather directs our attention to the tradition which it mediates. For to say the least which has to be said, without the tradition there is no shared memory and therefore no community. Our study of the canon has led to the conclusion that no one interpretation of the tradition can be accorded final and definitive status. The presence of prophecy as an essential part of the canon means that it will always be possible and necessary to remold the tradition as a source of life-giving power.[1]

Joseph Blenkinsopp's claim about the canon and its relation to prophecy and a community sufficient to sustain prophecy is crucial for understanding how scripture does and/or should function ethically. We currently have difficulty in appreciating the moral role of scripture because we have forgotten that the authority of scripture is a political claim characteristic of a very particular kind of polity. By "political" I do not mean, as many who identify with liberation theology, that scripture should be used as an ideology for justifying the demands of the oppressed. The authority of scripture derives its intelligibility from the existence of a community that knows its life depends on faithful remembering of God's care of his creation through the calling of Israel and the life of Jesus.

To construe the authority of scripture in this way, moreover, is most nearly faithful to the nature of biblical literature as well as the best insights we have learned from the historical study of the Bible. The formation of texts as well as the canon required the courage of a community to constantly remember and reinterpret its past. Such remembering and reinterpretation is a political task, for without a tradition there can be no community. That we no longer consider remembering as an ethical or political task manifests our questionable assumption that ethics primarily concerns decisions whereas politics brokers power.

When we so limit ethics and politics, the scripture, particularly in its narrative mode, cannot but appear as a "problem." For the narrative requires a corresponding community who are capable of remembering and for whom active reinterpreting remains the key to continuing a distinctive way of life. But when one begins to look to an ethic sufficient for guiding the wider society, the narrative aspects of scripture have to be ignored. Such an ethic, though often claimed to be biblically "inspired" or "informed," must be freed from the narratives of scripture if it is to be the basis for judging or making common cause with those who do not share those narratives in their own history. So what is presented as the "biblical ethic" has been made over into a universal ethic that does not depend on memory for its significance but turns on "reason" or "nature."

As a result, we could easily forget that a biblical ethic requires the existence of a community capable of remembering in the present, no less than it did in the past. Where such a community does not exist the most sophisticated scholarly and hermeneutical skills cannot make scripture morally relevant. What John Yoder describes as the free church understanding of the significance of community is necessary for any appreciation of the moral significance of scripture. He points out that the

> bridge between the words of Jesus or of the apostolic writings and the present is not a strictly conceptual operation, which could be carried out by a single scholar in an office, needing only an adequate dictionary and an adequate description of the available action options. The promise of the presence of Christ to actualize a definition of his will in a given future circumstance was given not to professional exegetes but to the community which would be gathered in his name (Mt. 18:19) with the specific purpose of "binding and loosing" (Mt. 18:18). Classical Protestantism tended to deny the place of this conversational process, in favor of its insistence on the perspicuity and objectivity of the words of Scripture. Catholicism before that has provoked that extreme Protestant answer by making of this hermeneutical mandate a blank check which the holders of ecclesiastical office could use with relative independence. The free church alternative to both recognizes the inadequacies of the text of Scripture standing alone uninterpreted and appropriates the promise of the guidance of the spirit throughout the ages, but locates the fulfillment of that promise in the assembly of those who gather around Scripture in the face of a given real moral challenge. Any description of the substance of ethical decision-making criteria is incomplete if this aspect of its communitarian and contemporary form is omitted.[2]

Failure to appreciate how the biblical narratives have and continue to form a polity is part of the reason that the ethical significance of scripture currently seems so problematic. Indeed, many of the articles written on the relation of scripture and ethics focus on ways scripture should not be used for ethical matters. Yet if my proposal is correct, that very way of putting the issue—i.e., how should scripture be used ethically—is already a distortion. For to put it that way assumes that we must first clarify the meaning of the text—in the sense that we understand its historical or sociological background—and only then can we ask its moral significance. David Kelsey has reminded us, however, that claims about the authority of scripture are in themselves moral claims about the function of scripture for the common life of the church. The scripture's authority for that life consists in its being used so that it helps to nurture and reform the community's self-identity as well as the personal character of its members.[3]

To reinstate the moral and political context required for the interpretation of scripture, moreover, demands that we challenge what Kelsey has characterized as the "standard picture" of the relation between scripture and theology. The "standard picture," supported by a variety of theological agendas, assumes that if scripture is to be meaningful it must be translated into a more general theological medium.[4] Such "translation" is often deemed necessary because of the texts' obscurity, cultural limits, and variety, but also because there seems to be no community in which the scripture functions authoritatively. As a result we forget that the narratives of scripture were not meant to describe our world—and thus in need of translation to adequately describe the "modern world"—but to change the world, including the one in which we now live. In the classic words of Erich Auerbach, scripture is not meant

> merely to make us forget our own reality for a few hours, it seeks to overcome our reality: we are to fit our own life into its world, feel ourselves to be elements in its structure of universal history. . . . Everything else that happens in the world can only be conceived as an element in this sequence; into it everything that is known about the world . . . must be fitted as an ingredient of the divine plan.[5]

I would only add that scripture creates more than a world; it shapes a community which is the bearer of that world. Without that community, claims about the moral authority of scripture—or rather the very idea of scripture itself—make no sense. Furthermore, I shall argue that claims about the authority of scripture make sense only in that the world and the community it creates are in fact true to the character of God. In order to develop this proposal, the concepts of "moral authority" and "scripture" must be analyzed to show how each gains its intelligibility only in relation to a particular kind of community. Before doing so, however, it should prove useful to examine how many current problems associated with the moral use of scripture are, in part, the result of attempts to ignore or avoid the necessity of a community in which it is intelligible for scripture to function authoritatively.

2.   The Scripture as a Moral Problem

James Gustafson has observed that "in spite of the great interest in ethics in the past thirty years, and in spite of the extensive growth of biblical studies, there is a paucity of material that relates the two areas of study in a scholarly way. Writers in ethics necessarily make their forays into the Bible without the technical exegetical and historical acumen and skills to be secure in the way they use biblical materials. But few biblical scholars have provided studies from which writers in ethics can draw."[6] Likewise, Brevard Childs suggests that "there is no outstanding modern work written in English that even attempts to deal adequately with Biblical material as it relates to ethics."[7]

No doubt the problem of specialization is a real one, but our current inability to use the scriptures ethically involves more fundamental conceptual and methodological issues. For, as we shall see, appeal to scripture is not equivalent to appeal to the text in itself, and it is the latter, rightly or wrongly, which is the subject of most current scholarly effort.[8] I am not suggesting that critical analysis of the development of the biblical text is theologically questionable, but that often it is simply unclear what theological significance such work should have. However, for Christian ethics the Bible is not just a collection of texts but scripture that makes normative claims on a community.

The confusion surrounding the relation of text to scripture has not resulted in ethicists (and theologians) paying too little attention to current scholarly work concerning the Bible; rather their attention is far too uncritical. It has been observed that there is finally no substitute for knowing the text, and it is often unfortunately true that theologians and ethicists alike know the current theories about the development of the text better than the text itself.[9] As a result, claims about an ethic being biblically informed too frequently turn out to mean that the ethic is in accordance with some scholar's reconstruction of "biblical theology," e.g., the centrality of covenant or love in the Bible.[10] And ironically, as James Barr has shown, the very notion of "biblical theology" distorts the variety of biblical material by failing to take the text seriously.[11]

The conceptual issues raised by the ethical use of scripture involve not only how we should understand scripture, but also how ethics should be understood. We often have a far too restricted understanding of the "ethical." For example, Childs asks "How does the Bible aid the Christian in the making of concrete ethical decisions," without considering whether "ethics" is or should be primarily about "decisions?"[12] Consequently, attempts to explicate the "ethics" of scripture have tended to concentrate on those aspects—Decalogue, the Sermon on the Mount, Wisdom books, the command to love—that fit our intuitive assumptions about what an "ethic" should look like. But this manner of locating the "biblical ethic" not only confuses the questions of the ethics in the scripture with the ethical use of scripture, but has the unfortunate effect of separating and abstracting the ethics from the religious (and narrative) contexts that make them intelligible.

Gustafson has often observed that how authors use scripture is determined as much by how they define the task of Christian ethics as how they understand the nature and status of scripture.[13] Birch and Rasmussen have also suggested that once the moral life is understood as not only involving decisions but also how actions mold the character of individuals and of a community, the narratives of scripture are as important as the commandments; the Psalms afford the most explicit moral teachings.[14] But pictures die harder even than habits and many persist in thinking that a biblical ethic must be one that tells us "what to do in circumstances X or Y." When ethics is equivalent to advice, issues of interpretation or community need not arise.

In fairness it should be said that the persistence of the idea that the Bible is some sort of "revealed morality"[15] has been deeply ingrained in our culture by the church itself. Moreover it is an idea shared by conservative and liberal alike as they appeal to different parts of scripture in support of ethical positions that they have ironically come to hold on grounds prior to looking to scripture. Thus claims about the moral significance of scripture are used to reinforce decisions about ethics derived from nonscriptural sources.

Though they may appear to be radically different, those who would have us obey everything in the scripture that looks like moral advice—e.g., that women should keep quiet in church (1 Cor. 14:34–36)—and those who would have us act according to the more general admonitions—e.g., that we should be loving (1 Cor. 13)—share many common assumptions. Both look to scripture as containing a revealed morality that must or should provide guidance. And each, often in quite different ways, has a stake in maintaining that the "biblical ethic" be distinctive or unique when compared with other ethics.[16]

The assumption that to be ethically significant the Bible must contain some kind of "revealed morality" not only creates a nest of unfruitful problems but finally betrays the character of the biblical literature. The very idea that the Bible is revealed (or inspired) is a claim that creates more trouble than it is worth. As Barr has pointed out, "the term *revelation* is not in the Bible a common general term for the source of man's knowledge of God, and some of the main cases found are eschatological, i.e., they look forward to a revealing of something *in the future*. Perhaps this suggests another way of thinking. The main relation of revelation to the Bible is not that of an antecedent revelation, which generates the Bible as its response, but that of a revelation which *follows upon* the existent tradition, or, once it has reached the fixed and written stage, the existent scripture. The scripture provides the frames of reference within which new events have meaning and make sense.''[17]

The problem of revelation aside, however, the view that the Bible contains a revealed morality that can be applied directly by the individual agent, perhaps with some help from the biblical critic, flounders when considering the status of individual commands. For some moral aspects of scripture—such as the *Haustafeln* (household codes: Col. 3:18–4:1; Eph. 5:21–6:9; 1 Pet. 2:13–3:7)—strike many today as not only morally irrelevant but morally perverse. The common strategy for dealing with such statements is to dismiss them as the product of the limitations of the early church's culture, which had not yet been sufficiently subjected to the searching transformation of the Gospel. But that strategy suffers from being too powerful, for why should the *Haustafeln* be singled out as culturally relative and texts more appealing to modern ears such as "there is neither Jew nor Greek, there is neither slave nor free, there is neither male nor female; for you are all one in Christ Jesus" (Gal. 3:28) be exempted?

Besides moral positions that simply strike us as wrong, scripture also contains commands that many feel are too "idealistic" to be workable. The admonition not to resist "one who is evil" (Matt. 5:39) may work at an interpersonal level, but most Christians assume that it makes no sense as a social policy. Attempts to "explain" such statements as "ideals," or as "law that provides consciousness of sin," or as requiring eschatological interpretation result in a feeling that we really do not need to treat them with moral seriousness after all.[18]

Thus attempts to formulate a "biblical ethic" result in the somewhat embarrassing recognition that the "morality" that is said to be "biblical" is quite selective and even arbitrary. Various strategies are used to justify our selectivity, such as appealing to "central" biblical themes or images, like love. No doubt love has a central place in the Bible and the Christian life, but when it becomes the primary locus of the biblical ethic it turns into an abstraction that cannot be biblically justified. Indeed when biblical ethics is so construed one wonders why appeals need be made to scripture at all, since one treats it as a source of general principles or images that once in hand need no longer acknowledge their origins. In fact, once we construe Christian ethics in such a way, we find it necessary to stress the "uniqueness" of the "biblical concept of love covenant," or some other equally impressive sounding notion.

Finally the attempt to capture the ethical significance of scripture by a summary image or concept makes it difficult to be faithful to our growing awareness that the ethics in the scripture are bound in an intimate way with the life of Christ; nor can they be dissociated from the life of the community that arose around his life.[19] The more we try to mine scripture for a workable ethic, the more we are drawn to separate such an ethic from the understanding of salvation that makes such an ethic intelligible in the first place.[20] Insisting that the biblical ethic is first an indicative before being an imperative[21] will hardly suffice to provide an account of the complex nature of the moral life manifest in the early Christian community, nor can that distinction inform us how we are to live and think in a manner appropriate to Christian convictions regarding God and his relation to our existence.

In an attempt to avoid separating the ethics of scripture from the theological context that makes them intelligible, the suggestion has been made that scripture is not so much a revealed morality as a revealed reality. Thus for H. R. Niebuhr the Bible is not morally important in that it gives us knowledge of itself, "but because it gives us knowledge of God acting on men, and of ourselves before God."[22] What the Bible makes known, then, "is not a morality, but a reality, a living presence to whom man responds."[23] The Bible does not so much provide a morality as it is the source of images and analogies that help us understand and interpret the nature of our existence.[24]

This suggestion that scripture is revealed reality has the virtue of being more appropriate to the nature of scripture than does the idea of "revealed morality." But it too lacks appreciation for the political nature of the very concepts of authority and scripture associated with the idea of "revealed morality." As a result, scripture is mined for concepts and images, which are claimed to be biblically warranted but have the effect of legitimating the loss of any continuing engagement of a community with the biblical narratives. Emphasis on the Bible as the revelation of God can give the impression that scripture can be known and used apart from a community that has been formed and sustained by the reality that gives substance both to the scripture and to that community. No image of God, no matter how rich, can substitute for the "life-giving power" which Blenkinsopp suggests arises from a community's capacity to sustain the prophetic activity of remembering and reinterpreting the traditions of Yahweh.

3. The Moral Authority of Scripture

Thus, the very definition of the problem of the relation of scripture and ethics, as well as the suggestions designed to deal with that problem, often suffer from a failure to appreciate how claims for the authority of scripture are political. Indeed, the overtly political assertion that scripture has authority is seldom analyzed. Rather it is accepted as a statement of fact, when it is by no means clear what it means to say that scripture or anything else has authority. Therefore it is necessary to provide an account of authority that may illumine how scripture is or should be used in the life of church.

Although my analysis of authority will be distinct from an explicit discussion of scripture, the very meaning of scripture entails authoritative judgment. As David Kelsey has reminded us, to say "these texts are Christian scripture" is but a way of saying "these texts are authoritative for the life of the Christian church." So claims about the authority of scripture are analytic, since the scriptural texts' "authority for theology is logically grounded in and dependent on their authority for the life of the church generally. But since, concretely speaking, the life of church taken as some sort of organic whole *is* 'tradition', that means that the texts' authority for theology is dependent on their being authority for 'tradition.' "[25] Therefore, to call certain texts "scripture" means in part that the church relies upon them in a normatively decisive manner.

This situation is not peculiar to the Christian community, for the very meaning of authority is community dependent. Though authority is often confused with power or coercion, it draws its life from community in a quite different manner. Like power, authority is directive; unlike power, however, it takes its rationale not from the deficiencies of community but from the intrinsic demands of a common life.[26] The meaning of authority must be grounded in a community's self-understanding, which is embodied in its habits, customs, laws, and traditions; for this embodiment constitutes the community's pledge to provide the means for an individual more nearly to approach the truth.

The language of community is open to a great deal of misunderstanding, given its association with small, tightly knit groups. Yet the fact that a community requires authority indicates that it is a mistake to think of community in personal rather than institutional terms. A community is a group of persons who share a history and whose common set of interpretations about that history provide the basis for common actions. These interpretations may be quite diverse and controversial even within the community, but are sufficient to provide the individual members with the sense that they are more alike than unlike.

The diversity of accounts and interpretations of a community's experiences is exactly the basis of authority. For authority is that power of a community that allows for reasoned interpretations of the community's past and future goals. Authority, therefore, is not contrary to reason but essential to it. Authority is the means by which the wisdom of the past is critically appropriated by being tested by current realities as well as by challenging the too often self-imposed limits of the present. A person or institution may be the way authority is exercised, but their authority derives only from their ability to justify their decision in terms of the shared traditions of the community.

Thus, there is an essential connection between authority, tradition, and change. Reasoning from tradition is the primary form and method of authority. As James Mackey has pointed out, tradition "is a dimension of life itself. It is the whole way of life of a people as it is transmitted from generation to generation. So tradition shares with life the characteristic of being something which we do (if that is the correct word) and may do very well indeed, and may do for a very long time, before we bother to provide ourselves with a general theory about what it is that we are doing."[27]

Traditions by their nature require change, since there can be no tradition without interpretation. And interpretation is the constant adjustment that is required if the current community is to stay in continuity with tradition. As Mackey suggests, "Change and continuity are two facets of the same process, the process we call tradition. So much so that continuity can only be maintained by continual development, and development or change is only such (and not simply replacement) because of continuity. Tradition means continuity and change, both together and both equally."[28]

This is even more true when the tradition of a community is based on witnessing to non-repeatable events. For such events must be fitted within a narrative that is an interpretation. But that interpretation must remain open to a new narrative display not only in relation to the future, but also whenever we come to a new understanding of our past. That is why, as Barr reminds us, it is so often the case that interpretation of the scripture does not mean the discovery of new meaning (as if there was no previous meaning there), but the reappropriation of the tradition with a greater depth of understanding.[29] Interpretation does not mean or require departure from the tradition, though justified discontinuity is not illegitimate, but rather that the scripture is capable of unanticipated relevancy through reinterpretation.[30]

It is particularly useful to note how fundamentally political is this understanding of the relation of tradition and authority. Although revolutions may occur without tradition,[31] politics depends on tradition, for politics is nothing else but a community's internal conversation with itself concerning the various possibilities of understanding and extending its life. In fact, the very discussion necessary to maintain the tradition can be considered an end in itself, since it provides the means for the community to discover the goods it holds in common. Without the authority of the tradition to guide such a discussion there would be no possibility of the community drawing nearer to the truth about itself or the world.

Yves Simon illustrates this feature by his refusal to justify authority from what he called a deficiency theory of community. The deficiency theory holds that authority is necessary to secure the unified action of a community because not everything is normal, because wills are weak or perverse and intellects ignorant or blinded.[32] In contrast Simon argued that authority is required, not because we are deficient, but because as the number of deficiencies in a society or individuals decreases, the number of available choices increases. Therefore, according to Simon, "The function of authority with which we are concerned, i.e., that of procuring united action when the means to the common good are several, does not disappear but grows as deficiencies are made up; it originates not in the defects of men and societies but in the nature of society. It is an essential function."[33]

Authority is required, not because there is any one perception of the common good that controls all the others, but because there are many ways of seeking such a good. The necessity of authority grows from the fact that morality unavoidably involves judgments that by their nature are particular and contingent—that is, they could be otherwise. Tradition is but the history of a community's sharing of such judgments as they have been tested through generations. Authority is not, therefore, an external force that commands against our will; rather it proceeds from a common life made possible by tradition. Authority is not only compatible with freedom, but requires it, since the continued existence and excellence of the community is possible only by forming and perfecting new members. Yet freedom is not an end in itself, but the necessary condition for a community to come to a more truthful understanding of itself and the world.

Particularly important in this respect is Simon's contention that true authority must always call a community to what it has not yet become. He does not deny that authority must be grounded in community, or that whatever is identified as the common good must be built on what the community is, but he sees that authority must always continue to act as a witness to the truth if it is to be legitimate. Authority, therefore, functions at those points where the tradition of a community engages in the discussion necessary to subject its politics to the search of and judgment by the truth.

The fact that truth is known only by the conversation initiated by the tradition and carried out through political means signals something essential about the character of truth. For if truth could be known without struggle, there would be no need for the kind of politics I am suggesting is integral to its discovery. Truth in this sense is like a "knowing how"—a skill that can only be passed from master to apprentice. Tradition and authority are crucial to such a process, as they must guide us to what others have found to be true, even though in the process we may well find that in order to be faithful to the tradition we must criticize our current guides. The place of tradition and authority in this sense is no less required for the development of intellectual disciplines, including science, than the more practical aspects of our existence.

In summary I have suggested that authority requires community, but it is equally true that community must have authority. For authority is that reflection initiated by a community's traditions through which a common goal can be pursued.[34] Authority is, therefore, the means through which a community is able to journey from where it is to where it ought to be. It is set on its way by the language and practices of the tradition, but while on its way it must often subtly reform those practices and language in accordance with its new perception of truth.

By regarding scripture as an authority Christians mean to indicate that they find there the traditions through which their community most nearly comes to knowing and being faithful to the truth. Scripture is not meant to be a problem solver. It rather describes the process whereby the community we call the church is initiated by certain texts into what Barr has called the "vivid and lively pattern of argument and controversy" characteristic of biblical traditions.[35]

The Scripture is not an authority because it sets a standard of orthodoxy—indeed the very categories of orthodoxy and heresy are anachronistic when applied to scripture—but because the traditions of scripture provide the means for our community to find new life.[36] Blenkinsopp reminds us:

> That those responsible for the editing of the biblical material did not on the whole expunge views in conflict with their own, but rather allowed them to exist side by side in a state of unresolved tension or unstable equilibrium, is clearly a fact of significance for the understanding of Judaism—and, *mutatis mutandis,* of Christianity also. It suggests that one may appeal to a fixed tradition with absolute seriousness and still affirm its "infinite interpretability" (Scholem). Given the formative influence of different interpretations of the tradition on the shape and self-understanding of the community at different times, it also suggests that the community must be prepared to accept creative tension as a permanent feature of its life.[37]

Therefore when Christians claim scripture as authority for their community they are not claiming that the Bible is without error; or that the genres of the Bible are unique; or that the Bible contains a unique understanding of man, history, or even God as opposed to Greek or some other culture; or that the Bible manifests a unique *Weltanschauung* or contains an implicit metaphysics that still remains largely misunderstood; or that the Bible contains images without which we cannot achieve an adequate self-understanding; and so on. Rather to claim the Bible as authority is the testimony of the church that this book provides the resources necessary for the church to be a community sufficiently truthful so that our conversation with one another and God can continue across generations.

4.   Scripture as Moral Authority

This analysis of the authority of scripture lacks concreteness, however, since it leaves what scripture means quite unanalyzed. One can agree formally that scripture has or should have such authority for Christians, but still ask what it is about scripture that compels such authority. Even before that, however, one must ask what is meant by *scripture,* for I have already noted that scripture cannot simply be identified with the collection of texts we find in the Bible.

David Kelsey's analysis of the way theologians use scripture demonstrates that theologians "do not appeal to some objective text-in-itself but rather to a text construed *as* a certain kind of whole having a certain kind of logical force. To call each different way of construing the text 'scripture' is to use 'scripture' in importantly different ways. In short, the suggestion that scripture might serve as a final court of appeals for theological disputes is misleading because there is no one, normative concept of 'scripture.' Instead, there seems to be a family of related but importantly different concepts of 'scripture.'"[38]

As a means for exploring the different concepts of scripture Kelsey suggests that in each case we must ask what aspect of scripture is taken to be authoritative. His book consists in an analysis of three ways that theologians have located the authoritative aspect of biblical writing, namely: (1) the Bible as containing doctrinal or conceptual content; (2) the Bible as the source of mythic, symbolic, or imagistic expression of a saving event; (3) the Bible as the recital of a narrative. One of the interesting results of Kelsey's analysis is that those who look at the Bible as a source of doctrine and those who criticize this approach as failing to appreciate the Bible as a record of God's action in history equally fail to appreciate the narrative mode of much of the material in scripture. Ironically, as Kelsey shows, the emphasis on "God acting in history" is structurally similar to the construal of scripture in terms of concepts such as covenant, promise, and so on.[39]

There is no need for me to repeat here the work that Kelsey has already done so well. But one aspect of his analysis is critical for the development of my proposal. Kelsey notes the difference between scripture's uses in the common life of the church and its uses in theology.[40] A theologian's "working canon" and the "Christian canon" are not identical, for the theologian is obliged to decide what it is *in* scripture that is authoritative. And such a decision often results in an appeal to certain patterns characteristically exhibited by whatever aspect of scripture the theologian takes to be authoritative.[41]

So a theologian's claim that the scriptures have authority for the church will involve ascribing some sort of wholeness to the text or set of texts.[42] But because various kinds of wholeness can be ascribed to the texts, there can be no one concept of scripture. The theologian's attempt to propose how scripture should be understood and used in the church derives from an act of imagination that Kelsey, borrowing from Robert Johnson, calls a *discrimen*—that is, "a configuration of criteria that are in some way organically related to one another as reciprocal coefficients."[43]

Therefore, according to Kelsey, the relationship between the church, scripture, and theology turns out to be formally similar to the notorious "hermeneutical circle." For "the concrete ways in which biblical texts are used as scripture in the church's common life help shape a theologian's imaginative construal of the way that use is conjoined with God's presence among the faithful. The determinate patterns in scripture suggest a range of images from which he may select or construct a root metaphor for that *discrimen*. The particularities of the concrete use of scripture unique to the common life of the church as he experiences it will shape which image strikes him as most apt. Then, secondly, it is that imaginative characterization of the central reality of Christianity, 'what it is finally all about,' that *is* decisive for the way the theologian actually construes and uses biblical texts as scripture in the course of doing theology."[44]

Kelsey's analysis is particularly illuminating for exposing the influence the church has on how we construe scripture. Theologians, to be sure, make suggestions about how scripture can or should be understood, but such suggestions must be fueled by the common life of the church in both its liturgical and moral forms. So a theologian may construe and use scripture in ways determined by a "logically prior imaginative judgment," but that is not all that needs to be said. For such judgment, as Kelsey suggests, must be schooled by a community whose life has been shaped by the narratives of the scripture. How we use scripture is finally an affair of the imagination, but it is nonetheless a political activity, since our imagination depends on our ability to remember and interpret our traditions as they are mediated through the moral reality of our community.

For all its perspicacity, however, Kelsey's analysis fails to do justice to the ways in which scripture morally shapes a community. The idea of a *discrimen* suggests a far too singular and unifying image, whereas the actual use of scripture in the church, in liturgy, preaching, and in morality, is not so easily characterized. In fact I would maintain that many of the difficulties attendant upon locating the authoritative aspect of scripture in doctrine, concepts, or saving event(s) revolve around the attempt to provide a far too coherent account of scripture. Put differently, one reason the church has had to be content with the notion of a canon rather than some more intellectually satisfying summary of the content of scripture is that only through the means of a canon can the church adequately manifest the kind of tension with which it must live. The canon marks off as scripture those texts that are necessary for the life of the church without trying to resolve their obvious diversity and/or even disagreements.

Still, it may be asked, why these texts? My answer is simply: these texts have been accepted as scripture because they and they alone satisfy what Reynolds Price has called our craving for a perfect story which we feel to be true. Put briefly, that story is: "History is the will of a just God who knows us."[45] Therefore the status of the Bible as scripture "separated both from other written works and from the continuous accretion of oral tradition, represents a fundamental decision to assign a special status to the material it contains and to recognize it as the classic model for the understanding of God."[46] We continue to honor that decision made by the ancient church, however, because it is a decision that makes sense "in relation to the basic nature of Christian faith. Faith is Christian because it relates itself to classically-expressed models. This is much the same as what people mean when they say, rather vaguely and ambiguously, that 'Christianity is a historical religion.' Christian faith is not whatever a modern Christian may happen to believe, on any grounds at all, but faith related to Jesus and to the God of Israel. The centrality of the Bible is the recognition of the classic sources for the expression of Jesus and of God."[47]

The scripture functions as an authority for Christians precisely because by trying to live, think, and feel faithful to its witness they find they are more nearly able to live faithful to the truth. For the scripture forms a society and sets an agenda for its life that requires nothing less than trusting its existence to the God found through the stories of Israel and Jesus. The moral use of scripture, therefore, lies precisely in its power to help us remember the stories of God for the continual guidance of our community and individual lives. To be a community which lives by remembering is a genuine achievement, as too often we assume that we can insure our existence only by freeing ourselves from the past.

5.   The Morality of Remembering: The Scripture as Narrative

Obviously I am convinced that the most appropriate image—or as Kelsey insists, *discrimen*—for characterizing scripture, for the use of the church as well as morally, is that of a narrative or a story. James Barr rightly points out that the dealings of God with man in the Bible are indeed describable as a cumulative process, "in which later elements do build upon what was said and done at an earlier time. As I have argued, the literature is meant to be read as a story with a beginning and a progression. All 'acts of God' and incidents of the story make sense because a framework of meaning has already been created by previous acts, remembered in the tradition; they are 'further acts of one already known, of one with whom the fathers have already been in contact and have passed on the tradition of this contact.' "[48]

It is certainly true, as Barr recognizes, that scripture contains much material that is not narrative in character. But such material, insofar as it is scripture, gains its intelligibility by being a product of and contribution to a community that lives through remembering. The narrative of scripture not only "renders a character"[49] but renders a community capable of ordering its existence appropriate to such stories. Jews and Christians believe this narrative does nothing less than render the character of God and in so doing renders us to be the kind of people appropriate to that character. To say that character is bound up with our ability to remember witnesses to the fact that our understanding of God is not inferred from the stories but is the stories.[50]

One of the virtues of calling attention to the narrative nature of scripture is the way it releases us from making unsupportable claims about the unity of scripture or the centrality of the "biblical view of X or Y." Rather, the scripture must be seen as one long, "loosely structured non-fiction novel" that has subplots that at some points appear minor but later turn out to be central.[51] What is crucial, however, is that the scripture does not try to suppress those subplots or characters that may challenge, or at least qualify, the main story line, for without them the story itself would be less than truthful.[52]

Through scripture we see that at crucial periods in the life of Israel and the church, questions about how to remember the stories were not just questions about "fact" or accuracy, but about what kind of community we must be to be faithful to Yahweh and his purposes for us. So the question of the status of the Davidic kingship for Israel now in Exile could not be avoided as Israel sought to survive as a community without being a "nation."[53] The issue is not just one of interpretation but of what kind of people can remember the past and yet know how to go on in a changed world.

Moreover one does not need to be a New Testament scholar to recognize that questions in the early church about how to tell the life of Jesus were also issues about the kind of community needed to live in keeping with the significance of that life. How the story should be told was basically a moral issue, since it was also a question about what kind of people we ought to be. The unity of the Gospels is not dependent, therefore, on whether they can be made to agree on the details of Jesus' life or even whether various theologies are compatible; rather, the unity of the Gospels is based on the unquestioned assumption that the unity of these people required the telling of the story of this man who claimed to be nothing less than the Messiah of Israel.[54]

The fact that we now have a canon and recognize its authority in the church does not mean that we can be any less concerned about what kind of community we must be to remember rightly through the biblical narrative. Our selectivity and arbitrariness in using scripture ultimately result from our attempt to be something less than a people capable of carrying God's story in the world. For who "wants to hear about brave deeds when he is ashamed of his own, and who likes an open, honest tale from someone he's deceiving."[55] The canon is not an accomplishment but a task, since it challenges us to be the kind of people capable of recalling the stories of our fathers and mothers, on which our existence continues to depend.

The temptation, now that we have the canon, is either to objectify scripture in a manner that kills its life, or to be willing in principle to accept the validity of any interpretation by way of acknowledging the scripture's variety. Both responses fail to meet the moral challenge of being a people who derive their identity from a book. The continued existence of Israel is alone enough to make us recognize that the question of what kind of community we must be to be faithful to God is not an issue settled by the mere fact we possess a canon. I have tried to show how the very nature of the biblical literature requires us to be as able to remember as those who produced the literature.

The question of the moral significance of scripture, therefore, turns out to be a question about what kind of community the church must be to be able to make the narratives of scripture central for its life. I have already argued that such a community must be capable of sustaining the authority of scripture through use in its liturgy and governance. But first and foremost the community must know that it has a history and tradition which separate it from the world. Such separation is required by the very fact that the world knows not the God we find in the scripture.[56]

The virtues of patience, courage, hope, and charity must reign if the community is to sustain its existence. For without patience the church may be tempted to apocalyptic fantasy; without courage the church would fail to hold fast to the traditions from which it draws its life; without hope the church risks losing sight of its tasks; and without charity the church would not manifest the kind of life made possible by God. Each of these virtues, and there are others equally important, draws its meaning and form from the biblical narrative, and each is necessary if we are to continue to remember and to live faithful to that narrative.

As I have suggested, Christians continue to honor the decision of their ancestors to fashion a canon because they believe the scripture reflects the very nature of God and his will for their lives. Put more concretely, scripture has authority for Christians because they have learned as a forgiven people they must also be able to forgive.[57] But to be a people capable of accepting forgiveness separates them from the world: The world, under the illusion that power and violence rule history, assumes that it has no need to be forgiven. Part of the meaning of the "world," therefore, is it is that which assumes it needs no scripture, since it lives not by memory made possible by forgiveness, but by power.

Being a community of the forgiven is directly connected with being a community sustained by the narratives we find in scripture, as those narratives do nothing less than manifest the God whose very nature is to forgive. To be capable of remembering we must be able to forgive, for without forgiveness we can only forget or repress those histories that prove to be destructive or at least unfruitful. But Christians and Jews are commanded not to forget, since the very character of their community depends on their accepting God's forgiveness and thus learning how to remember, even if what they must remember is their sin and unrighteousness.[58] By attending closely to the example of those who have given us our scripture, we learn how to be a people morally capable of forgiveness and thus worthy of continuing to carry the story of God we find authorized by scripture.

6. The Moral Use of "Biblical Morality"

Some may well wonder whether this account of the moral authority of scripture has really helped us advance beyond the problems concerning the use of "biblical morality" described in section two. It may be objected that all I have done is redescribe as "moral" aspects of scripture and the process of its development which we already knew.[59] I may be right that remembering is a moral activity that requires a particular kind of community, especially if the stories we find in the scripture are to be remembered, but that still does not help us to know what to do with the more straightforwardly "moral" aspects of scripture—i.e., the Decalogue or the Sermon on the Mount. Nor does it help us understand what we are to do with those aspects of scripture that now seem irrelevant or, even worse, morally perverse.

For example, the complexity of the analysis offered here tends to obscure the straightforward command "Thou shalt not commit adultery," (Ex. 20:14) or the equally significant, "Do not resist one who is evil" (Matt. 5:39). In spite of all that one must say about the need to understand such passages in context, I am impressed by those who live as if such commands should directly govern their affairs. None of us should lose the suspicion that our sophistication concerning the cultural and theological qualifications about "biblical morality" often hides a profound unwillingness to have our lives guided by it.

Yet I contend that the position developed here does help us better comprehend the more straightforwardly moral portions of scripture. It keeps us from turning commands found there into isolated rules or principles that are assumed to have special status because they are in the Bible. Rather it proposes that Christians (and we hope others) take them to heart (and mind) because they have been found to be crucial to a people formed by the story of God. Such commands stand as reminders of the kind of people we must be if we are to be capable of remembering for ourselves and the world the story of God's dealing with us.

To take the prohibition of adultery, it does not claim to be intelligible in itself, but draws its force from the meaning and significance of marriage in the Jewish and Christian communities. Marriage in those communities derives from profound hope in and commitment to the future, witnessed by the willingness and duty to bring new life into the world. Moreover for those traditions family and marriage have special significance as they are also an expression of the relation these people have with their God. The prohibition against adultery does not therefore derive from a set of premises concerned directly with the legitimacy of sexual expression, though without doubt it has often been so interpreted, but from the profoundest commitment of the community concerning the form of sexual life necessary to sustain their understanding of marriage and family.

Nor does the prohibition against resisting evil derive from an assumption about violence as inherently evil, but rather from the community's understanding of how God rules his creation. For how can a people who believe God is Lord of their existence show forth that conviction if they act as if the meaning of their existence, and perhaps even history itself, must be insured by the use of force? The nonviolence of the church derives from the character of the story of God that makes us what we are—namely a community capable of witnessing to others the kind of life made possible when trust rather than fear rules our relation with one another.

I do not assume that all the moral advice and admonitions found in scripture have the same significance or should positively be appropriated. Each must be evaluated separately and critically. Of course, before we decide that certain aspects of scripture are no longer relevant—e.g., the *Haustafeln*—we must make sure we understand them through an exegesis as accurate as we can muster. And we must remember that a set of historical-critical skills will not guarantee an accurate reading. Our analysis will also depend on the questions we learn to put to the text from participating in a community which acknowledges their formative role.

The command for wives to be subject to their husbands, for example, comes only after the admonition that everyone in the church must be subject to the other out of "reverence for Christ " (Eph. 5:21). It does not say that wives should be subject to husbands as an end in itself, but rather as "to the Lord." So the manner of being "subject" cannot be read off the face of the text nor can it be made clear by exegesis alone. In fact, exegesis itself points us to recall the ways in which we as members of the church have learned to be subject to one another as faithful disciples of Christ. That direction should effectively restrain a contemporary reader from trying to understand "subordinate" from a perspective that assumes all moral relations which are not "autonomous" are morally suspect.

There is no doubt that the *Haustafeln* are in danger of great distortion and harm if they are lifted out of their theological and community context and turned into general admonitions meant to apply to any community. But that is just what their existence in scripture should prohibit. One need not agree with Yoder's argument that the *Haustafeln* were necessary because the freedom established by this new community created the possibility of insubordination in order to appreciate how the *Haustafeln* are but reminders of the radical nature of the new community that has been called into existence—namely, one where service to the other is freed from concern with status and envy.[60]

Finally, there can be no ethical use of scripture unless we are a community capable of following the admonition to put " away falsehood, let every one speak the truth with his neighbor, for we are members of one another. Be angry but do not sin; do not let the sun go down on your anger, and give no opportunity to the devil. Let the thief no longer steal, but rather let him labor, doing honest work with his hands, so that he may be able to give to those in need. Let no evil talk come out of your mouths, but such as is good for edifying, as fits the occasion, that it may impart grace to those that hear. And do not grieve the Holy Spirit of God, in whom you were sealed for the day of redemption. Let all bitterness and wrath and anger and clamor and slander be put away from you, with all malice, and be kind to one another, tenderhearted, forgiving one another, as God in Christ forgave you" (Eph. 4:25-32).

4. The Church and Liberal Democracy: The Moral Limits of a Secular Polity

1. Christian Social Ethics in a Secular Polity

It has become commonplace that we live in a secular world and society. But attempts to describe and assess the significance of being "secular" are notoriously controversial.[1] I have no intention of adding further fuel to that particular debate. Rather I want to concentrate on a more limited, but I think no less important, set of challenges a secular polity, such as liberal democracy, presents for Christian social ethics.[2]

By calling attention to the secular nature of our polity I am not trying to provide or defend a theory about what it means to live in the "modern world" or to be a "modern woman or man." All I mean by secular is that our polity and politics gives no special status to any recognizable religious group.[3] Correlatively such a policy requires that public policies be justified on grounds that are not explicitly religious.

American religious groups have been particularly supportive of this understanding of the secular nature of our polity, in that it seems to allow for the free expression of religious convictions without limiting any one group. Of course particular religious groups have in fact been discriminated against socially and politically, but such discrimination, we feel, is not endemic to how our polity should work. Moreover some interpret the secular nature of our polity, that is, our government's acknowledgment of its noncompetency in religion, as a profound confession of the limits of the state appropriate to a recognition of God's sovereignty or as a realistic understanding of human sinfulness.[4]

This positive evaluation presents a decisive challenge to Christian social ethics that we have seldom understood. Even as Christians recover the profound social significance of the Gospel, they find that the terms of expression and justification of those convictions must be secular. Many Christians assume this presents no problem, as the inherent justice of our secular and democratic polity provides the appropriate means for the expression of Christian social concerns. Most recent Christian social ethics in America has thus derived from the largely unexamined axiom that Christians should engage in politics to secure a more nearly just society. Following the lead of the social gospel, social ethics presumes that the task of Christians is to transform[5] our basic social and economic structures in order to aid individuals in need. Thus political involvement is seen to be the best mechanism to deal with, and perhaps even transform, structures of injustice.

While Christians have sometimes naively overestimated the extent of such transformations, they have also developed extremely sophisticated and influential portrayals of the moral possibilities and limits of our polity. Reinhold Niebuhr took the enthusiasm of the social gospel and made it all the more powerful by suggesting the limits of what love could accomplish through the politics characteristic of our society. Niebuhr saw clearly that love without power is ineffective, but that power must at the same time limit the possibilities of the realization of love. Yet those limits do not lessen the Christian duty to use power to secure the forms of justice possible in our social and political system.[6] To do anything less is to be unfaithful to the Christian's understanding of history and our involvement in it.

Moreover, from this perspective attempts by Christians to avoid political involvement because of the "dirty" nature of politics are rightly condemned as irresponsible, if not unfaithful. Rather it is the task of Christians to be politically involved exactly because we recognize that our politics inherently involves compromise and accommodation. To withdraw from the political in order to remain pure is an irresponsible act of despair. Even more, such withdrawal is self-deceptive as it creates the condition by which the political realm may claim unwarranted significance.

It is my contention, however, that Christian enthusiasm for the political involvement offered by our secular polity has made us forget the church's more profound political task. In the interest of securing more equitable forms of justice possible in our society, Christians have failed to challenge the moral presuppositions of our polity and society. Nowhere is the effect of this seen more powerfully than in the Christian acquiescence to the liberal assumption that a just polity is possible without the people being just.[7] We simply accepted the assumption that politics is about the distribution of desires, irrespective of the content of those desires, and any consideration of the development of virtuous people as a political issue seems an inexcusable intrusion into our personal liberty.

The more destructive result is that the church has increasingly imitated in its own social life the politics of liberalism. We have almost forgotten that the church is also a polity that at one time had the confidence to encourage in its members virtues sufficient to sustain their role as citizens in a society whose purpose was to counter the unwarranted claims made by other societies and states. Indeed, only if such people exist is it possible for the state to be ''secular.'' Because the church rarely now engenders such a people and community, it has failed our particular secular polity: Christians have lacked the power that would enable themselves and others to perceive and interpret the kind of society in which we live. Christians have rightly thought that they have a proper investment in making this, and other societies, more nearly just, but have forgotten that genuine justice depends on more profound moral convictions than our secular polity can politically acknowledge.

Christians must again understand that their first task is not to make the world better or more just, but to recognize what the world[8] is and why it is that it understands the political task as it does. The first social task of the church is to provide the space and time necessary for developing skills of interpretation and discrimination sufficient to help us recognize the possibilities and limits of our society. In developing such skills, the church and Christians must be uninvolved in the politics of our society and involved in the polity that is the church. Theologically, the challenge of Christian social ethics in our secular polity is no different than in any time or place—it is always the Christian social task to form a society that is built on truth rather than fear. For the Christian, therefore, the church is always the primary polity through which we gain the experience to negotiate and make positive contributions to whatever society in which we may find ourselves.

2.   A Critique of Our Society

Insofar as many Christians assume that our liberal and secular society is at least neutral to, if not positively an advantage for, the church, we have failed to see and understand the depth of the moral challenge facing this society. Of course we all recognize our society has problems, but we assume our society and politics have the means to deal with them. We have no reason to question fundamentally our ''form of government'' or the ''American way of life.'' Rather, as Christians we assume we have a stake in America's extraordinary experiment to create a free people through the mechanism of democratic government.[9]

We thus feel puzzled by critiques of our society such as that of Solzhenitsyn. For it is the brunt of his charge that a polity is ultimately judged by the kind of people it produces, and from such a perspective our society can only be found wanting. He suggests that for all the injustice and terror of the

Russian and Eastern European societies, they have been through a spiritual training far advanced of the Western experience:

> Life's complexity and mortal weight have produced stronger, deeper, and more interesting characters than those generated by the standardized Western well-being. It is true, no doubt, that a society cannot remain in an abyss of lawlessness, as in our country. But it is also demeaning for it to elect such mechanical legalistic smoothness as you have. After the suffering of decades of violence and oppression, the human soul longs for things higher, warmer, and purer than those offered by today's mass living habits, introduced by the revolting invasion of publicity, by TV stupor, and by intolerable music.[10]

It is tempting to dismiss such attacks as failing to understand the character of the American people or our form of government. Some have suggested that Solzhenitsyn has confused a social and cultural critique with a political critique.[11] Yet to dismiss Solzhenitsyn in this way is but to manifest the problem he is trying to point out. For we have assumed that we can form a polity that ignores the relation between politics and moral virtue. In contrast, Solzhenitsyn takes the classical view that it should be the function of politics to direct people individually and collectively toward the good.[12]

Thus Solzhenitsyn's critique is radical insofar as it reaches to the roots of our societal presuppositions. In effect he is suggesting that when freedom becomes an end in itself people lose their ability to make sacrifices for worthy ends. The problem with our society is not that democracy has not worked, but that it has, and the results are less than good.[13] We have been freed to pursue happiness and "every citizen has been granted the desired freedom and material goods in such quantity and of such quality as to guarantee in theory the achievement of happiness. In the process, however, one psychological detail has been overlooked: the constant desire to have still more things and a still better life and the struggle to obtain them imprints many Western faces with worry and even depression, though it is customary to conceal such feelings. Active and tense competition permeates all human thoughts without opening a way to free spiritual development."[14]

Moreover, one of the great ironies of our society is that by attempting to make freedom an end in itself we have become an excessively legalistic society. As Solzhenitsyn points out, we feel there is little need for voluntary self-restraint, as we are free to operate to the limit of the law. Thus in condemning Richard Nixon, virtues of decency and honesty were invoked, but the legal system offered the only code by which the unacceptableness of those actions could be clearly and cogently expressed. An insightful commentator of the "Talk of the Town" column in the *New Yorker* observed that

Nixon's legal gymnastics to claim innocence in his interview with Frost was in a sense truthful—

> truthful in that he honestly did not know of any other moral framework by which to judge himself, truthful in that no other armature of principle was available to him on which to mold an understanding of his character. One searched for a hint of something in his character, some shred of belief or awareness, that might have given him the strength and the foothold—a motive—to act differently; but, save for the misgiving that his strategy might backfire, no such motive was there. . . . And yet if one asked onself what that foothold of belief might have been, there was no ready answer—only a prickling of dread. Each of us may have a sense of principle which he has generated himself, or has drawn from his particular background, but that is not a satisfactory answer here. What is called for is principles that can be pointed to as the mainstays of the culture, principles of which no disparate individuals but the society is the custodian. What is needed is something that could be called a tradition. Individual ethics can be very fine, but they cannot survive for long if they are not reinforced by the society, and even while they last they can have little public significance if they are not echoed in the general moral awareness of the world in which their possessor lives. Perhaps such an awareness does exist, but, if so, it has become so obscured that we cannot be sure what it is, or even whether it is there at all. Under these circumstances the only way in which we can clearly distinguish ourselves from Richard Nixon is by our view that the legal system is inadequate as a moral tradition. Unlike him, we are not at all comfortable when the legal system is made to assume this role. And we become even more uneasy as it occurs to us that there may be nothing sounder available to us.[15]

That our society has been brought to such a pass is no surprise to Solzhenitsyn, as he thinks it is the inevitable result of a social order whose base is the humanism of the Enlightenment, which presupposed that intrinsic evil did not exist, nor did man have any higher task than the attainment of his own happiness. "Everything beyond physical well-being and accumulation of material goods, all other human requirements and characteristics of a subtler and higher nature, were left outside the area of attention of state and social system, as if human life did not have any superior sense."[16] But such presumptions are profoundly false and any politics founded on them can only lead men to destruction, for

> if humanism were right in declaring that man is born to be happy, he would not be born to die. Since his body is doomed to die, his task on

earth evidently must be of a more spiritual nature. It cannot be unrestrained enjoyment of everyday life. It cannot be the search for the best ways to obtain material goods and then cheerfully get the most out of them. It has to be the fulfillment of a permanent, earnest duty so that one's life journey may become an experience of moral growth, so that one may leave life a better human being than one started it.[17]

Now it must be admitted that for those of us identified with religious traditions the kind of rhetoric Solzhenitsyn used in his Harvard address is a bit of an embarrassment. It is frankly religious rhetoric and somehow we have come to think such condemnations of the political order a bit out of place. Such rhetoric is for matters personal and best left to those institutions that specialize in such matters—that is, the family and the church. Solzhenitsyn seems not to realize that our society's commitment to "religious freedom" is based exactly on the understanding that the church will not challenge the primary assumption of our system. The very materialism and banality of American life that Solzhenitsyn condemns is the price, and not a high price at that, we must pay in order to make the state neutral in matters moral and religious. Solzhenitsyn wrongly assumes that the characteristics of the American people he finds so unappealing are matters of public concern rather than religious concern. Politically we are right to take up a stance of self-interest; morally and religiously we know however that self-interest is not an appropriate form of life for the rest of our lives.

Thus we console ourselves with the idea that Solzhenitsyn has failed to understand the genius of our polity because he fails to see the moral advance represented by the amorality of our politics. His view of us is therefore too myopic and narrow and he fails to appreciate those "non-political" aspects of our lives that should qualify his overly harsh judgments about the shallowness of American life. Yet I think Solzhenitsyn's critique remains accurate,[18] but to demonstrate that, it is necessary to pay closer attention to our profoundest political assumptions. For I want to suggest that the moral insufficiencies Solzhenitsyn finds so destructive about our society are necessarily built into the founding assumptions of America and have been reinforced by our best political practices and philosophy.

3. The Moral Assumptions of Political Liberalism

The American political system has been the testing ground for the viability of liberal theory. To be sure, "liberalism" is a many-faced and historically ambiguous phenomenon, and historically and culturally there were many factors in American life that served to qualify its impact.[19] But it is still the case that America, more than any nation before or after, has been the product of a theory of government.[20] Our assumption has been that, unlike other societies, we are not creatures of history, but that we have the possibility of a new beginning.[21] We are thus able to form our government on the basis of principle rather than the arbitrary elements of a tradition.

Our assumptions in this respect profoundly distort our history, but their power is hard to deny. Liberalism is successful exactly because it supplies us with a myth that seems to make sense of our social origins. For there is some truth to the fact that we originally existed as a people without any shared history, but came with many different kinds of histories. In the absence of any shared history we seemed to lack anything in common that could serve as a basis for societal cooperation. Fortunately, liberalism provided a philosophical account of society designed to deal with exactly that problem: A people do not need a shared history; all they need is a system of rules that will constitute procedures for resolving disputes as they pursue their various interests. Thus liberalism is a political philosophy committed to the proposition that a social order and corresponding mode of government can be formed on self-interest and consent.

From this perspective the achievement of the Constitution is not its fear of tyranny, or even its attempt to limit the totalitarian impulses of the majority. Rather the wisdom and achievement of the Constitution comes from the guiding "assumption that only by institutionalizing the self-interest of the leaders, on the one hand, and of the individual citizen, on the other, could tyranny be averted."[22] The ethical and political theory necessary to such a form of society was that the individual is the sole source of authority. Thus Hobbes and Locke, to be sure in very different ways, viewed the political problem as how to get individuals, who are necessarily in conflict with one another, to enter into a cooperative arrangement for their mutual self-interest.

Likewise, Madison assumed that "the causes of faction are sown into the nature of man," and since such causes cannot be eliminated without destroying "freedom," the primary task of government is to control the effects of conflict. He argues in the tenth *Federalist* essay that the chief advantage of an extended republic is that aggregates of self-interested individuals will find it difficult to interfere with the rights of others to pursue their self-interest. Thus, William Hixson argues, Madison justified his understanding of our political character on two suppositions, that

the only possible source of public authority is the private need of the independently situated political actors, each of whom is vested with a right to act according to self-defined standards of conscience and interest, and second, that the only legitimate function of "the sovereign" is the preservation of order through the management of conflict between such individuals.[23]

The irony is that our founders thought that the system of competing factions would work only if you could continue to assume that people were virtuous. John Adams in his first year as vice-president under the new constitution said: "We have no government armed with power capable of contending with human passions unbridled by morality and religion. Our constitution was made only for a moral and a religious people. It is wholly inadequate for the government of any other." Yet the very theory that has formed our public rhetoric and institutions gives no sufficient public basis for the development of such people. It was assumed that in making "morality" a matter of the "private sphere"—that is, what we do with our freedom—it could still be sustained and have an indirect public impact. But we know this has not been the case; our "private" morality has increasingly followed the form of our public life. People feel their only public duty is to follow their own interests as far as possible, limited only by the rule that we do not unfairly limit others' freedom. As a result we have found it increasingly necessary to substitute procedures and competition for the absence of public virtues. The bureaucracies in our lives are not simply the result of the complexities of an industrialized society, but a requirement of a social order individualistically organized.[24]

Many of our current political problems and the way we understand and try to solve them are a direct outgrowth of our liberal presuppositions. For example, the American government is often condemned for its inability to develop an economic or energy policy, but such policies must necessarily be public policies. Just as it has been the genius of the American political system to turn every issue of principle into an issue of interest, so it has been the intention of our polity to make impossible the very idea of public policy or public interest. Public policy cannot exist because society is nothing more than an aggregate of self-interested individuals. The policy which is formulated therefore must be the result of a coalescence of self-interests that is then justified in the name of the greatest good for the greatest number (but too often turns out to be the greatest good for the most powerful). Liberalism thus becomes a self-fulfilling prophecy; a social order that is designed to work on the presumption that people are self-interested tends to produce that kind of people.

It is often pointed out that there is a deep puzzle about the American people, for in spite of being the best off people in the world, their almost frantic pursuit of abundance seems to mask a deep despair and loss of purpose. I suspect that our despair is the result of living in a social order that asks nothing from us but our willingness to abide by the rules of fair competition. We have been told that it is moral to satisfy our "wants" and "needs," but we are no longer sure what our wants and needs are or should be. After all, "wants" are but individual preferences. Americans, as is often contended, are good people or at least want to be good people, but our problem is that we have lost any idea of what that could possibly mean. We have made "freedom of the individual" an end in itself and have ignored that fact that most of us do not have the slightest idea of what we should do with our freedom. Indeed, the idealists among us are reduced to fighting for the "freedom" or "right" of others to realize their self-interests more fully.

Such a system is defended because, whatever its faults, it is at least noncoercive. Therefore our public policies are formed in a manner that avoids as much as possible impinging on anyone's self-interest. As a result we fail to notice that "freedom" can become coercive by the very conception of "choice" it provides. For example, in his remarkable book *The Gift Relationship*, Richard Titmuss compares the blood distribution systems in America and Britain.[25] In Britain the only way one is allowed to obtain blood is through a voluntary donor who does not know to whom his or her blood is given. It is against the law to sell one's blood. In America we rely on diverse ways to obtain blood, ranging from voluntary programs to buying it. We feel that our system is inherently superior to the British because we do not prevent anyone from giving or selling their blood. We have a choice and are therefore free.

What we fail to notice is that by giving a "choice" we also create the assumption that blood, like cars and toothbrushes, can be bought and sold. We thus ignore the fact that the choice of selling blood trains us to see blood as simply one commodity among others. Put differently, what we have overlooked is that social policies should not only be efficient and fair, but they should also train us to have certain virtues as citizens. By concentrating on whether our policies are efficient, we have implicitly trained ourselves to assume that all human relationships should as much as possible take the form of an exchange model.[26] Thus Kenneth Arrow, in criticism of Titmuss' argument in favor of the British system, suggests

> I do not want to rely too heavily on substituting ethics for self-interest. I think it best on the whole that the requirement of ethical behavior be confined to those circumstances where the price system breaks down. Wholesale usage of ethical standards is apt to have undesirable consequences. We do not wish to use up recklessly the scarce resources of altruistic motivation, and in any case ethically motivated behavior may even have a negative value to others if the agent acts without sufficient knowledge of the situation.[27]

We should not be too hasty in criticizing Arrow's claim that the economic model should prevail for as many relations as possible, since he is stating the profoundest assumptions of a liberal polity. For liberal polity is the attempt to show that societal cooperation is possible under the conditions of distrust. The very genius of our society is to forge a political and social existence that does not have to depend on trusting others in matters important for our survival. Thus to leave our destiny to the gift of blood from a stranger simply becomes unthinkable.

Of course the more it becomes unthinkable to trust a stranger, the more we must depend on more exaggerated forms of protection. But the human costs of distrust are perhaps the most destructive. For we are increasingly forced to view one another as strangers rather than as friends, and as a result we become all the more lonely. We have learned to call our loneliness "autonomy" and/or freedom, but the freer we become the more desperate our search for forms of "community" or "interpersonal relationship" that offer some contact with our fellows. Even the family is not immune from this development, since we now assume that children should have "rights" against the parents, as if the family itself were but a contractual society.[28]

In spite of our claim that the family is the bedrock of our society, the family has always been an anomaly for the liberal tradition. Only if human beings can be separated in a substantial degree from kinship can they be free individuals subject to egalitarian policies. Thus we assume—and this is an assumption shared by political conservatives and activists alike—that it is more important to be an "autonomous person" than to be a "Hauerwas" or a "Pulaski" or a "Smith." For example, the Supreme Court recently held in *Planned Parenthood* vs. *Danforth* that a husband has no rights if his wife wishes an abortion, because "abortion is a purely personal right of the woman, and the status of marriage can place no limitations on personal rights."[29]

Or, for example, Milton Friedman, the paradigm liberal whom we mistakenly call "conservative," claims that for liberals "freedom of the individual or perhaps the family, is our ultimate goal in judging social arrangements. In a society freedom has nothing to say about what an individual does with his freedom; it is not an all-embracing ethic. Indeed, a major aim of the liberal is to leave the ethical problem for the individual to wrestle with."[30] But Friedman fails to recognize that the kind of freedom gained by the individual in our society is incompatible with freedom of the family. A society that leaves the "ethical problem to the individual" cannot engender or sustain the virtues necessary for providing the individual or the family the power to resist the state.[31]

Shorn of particularistic commitments essential to our public life, we exist as individuals, but now "individuals" is but a name for a particular unit of arbitrary desires. As C. B. Macpherson argues, liberalism's embrace of the market as the dominant institution of society involved a fundamental change in the conception of human nature. The traditional view of man was that of a being whose activity was an end in itself. With the rise of the market society the essence of rational purpose was taken to be the pursuit of possessions—we are what we own. But as soon as you

> take the essence of man to be the acquisition of more *things* for himself, as soon as you make the essential human quality the striving for possessions rather than creative activity, you are caught up in an insoluble contradiction. Human beings are sufficiently unequal in strength and skill that if you put them into an unlimited contest for possessions, some will not only get more than others, but will get control of the means of labor to which the others must have access. The others then cannot be fully human even in the restricted sense of being able to get possessions, let alone in the original sense of being able to use their faculties in purposive creative activity. So in choosing to make the essence of man the striving for possessions, we make it impossible for many men to be fully human.[32]

Ironically, however, when such a view of man prevails scarcity becomes an ever-present necessity. For scarcity is a necessary social creation when men are defined as having unlimited desires. The genius of liberalism was to make what had always been considered a vice, namely unlimited desire, a virtue. Thus it became legitimate for us to assume that the governing law of human nature is "the insatiable desire of every man for power to render the person and properties of others subservient to his pleasures."[33] Indeed such a view has us so strongly in its grip that we are now unable to think what might sustain a society that did not make scarcity integral to its understanding of man. No matter how great our abundance, we assume it is necessary to make and want more, even if the acquisition of more requires the unjust exploitation of "less developed lands." In truth we have no choice, for in a social order where distrust is primary we can only rely on abundance and technology to be a substitute for cooperation and community.

The recent emphasis on "justice" in the elegant ethical and political theory eleborated by John Rawls might be taken to indicate that liberalism is capable of a profounder sense of justice than I have described. Without going into the detailed argument necessary to criticize Rawls, his book stands as a testimony to the moral limits of the liberal tradition. For the "original position" is a stark metaphor for the ahistorical approach of liberal theory, as the self is alienated from its history and simply left with its individual preferences and prejudices.[34] The "justice" that results from the bargaining game is but the guarantee that my liberty to consume will be fairly limited within the overall distributive shares. To be sure, some concern for the "most disadvantaged" is built into the system, but not in a manner that qualifies my appropriate concern for my self-interest. Missing entirely from Rawls' position is any suggestion that a theory of justice is ultimately dependent on a view of the good; or that justice is as much a category for individuals as for societies. The question is not only how should the shares of any society be distributed equitably, but what bounds should individuals set for themselves if they are to be just. In an effort to rid liberalism of a social system built on envy, Rawls has to resort to the extraordinary device of making all desires equal before the bar of justice. As a result he represents the ultimate liberal irony: individualism, in an effort to secure societal cooperation and justice, must deny individual differences.

Perhaps Solzhenitsyn's critique is truer than even he suspected, for his criticisms reach to the basic moral presumptions of our society. Perhaps what he criticizes in us results not from our having been untrue to our best insights, but because we have been true to them. Of course, there have always been richer experiences of trust and community in our polity, but the problem is that such experience and community have no way to find political expression.[35] Thus blacks are encouraged to participate fully in our political process so that their interests might be known, yet there is no political recognition that the history of their suffering might or should be recognized as a valuable political resource.[36] Such concerns make good political rhetoric, but have little to do with the reality of politics which deals with the satisfaction of interests as articulated through group conflict and cooperation.

4.   The Church as a School for Virtue

If this analysis of our society's polity is even close to being correct, then it is by no means clear what the church's stance ought to be. The temptation is to assume that the task of the church is to find a political alternative or ways to qualify some of the excesses of liberalism. But such a strategy is both theologically and ethically problematic, for it fails to recognize that our society offers no ready alternatives to liberalism. We are all liberals. In fact for us in America, liberalism, a position dedicated to ending our captivity to nature, custom, and coercion, ironically has become our fate. The great self-deception is in thinking that the tradition of liberalism gives us the means to recognize that it is indeed a tradition. Instead it continues to promise us new tomorrows of infinite creation. And the more we are convinced we are free, the more determined we become.

For the church to adopt social strategies in the name of securing justice in such a social order is only to compound the problem. Rather the church must recognize that her first social task in any society is to be herself.[37] At the very least that means that the church's first political task is to be the kind of community that recognizes the necessity that all societies, church and political alike, require authority. But for Christians our authority is neither in society itself nor in the individual; it is in God.[38] As a result the church must stand as a reminder to the pretensions of liberalism that in spite of its claims to legitimate authority, some necessarily rule over others as if they had the right to command obedience.

The church also has a constitution that requires consent, but its constitution takes the form of the story of a savior who taught us to deal with power by recognizing how God limits all earthly claims to power.[39] Because we have been so called and formed, Christians should be free from the fear that fuels the power of coercion for liberal and illiberal states alike. The moral adventure represented by liberalism has been to diffuse the coercive nature of the state and society by developing a culture and government that left the individual to his or her own desires. As a result the coercive aspects of our social order are hidden, since they take the appearance of being self-imposed. Yet the distrust of the other inherent in liberal social and political theory cannot help but create powers that claim our loyalties and destructively run our lives.

Ironically, the most coercive aspect of the liberal account of the world is that we are free to make up our own story. The story that liberalism teaches us is that we have no story, and as a result we fail to notice how deeply that story determines our lives. Accordingly, we fail to recognize the coercive form of the liberal state, as it, like all states, finally claims our loyalty under the self-deceptive slogan that in a democracy the people rule themselves because they have "consented" to be so ruled. But a people who have learned the strenuous lesson of God's lordship through Jesus' cross should recognize that "the people" are no less tyrannical than kings or dictators.

In the absence of anyone knowing the truth, it has been the liberal assumption that "the people," particularly as they balance one another's desires, limit the power of falsehood. The church accepted such a strategy because it seemed to express a humility about the status of the state that, if not founded on the confession of God's lordship, at least was appropriate to our conviction that God limits all earthly power. Moreover, such a strategy seemed to offer the church freedom to preach the Gospel in a manner few societies had ever been willing to allow. While reveling in such "freedom" we failed to notice that the church had again been coopted into accepting the assumption that the destiny of a particular state and social order was intrinsic to God's Kingdom.

The challenge of the political today is no different than it has always been, though it appears in a new form. The challenge is always for the church to be a "contrast model" for all polities that know not God. Unlike them, we know that the story of God is the truthful account of our existence, and thus we can be a community formed on trust rather than distrust. The hallmark of such a community, unlike the power of the nation-states, is its refusal to resort to violence to secure its own existence or to insure internal obedience. For as a community convinced of the truth, we refuse to trust any other power to compel than the truth itself.

It is in that connection that the church is in a certain sense "democratic," for it believes that through the story of Christ it best charts its future. We rejoice in the difference and diversity of gifts among those in the church, as that very diversity is the necessary condition for our faithfulness. Discussion becomes the hallmark of such a society, since recognition and listening to the other is the way our community finds the way of obedience.[40] But the church is radically not democratic if by democratic we mean that no one knows the truth and therefore everyone's opinion counts equally. Christians do not believe that there is no truth; rather truth can only be known through struggle. That is exactly why authority in the church is vested in those we have learned to call saints in recognition of their more complete appropriation of that truth.

Put starkly, the way the church must always respond to the challenge of our polity is to be herself. This does not involve a rejection of the world, or a withdrawal from the world; rather it is a reminder that the church must serve the world on her own terms. We must be faithful in our own way, even if the world understands such faithfulness as disloyalty. But the first task of the church is not to supply theories of governmental legitimacy or even to suggest strategies for social betterment. The first task of the church is to exhibit in our common life the kind of community possible when trust, and not fear, rules our lives.

Such a view of the political task of the church should not sound strange to Christians, whose very existence was secured by people who were willing to die rather than conform to the pretentious claims of government. And we must remember that the demand that religion be freed from state control was not simply an attempt to gain toleration, but to make clear that the church represented a polity truer and more just than the state can ever embody. Simply because we live in a society that has institutionalized "freedom of religion" does not mean the church's political task has thereby been accomplished.

This kind of challenge is all the more needed in a society like ours that is living under the illusion that justice can be based on the assumption that man rather than God controls the world. As John Howard Yoder has suggested, "it is more important to know with what kind of language we criticize the structures of oppression than to suggest that we have the capacity to provide an alternative which would not also be a structure of oppression."[41] As Christians we have a language to describe the problems of liberalism, but we have become hesitant and embarrassed to use it. We must take courage from Solzhenitsyn's example and clearly say that the problem with our society and politics is its sinful presumption that man is born to be happy, when he clearly has to die. A truthful politics is one that teaches us to die for the right thing, and only the church can be trusted with that task.[42]

Moreover, by taking seriously its task to be an alternative polity, the church might well help us to experience what a politics of trust can be like. Such communities should be the source for imaginative alternatives for social policies that not only require us to trust one another, but chart forms of life for the development of virtue and character as public concerns. The problem in liberal societies is that there seems to be no way to encourage the development of public virtue without accepting a totalitarian strategy from the left or an elitist strategy from the right. By standing as an alternative to each, the church may well help free our social imagination from those destructive choices. For finally social and political theory depends on people having the experience of trust rather than the idea of trust.

But we must admit the church has not been a society of trust and virtue. At most, people identify the church as a place where the young learn "morals," but the "morals" often prove to be little more than conventional pieties coupled with a few unintelligible "don'ts." Therefore any radical critique of our secular polity requires an equally radical critique of the church.

And it is a radical critique, for I am not calling for a return to some conservative stance of the church. My call is for Christians to exhibit confidence in the lordship of Yahweh as the truth of our existence and in particular of our community. If we are so confident, we cannot help but serve our polity, for such confidence creates a society capable of engendering persons of virtue and trust. A people so formed are particularly important for the continued existence of a society like ours, as they can provide the experience and skills necessary for me to recognize the difference of my neighbor not as a threat but as essential for my very life.

PART TWO

Church and World: History, Politics, and the Virtues

5. The Church in a Divided World: The Interpretative Power of the Christian Story

1.   Truthfulness, Narrative, and Christian Ethics: Some Preliminary Considerations

Christian ethics as a self-conscious activity is a rather recent development. Of course being a Christian has always involved moral claims, but rarely before the nineteenth century was it thought necessary to analyze the conceptual and logical relation between Christian belief and action. Insofar as Christian ethics existed as a recognizable activity, among Protestants it took the form of practical moral guidance designed to help believers conform more completely to their beliefs. Catholic moral theology seemed to be more critically self-conscious, but impressive as the accomplishments of that tradition are, its close connection with penitential practice did not require theological analysis of the relation of religious convictions to moral judgments. In fact, Catholic claims about the status of natural law in principle implied that theological claims were not required to justify basic moral judgments.[1]

The preoccupation with Christian ethics as a, if not *the*, central enterprise of Christian theology is primarily a legacy of Protestant liberalism. As the central Christian beliefs came under increasingly successful philosophical and historical challenges, an emphasis on the moral significance of those beliefs seemed to offer a strategy to save their meaningfulness. Therefore Christian ethics, as a self-conscious endeavor, represented a retrenchment to secure some meaning, if not truth, for religious belief. The moral implications of the doctrines of God, Jesus, and reconciliation appeared to be the nail on which the continued viability of Christianity could hang. Of course this strategy was beset by deep problems in that no necessary relation could be shown between morality and increasingly isolated and abstract religious symbols and doctrines. While the very meaningfulness of religious discourse depended on a satisfactory account of the relation of "religion" and "morality," such accounts always seemed to involve fatally reductionistic accounts of religious beliefs. The "moral" kernel did not seem to require the "religious" claims associated with it.

This endeavor was partially obscured by the recovery of the social significance of the Gospel. The social gospel movement gave birth to a generation of Christian social critics and reformers who, often influenced by nineteenth-century theologians, turned their attention to developing strategies for the realization of justice in the social realm. They were little interested in how their conception of "justice" was derived from or informed by their religious convictions. They simply assumed that one was in some manner connected with the other. Nor were they much interested in questions of the truthfulness of their religious convictions, as they were more concerned with the social implications of those convictions.

But the question of the truth of religious convictions cannot or should not go away; it simply needs to be asked in the right way. Nineteenth-century theologians were right that moral concerns are central for understanding the power of religious convictions, but they provided a too limited account of the nature of those convictions and how they work morally. By calling attention to the narrative character of Christian convictions, however, the reductionistic assumptions associated with the ethics sponsored by Protestant liberalism can be avoided. For the fact is that there are no doctrines for which one must search out moral implications; rather "doctrines" and "morality" gain their intelligibility from narratives that promise to help us see and act in a manner appropriate to the character of our existence.

The narrative nature of Christian convictions helps us see that "ethics" is not what one does after one has gotten straight on the meaning and truth of religious beliefs; rather Christian ethics offers the means for exploring the meaning, relation, and truthfulness of Christian convictions. That is not to say that Christian convictions are proven meaningful or true by showing their ethical implications; rather they are both true and ethical in that they force us to a true understanding of ourselves and our existence. Christian ethics must deal with the fact that either separation or too close an identity between theology and ethics distorts the character of Christian convictions, as the beliefs that claim to provide a truthful understanding of God, self, and the world do so only as they also transform the self. Religious convictions, at least Christian convictions, are not primitive worldviews that must be given more sophisticated metaphysical or literal expression before they can be tested for their truth. Rather the claims they make about the way things are involve convictions about the way *we* should be if we are to be *able* to see truthfully the way things are.

If we are to understand how Christian convictions help us to form our lives truthfully the narrative nature of our lives must be recognized. To stress the significance of narrative at the very least helps remind us that the documents crucial to the life of the Christian community take the form of a narrative. Of course some of the material in those documents is not immediately narrative in form, but such material could not exist without the narratives and indeed draws its intelligibility from them. To insist on the significance of narrative for theological reflection is not, however, just to make a point about the form of biblical sources, but involves claims about the nature of God, the self, and the nature of the world. We are "storied people" because the God that sustains us is a "storied God," whom we come to know only by having our character formed appropriate to God's character.

The formation of such character is not an isolated event but requires the existence of a corresponding society—a "storied society." Therefore the truthfulness of Christian convictions can only be tested by recognizing that they involve the claim that the character of the world is such that it requires the formation of a people who are clearly differentiated from the world. For the church, as H. R. Niebuhr suggested,

> lives and defines itself in action vis-a-vis the world. World, however, is not object of Church as God is. World, rather, is companion of the Church, a community something like itself with which it lives before God. The world is sometimes enemy, sometimes partner of Church, often antagonist, always one to be befriended; now it is the co-knower, now the one that does not know what the Church knows, now the knower of what the Church does not know. The world is the community of those before God who feel rejected by God and reject him; again it is the community of those who do not know God and seem not to be known by him; or, it is the community of those who knowing God do not worship him. In all cases it is the community to which the Church addresses itself with its gospel, to which it gives account of what it has seen and heard in divine revelation, which it invites to come and see and hear. The world is the community to which Christ comes and to which he sends his disciples.[2]

Through the church, therefore, the world is given a history.[3] Indeed the term "world" derives its intelligibility from there being a people who can supply a history for the world. Of course such a history cannot ignore the fact that the world involves many separate stories that cannot be easily reconciled or even related. It is not the task of the church to deny the reality of the multiplicity of stories in the world or to force the many stories into an artificial harmony. Rather the task of the church is to be faithful to the story of God that makes intelligible the divided nature of the world.

The existence of the church, therefore, is not an accidental or contingent fact that can be ignored in considerations of the truth of Christian convictions. The church, and the social ethic implied by its separate existence, is an essential aspect of why Christians think their convictions are true. For it is a central Christian conviction that even though the world is God's creation and subject to God's redemption it continues eschatologically to be a realm that defies his rule. The church, which too often is unfaithful to its task, at the very least must lay claim to being the earnest of God's Kingdom and thus able to provide the institutional space for us to rightly understand the disobedient, sinful, but still God-created character of the world. The ethical significance of Christian convictions depends on the power of those convictions to shape a community sufficient to face truthfully the nature of our world.

Christian social ethics should not begin with attempts to develop strategies designed to make the world more "just," but with the formation of a society shaped and informed by the truthful character of the God we find revealed in the stories of Israel and Jesus. The remarkable richness of these stories of God requires that a church be a community of discourse and interpretation that endeavors to tell these stories and form its life in accordance with them. The church, the whole body of believers, therefore cannot be limited to any one historical paradigm or contained by any one institutional form. Rather the very character of the stories of God requires a people who are willing to have their understanding of the story constantly challenged by what others have discovered in their attempt to live faithful to that tradition. For the church is able to exist and grow only through tradition, which—as the memory sustained over time by ritual and habit—sets the context and boundaries for the discussion required by the Christian stories. As Frank Kermode has recently reminded us, the way to interpret a narrative is through another narrative;[4] indeed, a narrative is already a form of interpretation, as the power of a narrative lies precisely in its potential for producing a community of interpretation sufficient for the growth of further narratives.

Inevitably, calling attention to the narrative shape of Christian convictions means that Christian ethics must be taken seriously as Christian. To do that seems to risk the cooperation Christians have achieved with those who do not share their convictions; or worse, it might provide justification for the church to withdraw into a religious ghetto no longer concerned to serve the world. Such a result would indeed be a new and not even very sophisticated form of tribalism. The church, however, is not and cannot be "tribal"; rather the church is the community that enables us to recognize that, in fact, it is the world we live in which has a splintered and tribal existence.

The ability of the church to interpret and provide alternatives to the narrow loyalties of the world results from the story—a particular story, to be sure—that teaches us the significance of lives different from our own, within and without our community. Indeed, we only learn what that story entails as it is lived and lives through the lives of others. If we are to trust in the truthfulness of the stories of God, we must also trust that the other's life, as threatening as it may first appear, is necessary for our own.[5]

Christians, then, must not only discern the various gifts of individuals, they must also recognize the difference between church and world, and the differences that divide the world. It has often been assumed that acknowledgment of the divided character of the world calls into question the universality of the Christian story. If the God of Abraham, Isaac, and Jacob could lay claim to the allegiance of all people, then it seemed that some universal *theory* of truth and morality (such as natural law theory) would be required to establish the basis of such a claim. Christian claims of universal salvation and the corresponding missionary enterprise seemed to intensify the need for such an account. From such a perspective the dividedness of the world could only be interpreted as an appearance of differences that masked a deeper commonality.

But the dividedness of the world cannot so easily be overcome or dismissed; rather it must first be acknowledged. Nor should the dividedness of our existence be surprising to a people who are schooled by a story that makes clear that dividedness is the character of existence for a world that knows not God.

That does not mean that Christians can give up claims of universality, but that the basis of our universalism comes by first being initiated into a particular story and community. As John Howard Yoder has argued, the universality of Christian convictions does not presume the "adequacy of the religious expression of almost everyone or at least every people in every condition, sometimes in other religions or perhaps in no religion, because of some inherent human qualities for which one considers the label 'Christ' to be a symbol.''[6] (Yoder sees this as a temptation for the mainstream of Christendom, however, "which even when the church has lost position and privileges still wants to be taking responsibility for and giving meaning to the cultural mainstream.'') In contrast, the universalism that derives from faith in the God of Israel and Jesus, a God who challenges all the narrow loyalties that constitute the world, comes from believing that his lordship "can reach beyond the number of those who know him by his right name.''[7]

The truthfulness of Christian convictions, therefore, is not dependent on being able to generate a theory of truth that *a priori* renders all other accounts false, or that promises to demonstrate that underlying the differences between people is a deeper and more profound common morality. Rather the truthfulness of Christian convictions resides in their power to form a people sufficient to acknowledge the divided character of the world and thus necessarily ready to offer hospitality to the stranger. They must be what they are, i.e., the church, exactly because the story of God that has formed them requires them to understand and acknowledge the divided character of the world. The task of

Christians is not, therefore, to demonstrate that all other positions are false, though critical questions may often be appropriate, but to be a witness to the God that they believe embraces all truth.

2.   Narrative and Character: The Constructive Intent and Philosophical Objections[8]

Many, however, assume that the kind of particularity defended above cannot avoid vicious relativism. To introduce the category of narrative appears, at best, to be a confusing and soft-headed popularization of important philosophical and theological issues; at worse it seems "morally bankrupt,"[9] as it renders impossible the development of significant moral discourse and action between people of different beliefs and customs just at a time when we confront problems where such discourse and actions are so much needed. "Story theology and ethics" thus manifest and reinforce some of the difficulties raised by a pluralistic culture, for such a culture offers no account of morality that can provide the basis for cooperation between different people in order to secure justice. In the interest of protecting religious convictions from critical analysis, the emphasis on story seems to encourage the attitude that every community—and worse, every individual—has their own story and there is no means for deciding that one story can be preferred to another.

From this perspective, the category of story is but a new and not very promising wrinkle on a standard form of recent Christian apologetics. By claiming that every intellectual activity, including science, rests on presuppositions that cannot be proved true, religious and, in particular, Christian convictions can be protected from radical analysis and doubt. All human activity, it is claimed, involves a kind of "faith," and religious faith therefore cannot be dismissed on grounds that it involves holding some unprovable assumptions. The emphasis on story, then, seems to be but a new word for faith, ultimate perspective, or absolute presupposition that seeks to make this apologetic move more compellingly. Insofar as some of the recent emphasis on "story theology" involves this strategy, the critics correctly argue that the category of narrative adds little illumination and a good deal of confusion for serious consideration of the status of religious belief.

However, the usefulness of the category of narrative for theology should not be dismissed because it has been and will no doubt continue to be ill used. The significance of narrative for illuminating the grammar of religious convictions is not and should not be primarily an apologetic strategy. Instead, approaching Christian convictions via their narrative character involves an attempt to do constructive Christian theology and ethics in a nonreductionistic manner, so that questions of truth may be rightly asked. Without denying the place of abstract and general images and concepts in scripture and theology, it is nonetheless true that the most significant claims about God and the moral life take the form of or presuppose a narrative context. Any theological account of narrative, therefore, must involve an attempt to show that this is not just an accidental category but a necessary one for any true knowledge of God and the self.

The understanding and significance of narrative I wish to defend is crucial in the task of doing constructive Christian theology and ethics. Narrative provides the conceptual means to suggest how the stories of Israel and Jesus are a "morality" for the formation of Christian community and character. Thomas Ogletree may be right to suggest that narrative is or should be more central than the notion of character, but constructively I think of them as but two sides of the same coin.[10] As Kermode has observed,

> That character, in the modern sense of the word, takes precedence over story (or "agent" over "fable") seems natural enough after two and a half centuries of the novel, and after endless practice in reading the narrative clues on which—with the help of our memories of other books, our knowledge of character codes—we found our conventional notions of individuality. Yet there is nothing natural about it; it is a cultural myth. For Aristotle the fable came first, and character followed; though this does not mean character is without importance, only that it lacks autonomy, could never originate a narrative. Character does generate narrative, just as narrative generates character. The more elaborate the story grows—the more remote from its schematic base—the more these agents will deviate from type and come to look like "characters."[11]

The necessary interrelation of narrative and character provides the means to test the truthfulness of narratives. Significant narratives produce significant and various characters necessary for the understanding and richness of the story itself. Just as scientific theories are partially judged by the fruitfulness of the activities they generate, so narratives can and should be judged by the richness of moral character and activity they generate. Or just as significant works of art occasion a tradition of interpretation and criticism,[12] so significant narratives are at once the result of and continuation of moral communities and character that form nothing less than a tradition. And without tradition we have no means to ask questions of truth and falsity.[13]

Therefore the emphasis on narrative and character is not an attempt to avoid analyzing the status of Christian convictions, but to enliven the discussion by reminding us of what kind of community we must be to sustain the sort of discussion required by the stories of God. Those stories are, of course, the ones found in scripture, but by their nature they have given and continue to give birth to diverse narrative traditions which are essential to understanding the original stories. The church is nothing less than that community where we as individuals continue to test and are tested by the particular way those stories live through us.

The very variety of those stories and the corresponding variety of lives requires theological and moral reflection if we are to understand their meaning and significance.[14] Part of the test of the truthfulness of the church is whether it can provide a polity sufficient to sustain the differences necessary for discussion. For such differences are not just matters of variety in personal opinion or interpretation, but are required for understanding the self, God, and the world.

The crucial interaction of story and community for the formation of truthful lives is an indication that there exists no "story of stories" from which the many stories of our existence can be analyzed and evaluated. This is not to deny that a taxonomy and classification of various kinds, forms, and elements of stories and narratives might prove illuminating for certain purposes. But the constructive theological task remains primary. Our concern must be to understand better how to live appropriate to the God whom we find in the narratives of Israel and Jesus, and how these stories help provide the means for recognizing and critically appropriating other stories that claim our lives. For it is true that we always find ourselves enmeshed in many histories—of our families, of Texas, America, European civilization, and so on—each of which is constituted by many interrelated and confusing story lines. The moral task consists in acquiring the skills, i.e., the character, which enable us to negotiate these many kinds and levels of narrative in a truthful manner.

Some of these skills involve questions about how accurately and from whose point of view the story has been told. But accuracy of the narration of a history cannot be determined solely by the historian's craft, for the historian is not freed from being part of a community and a history.[15] Objectivity—or better, disinterestedness—is no less important for the moral life than for the work of the historian. But neither is objectivity achieved by positing a position that assumes we can find a place to stick our heads above history. Rather objectivity comes from being formed by a truthful narrative and community within history.

As Christians we claim that by conforming our lives in a faithful manner to the stories of God we acquire the moral and intellectual skills, as a community and as individuals, to face the world as it is, not as we wish it to be. Of course this remains a "claim," for there is no way within history to prove that such a story must be true. But that does not mean we are without resources for testing such a claim. The very story people hold directs us to observe the lives of those who live it as a crucial indication of the truth of their convictions.

From such a perspective it is impossible to distinguish, as Wes Robbins claims, questions regarding the truth of the narrative from its normative status.[16] At least part of what it means to call a significant narrative true is how that narrative claims and shapes our lives.

My refusal to posit a "story of stories" in order to provide a foundation for "morality" strikes many contemporary ethicists, both philosophical and theological, as profoundly mistaken. For it has been the intent of ethical theory, at least since Kant, to free morality from historic communities and traditions. Such theories assume that only a universal morality could be worthy of forming lives and securing moral agreement between peoples short of war. One cannot help but appreciate the moral project involved in this attempt to find a foundation for morality that might be sufficient to begin to work for a peaceful world, but the attempt was radically misconceived; it results in the positing of a moral order and rational community that simply does not exist.

Of course Gene Outka may well be right that it is a mistake to read philosophical ethics in this manner.[17] Instead of such a grand project, contemporary moral philosophers are best understood as involved in the more humble enterprise of providing the moral procedures necessary to sustain a society of fairness and relative justice. Without denying that there is a good deal of truth to such an interpretation, it can also be pointed out that fairness is not sufficient to sustain a good society; and such accounts of fairness, or justice, become self-deceptive insofar as they pretend to be ahistorical. Christians must be very careful how they use such accounts of "fairness," as these accounts often entail anthropological commitments that as Christians they cannot accept.

Moreover, the concentration on fairness, or promises, as the central concern of the moral life has led to a failure to appreciate the significance of character and virtue for the moral life. I have, perhaps, overstated this neglect by suggesting that a concentration on the language of duty necessarily involves a failure to provide an adequate account of virtue and character. Every account of morality, explicitly or implicitly, involves some sense of character and virtue as well as some suggestion as to which virtues ought to be central. But it is correct that in more Kantian and utilitarian moral theories[18] the attention paid to the concepts of character and virtue has clearly been subordinate to accounts of obligations and that, from such a perspective, if the virtues have been treated at all, they have become abstract qualities with little or no analysis of how they form or are possessed by the self. Such theories have concentrated on the concept of duty, since it alone seemed to offer the means to generate the minimal morality necessary to achieve cooperation between diverse people and thus to sustain a morally pluralistic civilization.

As a result, the relation of virtue and obligation became a "problem"

created by an unwarrantedly abstract concept of "duty" divorced from any
community presuppositions that make our "duties" intelligible. Indeed, the
very distinction between teleological (which is too often mistakenly limited in
consequentialist accounts of morality) and deontological ethics distorts our
moral alternatives rather than illuminating them.[19] As Alasdair MacIntyre has
suggested, there is no inherent incompatibility between a *telos,* virtue, and
law. He asks us to

> imagine a community who have come to recognize that there is a good
> for man and that this good is such that it can only be achieved in and
> through the life of a community constituted by this shared project. We
> can envisage such a community as requiring two distinct types of pre-
> cept to be observed in order to ensure the requisite kind of order for its
> common life. The first would be a set of precepts enjoining the virtues,
> those dispositions without the exercise of which the good cannot be
> achieved, more particularly if the good is a form of life which includes
> as an essential part the exercise of the virtues. The second would be a set
> of precepts prohibiting those actions destructive of those human rela-
> tionships which are necessary to a community in which and for which
> the good is to be achieved and in which and for which the virtues are to
> be practised. Both sets of precepts derive their point, purpose and jus-
> tification from the *telos,* but in two very different ways. To violate the
> second type of precept is to commit an act sufficiently intolerable to
> exclude oneself from the community in which alone one can hope to
> achieve the good. Thus the absolute prohibition of certain specifiable
> kinds of action finds a necessary place within a certain type of teleologi-
> cal framework; and since the Christian doctrine of ethics appears to be a
> teleology of just this type, the existence of Christian theologians who
> deny that there are any such absolute prohibitions would be *prima facie*
> puzzling.[20]

So the issue is not whether virtues or obligations are primary; that
simply divorces virtues and obligations from the community context that
makes them intelligible. Moreover, once the community aspect and the historical, dependent nature of ethical theory are recognized, there is no possibility,
as Robbins argues,[21] of our having a choice between "pure-narrative and
non-narrative" versions of ethical theory. Indeed the latter is but the ideology
of a dominant culture that no longer has the confidence to acknowledge the
contingent nature of their understanding of duties and virtues. Under the spell
of Kantian accounts of rationality, there lingers the fear that if we recognize
the historic nature of our moral convictions we will have to acknowledge them
as arbitrary and possibly even false. But such fear is ill founded, as there is no

other basis of moral convictions than the historic and narrative-related experience of a community.

Ogletree[22] is right, therefore, to suggest that the issue between William Frankena[23] (and many others who share his general perspective on moral philosophy) and me is not simply what constitutes an adequate moral psychology, but the "normative framework within which actions and lives are to be morally assessed." And I have suggested that such a framework is best thought of as a narrative, not simply because Christian convictions take the form of a narrative, but because all significant moral claims are historically derived and require narrative display. What is peculiar about Christian convictions is not that they involve a narrative, but the kind of narrative they involve. Appeal to the narrative dependence and structure of moral rationality is not a form of special pleading for Christian convictions but an attempt to illuminate, in a formal manner, the character of our moral existence as historic beings.

For example, MacIntyre, in contrast to most interpreters of Kant as well as the intention of most neo-Kantians, has pointed out that crucial for the intelligibility of Kant's account of morality is the metaphor

> of the life of the individual and also of that of the human race as a journey toward a goal. The journey has two aspects. There is the progress toward creating the external conditions for the achievement of moral perfection by individuals: "with advancing civilization reason grows pragmatically in its capacity to realize ideas of law. But at the same time the culpability for the transgression also grows." Within the framework of law and civility the individual progresses toward moral perfection, a progress "directed to a goal infinitely remote." It follows that the significance of a particular moral action does not lie solely in its conformity to the moral law; it marks a stage in that journey the carrying through of which confers significance on the individual's life. Thus a link does exist between the acts of duty and the *summum bonum* conceived as the goal of the individual's journey.[24]

Moreover MacIntyre goes on to observe that Kant's moral philosophy has kinship to a whole family of narrative portrayals of human life, of which the Grail legends are prime examples. "Human life is a quest in which a variety of dangers and harms may befall me; unless I am prepared to sacrifice my life on occasion I cannot achieve that which I seek. To fail to sacrifice my life, necessarily will be to fail as a man."[25] MacIntyre suggests that while such themes may originally be Pythagorean or Orphic, and reappear in Plato's myths and Socrates' death, they are crucial to Jewish and Christian accounts of the world. In both Platonic and Judeo-Christian versions it turns out that only if I am prepared to lose my life can I achieve the goal. "Only if I place my own physical survival lower on the scale of values than other goods, can my self be perfected. Teleology has thus been restored but in a form very alien to either Aristotle's thought or Mill's. It is no wonder that Kant finds in Greek ethics no adequate conceptual scheme for the presentation of morality, but views Christianity as providing just such a scheme."[26]

I do not intend to try to substantiate MacIntyre's interpretation of Kant, though I find it persuasive.[27] It is sufficient that Kant simply be open to such an interpretation to suggest that moral philosophy presupposes a narrative context in its actual functioning. Nor does calling attention to the narrative presuppositions of Kant's ethics or any other moral philosophy show that a Christian understanding of our journey with God is either necessary or true. But at least it puts the issue in the right context, as "the individual who knows himself to be part of a moral history whose outcome is as yet unsettled may be less likely to claim prematurely that title of universal moral legislator that Kant bestowed on all rational agents and which has had such great effects on the character of moral activity."[28] Rather, we learn that our first moral question must be Of what history am I a part and how can I best understand it?

To answer such a question it is necessary that the stories we hold about our history be true, but again, as MacIntyre observes, "the criterion of truth for extended historical narratives is notoriously complex, and there may be periods in which the conflicting claims of rival historical interpretations cannot be put to a finally decisive test."[29] Yet morally we cannot live indecisively, for we must ask sacrifices from ourselves and others that seem justified only if we know our story is true. We are thus tempted to assert that we do in fact share non-narrative-dependent values or norms such as justice or benevolence.[30] But justice is always someone's justice and benevolence someone's benevolence; indeed the very distinction between justice and benevolence turns out to be relative to the self-understanding of historic communities. As concepts, justice and benevolence are capable of abstract display and analysis, but like all moral notions they derive their force from paradigmatic display and imagination disciplined by analogies.

The Kantian-inspired attempt to make justice integral to the allegedly rational and universal requirement to respect all persons as ends in themselves is a noble endeavor. Indeed such a vision, I suspect, draws its inspiration from the Christian hope of the realization of a kingdom where peace and not war will characterize the relation between peoples and nations. But for Christians such a kingdom remains an eschatological hope that cannot be made present by heightening the status of human rationality. From the Christian perspective Kant's account of the universal requirements of reason is a secularized version of Christian hope. Kant sought to make Christian hope into a necessary condition for rational living, but in the process hope is trivialized, for if the kingdom can be based on or come from within humankind, then there is no reason to hope. Kant's hope is one that no longer knows how to be patient in the face of the dividedness of the world and in desperation seeks peace by making God's Kingdom a human possibility. Yet peace, Christians believe, cannot be founded on false accounts of our rational powers but depends on our learning to acknowledge God's lordship over all life. The Christian commitment to peace is based not on the inherent value of life, but on the conviction that war cannot be consistent with the Kingdom we have only begun to experience through the work of Christ and his continuing power in the church.

It must be admitted that to stake one's life on such a view is indeed dangerous. For there are many who claim their convictions to be true and assume that those who do not hold similar beliefs should be forced to do so. They are even willing to kill in defense of what they hold dear. To abandon the attempt to develop a "universal" ethic, as I have done, therefore appears as an act of despair, as we are left at the mercy of such people.

The Christian, however, does not claim that the world is safe but only that it is under God's lordship. Christian confidence in God's lordship provides the church with the power to exist amid the diversity of this world, trusting that the truth "will out" without resorting to coercion and violence for self-protection or to secure adherents. Therefore the non-resistant character of Christian community, which is often sadly absent, is a crucial mark of the power of the Christian story to form a people in a manner appropriate to the character of God's providential rule of the world.

3.   Relativism and Tragedy

This way of putting the matter, however, will not satisfy those who are haunted by the ghost of relativism. Though the position I hold involves a certain kind of relativism, as I have tried to suggest elsewhere it is not a vicious relativism; there is no conceptual reason that prevents me from making judgments or from seeking to change the mind of those from other traditions.[31] The kind of relativism which must be acknowledged as part of our moral existence will appear destructive to those who want to supply a foundational account of knowledge and morality. Once that enterprise is recognized as illusory, however, then it is possible to appreciate how rational discourse and argument are possible without denying that there are often tragic and unbridgeable divisions between people.

One of the difficulties is that any account of relativism or the assumed "problem of relativism" is theory-dependent—i.e., we all know that people and cultures are different but the characterization and status of those differences depend on putative accounts of "morality." Therefore it is a mistake to assume that there is any one version of relativism that must be accepted. The kind of relativism I am willing to defend is similar to what Gilbert Harman[32] has described as his "soberly logical thesis" that morality arises when a group of people reach an implicit agreement or come to a tacit understanding about their relations with one another. Moral judgments, therefore, only make sense in relation to and with reference to one or another such agreement or understanding. Harman's use of the language of "agreement" is misleading, however, in that it gives the impression that a people's morality may be much more coherent than we know almost all significant moral traditions to be. In contrast, I assume, as I suspect Harman also does, that our morality is much less the product of an agreement than it is the ongoing experience and conversation of a people that enables them to have a history sufficient for community identity.[33]

Rather than discussing relativism so abstractly, I think it best to turn to the kind of concrete issue which we fear that admission of the truth of relativism will not let us handle—namely, would it mean that we would not say that slavery in a society different from ours is wrong? At the very outset we must be careful not to let the force of such a question mislead us. For it is far from clear that slavery is morally the same no matter what society and what kind of system of beliefs supports it. I suspect that there are many different kinds of slavery, each with its own peculiar moral difficulties and advantages. If that is so, then no single set of considerations could ever be sufficient to tell us what is always wrong with "slavery." This may be the source of some of our deepest frustrations with relativism, as we often wish to think we have a real confrontation when actually we are not even agreeing about what set of moral "facts" is involved.

In order to discuss slavery we retreat to the theoretical mode, so that its features are derived from our assumption about what slavery must have been like in pre-Civil War America. Thus Harman asks us to conceive of a society where there is a well-established and long-standing tradition of slavery in which everyone accepts the institution, including the slaves.[34] However, in this society there are aspects of the basic moral agreement—or as I would prefer, their narrative traditions—that call slavery into question. In such a society, justifications for slavery would be defective, though the deficiencies might be hidden by self-deceptive accounts or myths concerning the physical and mental limits of slaves. If the myth were exposed and the incoherence became manifest, then society would in time have to change its acceptance of slavery.

However, Harman also suggests that it is possible to imagine a society where there are no aspects of a tradition that speak against slavery. In such a situation, no dissonance would ever appear in the underlying precepts of the society and slave owners could never even understand, much less act upon, the idea that they ought to free their slaves. While there might come an external threat that would cause them to modify their views, there would be no internal moral necessity for them to do so. Harman notes that we feel much more at home making judgments about the first mentioned society because we can invoke principles that they share with us and thus we can say that they ought not to have slaves. However, this sort of judgment becomes increasingly inappropriate the more distant such a society is from us, for it is less easy for us to think of their moral understanding as being continuous with our own. We find it inappropriate to say it is morally wrong for slave owners in the second society to own slaves, though we can certainly say that the society is unfair and unjust insofar as it allows slavery.

This would seem to be a damaging admission. After all, we seem prevented from making the kind of judgments about people in the second society we feel we ought to be able to make. Relativism, even the kind defended by Harman, seems to entail the possibility that we can have two or more systems of belief which are to some extent self-contained. Yet there are empirical and conceptual limits to that kind of self-containment. First, it is implausible to assume that any group of humans will or can have a belief system that is fully coherent. Our common historical nature means it is very likely that we will find we share something in common, though what we share may not be sufficient to gain agreement concerning such issues as slavery. Secondly, the conceptual difficulties in stating the problem of relativism imply presuppositions that qualify the extent of relativism; i.e., "the application of a notion such as 'a culture' presupposes the instantiation in the subject-matter of a whole set of relations which can be adequately expressed at all only via the concepts of one culture rather than another. Any relativism which denied the non-relative validity of concepts involved in setting up its problem at all would be refuted."[35]

Yet neither of the qualifications is sufficient to ground a universal morality capable of refuting moral relativism. In contrast Bernard Williams has suggested that the "truth in relativism" is our inability to envision something about another life as a "real option" for me. For Williams a "real option" would mean the ability of people to change their convictions so that they can live within and retain their hold on reality while making rational comparisons between the new option and their present outlook and then acknowledge their transition to the new option in the light of such comparisons.[36] To speak of people who have made such a "real option" as "retaining their hold on reality" is to imply that it is possible for them to change without engaging in extensive self-deception, paranoia, or other such things.

Williams suggests that most discussions of relativism are misleading, because they only deal with notional confrontations.[37] A notional confrontation resembles a real confrontation, that is, a confrontation where a real option is a possibility, but it differs from the latter exactly because one or the other position is not a real option for me. Thus, examples used to create the problem of relativism—i.e., the life of a Greek Bronze Age chief, or a medieval Samurai—do not serve well, since those ways of life are not real options for us. We simply have no idea what it would mean to live them.[38] Reflection on such examples may help us think about elements missing from our own lives, but there is no question of our becoming one or the other.

Williams argues that only in situations of real confrontation do we appropriately employ the vocabulary of appraisal—"true-false," "right-wrong," "acceptable-unacceptable." Such a vocabulary is employed because where there is a different system of belief that is a real option for us we feel we must organize what is to be said in order to accept or deny it as our own. That we often do not feel the need to employ such language reveals the truth in relativism, as we find that many confrontations do not involve questions of a real option at all and thus issues of appraisal simply do not arise, or they arise only notionally.

Williams maintains that this understanding of relativism, unlike most of the alternatives, is coherent. It manages to cohere with two propositions, both of which are true: first, that we must have a form of thought not relativized to our own existing system of beliefs for thinking about and expressing other systems of beliefs which may be of concern to us; but, second, we can nevertheless recognize that there can be many systems of beliefs "which have insufficient relation to our concerns for our judgments to have any grip on them, while admitting that other persons' judgment could get a grip on them, namely, those for whom they were real options."[39] Williams rightly notes that most traditional forms of relativism have paid insufficient attention to the first proposition relativizing the categories of appraisal into "true for us," or "true for them." The problem with such formulations is that they cannot account for the reality of real confrontations. In like manner, vulgar relativism, the view that combines a relativistic account of ethical terms with a non-relativistic principle of toleration, fails to deal with real confrontation, since it assumes the impossibility or pointlessness of choosing between options that do not matter to anyone. The problem with vulgar relativism is it treats all moral convictions as if they were only notional commitments.

Williams' account of the truth of relativism shows why there can be no way of formulating a moral theory capable of defeating relativism in principle. Rather, once we rightly understand the nature of relativism, we see that morally we must deal with one confrontation at a time, because that, in effect, is the nature of our world. What we require, therefore, is not an argument that provides an *a priori* defeat of relativism, but an interpretation of and the corresponding skills to live in a world where others exist who do not share my moral history. I have tried to suggest above that Christian understanding of the divided character of our existence provides just such an interpretation as well as a context in which we have the means to negotiate such a world.

Christians are forbidden to despair in the face of the dividedness of the world. On the contrary, we are commanded to witness to others that there is a God that overcomes our differences by making them serve his Kingdom. The task of the Christian is not to defeat relativism by argument but to witness to a God who requires confrontation. Too often the epistemological and moral presuppositions behind the Christian command to be a witness to such a God have been overlooked. The command to witness is not based on the assumption that we are in possession of a universal truth which others must also "implicitly" possess or have sinfully rejected. If such a truth existed, we would not be called upon to be witnesses, but philosophers. Rather the command to be a witness is based on the presupposition that we only come to the truth through the process of being confronted by the truth.

The command to be a witness does not entail *a priori* judgments about the beliefs and life of others—e.g., what is right or wrong with Hinduism or Islam—though such judgments after time may be appropriate, but rather witness derives from no other source than that which invites us to "look what manner of life has been made possible among us by the power of the cross and resurrection of Christ." The invitation to join such a life is made not on the assumption that there is something wrong with the others' beliefs, but it is made because we are all sinners and through participation in this community we have the possibility of finding redemption. We are not sinners because we are Hindu, Muslim, secularist, or Christian, but because we are people who live as though we can be our own creator and redeemer.

In the terms used above, therefore, the task of Christians is to be the sort of people and community that can become a real option and provide a real confrontation for others. Unless such a community exists, then no real option exists. The manner of providing such an option, moreover, entails that Christians go to every land and every people in the hope that they can elicit a real confrontation on matters that matter. Such confrontation may sometimes take the form of explicit argument, but the validity and power of such argument ultimately depends on the church being a society where people manifest the unity that can come only from worship of the true Lord of our existence. Therefore the kind of unity in diversity characteristic of the church must always stand in sharp judgment of the diversity in the world where most of our confrontations are either notional or violent.

The kind of alternative the church provides will differ from society to society, system of belief to system of belief, from culture to culture, state to state. Indeed the church will often learn from different cultures what is and is not essential to its own life. Too often the church becomes but a mirror of one cultural option rather than a mirror to which each culture should compare itself. Confronting and learning to live in many cultures is the necessary condition for Christians to test what is and is not essential for their life together. Christians must always remember the God they serve is found among all people. That God speaks through the stranger, however, is no reason or basis for melding all differences through self-deceptive tolerance; rather it is the reason why the church must be a universal community capable of showing forth our unity in our diversity. Such unity comes not from the assumption that all people share the same nature, but that we share the same Lord. Though certainly the fact that we believe that we have a common creator provides a basis for some common experience and appeals.

The existence of a community characterized by such unity is crucial, moreover, for moral argument. For if societies such as Harman's second slave society are to be confronted, there must exist a society that provides an alternative. Their assumptions about slavery cannot be susceptible to argument unless an alternative society exists that witnesses and manifests a unity that comes from worship of the single God. The problem with slavery is not that it violates the "inherent dignity of our humanity," but that as a people we have found that we cannot worship together at the table of the Lord if one claims an ownership over others that only God has the right to claim. We have no guarantee, of course, that others will accept such a way of life, but Christians must live with the confidence that others will find that such a life frees them from the fears that give birth to slavery and injustice. God has promised the church that if we are faithful our life will not be without effect. The church's task does not depend on nor is it sustained by such effectiveness, however; it is sustained by our experience that by living faithfully we do find God is the truth of our existence.

It must be admitted that the Christian willingness to accept existence amid the dividedness of the world means that we cannot live without appreciating the tragic character of our world. Elsewhere I have argued that tragedy often involves the conflict of right with right, but such conflict is but a form of a more profound sense of tragedy inherent in living in a divided world. For tragedy consists in the moral necessity of having to risk our lives and the lives of others in order to live faithful to the histories that are the only means we have for knowing and living truthfully.[40]

It is not accidental that this sense of tragedy is particularly useful for an understanding of the moral life that stresses the significance of character. For tragedy and character are but two sides of the same coin. Tragedy is not the result of a "flaw" of character, but the result of living faithful to what is best about our character. Moralistic judgments about weakness of character or the flaw in an otherwise strong person's character result finally in a failure to appreciate how character is at once necessary and the cause of tragedy. No one narrative, much less any one character, is sufficient to embody the richness of the moral values and virtues of our existence. Our character is therefore the source of our strength, as it provides us with a history of commitment, but in doing so it also sets the stage for the possibility of tragedy.

As John Barbour has suggested, the tragic arises through the "radical incongruity of a basically good person performing actions which lead to evil and self-destructive consequences."[41] The source of each tragedy is a situation in which a character's multiple responsibilities and obligations conflict not only with self-interest, but with each other. Moral choice is potentially tragic when several moral obligations are juxtaposed with the necessity of a single decision having irreversible consequences. "The tragedy is realized when the pursuit of one of a person's duties leads not simply to neglect, but to destruction of the others, and thus to moral evil. And the tragic nature of such a moral dilemma is exacerbated when the moral agent involved is basically a virtuous person—someone who desires to carry out his moral obligations and aspirations, feels his dilemma keenly, and persists in the struggle to act rightly when a less conscientious person would compromise his ideals or shirk his obligations."[42]

I have a hunch that behind those moral theories that seek to deny the radical dividedness of our world, whether they take deontological or utilitarian form, lies a profound attempt to deny this sense of the tragic. But the very attempt to avoid the tragic only makes us more susceptible to it; and, worse still, it leads us to seek to avoid the tragic through violence. As Stanley Cavell has suggested,

> In the typical situation of tragic heroes, time and space converge to a point at which an ultimate care is exposed and action must be taken which impales one's life upon the founding care of that life. Death, so caused, may be mysterious, but what founds these lives is clear enough: the capacity to love, the strength to found a life upon a love. That the love becomes incompatible with that life is tragic, but that it is maintained until the end is heroic. People capable of such love could have removed mountains; instead it has caved in upon them. One moral of such events is obvious: if you would avoid tragedy (and suffering), avoid love; if you cannot avoid love, avoid integrity; if you cannot avoid integrity, avoid the world; if you cannot avoid the world, destroy it. Our tragedy differs from this classical chain not in the conclusion but in the fact that the conclusion has been reached without passing through love, in the fact that no love seems worth founding one's life upon, or that society—and therefore I myself—can allow no context in which love for anything but itself can be expressed. Our problem, in getting back to beginnings, will not be to find the thing we have always cared about, but to discover whether we have it in us to care about something.[43]

In a divided world tragedy cannot be denied, but we can find the patience to sustain one another through our tragedies and in so doing provide an alternative to the violence that would force the world into a premature unity. The church in its profoundest expression is the gathering of a people who are able to sustain one another through the inevitable tragedies of our lives. They are able to do so because they have been formed by a narrative, constantly reenacted through the sharing of a meal, that claims nothing less than that God has taken the tragic character of our existence into his very life.

4.   The Church and Social Ethics

Of course it may be objected that such a church simply does not exist. Thus Robbins asserts that Christians and the church are at least as fragmented, as far as substantive moral values and judgments are concerned, as any group in contemporary society.[44] Therefore, even if the position I am trying to develop is correct in principle, it fails, for Christians no longer provide the kind of witness and unity I allege they must.

However I refuse to accept Robbins' characterization of the church either as descriptive or normatively correct. To be sure, Christians can often be found on nearly every side of any issue, but they may not be found there as Christians. Theologically the question is not what Christians do think, but what they ought to think given their basic convictions. The modest task of theologians is to help contribute to the discussion of what they ought to think by thinking as clearly as we can. But the theologian must always remember that those not schooled in theology will often lead the way.

Moreover there is no inherent reason that Christians must agree about every issue—after all, as Aristotle reminds us, ethics involves matters that can be other. What is required is not that Christians always agree, but that their agreements and their disagreements reflect their theological convictions. The church no less than any community must provide the political process through which moral issues can be disposed and adjudicated. What is unique about the church is not that such a process is required, or that it does not always produce agreement; what is unique is the kind of concerns that are made subject to the process, the theological convictions that shape our reasoning, and the way the discussion is governed by love.

That such a discussion does not occur often enough in the church is surely regrettable, but even there it is easy to misread the reality of church life. For it is my contention that the church is not nearly as dead as many think. Claims about the moral failure of the "church" characteristically employ a far too restricted sense of "church"—i.e., the Protestant church of America, "Western Christendom," the Roman Catholic Church, and so on.

The church is none of these, but rather the church is where people faithfully carry out the task of being a witness to the reality of God's Kingdom.

Indeed the very selectivity implied in our criticism of the church often is but a sign of our unfaithfulness. Thus many of us criticized the "church" of the South for its failure to provide a prophetic critique and leadership against racism. In our enthusiasm for exposing the "failure" of the church, it was forgotten that the white churches of the South were not the only church there. Indeed, the church did not fail in the South, as black church congregations continued to do the patient work of preparation necessary to create a people sufficient for the coming struggle.

For theologians, therefore, to accept as normative the limits of the current church is an act of irresponsibility. The church that is the subject of theological reflection can never be limited to the present moment but reaches back into history and forward into the future, as both directions provide an indication of what we ought to be. For it is an article of our faith that God will not abandon his church but, generation after generation, will continue to provide faithful witnesses to his Kingdom.

There is a further objection, however, that acknowledges this depiction of the church as a possibility but insists that such a church involves an illegitimate withdrawal from the world. It is certainly true that I think the first social task of the church is to be the church, but there is nothing about that description of the task that warrants the charge of "withdrawal." Rather, such a description, with its corresponding understanding of church polity, requires a rethinking of what most mean by "social ethics."

"Social ethics" is not what the church does after it has got its theological convictions straight and its own house in order. But our theological convictions and corresponding community are a social ethic as they provide the necessary context for us to understand the world in which we live. The church serves the world first by providing categories of interpretation that offer the means for us to understand ourselves truthfully, e.g., we are a sinful yet redeemed people. Interpretation does not preclude action, but our actions can only be effective when they are formed according to a truthful account of the world.

And part of what such an account entails is that the world can never be the church. If this is what is meant by the "withdrawal" charge, then I must accept it as an accurate account of my position. The world cannot be the church, for the world, while still God's good creation, is a realm that knows not God and is thus characterized by the fears that constantly fuel the fires of violence. We live in a mad existence where some people kill other people for abstract and unworthy entities called nations. The church's first task is not to make the nation-state system work, but rather to remind us that the nation, especially as we know it today, is not an ontological necessity for human living. The church, as an international society, is a sign that God, not nations, rule this world.

The Christian's distrust of violence—and it must be remembered that the just war tradition distrusts violence no less than the pacifist[45]—is but an indication of the church's commitment to the unity denied by the disunity created by nations, cultural systems, and other limited commitments. This distrust of violence does not mean that Christians are prohibited from trying to make nations in which they find themselves more just, unless one has concluded that justice can be accomplished only through violence or the threat of violence. As Christians we are committed to the view that justice is possible between peoples because trust is finally a deeper reality in our lives than distrust, because God's justice is more profound than injustice. Such a view is not an unrealistic, idealistic, or utopian strategy; it is built on the profoundly realistic hope that God, not man, rules the world.

The concrete form of the church's social ethic will differ from one social setting to another. General claims about the relation of church to world are never sufficient and cannot be substituted for the hard work of social analysis and of particular societies. Certainly philosophical and scientific tools are extremely useful for such analysis. Yet the church must be careful that such tools do not substitute for the necessity of making clear that its social ethic can never be identical with what appear to be the progressive programs of a particular society.

This is a particularly important challenge for the church that continues to exist in Western civilization. For our identification with that civilization has been so complete that we have tended to forget that the church's future is not the future of "western democracies." There is, to be sure, much that is positive about these social systems that Christians should rightly value.[46] But we must also remember that their liberty is not the liberty of God, nor is their justice the justice that we have come to know through being a member of God's people. Our task is not to make these nations the church, but rather to remind them that they are but nations. From the world's perspective, that may not seem like much, but the perspective of the people formed by the story of God's redemption shows us how important a task it is. For the idolatry most convenient to us all remains the presumed primacy of the nation-state.

6. The Virtues and Our Communities: Human Nature As History

1. The Virtues: Past and Current Status

In common discourse there is a general agreement that virtue and the virtues are important, but philosophically or theologically there is no consensus on how the virtues should be understood or the significance they have or ought to have in accounts of morality. Whether virtue is one or many, what the individual virtues are or which are primary, whether the virtues can conflict, how they are acquired, the locus of the virtues, are all questions on which there is little agreement and even less discussion. Such questions assume that virtue is a central concept for moral reflection, a presupposition that most current theories of morality do not share.

For the Greeks, as well as the Christians, virtue was the central concept for moral reflection. Although there was no complete consensus about what constitutes virtue or which virtues should be considered primary, it was accepted that consideration of morality began with descriptions of the virtuous life. Ethics grew from questions of what individuals should be; armed with answers, the ancients then turned to prescriptive modes.

For the Greeks the term virtue, *arete,* meant that which causes a thing to perform its function well. *Arete* was an excellence of any kind that denotes the power of anything to fulfill its function.[1] Thus the virtue of the eye is seeing; the virtue of a knife is cutting; the virtue of a horse is running, and so on. All accounts of virtue involve some combination of excellence and power. One cannot exist without the other. Later Aquinas defined virtue as simply a "certain perfection of power."[2]

On the analogy that virtue was that which caused a thing to perform its function well, it seemed that human virtue would be that which caused us to fulfill our function as humans. But then the meaning and content of virtue would be relative to the controverted issue of what is "human nature." To add complexity, some accounts insisted that the virtues were not "in" one, but "added" to our powers, thereby creating "powers," not simply perfecting potential.

111

As a result, there has been no satisfactory, unambiguous moral definition of the virtues. Although Plato asserts that "virtue is knowledge," the
knowledge involved is not easily depicted or acquired. For Aristotle virtue "is
a characteristic involving choice, and it consists in observing the mean relative to us, a mean which is defined by a rational principle, such as a man of
practical wisdom would use to determine it."[3] Aquinas accepts Aristotle's
definition, but speaks of a "mean between the passions."[4] Kant described
that which brings inner rather than outer freedom under the laws."[5] More recently James Wallace has appealed to those "capacities or tendencies that suit an
individual for human life generally";[6] and Donald Evans argues that "a moral
virtue is a pervasive, unifying stance which is an integral part of a person's
fulfillment as a human being, and which influences his actions in each and
every situation, especially his dealings with other human beings, where it
helps to promote their fulfillment."[7]

While this is but a random sample of definitions, little would be gained
by trying to make the list more comprehensive. No such list would or could
yield any satisfactory understanding. The very plurality of different notions of
virtue indicates that any account of the virtues is context-dependent. The
significance of this point for my perspective cannot be overestimated, since I
will make no attempt to develop an "ethics of virtue" satisfactory for any
society. Rather I will try to show how an analysis of virtue turns on an
understanding of human nature as historical and why, therefore, any account
of virtue involves the particular traditions and history of a society.

I have no intention, therefore, of trying to formulate or defend one
definition of virtue as most adequate. It is, however, important to note that
there is a significant grammatical difference between trying to define and
analyze the concept of virtue and an individual virtue (or the virtues). Admittedly, the extent of this difference is relative to differing theoretical accounts
of virtue, but grammatically the assumptions involved in trying to give an
account of virtue are different from those necessary to focus on the virtues.
Virtue seems to denote a general stance of the self that has more remote
normative significance than do the individual virtues. For example, virtues
such as humility, honesty, kindness, and courage embody immediate judgments of praise, whereas to be a "person of virtue" is more ambiguous. Thus,
many accounts of the virtues do little more than list the qualities generally
praised by a society. A person who exhibits such qualities may not necessarily
be a person of virtue.[8] For even though "being a person of virtue" is morally
ambiguous, we still assume that "a person of virtue or character" describes a
self formed in a more fundamental and substantive manner than the individual
virtues seem to denote.

As a result, discussions of virtue or character involve an analysis of the nature of the self, which seems unnecessary for depiction of the individual virtues. It remains unclear, however, how virtue and the virtues are related. Though discussions of virtue often treat them as if they were the same, how they impinge is seldom made explicit. This creates confusion in critic and defender of virtue alike, in that what is questioned is not the significance of virtue for the moral life but claims for the significance of specific virtues.

It is tempting to interpret the affinity between virtue and the virtues as a unity between formal and material principles. The age-old claim that a person of virtue embodies all virtues seems, moreover, to suggest that virtue as a formal category derives its material content from the individual virtues. This prevailing notion must be counterbalanced by the equally significant concept that to have virtue or character involves more than a sum of the individual virtues. Indeed to have the virtues rightly, it has often been argued, requires that one must acquire and have them as a person of character.[9]

I will make no attempt to suggest how the relation between virtue and the virtues should be understood. Indeed I remain unconvinced that any one account of this interaction is necessary. For the purposes of this essay it is sufficient to mark the significance of the distinction in hopes of avoiding some of the confusions that often arise in discussions concerning the nature and significance of virtue and the virtues for the moral life.

2. An Ethic of Virtue

An ethic of virtue centers on the claim that an agent's being is prior to doing. Not that what we do is unimportant or even secondary, but rather that what one does or does not do is dependent on possessing a "self" sufficient to take personal responsibility for one's action.[10] What is significant about us morally is not what we do or do not do, but how we do what we do. A person of virtue is often said to be a person of style or class in that he or she may well do what others do but in a distinctive manner. Nevertheless, virtue is not the same as "style"; we associate virtue with a more profound formation of the self.

How persons of virtue or character act is not just distinctive: the manner of their action must contribute to or fulfill their moral character. This has sometimes been misinterpreted to imply that emphasis on virtue encourages a self-involvement or even egoism that is antithetical to the kind of disinterestedness appropriate to the "moral point of view." It may be true that an ethic of virtue does not exclude a kind of interestedness in the self circumscribed by some Kantian interpretation of moral rationality; but attempts to designate all accounts of an ethic of virtue as perversely self-involving or egoistic are clearly unjustified. The concern that our behavior contribute to our moral character is but a recognition that what we do should be done in a manner befitting our history as moral agents.

In this respect attempts to contrast an ethic of virtue with that of duty are often misleading. Neither the language of duty nor of virtue excludes the other on principle, though often theoretical accounts fail to describe adequately the ways virtue and duty interrelate in our moral experience. Moreover, while certain moral traditions seem to be more appropriately expressed conceptually in terms of one rather than the other, at a formal level there is no inherent conflict between duty and virtue. The recognition and performance of duty is made possible because we are virtuous, and a person of virtue is dutiful because not to be so is to be less than virtuous.

Perhaps the assumption that there is conflict between ethics of duty and virtue derives from awareness that we often have duties that we must do because they are the responsibilities of roles in which we find ourselves or because there simply seems to be no other alternative, even though "personally" we would prefer not to do what we feel we must do. Thus our "duties" seem to require choices and decisions, whereas virtues do not. From the perspective of an ethic of duty we should do what we are obligated to do even though it may not reflect or contribute to our character.

Without denying that this frequently may be an appropriate interpretation of our experience, there is nothing peculiar about it that would favor an account of morality in terms of duty rather than virtue. For the claim that we must do our duty even though it does not contribute to our character speaks to the kind of character we ought to have—namely, we ought to be people who can be trusted because we are faithful. And who would trust persons who think their moral responsibility reaches no further than fulfilling duties?

There is, perhaps, a stronger emphasis on the significance of decision associated with the language and concept of duty than that of virtue. Duties imply matters that we must decide and act upon, whereas virtues involve dispositions that may or may not entail decisions. And from the perspective of virtue, in a certain sense decisions are morally secondary. Of course the virtuous person makes decisions, but they are viewed as dependent on a more profound moral reality. Thus persons of character or virtue may, from the perspective of others, make what appear to have been momentous and even heroic decisions, but feel that in their own lives they "had no choice" if they were to continue to be faithful to their characters.

Individuals of character have decisions or choices forced on them, just as anyone else does. But an ethic of virtue refuses to make such decisions the paradigmatic center of moral reflection. Morality is not primarily concerned with quandaries or hard decisions; nor is the moral self simply the collection of such decisions. As persons of character we do not confront situations as mud puddles into which we have to step; rather the kind of "situations" we confront and how we understand them are a function of the kind of people we are. Thus "training in virtue" often requires that we struggle with the moral situations which we have "got ourselves into" in the hope that such a struggle will help us develop a character sufficient to avoid, or understand differently, such situations in the future.

To be a person of virtue, therefore, involves acquiring the linguistic, emotional, and rational skills[11] that give us the strength to make our decisions and our life our own. The individual virtues are specific skills required to live faithful to a tradition's understanding of the moral project in which its adherents participate. Like any skills, the virtues must be learned and coordinated in an individual's life, as a master craftsman has learned to blend the many skills necessary for the exercise of any complex craft. Moreover, such skills require constant practice as they are never simply a matter of routine or technique.[12] For skills, unlike technique, give the craftsman the ability to respond creatively to the always unanticipated difficulties involved in any craft in a manner that technique can never provide.[13] That is why the person of virtue is also often thought of as a person of power, in that their moral skills provide them with resources to do easily what some who are less virtuous would find difficult.

But it is also the case that the virtuous person confronts some difficulties exactly because he or she is virtuous. For the virtuous life is not premised on the assumption that we can avoid the morally onerous; rather, if we are virtuous, we can deal with the onerous on our terms. The directive that we be virtuous necessarily challenges us to face moral difficulties and obstacles that might not be present if we were less virtuous. The coward can never know the fears of the courageous. That is why an ethic of virtue always gains its intelligibility from narratives that place our lives within an adventure. For to be virtuous necessarily means we must take the risk of facing trouble and dangers that might otherwise be unrecognized. The rationality of taking such risks, and corresponding opportunities, can only be grounded in a narrative that makes clear that life would be less interesting and good if such risks were absent from our lives.

From the perspective of an ethic of virtue, therefore, freedom is more like having power than having a choice. For to have "had a choice" may only mean that there were but few options, or the limit may in part be the result of the insufficiency of one's own character. For the virtuous person, being free does not imply a choice but the ability to claim that what was or was not done was one's own. As Frithjof Bergmann has argued,

> If it is now understood that the making of a choice gives rise to freedom
> only if I identify with the agency that does the choosing (i.e., if I regard

the thought-process that makes the decision as truly mine, despite its being conditioned, or influenced, or so forth), then it should be clear that freedom can also result from my identifying with an agency other than those processes of thought—and this means that I may be free even if the decisive difference between two alternatives was not made by my choice, as long as I identify with (i.e., regard as *myself*) the agency that did tip the scales.[14]

But what allows us to claim our action as our own is the self-possession that comes from being formed by the virtues.

Some have advanced from this argument that virtuous persons could be free no matter what their circumstances—slavery, rack, or the throne. There is a sense in which this may be true, though it is probably wrongly put, for the question is not whether they are "free" but whether they have ceased to be virtuous. Nevertheless, I would deny the secondary implication that an ethic of virtue is therefore indifferent to social circumstance. Indeed, I argue our capacity to be virtuous depends on the existence of communities which have been formed by narratives faithful to the character of reality.

The connection between freedom and self-possession in the virtuous person points to the centrality of the agent for an ethic of virtue. For the subject of virtue can be none other than the self, which has its being only as an agent with particular gifts, experiences, and history. Thus a person of virtue or character is often described as "his own man"; possessing "character" is equated with being a person of integrity.[15] By definition, integrity denotes the courage to march to a different drummer.

While we may admire these people, we assume that a full ethical life demands more than integrity. After all, Gordon Liddy seems to have had integrity of a sort, and persons of integrity sometimes commit extreme deeds in the interest of preserving their fortitude. Because of this many assume that the very meaning of morality implies the qualification of our agency by a more universal or disinterested point of view. In such a view the moral life would not be lived, as an ethic of virtue seems to imply, from the perspective of the artist, but from the perspective of the art-critic.

No doubt judges and disinterested observers have characteristics appropriate to such stances, but they cannot be those necessary for the person of virtue. For it is morally necessary, if one is to have character or to be a person of virtue, that it be one's *own* character. Therefore an ethic of virtue seems to entail a refusal to ignore the status of the agent's "subjectivity" for moral formation and behavior. Even as integrity requires that one live faithful to personal history, so the development of a person of virtue mandates living faithful to a community's history. Exactly because an ethic of virtue has such a stake in the agent's perspective, it is profoundly committed to the existence of communities convinced that their future depends on the development of, and trust in, persons of virtue.

3. The Politics of Ethics and the Neglect of Virtue

In spite of recent interest in the ethics of character and virtue,[16] it is generally conceded that modern moral philosophy has neglected the virtues.[17] Much of this neglect can be attributed to the concern of moral philosophers to expurgate and deny status to the "subjective" in moral argument and justification. Many assume that giving credence to the subject, in the manner an ethic of virtue seems to involve, would prevent us from demonstrating how relativism (and perhaps even egoism) are morally untenable. Some contend that the defeat of relativism and egoism is the great project and task of modern ethics. Yet the primary reason for neglecting the subject, I think, is more revealing. I suspect that it originated in a tacit fear that we lack the kind of community necessary to sustain development of people of virtue and character.[18] It is not primarily an issue of ethical theory then, but of politics. That is, contemporary ethicists are attempting an account of the moral life while avoiding the necessary risks concomitant to all significant attempts at community and corresponding ethics of virtue.

My suggestion as to why virtue is currently neglected in moral theory may appear too dramatic, as it can be objected that there are some quite plausible and more mundane reasons for the neglect of virtue in contemporary moral discussion. It is often pointed out that there is hardly any way to portray "the virtuous person" or the "person of character" without reference to some antecedent criteria of good or right.[19] Thus concepts of virtue are parasitic on prior concepts of good or duty. That is why, in spite of deep disagreements, both the teleologist and the deontologist assume that questions of the nature of virtue are secondary to genuine ethical issues.

This presumption is often reinforced by the commonplace assumption that a "person's moral character is typically approached via questions of the worth of the things he or she does (or is disposed to do) and the motives and intentions behind those acts. Thus, matters of moral character seem not only dependent upon but exhaustively definable in the language of act morality."[20] Many argue, therefore, that an ethics of virtue depends first on an account of what acts should or should not be done; only when such an account is compiled will we have a basis for knowing what kind of virtues we ought to have.

Hence William Frankena delineates three primary theories of virtue necessarily dependent on prior theories of normative ethics—i.e., trait-egoism, trait-utilitarianism, and trait-deontological theories. Frankena defends a form of the latter, pointing out that ''an ethics of duty or principles also has an important place for the virtues.''[21] For ''principles without traits are impotent and traits without principles are blind.''[22] While virtues are important to insure that we know what we *should* do, Frankena contends against anyone advocating an ethic of virtue that it is not the function of virtue to tell us *what* to do. For that we must rely on the two deontic principles, beneficence and equal treatment, plus ''the necessary clarity of thought and factual knowledge.''[23]

Utilitarians are often even less interested in the agent and the virtues than are the many kinds of deontologist. Thus R. M. Hare has argued,

> It is important to distinguish between judgments about the moral rightness of an act and those about the moral worth of the agent. The use, in theological discussions about the morality of acts, of expressions such as 'sinful' obscures this distinction. This word applies most naturally to the agent. If so applied, the agent's intentions and motives will be highly relevant; the same act done with one intention or one motive may justify the imputation of sin to the agent, but done with another, not. Theologians are commonly interested in what will happen on Judgment Day; and for deciding the final disposal of souls it is important to know what state they are in.
>
> Utilitarianism, however, has seldom been advocated primarily as a way of judging agents. If it is so used, it will have to pay as much attention to motives and intentions as any other theory. Good motives and intentions will be benevolent ones, arising from the desire to do what is best for the people affected by our acts. As we shall see this may engender a respect (because of the good which comes therefrom) for the moral principles which anti-utilitarians too revere. But utilitarians have generally been less interested in the question ''Will this act put me in the category of good or of sinful men?'' than in the question ''Ought I now to do this Act? Would it be the right thing to do?'' and they have said that we must answer this question by examining the consequences.[24]

Proponents of an ethic of virtue would not deny that every society rightly singles out certain forms of behavior which it either prohibits or recommends irrespective of the character or intentions of the agents. Yet this ''fact'' is not sufficient to establish the further claim that the rightness or wrongness of any behavior, whether teleologically or deontologically justified, is logically prior to an account of virtue. The assumption of such priority necessarily distorts our moral psychology. For we as agents know that our actions, both what we have done and what we have not done, are seldom good indications of our moral worth. Assessment of one another solely on the basis of our actions is insufficient to describe ourselves. (Though often what we do may well be a crucial test case to show that our assumption about what we "really are" is or is not in fact congruent with what we are.)[25] Rather we wish to be judged by the way our "actions" gain their intelligibility as they are understood in the context of our history, our character.

Lawrence Becker has suggested that self-esteem is often the crux in evaluations of our own conduct. "And self-esteem is not built entirely on estimates of the value or dutifulness of one's performance. No matter how many successes some people have, they still feel like they are failures; no matter how many lies some people tell, they still feel they 'are' fundamentally honest. Moral theorizing which ignores or slights this—as act theory tends to do—is very often beside the point in concrete moral situations."[26] Moreover, self-esteem, and subsequent respect for others, seems to involve the willingness to accept responsibility not just for acts, but for ourselves as "having a self-reality that is always both to be discovered and recognized on the one hand and further constituted and determined on the other."[27] The essence of such self-esteem depends on our having the self-constitutive ability to conceive and live it—i.e., the very power commensurate with being a person of virtue or character.

Recognizing the significance of virtue does not imply that questions of performance or behavior are irrelevant for moral evaluations. As I suggested above, it is certainly appropriate, especially in legal contexts, for a society to single out certain kinds of behavior which are excluded, irrespective of the agent's interests. Yet I suspect that such "abstractions" gain their rationale from an interest in reminding us not just what our conduct should and should not be, but what *we* should be. It could thus be that common prohibitions, such as that against murder, also function to remind us that we should be people who respect the life of the other.

Moreover, evaluations of "acts" are crucial for the growth of our own character and virtue. For it is through descriptions of our behavior tested against other accounts that we check ourselves against self-deception and self-righteousness.[28] Nevertheless, the truthfulness of such accounts is not guaranteed by their being formed allegedly from "the moral point of view," but depends on their representing the wisdom of virtuous persons from a community's past and present.

Current theories of normative ethics, in concentrating on acts[29] prior to any account of virtue, are problematic, since they miss something we think vital to the moral life. Indeed, it is my suspicion that prescriptions of moral justification of conduct from the "moral point of view" have appeared intelligible only in that we have continued to expect that people would be trained to be virtuous in the future. The difficulty is that such theories cannot supply, and perhaps even tend to impede, considerations crucial to the development of such people.

The focus on acts, as Lawrence Becker has reminded us, cannot explain why

> there are people whose performance is consistently good—even saintly—who seem untouched by ignoble purposes to the degree we have come to expect in our fellows, and whom we still will not call, in any unreserved sense, "good people." We will not so describe them when we think that their virtue is simply blind adherence to authority training, for example—or, as one of Steinbeck's characters, merely due to lack of energy. Similarly, there are people whose performance is consistently bad—even malevolent—but who exhibit not just remorse after the fact, and surely not just regret, but rather a tragically accurate self-perception which makes us unable to call them, in any unreserved sense, "bad people."[30]

No theory of "moral rationality" or the "moral point of view" can in itself supply an account sufficient to explain why we think such judgments appropriate. Rather we need to appreciate how significant depictions of morality presuppose and require the existence of societies who know that their moral life relies on the vitality of persons of character and virtue.

But as I suggested, contemporary discussions of morality which neglect or, at any rate, make virtue secondary are attempts to develop ethical theory not founded on such a moral community. Morally and politically, we act as though we are members of no community, share no goods, and have no common history. Thus, the challenge is to provide a theory of how moral "objectivity" can be achieved in such a society. By providing an impersonal interpretation of "moral rationality" in which the emotions and history of the agent are relegated to the "private," recent moral theory has tried to show how moral argument (and even agreement) is possible between people who otherwise share nothing in common. Thus, it is thought, "morality" can be grounded in human nature, only now "nature" is limited to "rationality," abstracted from any particular community's history.

Rather than condemn contemporary moral theory for being trivial and/or abstractly irrelevant, it must be seen as an extraordinary moral project that seeks to secure societal cooperation between moral strangers short of reliance on violence.[31] Such an endeavor should not be lightly criticized or dismissed. But neither can it be accepted, since its failure to properly account for the moral agent distorts our nature. In the interest of securing tolerance between people, we are forced to pay the price of having our differences rendered morally irrelevant, for recognition of such differences is the basis for fear and envy. As a result, our nature as agents in and of history is obscured.

Only from the perspective of an ethic that tries to free morality from history would an ethic of virtue look like a subjectivistic threat to morality.

While an ethic of virtue is certainly an agent morality, virtue does not thereby denote a private morality in contrast to a more fundamental and important public morality. Indeed, the very distinction between public and private, social and individual morality is a theory-dependent distinction that is antithetical to an ethic of virtue.[32] An ethic of virtue necessarily involves an account of how every polity, implicitly or explicitly, entails a narrative which depicts what a person of character should be, as well as how certain virtues, in their interrelation, are central to the moral life. But even more strongly, we must see how every polity is ultimately tested by the kind of people it develops.

In this sense, then, there can be no theory of virtue, for any such is necessarily relative to the history of a particular community.[33] All renderings of the virtues imply, implicitly or explicity, an understanding of human nature and history. Thus follows my assessment of the concepts of "human nature" and "history" I think most appropriate for more explicit formulation of an ethic of virtue.

4.   The Virtues and Human Nature

The most striking indication of the historical nature of virtue must be the diversity of virtues recommended by different societies and thinkers. Indeed, from the point of view of modern philosophical ethics one of the things that must make attention to the virtues so unappealing is the lack of consensus about which virtues are morally central; and perhaps even more frustrating is the absence of any principle or method to determine what the primary virtues are or how they might be interrelated. It is no wonder that we are tempted to abandon all interest in the virtues for the less messy and seemingly more fundamental task of providing a rational foundation for morality.

Certainly, no agreement exists about which virtues should be considered central. Plato, for example, emphasized in the *Republic* the virtues of courage, temperance, wisdom, and justice.[34] These became known as the "cardinal virtues," though quite different reasons have been given for why they should be so named.[35] For Plato they are the central virtues because he thought them crucial for functions necessary in the *Republic,* but he also suggested they fulfill or perfect various aspects of the soul.

Plato's account of the virtues has often been criticized because of what many take to be his faulty psychology. However, such criticism fails to touch the significant insight contained in his argument. For Plato rightly suggested that any analysis of the virtues requires some account of how they are necessary for the fulfillment of our nature and for the working of the good society. When the virtues are simply treated as "excellences" for the fulfillment of our human nature, divorced from any political context, they cannot help but appear arbitrary.[36] But, of course, that is exactly what happened as the increasing disintegration of Greek society made implausible the political significance of the virtues. As a result, it became necessary to try to show that particular virtues gained their meaning and intelligibility as forms of fulfillment of particular aspects of human nature.

But such strategy, while often ingenious, was doomed to fail. For as Aristotle argued, our nature does not dictate what the virtues should be; instead, they "are implanted in us neither by nature nor contrary to nature: we are by nature equipped with the ability to receive them, and habit brings this ability to completion and fulfillment."[37] Aristotle was no less insistent than Plato that ethics was but a branch of politics; yet, unlike Plato, he made no attempt to establish a list of central virtues. Struck by the diversity of constitutions, and considering it impossible to provide any one account of the ideal state and a corresponding set of virtues, Aristotle was forced to rely on the clumsy device of the mean in order to compile what is almost a grocery list of virtues. Courage, self-control, generosity, magnificence, high-mindedness, gentleness, friendliness, truthfulness, wittiness, justice, and even a nameless virtue that was a mean between ambition and lack of ambition are those qualities which he deemed characteristic of the Greek gentleman.[38]

In Christian theology accounts of the virtues were even less systematic. Listed among the "fruits of the Spirit" by St. Paul are love, joy, peace, patience, kindness, goodness, faithfulness, gentleness, and self-control (Gal. 5:22-23). Christians, especially in the early centuries, made no attempt to establish any one list of the virtues or to show why certain virtues were more fundamental or grounded in our nature. Indeed the Christian appropriation of the concept of virtue introduced some difficulty. Augustine argued that in a significant sense virtue cannot be a possession of the soul. On the contrary, as a gift of God "either virtue exists beyond the soul, or if we are not allowed to give the name of virtue except to the habit and disposition of the wise soul, which can exist only in the soul, we must allow that the soul follows after something else in order that virtue may be produced in itself."[39] Unless this "something else" is God, the virtues are but forms of self-love and become nothing more than glorious vices. The fourfold division of virtue in Augustine's writings must be understood as four forms of love: "temperance is love giving itself entirely to that which is loved; fortitude is love readily bearing all things for the sake of the loved object; justice is love serving only the loved object, and therefore ruling rightly; prudence is love distinguishing with sagacity between what hinders it and what helps it. The object of this love is not anything, but only God, the chief good, the highest wisdom, the perfect harmony."[40]

Aquinas in many ways is the high point for reflection on virtue, as his compilation combines the influence of Plato, Aristotle, the Stoics,[41] and Augustine in an extraodinarily complex manner. Though his account of the nature of the virtues as habits and how we acquire them is primarily dependent on Aristotle, he attempted to correlate the individual cardinal virtues with functions of the soul. Just as temperance directs and fulfills the concupiscible passions, courage the irascible, prudence perfects the practical intelligence, and justice guides all our "operations."[42] The simplicity of this scheme, however, betrays the complexity of Aquinas' account. He was well aware that a "diversity of objects" could cause a "diversity of passions without causing diversity of virtues, as when one virtue is about several passions," or a diversity of objects can cause "different virtues without causing a difference of passions, since several virtues are directed towards one passion, for example, pleasure."[43] Moreover, Aquinas maintains, following Augustine, that the theological virtues of faith, hope, and charity must be infused in us if the "natural virtues" are to be properly formed and directed.

Other descriptions of the virtues and how they may be thought to perfect human nature could be cited, but such a listing neither would nor could provide lucidity in this matter. Even if it were possible to cull from these lists some virtues common to all, that would not demonstrate that there is a unique set of virtues required by our common human nature. Although there might be widespread consensus on the importance of such virtues as temperance and courage, agreement often extends no further than the name.[44] As soon as the question of substance is raised, sharp disagreements appear as to what courage or temperance entail. For the meanings of courage and temperance vary depending on what society considers paradigmatic examples of temperance or courage.[45]

The diversity of the meaning and kinds of virtues does not imply, however, that all attempts to depict the virtues are arbitrary. For rather than revealing there is no human nature, it reveals the historical nature of our human existence, which requires virtues for the moral life of the individual and society.[46] As humans we cannot be anything we wish, but, as the virtues show, our nature demands that we wish to be more than our nature. Aristotle and Aquinas suggest that it is through our habits that we acquire a "second nature"; and insofar as those habits are virtuous they furnish us with a nature befitting our moral stature.

Some, dissatisfied with the "looseness" of such accounts, have sought to provide a depiction of human nature sufficient to show why one set of virtues, or at least certain virtues, must be preferred over all others. This often involves the claim that there is clearly one aspect of being human that distinguishes us from all other species—i.e., rationality. But as Mary Midgley has argued, what is special about each creature, including humans, "is not a single, unique quality but a rich and complex arrangement of powers and qualities, some of which it will certainly share with its neighbors. And the more complex the species, the more true this is. To expect a single differentia is absurd. And it is not even effectively flattering to the species, since it obscures our truly characteristic richness and versatility."[47]

Perhaps more troubling, when rationality is claimed as our distinctive nature, undue emphasis is placed on intellect as the sole source and basis of virtue. To be sure, there are powerful and profound reasons for this, as Aquinas is certainly right to claim that moral virtue cannot obtain without prudence.[48] Moreover, since the human condition involves many activities which often seem without coherence, it is only with our "minds" that we exact order in our lives at all. Thus reason has been conjectured as the basis for our historicity because it alone gives us the power to act. But as Bernard Williams has suggested, claims that rationality is the distinguishing mark of man tend

> to acquire a Manichean leaning and emphasize virtues of rational self-control at the expense of all else. There is no reason why such an outlook should inevitably follow; apart from anything else, it involves a false and inhuman view of the passions themselves as blind causal forces or merely animal characteristics. To be helplessly in love is in fact as distinctively a human condition as to approve rationally of someone's moral dispositions. But it is easy to see why, in the present direction, Manicheanism looks inviting. If rationality and consistent thought are the preferred distinguishing marks of man, then even if it is admitted that man, as a whole, also has passions, the supremacy of rational thought over them may well seem an unquestionable ideal. This is all the more so, since it is quite obvious that gaining some such control is a basic condition of growing up, and even, at the extreme, of sanity. But to move from that into making such control into the ideal, rules out a priori most forms of spontaneity. And this seems to be absurd.[49]

Indeed when reason is made the primary source and basis of the virtues their very substance is distorted, for then they appear to be the means to control our nature and passions. But as Aristotle and Aquinas insisted, the virtues are a unique blend of "nature" and "reason," since our passions do not so much need control as they need direction.[50] Thus Aquinas argued that only because the Stoics mistakenly understood passion as any affection in discord with reason did they argue that virtuousness required the supression or eradication of all passion.[51] Once passions are correctly understood as "movements of the sensitive appetite," the virtuous man cannot be without them.[52]

What must be rejected is what Robert Solomon has called the "myth of the passions" that interprets the passions as the antithesis to "reason." On the basis of this myth, the passions are seen as animal intrusions and physiological disruptions that reason must control.[53] In contrast to the myth, Solomon argues that the passions are our "self-esteeming representations of emotions as our own judgments, with which we structure the world to our purposes, carve out a universe in our own terms, measure the facts of reality, and ultimately 'constitute' not only our world but ourselves. Rather than disturbances or intrusions, these emotions, and the passions in general, are the very core of our existence, the system of meanings and values within which our lives either develop and grow or starve and stagnate."[54]

The passion of reason and the reason of the passions involved in any account of virtue are an indication of our historical nature.[55] Just as history cannot be separated from the natural, since nature is the very stuff of history, neither can reason be separated from the passions. Being human means our reason and our passions find their fulfillment in and through the virtues. Put more strongly, it is a mistake to argue whether reason or passion is more basic to human nature, since both reason and passion are essential for the development and life of virtue. The only way to be human is to be habitual—which is to say, historical.

Indeed the virtues are the prerequisites illuminating our history as our destiny rather than our fate. Virtue provides the power of self-possession necessary to avoid the parameters of life that others would impose. That virtue provides such power is the basis for the axiom that virtue is "its own reward," though such a claim does not mean that the virtues offer no other benefits. According to Peter Geach, "men need virtues as bees need stings. An individual bee may perish by stinging, all the same bees need stings; an individual man may perish by being brave or just, all the same men need courage and justice."[56] "Virtue as its own reward" is a reminder that we choose to be virtuous for no other reason than that to be so is the only condition under which we would desire to survive. Only by so embodying the virtues have we the power to make our lives our own.

5.   The Virtues and the Histories of Our Communities

This analysis of the nature and significance of virtue should enable us to understand today's peculiar moral situation. For if, as argued above, an ethic of virtue depends on a particularly strong claim and commitment to the historical nature of human existence, and if the specification of individual virtues and their relation derives from the traditions of a particular community, then we develop some inkling why many currently feel so morally lost. As individuals we express a lack of common history or community sufficient to provide us with the resources necessary for us to make our lives our own. Yet our problem is not that we have inherited an oppressive history or that we exist in coercive societies, but that we inherit too many histories and participate in too many communities, each with its own account of what constitutes being virtuous.[57]

I am not suggesting that there once was a golden age in which there was a society so coherent that a person of virtue could avoid any internal or external moral conflict. Every substantive tradition generates diverse interpretations which give rise to conflict. Fortunately no society is so well ordered that all moral conflicts are excluded. The peculiar circumstance of our current situation is that we lack any schema for resolving such conflicts societally and, even more significantly, in our own souls. Bereft of virtues sufficient to structure either self-esteem or self-possession, in the absence of the faculties that are developed only through virtue, we employ forms of power and violence which seem to guarantee our only security.[58]

The plurality of communities, moreover, helps to explain the peculiar moral power of the traditional professions. If every polity derives from a corresponding training in virtue, the professions must be regarded as some of the few remaining coherent polities. That is why, in spite of claims of moral neutrality, medical and law schools survive as the closest modern analogs to ancient schools of virtue. In the commitment to their clients' welfare through the practice of developed skills, they exemplify a training in virtue from which they derive profound self-esteem. That is why their professions become the source of their identity and justification, as occupation is one of the few areas in life which leads itself to exposition.

Moral coherence, however, cannot be supplied even by the professions. For not only are their traditional commitments increasingly qualified by our moral pluralism, no one can live morally as a professional only. Efforts to deal with human existence solely as a ''lawyer'' or ''doctor'' cannot succeed. The virtues and skills of the professions were not, nor can they ever be, sufficient to negotiate the moral demands our lives inevitably place upon us.

Because we find ourselves always involved in intricate webs of conflicting relationships and duties, it is imperative that the ultimate guide issue from personal resources. Authenticity thereby is signaled as the hallmark of our morality, through which we can initiate the ''downward movement through all the cultural superstructures to some place where all movement ends.''[59] Conscience thus becomes the ultimate authority for our behavior.

Yet conscience, David Little has observed, works in a peculiar relation to the possesser of conscience, to our identity as a self. The very notion of conscience involves the ''business of sustaining the identity and continuity, of protecting the integrity of the person as actor, at the deepest levels of the self.''[60] But if the primary task of conscience is to sustain the achievement through time of personal identity and integrity, it seems to require some combination of virtues such as wisdom, courage, honesty, temperance.[61] Perhaps that is why many in the past have said that the duty to be a person of conscience is not just a personal necessity, but a social responsibility.[62]

But if conscience requires some account of the virtues, then appeal to it as a court of last resort is more a symptom of our moral situation than its solution.[63] That may be why so many today rely on cynicism to sustain the self. When the presuppositions necessary to uphold a society's ethic of honor are no longer tenable, cynicism becomes morally indispensable.[64] Through our cynicism—that is, the rigorous and disciplined attempt to investigate the self-interest behind every moral claim—we seek to avoid the loss of the self by denying overriding loyalty to any cause or community.

Yet in the process we lose the very soil crucial to the growth of virtue—the self-esteem cultivated by the sense of sharing a worthy adventure. For a rigorous cynicism is too powerful. Even as it calls into question the moral commitments of others, we cannot save ourselves from its destructive gaze. Cynicism leaves us only with the consolation that because we recognize our own deception we are not hypocrites or fools. Of course, there is no deeper deceit than the assumption that we are among those free from deception.

Moreover, cynicism cannot sustain itself, as it is too easily captured by powers it does not have the means to name, much less avoid. As historical beings we cannot avoid living someone's history, even if we think our cynicism has freed us from all commitments. We are not free from all narratives, nor can we choose any story. Our only escape from destructive histories consists in having the virtues trained by a truthful story, and that can come solely through participation in a society that claims our lives in a more fundamental fashion than any profession or state has the right to do.

Only through such a society do we have the possibility of acquiring those virtues capable of countering cynicism—hope and patience. For as I suggested, the virtuous life is inherently adventurous; people of virtue claim, in spite of all evidence to the contrary, that our existence is responsive to moral endeavor. We are thus sustained by hope that the adventure of living virtuously will be worth the risk. Hope thus forms every virtue, for without hope the virtuous cannot help but be ruled by despair.

But hope without patience results in the illusion of optimism or, more terrifying, the desperation of fanaticism. The hope necessary to initiate us into the adventure must be schooled by patience if the adventure is to be sustained. Through patience we learn to continue to hope even though our hope seems to offer little chance of fulfillment. Patience is training in how to wait when there seems no way to resolve our moral conflicts or even when we see no clear way to go on.[65] Patience is able to wait because it is fueled by the conviction that our moral projects, and in particular our central moral project we call the self, will prevail. Yet patience equally requires hope, for without hope patience too easily accepts the world and the self for what it is rather than what it can or should be.

Only by hope and patience, therefore, are we able to sustain a self capable of withstanding the disintegration that is threatened by the inescapable plurality and often unresolved nature of our moral existence. We do not live in a world that is capable of being negotiated by one virtue, but neither can we live without a self formed by the hope and patience sufficient to make our life our own. Without hope we lack the resource even to have a self befitting our moral nature; but without patience we lack the skills for the self to acquire a history sufficient to be a self.

Without denying that there may be non-religious accounts of hope and patience, Jews and Christians have been the people that have stressed the particular importance of these virtues.[66] For they are the people formed by the conviction that our existence is bounded by a power that is good and faithful. Moreover they are peoples with a deep stake in history; they believe God has charged them with the task of witnessing to his providential care of our existence. They believe their history is nothing less than the story of God's salvation of them and all people. Such a history does not promise to make the life of virtue easier or our existence safer. Rather such a story, and corresponding society, offers training in the hope and patience necessary to live amid the diversity of the world while trusting that its very plurality reflects the richness of God's creating and redeeming purposes.

Whether hope and patience can be sustained in a world, and more particularly, a society like ours that no longer thinks such trust is warranted remains to be seen. I am not suggesting that in the absence of God people lack the resources to live morally. People will usually find the means to live decently. I am raising a more profound question—namely, whether in the absence of God people can find the resources, socially and personally, to form and sustain the virtues necessary for the recognition and fulfillment of our historical nature.

7. Character, Narrative, and Growth in the Christian Life

1. Moral Development and the Christian Life

Recent attention to the nature and process of development occasioned by the work of Jean Piaget and Lawrence Kohlberg is a welcome occurrence. Philosophers and theologians have for too long left the analysis of moral development to educators and psychologists. Yet it is important that we not forget that the experience and necessity of moral growth has always been the subject of philosophical reflection and theological inquiry, and of course has been embodied in actual religious practices and disciplines. Every community has to provide some account and means to initiate their young into their moral traditions and activities, and it seems every community finds some way to encourage its members to move from the less good to the better, and from the good to the excellent.

The fact that some sense of moral development is implicit in any account of morality is not, however, sufficient to allow us to make generalizations about what moral development means and how it must take place.[1] It may be that there are certain biological and social aspects of human nature that allow us to draw some generalizations about moral development,[2] but I remain skeptical that these are sufficient to provide an account of moral development that is independent of content.

The phrase "moral development" is seductive, as it seems to imply that we know what we mean by "moral." Since the Enlightenment, moreover, powerful philosophical accounts have attempted to provide a foundation for sustaining the assumption that "moral" is a univocal concept. In contrast I assume that the notion of morality has no one meaning and any attempt to talk in general about morality will require analogical control. Correlatively, this means that one community's sense of moral development may be quite different from another's.

This is particularly important for trying to understand how and why Christians have been concerned with moral development. While it is certainly true that Christians have emphasized the necessity of moral development, it is

129

equally interesting to note that they have seldom used phrases like "moral development" to talk about it. Rather they have talked about the necessity of spiritual growth, growth in holiness, the pilgrimage of the self, being faithful to the way, and the quaint, but still significant, notion of perfection. It is quite legitimate, of course, to suggest that these are simply more colorful ways to talk about moral development, but such a suggestion fails to do justice to the kind of life Christians have been concerned to promote. For the language of spiritual growth, holiness, and perfection directs attention to the development of the moral self in a manner quite different from the contemporary concern with moral development.[3]

It is equally true that Christians have failed to develop the conceptual categories necessary to illuminate the kind of morality appropriate to their language.[4] Because of their lack of conceptual paradigms, in recent years Christians have eagerly adopted the language of moral development as their own. The translation of the language of perfection into the language of development, however, involves a transformation that robs the language of its religious import.

There are a number of ways such a contention might be stated, but here are only three: (1) the Christian thinks it important to live in recognition that life is a gift rather than to live autonomously; (2) Christian ethics involves learning to imitate another before it involves acting on principles (though principles are not excluded); and (3) the Christian moral life is finally not one of "development" but of conversion. We can examine each of these only briefly.

It is often assumed that Christians cannot be wholly satisfied with the language of moral development because they are also concerned with a dimension beyond the moral which is suggested by the term "faith." So construed, faith does not change or add anything, but denotes something beyond the moral or provides a different perspective.[5] Not only is this a misunderstanding of faith; more significantly, it fails to see that the kind of life Christians describe as faithful is substantively at odds with any account of morality that makes autonomy the necessary condition and/or goal of moral behavior. For the Christian seeks neither autonomy nor independence, but rather to be faithful to the way that manifests the conviction that we belong to another. Thus Christians learn to describe their lives as a gift rather than an achievement.

From the perspective of those who assume that morality is an autonomous institution, the idea that life is a gift can only appear heteronomous. For it is supposed that autonomy entails freeing oneself from all relations except those freely chosen, while the language of gift continues to encourage dependence.[6] Yet, for the Christian autonomous freedom can only mean slavery to the self and the self's desires. In contrast, it is the Christian belief that true freedom comes by learning to be appropriately dependent, that is, to trust the one who wills to have us as his own and who wills the final good of all. In more traditional language, for the Christian to be perfectly free means to be perfectly obedient. True freedom is perfect service.

Yet it may be objected that the contrast between gift and autonomy is overdrawn. For Kant also argued that autonomy consists of doing our duty in accordance with the universal law of our being. Such an objection, however, fails to appreciate that for Christians freedom is literally a gift. We do not become free by conforming our actions to the categorial imperative but by being accepted as disciples and thus learning to imitate a master. Such discipleship can only appear heteronomous from the moral point of view, since the paradigm cannot be reduced to, or determined by, principles known prior to imitation.[7] For the Christian, morality is not chosen and then confirmed by the example of others; instead, we learn what the moral life entails by imitating another. This is intrinsic to the nature of Christian convictions, for the Christian life requires a transformation of the self that can be accomplished only through direction from a master. The problem lies not in knowing *what* we must do, but *how* we are to do it. And the how is learned only by watching and following.[8]

Finally, to be holy or perfect suggests more radical transformation and continued growth in the Christian life than can be captured by the idea of development. The convictions that form the background for Christian growth take the form of a narrative which requires conversion, since the narrative never treats the formation of the self as completed. Thus the story that forms Christian identity trains the self to regard itself under the category of sin,[9] which means we must do more than just develop. Christians are called to a new way of life that requires nothing less than a transvaluation of their past reality—repentance.

Moreover, because of the nature of the reality to which they have been converted, conversion is something never merely accomplished but remains also always in front of them. Thus growth in the Christian life is not required only because we are morally deficient, but also because the God who has called us is infinitely rich. Therefore conversion denotes the necessity of a turning of the self that is so fundamental that the self is placed on a path of growth for which there is no end.

1.1 Character, Narrative, and the Christian Life

Nevertheless, Christian reflection has largely failed to provide conceptual categories for understanding and articulating the kind of moral development appropriate to these Christian convictions. As a result, claims about the

Christian life have too often appeared to be assertions that certain kinds of behavior or actions were to be done simply because "that is the way Christians do things." The relationship between behavior and belief was assumed rather than analyzed.[10] This has had many unfortunate consequences, as it has often created the context for and even encouraged the growth of legalism, self-righteousness, and a refusal to analyze the rationality of Christians' moral convictions. On a more theoretical level the Christian life was divided into internal matters dealing with the spiritual life and external concerns about morality. Indeed, in some traditions distinct disciplines developed to deal with each aspect of the Christian life: thus moral theology dealt with matters of right and wrong abstracted from concern with the agent's moral growth, while ascetical or spiritual theology dealt with the spiritual growth of the inner man.[11]

The Protestant condemnation of moral theology did not help, as Protestants did little more than assert that good works "flow" from faith. Concern for moral development from the Protestant perspective was thus seen as a form of works righteousness. And in the absence of any way to talk about and form the behavior of Christians, Protestants were left vulnerable to whatever moralities happened to pertain in their cultures. Thus, being Christian often simply became a way to indicate what the society generally regarded as decent.

Because of the lack of conceptual categories, attempts to deal with moral development in the Christian life always seem to call forth irresoluble issues, such as the relation between faith and works, and so on. I will try to avoid these issues by providing conceptual categories that may help us see that such alternatives fail to do justice to the nature of the Christian life. In particular I will argue that the language of virtue and character is especially fruitful in providing moral expressions appropriate to Christian convictions.[12] Moreover, I hope to show how the concepts of virtue and character help account for the kind of moral development required of those who have undertaken to live faithful to the Christian story. It is my view that language of virtue or character might well be useful to *most* accounts of moral development, but I am content here merely to make the case that they are conceptually crucial for articulating the kind of growth commensurate with Christian convictions.

Even though the concepts of virtue and character help situate the appropriate locus for Christian growth, they do not in themselves provide a sufficient account of the kind of growth required. "Character" is but a reminder that it is the self that is the subject of growth. But the kind of character the Christian seeks to develop is a correlative of a narrative that trains the self to be sufficient to negotiate existence without illusion or deception.[13] For our character is not the result of any one narrative; the self is constituted by many different roles and stories. Moral growth involves a constant conversation between our stories that allows us to live appropriate to the character of our existence. By learning to make their lives conform to God's way, Christians claim that they are provided with a self that is a story that enables the conversation to continue in a truthful manner.

1.2   *Puzzles of Moral Growth and the Ethics of Character*

I am acutely aware that the concepts of character and narrative have received scant attention in recent moral theory.[14] In this essay I cannot hope to provide an analysis of character and narrative sufficient to defend the significance I have claimed for them. However, I can show how the ideas of character and narrative provide natural or useful ways to think about moral growth by analyzing some of the puzzles that bedevil most theories of moral development—i.e., (1) growth as a threat to moral integrity; (2) how someone can be held responsible for acting in a manner that requires moral skills that he has not yet developed, and (3) how moral growth increases our capacity for moral degeneracy. By providing a brief discussion of each of these puzzles I hope not only to demonstrate how the concepts of narrative and character may help explicate moral growth, but also to introduce themes necessary for the development of the more constructive aspect of this essay.

The general assumption that it is a good thing for anyone to grow morally involves a paradox that is seldom noticed—for how can we grow and yet at the same time remain faithful to ourselves? We have little respect for people who constantly seem to be "changing," as we are not sure we can trust them to be true to themselves. Or even more troubling, we sometimes find ourselves unable to grow as we think we should, because such growth requires a betrayal of relationship dependent on my being "true to my past self." Marriage often provides a particularly intense example of this kind of problem.

I suspect this to be the underlying reason why moral philosophy generally has been so disinclined to analyze the different "stages" of moral growth. Modern moral philosophy has been written from the perspective of some last stage, as if everyone were already at that stage or at least should have it in sight and should be working to achieve it.[15] The problem of moral development is then taken to be how to reach the last stage of morality where moral growth ceases. Childhood is largely ignored because it is taken to represent a pre- or non-moral stage of development.[16]

To proceed in this manner seems to assume that there is no way to account for present moral integrity *and* moral growth. Theories of morality are thus constructed to insure grounds for integrity by supplying monistic moral principles that might render coherent all our activities. The two dominant contemporary moral theories, utilitarianism and formalism, share a common presumption that in the absence of any one moral principle our lives cannot help but be chaotic. They assume the possibility of integrity or moral identity depends on a single moral principle sufficient to determine every moral situation. The moral self results from or is the product of discrete decisions that have been justified from the moral point of view. The integrity of the self, in terms of these accounts, ironically results from always acting as if we are a moral judge of our own actions. For we can claim our actions morally as our own only if they were done from the point of view of anyone.[17]

The concepts of character and narrative provide a means, however, to express the moral significance of integrity without assuming that any one moral principle is available, or that moral development requires that there be a final stage. Indeed, the necessity of character for the morally coherent life is a recognition that morally our existence is constituted by a plentitude of values and virtues, not all of which can be perfectly embodied in any one life. Integrity, therefore, need not be connected with one final end or one basic moral principle, but is more usefully linked with a narrative sufficient to guide us through the many valid and often incompatible duties and virtues that form our selves. From such a perspective growth cannot be antithetical to integrity, but essential to it; our character, like the narrative of a good novel, is forged to give a coherence to our activities by claiming them as "our own."

But if our character is always in process, how can we ever attribute responsibility to anyone? The reason deontological theories seem to have such explanatory power is that they seem to allow us to be held responsible for our behavior even though we were personally not able to avoid what we did or did not do. Thus, children grow by being held responsible, not by becoming responsible. But there are the more troubling cases, like that of Patty Hearst, where we hold a person responsible though we are not sure she was herself, but we think she should have been. Thus Patty Hearst, it is alleged, may not have known how to deal with the SLA, but anyone her age and with her experience should have known how. As a result, we hold her morally and legally responsible for bank robbery.

Such a judgment, though harsh, seems unavoidable. If responsibility were to be relative to each agent's character, public morality would be undermined. But to attribute responsibility to the agent from the perspective of public morality often seems unjust. Recent moral theories have tried to solve this tension by writing moral philosophy from the perspective of the moral observer. To become moral thus entails that each person learn to describe and judge his or her own behavior "from the perspective of anyone." As a result, the subject of moral development—the agent—ironically seems to be lost.

By contrast I assume that no moral theory is capable in principle of closing the gap between what I should do (my public responsibility) and what I can or have to do (my own responsibility). What is needed is not a theory that will insure correspondence between public and agent responsibility, but an account of how my way of appropriating the convictions of my community contributes to the story of that people. I am suggesting it is useful to think of such an account as a narrative that is more basic than either the agent's or observer's standpoint. To claim responsibility for (or to attribute responsibility to) the agent is to call for an agent to be true to the narrative that provides the conditions for the agent to be uniquely that agent.

Finally, there is the problem of moral degeneracy. From the perspective of moral development the possibility of degeneracy simply should not exist. For why would anyone backslide if they had reached a higher stage of morality? And yet empirically there simply seems to be the stubborn fact that we do backslide. The only explanation offered by advocates of "the moral point of view" is that backsliders had yet to form every aspect of their life according to the supreme moral principle—i.e., it was not really backsliding.

But such an explanation fails to do justice to the struggle we all feel in learning to lead decent lives. What we need is an account that will help us deal with the "war that is in our members," that requires constant vigilance if growth is to occur. For as soon as we feel we have "made it," we discover that we have lost the skills necessary to sustain the endeavor. Ironically the demand for moral growth requires an account of morality that allows us to understand that with every advance comes a new possibility of higher-level degeneracy.[18] The greater the integrity of our character, the more we are liable to self-deception and fault.[19] Moral growth, thus, requires a narrative that offers the skills to recognize the ambiguity of our moral achievements and the necessity of continued growth.

2. Moral Virtues and the Unity of the Self

So far I have tried to suggest that the categories of character and narrative offer a promising way to discuss the moral formation of the self—how Christian convictions may or should function to form lives. I have also hinted that the self can be held to have sufficient coherence to deal with the diversity of our moral existence only if that self is formed by a narrative that helps us understand that morally we are not our own creation, but rather our life is fundamentally a gift. In order to supply a more disciplined discussion of this latter contention, I am going to analyze some of the interesting suggestions and problems found in Aristotle's and Aquinas' ethics.

Aristotle and Aquinas, more than any other philosophers, were concerned with how the self, through its activity, acquires character. It is obviously not possible, nor is it necessary, to provide here a complete account of their extremely complex and often quite different accounts of moral virtue. Rather it is my intention to explore certain unresolved problems in their accounts so as to illuminate the meaning and necessity of character and the importance of narrative.

I will call particular attention to Aristotle's and Aquinas' insistence that only behavior that issues from a "firm and unchangeable character," i.e., those actions I am able to claim as mine, can constitute moral virtue. Such a contention appears circular, since those capable of claiming their action as their own must already possess "perfect virtue." This is further complicated by Aristotle's and Aquinas' view that to be virtuous requires that one possess all the virtues, since they assumed that the virtues formed a unity. A perspective like theirs seems to pose insoluble problems for moral development, since one must already be morally virtuous to act in a manner that contributes to moral growth.

I shall try to show that Aristotle and Aquinas are right to think that moral growth is dependent on the development of character sufficient to claim one's behavior as one's own. But they were incorrect to assume that the development of such a self is but the reflection of the prior unity of the virtues. What is required for our moral behavior to contribute to a coherent sense of the self is neither a single moral principle nor a harmony of the virtues but, as I have already said, the formation of character by a narrative that provides a sufficiently truthful account of our existence. If I can show this to be the case, then at least I will have found a way to make intelligible the Christian claim that understanding the story of God as found in Israel and Jesus is the necessary basis for any moral development that is Christianly significant.

2.1   Acting as a Virtuous Man

There are certainly aspects of Aristotle's account of the moral life that might lead one to think that for him "moral character consists of a bag of virtues and vices."[20] If that is Aristotle's view, he seems to have no way to avoid the difficulty that "everyone has his own bag." The problem is not only that a virtue like honesty may not be high in everyone's bag, but that my definition of honesty may not be yours. The objection of the psychologist to the bag of virtues should be that virtues and vices are labels by which people award praise or blame to others, but the ways people use praise and blame toward others are not the ways in which they think when making moral decisions themselves."[21] The issue thus seems to be that the language of virtue reinforces an unreflective habituation to do the moral thing while ignoring the morally central issue—namely, that we not only do the right thing but for the right reason as well.

It is certainly true that Aristotle's resort to the mean fails to give an adequate explanation for the individuation of the various virtues.[22] Nor does he seem to appreciate the theoretical significance of the fact that the meanings of individual virtues are relative to different cultural and societal contexts. In the language I used above, he fails to see that the virtues are narrative-dependent.

Moreover, Aristotle at times seems to claim that becoming virtuous is simply a matter of training. Thus "moral excellence is concerned with pleasure and pain; it is pleasure that makes us do base actions and pain that prevents us from doing noble actions. For that reason, as Plato says, men must be brought up from childhood to feel pleasure and pain at the proper things; for this is correct education" (*Ethics*, 1104b10–12).[23] Aristotle thinks it does little good, therefore, to argue with people who have not been "well brought up," for they

> do not even have a notion of what is noble and truly pleasant, since they have never tasted it. What argument indeed can transform people like that? To change by argument what has long been ingrained in a character is impossible or, at least, not easy. Argument and teaching, I am afraid, are not effective in all cases: the soul of the listener must first have been conditioned by habits to the right kind of likes and dislikes, just as land must be cultivated before it is able to foster seed. For a man whose life is guided by emotion will not listen to an argument that dissuades him, nor will he understand it. And in general it seems that emotion does not yield to argument but only to force. Therefore, there must first be a character that somehow has an affinity for excellence or virtue, a character that loves what is noble and feels disgust at what is base. (*Ethics*, 1179b15–30)

Of course, Aristotle does not mean to imply that someone can become virtuous simply by being taught to be virtuous. The virtues must be acquired by putting them into action.

> For the things which we have to learn before we can do them we learn by doing: men become builders by building houses, and harpists by playing the harp. Similarly, we become just by the practice of just actions, self-controlled by exercising self-control, and courageous by performing acts of courage. . . . In a word, characteristics develop from corresponding activities. For that reason, we must see to it that our activities are of a certain kind, since any variations in them will be reflected in our characteristics. Hence, it is no small matter whether one habit or another is inculcated in us from early childhood; on the contrary

it makes a considerable difference, or rather, all the difference.'' (*Ethics* 1103a30–1103b25)[24]

The behavioristic overtones of these passages have led some to misinterpret Aristotle as an early Skinnerian. Yet he was acutely aware that people do not become just simply by doing just acts. Though some people do what is laid down in the laws, he knows that if they do so involuntarily, or through ignorance, or for an ulterior motive, they do not become just. They cannot be just, "despite the fact that they act the way they should, and perform all the actions which a morally good man ought to perform" (*Ethics* 1144a15–17).

Aristotle was no less concerned than Kant (or Kohlberg) that the morally right thing be done for the right reason. Where he differs from Kant is in his characterization of the kind of reason that forms our agency so we are capable, not just of acting, but of becoming moral through our activity. A formal principle of rationality could not be sufficient, as the self must be formed to desire and act as a man of virtue desires and acts. Even though, as Kohlberg observes, Aristotle distinguishes between the intellectual and moral virtues,[25] the latter are only formed rightly when they are the result of practical wisdom.

2.2   The Circularity Involved in the Acquisition of Virtue

Aristotle notes that we are capable of performing just actions without becoming just, yet "it is possible for a man to be of such a character that he performs each particular act in such a way as to make him a good man—I mean that his acts are due to choice and are performed for the sake of acts themselves" (*Ethics*, 1144a17–20). Or again

in the case of the virtues an act is not performed justly or with self control if the act itself is of a certain kind, but only if in addition the agent has certain characteristics as he performs it: first of all, he must know what he is doing; secondly, he must choose to act the way he does, and he must choose it for its own sake; and in the third place, the act must spring from a firm and unchangeable character. In other words, acts are called just and self-controlled when they are the kind of acts which a just or self-controlled man would perform; but the just and self-controlled man is not he who performs these acts, but he who also performs them in the way just and self-controlled men do. (*Ethics* 1105a30–1105b8)

Note that this seems clearly to be circular.[26] I cannot be virtuous except as I act as a virtuous man would act, but the only way I can become a virtuous man is by acting virtuously. Aristotle seems to have thought that there was something about the very exercise of practical reason itself that, if rightly used, made us virtuous.[27] Yet, even if there is some truth to that, it cannot be sufficient, since he also argues that without virtue rational choice can at best be cleverness. A man can only have practical wisdom if he is good, for only the good man can know and judge his true end (*Ethics* 1144a25–36).

The obvious circularity of the arguments did not bother Aristotle. He assumed that if people were started off rightly they would naturally over time become people of character capable of moral development.[28] At least one of the reasons he felt no need to explore the issue further was that he assumed we are capable of acting voluntarily—so that we can claim our actions as our own. In Aristotle's language we are capable of choice, that is "deliberate desire for things within our power" (*Ethics* 1113a10). Therefore the acquisition of virtue is possible, since we are capable of acting in such a manner that the "initiative lies in ourselves" (*Ethics* 1113b20).[29]

2.3   On Being Responsible for Our Character

Indeed, Aritotle even goes so far as to suggest that we must finally be responsible for our character. He notes, for example, that some may object that carelessness is simply part of a man's character.

> We counter, however, by asserting that a man is himself responsible for becoming careless, because he lives in a loose and carefree manner; he is likewise responsible for being unjust or self-indulgent, if he keeps on doing mischief or spending his time in drinking and the like. For a given kind of activity produces a corresponding character. This is shown by the way in which people train themselves for any kind of contest or performance: they keep on practicing for it. Thus, only a man who is utterly insensitive can be ignorant of the fact that moral characteristics are formed by actively engaging in particular actions. (*Ethics,* 1114a4–10)

Aristotle is prepared to admit, however, that once an unjust or self-indulgent man has acquired these traits voluntarily "then it is no longer possible for him not to be what he is" (*Ethics* 1114a 20).

Finally, Aristotle asks what we are to make of the theory put forward by some that the end is not determined by choice of the individual himself, but is a natural gift of vision which enables him to make correct judgments and to choose what is truly good. In contrast he argues such a theory cannot be true, for how then can

> virtue be any more voluntary than vice? Thus whether the end that appears (to be good) to a particular person, whatever it may be, is not simply given to him by nature but is to some extent due to himself; or whether, though the end is given by nature, virtue is voluntary in the sense that a man of high moral standards performs the actions that lead up to that end voluntarily: in either case vice, too, is bound to be no less voluntary than virtue. For, like the good man, the bad man has the requisite *ability to perform actions through his own agency,* even if not to formulate his own ends. If, then, our assertion is correct, viz., that the virtues are voluntary because we share *in some way* the responsibility for our own characteristics and because the ends we set up for ourselves are determined by the kind of person we are, it follows that the vices, too, are voluntary; for the same is true of them. (*Ethics,* 1114b14–25, italics mine)

But obviously everything depends on the ambiguous phrase "in some way." Aristotle has suggested we can become virtuous because we have the ability to make our actions our own—that is, to do them in a manner appropriate to our character. Yet our ability to act so seems to depend on our having become a person of virtue. Indeed that is why Aristotle (and Aquinas) are doubtful that a morally weak person can be said to be acting at all, since such a person lacks the strength of character to make his actions his own.[30]

From within Aristotle's position I think there is no satisfactory way to deal with the circularity of his position. Yet for our purposes the circularity is extremely instructive, since it suggests that the ability to act and to claim my action as my own depends on my "having" a self through which I am able to give an intelligibility to that which I do and to that which happens to me. But Aristotle simply lacked the conceptual means to articulate the nature of such a self, and as a result he finally has no alternative but to assume that the conventions of Greek society will be sufficient to provide the conditions necessary for us to be morally virtuous.

2.4   Aquinas on Acquiring the Virtues

I suspect that some circularity will bedevil any account of moral development. For we must all begin somewhere, and Aristotle cannot be faulted for insisting that we must develop certain sorts of habits early if we are to learn how to be moral in a more refined and nuanced sense.[31] The question is not whether such habits are necessary, but what kind would encourage the development of truthful character. Aristotle, and Aquinas, however, too easily assumed that ''character'' would result if we rightly embodied all the virtues.

This is perhaps more evident in Aquinas than in Aristotle. For Aquinas argued explicitly that all the virtues are united in the virtue of prudence; indeed every virtue ''is a kind of prudence'' (I-II, 58, 4 and 2). Like Aristotle, Aquinas emphasized the centrality of practical wisdom, since the doing of good deeds is not sufficient to make a man virtuous: ''it matters not only what a man does but also how he does it'' (I-II, 57, 5). And the ''how'' is always determined by prudence.

As a result we find the same kind of circularity in Aquinas that we saw in Aristotle: the practice of any virtue requires prudence, yet prudence cannot be developed without moral virtue. The reason for this, according to Aquinas, is

> prudence's right reason about things to be done, and this not merely in general but also in particular. Now right reason demands principles from which reason proceeds. And when reason argues about particular cases, it needs not only universal but also particular principles. Consequently, just as one is rightly disposed in regard to the universal principles of action by the natural understanding or by the habit of science, one needs to be perfected by certain habits by which it becomes connatural, as it were, to judge rightly particular ends. This is done by moral virtue; for the virtuous man judges rightly of the end of virtue because such as a man is, such does the end seem to him (Aristotle, *Ethics,* 1114a32). Consequently the right reason about things to be done, namely prudence, requires man to have moral virtue. (*Summa Theologica* I-II, 58, 5)

2.5   The Unity of the Virtues

Unlike Aristotle, however, Aquinas tried to provide a rational scheme to suggest why certain virtues are more prominent than others—thus prudence is the perfection of the practical intellect, temperance perfects the concupiscible passions, courage perfects the irascible passions, and justice perfects all operations. These are, of course, the classical cardinal virtues which Aquinas claims are called such because they ''not only confer the power of doing well, but also cause the exercise of the good deed'' (*Summa Theologica* I-II, 61, 1).

Even though Aquinas defends the view that each of the virtues is distinct, he also maintains that they

> qualify one another by a kind of overflow. For the qualities of prudence overflow on to the other virtues insofar as they are directed by prudence.

And each of the others overflow onto the rest, for the reason that whoever can do what is harder, can do what is less difficult. Therefore, whoever can curb his desires for the pleasures of touch, so that they keep within bounds, which is a very hard thing to do, for this very reason is more able to check his daring in dangers of death, so as not to go too far, which is much easier; and in this sense fortitude is said to be temperate. Again, temperance is said to be brave, by reason of fortitude overflowing into temperance, insofar, namely, as he whose soul is strengthened by fortitude against dangers of death, which is a matter of great difficulty, is more able to stand firm against the onslaught of pleasures. (*Summa Theologica* I-II, 61, 4)[32]

Aquinas, therefore, maintains that if anyone has "perfect moral virtue"—that is, a "habit that inclines us to do a good deed well"—then they have all the virtues. He thus assumes that perfect moral virtue necessarily provides a unity to the self, since there is no possibility of the virtues conflicting. However, he is able to make such an assumption only because he asserts that all men have a single last end which orders the various virtues appropriately. Aquinas' claim that "charity is but the form of the virtues" (I-II, 24, 8) is but a theological restatement of his assumption that the unity of the virtues (and the self) is a correlative of men having a single "last end."

Before criticizing Aquinas' (and Aristotle's) views on the unity of the virtues, I think it is well to call attention to the strength of their analysis. For by calling attention to the virtues they at least make the question of the self central to ethical reflection—"the form of an act always follows from a form of the agent" (II-II, 24, 2). Moreover, they do not assume that there is any one external or neutral standpoint from which

the various conditioned moralities can be judged. Precisely the force of the Aristotelian good for man is that it does single out, in necessarily vague terms, the perfect life of a man, taking account of his unconditioned powers of mind; and that this abstract ideal constitutes the permanent standard or norm to which the historically conditioned moralities can be referred when they are to be rationally assessed. In fact, the historically conditioned moralities do converge upon a common core and are not so diverse as the relativists claim. Courage, justice, friendship, the power of thought and the exercise of intelligence, are the essential Aristotelian virtues, although the concrete forms that they take greatly vary in the different socially conditioned moralities. The virtues of splendid aristocratic warriors are not the same as the virtues of a Christian monk; but they are not merely different.

Each of the two ways of life demands courage, fairness or justice, loyalty, love and friendship, intelligence and skill, and self control.[33]

2.6 *The Disunity of the Virtues and the Unity of the Self*

But Aristotle and Aquinas were unable to conceive that we live in a world in which we must choose between ways of life that are inherently incompatible. No positing of a single end or good for man is sufficient to provide a solution for that fact. As Stuart Hampshire has observed,

> the ways of life which men aspire to and admire and wish to enjoy are normally a balance between, and combination of, disparate elements; and this is so, partly because human beings are not so constructed that they have just one overriding concern or end, or even a few overriding desires or interests. They find themselves trying to reconcile, and to assign priorities to widely different and diverging and changing concerns and interests, both within the single life of an individual, and within a single society. They also admire, and pursue, virtues which could not be combined without abridgement in any possible world: for instance, literal honesty and constructive gift of fantasy, spontaneity and scrupulous care, integrity and political skill in manoeuvre. Serious moral problems typically take the form of balancing strict but conflicting requirements, which Plato dramatized in the *Republic* by representing the man educated to be just as educated to combine and balance gentleness and firmness. As there must be conflicts in society, so there must be conflict in the soul, and it is the same virtue that strikes the right balance in situations of conflict.[34]

Aristotle and Aquinas seemed to assume that no self could bear such conflict. It was necessary, therefore, to assert that there could be no inherent incompatibility between the virtues. Rather the right balance between the virtues could be exercised within a single complete life. As a result they failed to see that we often find ourselves involved in ways of life that require that certain virtues go undeveloped or be essentially transformed. We cannot depend on "the virtues" to provide us with a self sufficient to give us the ability to claim our actions as our own. Rather, virtues finally depend on our character for direction, not vice versa.

2.7 *The Narrative Unity of the Self*

Aristotle's and Aquinas' difficulty in accounting for the unity of the self helps one to appreciate the way Kohlberg has approached the problem of moral development. Like Aristotle and Aquinas he is concerned to articulate, or perhaps better, discover, the structure of our moral existence which enables us to make our actions and our life our own. But, unlike them, he feels it is hopeless to confuse the issue of "ego development" with moral development. "For the requirements for consistency in logic and morals are much tighter than those for consistency in personality, which is a psychological, not a logical, unity. Furthermore, there are relatively clear criteria of increased adequacy in logical and moral hierarchies, but not in ego levels."[35]

This does not mean that Kohlberg is uninterested in "ego development," or character, but rather his assumption seems to be that "consistency" of self depends on our willingness to guide our life from the perspective of a universal moral standpoint. "A more differentiated and integrated moral structure handles more moral problems, conflicts, or points of view in a more stable or self-consistent way. Because conventional morality is not fully universal and prescriptive, it leads to continual self-contradictions, to definitions of right which are different for Republicans and Democrats, for Americans and Vietnamese, for fathers and sons. In contrast, principled morality is directed to resolving conflicts in a stable self-consistent fashion."[36]

Kohlberg is looking for something equivalent to Aristotle's and Aquinas' last end, but no moral principle (not even the most universal) or last end is sufficient to provide the self with the kind of unity he seeks. For even if such a principle existed, any attempt to guide our lives by it would necessarily require the moral confinement of the self. What we need is not a principle or end but a narrative that charts a way for us to live coherently amid the diversity and conflicts that circumscribe and shape our moral existence.

In summary, I am suggesting that descriptively the self is best understood as a narrative, and normatively we require a narrative that will provide the skills appropriate to the conflicting loyalties and roles we necessarily confront in our existence. The unity of the self is therefore more like the unity that is exhibited in a good novel—namely with many subplots and characters that we at times do not closely relate to the primary dramatic action of the novel. But ironically without such subplots we cannot achieve the kind of unity necessary to claim our actions as our own.

Yet a narrative that provides the skill to let us claim our actions as our own is not the sort that I can simply "make mine" through a decision. Substantive narratives that promise me a way to make my self my own require me to grow into the narrative by constantly challenging my past achievements. That is what I mean by saying that the narrative must provide skills of discernment and distancing. For it is certainly a skill to be able to describe my behavior appropriately and to know how to "step back" from myself so that I might better understand what I am doing. The ability to step back cannot come by trying to discover a moral perspective abstracted from all my endeavors, but rather comes through having a narrative that gives me critical purchase on my own projects.

3. Growth in the Christian Life: A Story

As a way of trying to bring the disparate parts of my argument together I am going to tell a story. It is not a complicated story, but I think it suggests nicely how character and narrative can help us understand how the self can and should be capable of moral growth. Moreover I hope this story will serve to suggest how the convictions peculiar to the Christian story require the development of certain kinds of skills. The story relates an incident between me and my father that occurred in a instant but has stayed with me for many years. In order to make it intelligible, I need to supply a little background.

My father is a good but simple man. He was born on the frontier and grew up herding cows. Living with a gun was and is as natural to him as living with an automobile is for me. He made his living, as his father and five brothers did, by laying brick. He spent his whole life working hard at honest labor. It would have simply been unthinkable for him to have done a job halfway. He is after all a craftsman.

I have no doubt that my father loves me deeply, but such love, as is often the case among Westerners, was seldom verbally or physically expressed. It was simply assumed in the day-to-day care involved in surviving. Love meant working hard enough to give me the opportunity to go to college so that I might have more opportunity than my parents had.

And go on I did in abstruse subjects like philosophy and theology. And the further I went the more unlike my parents I became. I gradually learned to recognize that blacks had been unfairly treated and that the word "nigger" could no longer pass my lips. I also learned the Christianity involved more than a general admonition to live a decent life, which made belief in God at once more difficult and easy. And I learned to appreciate art and music which simply did not exist for my parents.

Married to a woman my parents would always have difficulty understanding, I then made my way to Yale Divinity School, not to study for the ministry, but to study theology. During my second year in divinity school, every time we called home the primary news was about the gun on which my father was working. During the off months of the winter my father had undertaken to build a deer rifle. That meant everything from boring the barrel and setting the sight, to hand-carving the stock. I thought that was fine, since it certainly had nothing to do with me.

However, that summer my wife and I made our usual trip home and we had hardly entered the door when my father thrust the now completed gun into my hands. It was indeed a beautiful piece of craftsmanship. And I immediately allowed as such, but I was not content to stop there. Flushed with theories about the importance of truthfulness and the irrationality of our society's gun policy I said, "Of course you realize that it will not be long before we as a society are going to have to take all these things away from you people."

Morally what I said still seems to me to be exactly right as a social policy. But that I made such a statement in that context surely is one of the lowest points of my "moral development." To be sure there are ready explanations supplied by the Freudians to account for my behavior, but they fail to do justice to the moral failure my response involved. For I was simply not morally mature enough or skillful enough to know how to respond properly when a precious gift was being made.

For what my father was saying, of course, was someday this will be yours and it will be a sign of how much I cared about you. But all I could see was a gun, and in the name of moral righteousness, I callously rejected it. One hopes that now I would be able to say, "I recognize what this gun means and I admire the workmanship that has gone into it. I want you to know that I will always value it for that and I will see that it is cared for in a manner that others can appreciate its value."

I have not told the story to give an insight into my family history or because I get some pleasure from revealing my moral shortcomings. Rather, I have told it because I have found it illuminating for reflecting generally about moral growth. For the insensitivity of my response to my father did not reflect my failure to grasp some moral principle, or to keep the maxim of my action from being universalized, but showed that I did not yet have sufficient character to provide me with the moral skills to know that I had been given a gift and how to respond appropriately. On the surface my response was morally exemplary—I was straightforwardly honest and my position was amply justified. But in fact what I did was deeply dishonest, as it revealed a lack of self, the absence of a sustaining narrative sufficient to bind my past with my future.[37]

For my response was meant only to increase further the alienation between my father and myself in the interest of reinforcing what I took to be more "universal" and objective morality. I discovered that the person who responded so insensitively to my father was not "who I was" or at least not what "I wanted to be." I was and am destined to be different from my parents, but not in a manner that means I no longer carry their story with me. But my own self, my story, was not sufficient to know how that might be done.

And I am struck by how little I would have been helped by becoming more sophisticated in ethical theory or even by conforming my life more completely to the best ethical theory of our day. My problem was not that I lacked skill in moral argument and justification, but that I lacked character sufficient to acknowledge all that I owed my parents while seeing that I am and was independent of them. Indeed it has taken me years to understand that their great gift to me was the permission to go on, even though they sensed my "going on" could not help but create a distance between me and them that love itself would be unable to bridge.

Equally interesting to me has been the attempt to explain to myself how I could have been so unbelievably self-righteous. My temptation has always been to think that what I said "was not the real me." Moreover there is some good reason to accept that kind of explanation, since I certainly would not have said what I did had I "known better." Therefore, I was not responsible for what I did, though I clearly did it at the time.

But such an explanation is a "temptation," as it is equally clear to me that my moral growth depends on taking responsibility for what I said as something done by me. Not to take responsibility for my response is to remain the person who made that kind of response. Philosophically that seems to be a puzzle, for how am I to explain that I must take responsibility for what "I did 'unknowingly'" in order that I can now claim responsibility for what I am and have become? As puzzling as the philosophical problem is, the moral intelligibility of claiming such an action as mine is just as sure. For retrospectively all my actions tend to appear more like what "happened to me" than what I did. Yet to claim them as mine is a necessary condition for making my current actions my own. Our ability to make our actions our own—that is, to claim them as crucial to our history—even those we regret, turns out to be a necessary condition for having a coherent sense of self—that is, our character. But such a coherence requires a narrative that gives us the skill to see that our freedom is as much a gift as it is something we do.

For our freedom is dependent on our having a narrative that gives us skills of interpretation sufficient to allow us to make our past our own through incorporation into our ongoing history. Our ability to so interpret our past may often seem to require nothing less than conversion as we are forced to give up false accounts of ourselves. Because of the pain such conversions often entail, the language of discontinuity tends to predominate in our accounts of our moral development. But the freedom acquired through our reinterpretations is dependent on our having a narrative sufficient to "make sense" of our lives by recognizing the continuity between our past and present and our intended future. In order to see that, we need a story that not only provides the means to acknowledge the blunders as part of our own story, but to see ourselves in a story where even our blunders are part of an ongoing grace, i.e., are forgiven and transformed for "our good and the good of all the church."[38]

3.1   Gifts, Sociality, and Growth

These last claims obviously require a defense more elaborate than I can hope to develop here. Indeed, I am unsure I even know how to defend such a claim or know what defense would or should look like. In fact, I have suggested two related but different points: (1) that the self is a gift and (2) that we need a story that helps us accept it as a gift. It is from the story that we gain the skills to recognize the gift on which our life depends, as well as ways of acting appropriate to such a gift. For the language of gift, without an appropriate account of the gift itself, can be just as destructive as the claim that we are our own possession.

Yet the language of gift at least offers us a way to deal with Aristotle's claim that we are responsible for having a careless character. Even though we may intuitively think that to be correct, it remains quite unclear how we can be said to be responsible for our character. For the very condition required to claim responsibility seems to be character itself. Therefore Aristotle seems right in suggesting that it does not just make considerable difference how we are brought up, it makes "all the difference."

And it is certainly true that we need to be trained to acquire certain habits. But it is equally important to be introduced to stories that provide a way to locate ourselves in relation to others, our society, and the universe. Stories capable of doing that may be thought of as adventures, for there can be no self devoid of adventure. What we crave is not dignity as an end in itself, but the participation in a struggle that is dignifying. Without self-respect, integrity is impossible. And self-respect comes from a sense of the possession of a self correlative to our participation in a worthy adventure. Yet my very ability to take on a role in the adventure is dependent on my understanding that there are other roles I am not called on to play or cannot play. But the very existence of these other roles gives me the ability to step back and test my own involvement in the adventure. They provide a standpoint that helps me see the limits and possibilities of my own role. Moral growth comes exactly through the testing of my role amid the other possibilities in the adventure.

Moreover, through initiation into such a story I learn to regard others and their difference from me as a gift. Only through their existence do I learn what I am, can, or should be.[39] To be sure, the other's very existence necessarily is a threat to me, reminding me that I could have been different than I am. The truthfulness of the adventure tale is thus partly tested by how it helps me negotiate the existence of the other both as a threat and a gift for the existence of my own story.

The necessary existence of the other for my own self is but a reminder that the self is not something we create, but is a gift. Thus we become who we are through the embodiment of the story in the communities in which we are born. What is crucial is not that we find some way to free ourselves from such stories or community, but that the story which grasps us through our community is true. And at least one indication of the truthfulness of a community's story is how it forces me to live in it in a manner that gives me the skill to take responsibility for my character. That does not mean that there will ever be a point at which I can say "I am now what I have made myself," for the story must help me see that claiming myself as my own is not the same as claiming that I have made or chosen what I am. Rather it means I am able to recognize myself in the story that I have learned to make my own.

This is a particularly foreign perspective for most of us today. For our primary story is that we have no story, or that the stories that we have must be overcome if we are to be free. Thus we demand a universal standpoint so that the self may reach a point from which it can judge and choose objectively between competing particularistic stories; in short, we seek a story that frees us from the adventure. Ironically, the story that we have no story is one that prevents moral growth. For it provides us with a self-deceptive story that fails to adequately account for the moral necessity of having a story and of being a self in the first place.

What we require is not no story, but a true story. Such a story is one that provides a pilgrimage with appropriate exercises and disciplines of self-examination. Christians believe scripture offers such a story. There we find many accounts of a struggle of God with his creation. The story of God does not offer a resolution of life's difficulties, but it offers us something better— an adventure and struggle, for we are possessors of the happy news that God has called people together to live faithful to the reality that he is the Lord of this world. All men have been promised that through the struggle of this people to live faithful to that promise God will reclaim the world for his Kingdom. By learning their part in this story, Christians claim to have a narrative that can provide the basis for a self appropriate to the unresolved, and often tragic, conflicts of this existence. The unity of the self is not gained by attaining a universal point of view, but by living faithful to a narrative that does not betray the diversity of our existence. No matter how hard such a people work to stay faithful to such convictions, they never can forget that it is only through a gift that they are what they are.

To argue that what we need is a true story if we are to grow in a morally appropriate way is not to deny the importance of the "universal." But the test of the truthfulness of any story does not reside in its conforming to or embodying a prior universal norm, but rather in how we and others find their lives illuminated and compelled by the accuracy and truthfulness of its particular vision. There is no "story of stories," but only particular stories which more or less adequately enable us to know and face the truth of our existence. Thus, there is no universal point of view, a point of view that does not bear the marks of a particular history. The recognition of that is one of the first indications that we are dealing with a story that should demand our attention for its power to reveal the truth.

3.2 How Can We Be Taught and Grow into the Story?

Every account of moral development must necessarily have educational implications. We must be given some exercises appropriate to the kinds of moral growth desired. That is an incontrovertible risk. The various sets of exercises through which Christians learn to understand and live appropriate to the story of God's dealing with them in Israel and Jesus may be called tradition. The Christian life requires the development of certain kinds of habits, but those very habits require us to face ambiguities and conflicts through which our virtues are refined. Therefore, there is every reason to think that Christians have always been prescribing a form of moral development for training in their own community.

Growth in the Christian life may well involve encouraging a greater conflict between the self and wider society than is generally approved. Thus Christians train or should train their children to resist the authority of the state, not in the name of their ''rights'' as individuals, but because the ''justice'' of the state is to be judged against God's justice. Such training is ''risky,'' as it separates the young of the Christian community from powerful support necessary to being ''a self.'' To be trained to resist the state, therefore, requires nothing less than an alternative story and society in which the self can find a home.

Such a society can never be satisfied with external compliance with the story. For the story itself demands that only those who are willing to be the story are capable of following it. That is why it has been the brunt of Christian spirituality through the ages to provide exercises and examples through which Christians might better be what they are. What is crucial is not that Christians know the truth, but that they be the truth. ''For if the doctrines of Christianity were practiced, they would make a man as different from other people as to all worldly tempers, sensual pleasures, and the pride of life as a wise man is different from a natural; it would be as easy a thing to know a Christian by his outward course of life as it is now difficult to find anybody that lives it.''[40]

I suspect that the insistence on learning to live as you are and be as you live is part of the reason that Christians have maintained that the Christian life finally requires attention to masters of that life. For it is from the masters that we learn skills necessary to have lives appropriate to the claim that we are nothing less than God's people. For the most central of Christian convictions is the assumption that no statement or principle of morality can be sufficient to make us moral. Rather to be moral requires constant training, for the story that forms our lives requires nothing less than perfection—i.e., full participation in an adequate story.

4. Conclusion

I am acutely aware that the twisting and turnings in this chapter are enough to test the patience of even the most sympathetic reader. Therefore some attempt at summing up seems called for. I began with the claim that Christians have always been concerned with moral development, but that the kind of moral growth they wish to promote is not equivalent with current theories of moral development. For Christian convictions require that the self be transformed in a manner that befits their conviction that the world is under the lordship of Jesus Christ—that is, that the fundamental character of our life is that of a gift. By exploring some of the puzzles endemic to accounts of moral growth, I suggested that the concepts of character and narrative are particularly important for understanding moral growth and in particular the kind of growth appropriate to Christians.

The exploration of these puzzles also allowed me to suggest some of the difficulties of theories of moral development inspired by Kant. By analyzing the strength and weakness of Aristotle's and Aquinas' understanding of the acquisition of virtue, I tried to suggest how the growth of character, and the corresponding ability to claim our actions as our own, is a correlative of our being initiated into a determinative story. For it is only through a narrative which we learn to "live into" that we acquire a character sufficient to make our history our own.

By telling and analyzing a story from my own experience, I sought to suggest in a more concrete manner the rather abstract analysis of Aristotle and Aquinas. The development of character involves more than adherence to principles for their own sake; rather, it demands that we acquire a narrative that gives us the skill to fit what we do and do not do into a coherent account sufficient to claim our life as our own. Such narratives may of course be false and as a result produce false character. Indeed, an indication of a truthful narrative is one that remains open to challenge from new experience. That is why a truthful narrative necessarily must be one that can provide integrity in a manner that does not deny the diversity of our lives and the necessity to claim as mine what I wish I had not done, as well as what I have done well.

By suggesting how the story Christians tell offers them a place in an adventure, I have tried to indicate how such a theory provides a pattern for moral growth. But this suggestion remains enigmatic, apart from my few suggestions concerning learning to trust in our existence as a gift. A more detailed account would require showing how that claim is spelled out through the story of God's dealing with his people and how the struggle that always goes with learning is necessary to make that story ours. For internal to the story itself is the claim that we cannot know the story simply by hearing it, but only by learning to imitate those who now are the continuation of the story.

PART THREE

The Church and Social Policy: The Family, Sex, and Abortion

8. The Moral Value of the Family

1. The Crisis of the "Family"

One of the few issues on which there is consensus today is that the family seems to be going through some kind of crisis. Indeed the account of why this crisis exists is beginning to take on a boring familiarity. This account usually begins by observing that the family is a very good thing—the backbone of the nation and society, or something equally impressive. It is thus assumed that the family is inherently valuable—an end in itself—without which we could not develop as full moral beings. But then divorce statistics, examples of wife and child beating, the rates of delinquency, the demands of women's liberation, and rising sexual immorality are cited as evidence that the family is in deep trouble. It is alleged that we are living at a time when there is a breakdown of morality, or rather that a hedonistic self-fulfillment ethic has replaced past commitments to duty and responsibility, and the family is among the first and the most important casualties of this breakdown. This usually sets the stage for a call to return to traditional values in an effort to save the family from the acids of immorality. And by saving the family we can save our society.

It is a temptation for anyone reflecting on issues of the family to accept this account; issues concerning the family are so confusing that any pattern of explanation seems better than none at all. Yet such an account fails to help us determine the moral importance of the family and what is happening to it. This pattern encourages us to think of the family in simplistic terms. In fact, appeals to the "moral value of the family" too often succeed in obscuring the more profound issues concerning the moral status of the family in our society.

Of course, some are suggesting that the very idea that the family is in crisis is a mistake. It only appears a crisis to those who cannot distinguish change from crisis. Thus Dr. Tamara Hareven argues:

> The family has never been a utopian retreat from the world, except in the imagination of social reformers and social scientists. Some of the major problems besetting family life today emanate from the heavy demands placed upon it by individuals in society who require that it be a

haven of nurture and a retreat from the outside world. The modern family's growing discomfort suggests the need for expansion and diversity in what we expect from it and its adaptation to a new social condition with diverse timing schedules and multiplicity of roles for its members, rather than seeking refuge in a non-existent past.[1]

Some have come to realize that the rising divorce rate in our society does not indicate the family has broken down. The fact that an extremely high percentage of those who divorce remarry may indeed suggest just the opposite. They even seem to remarry someone remarkably like their former spouse. The family remains a tough institution, not easily defeated.

In spite of everything, people seem to end up living together, and some even have children. It would seem that in many cases those who decry the loss of familial relationships are arbitrarily asserting a preference for one style of family constellation over others. The issue becomes not really whether the family will continue to exist, but what kind of family should exist and what moral presuppositions are necessary to form and sustain it. Considered in these terms, it makes sense to suggest that the family is in a crisis, but our problem is that we can no longer describe what the family should be and/or why we think of it as our most basic moral institution.

Because we have all had an experience of family and most of us are involved in families, it seems bizarre to say that we do not know what our involvement means. I am suggesting that we lack the moral and linguistic skills to express adequately what has happened to us and what we do in families. More importantly, I want to try to show that the moral language our culture supplies tends to distort the very experience we are trying to describe.

Ethicists provide little help in recovering the experience of the family. For modern ethical reflection the family is simply an anomaly, a curiosity left over from previous ages. From the "moral point of view" identification with relatives appears at best a sentimental attachment—more likely an irrational commitment. Nowhere in contemporary ethical literature is there discussion of the simple but fundamental assumption that we have a responsibility to our own children that overrides responsibility to children who are not ours. Although a powerful assumption, there is no adequate account in contemporary ethical reflection of why we hold it or if it is justified. Instead, the best my colleagues can offer is the doubtful thesis that children ought to have rights.[2]

Certainly, it may be suggested, the lack of such an account is no serious matter. People seldom know what they are doing, and yet they come out all right. While that is correct, in the absence of any determinative account we can too easily be captured by descriptions that provide little aid in knowing what it means to be a family. For example my course on marriage and the family at Notre Dame is structured by questions such as "What is it?" and "Why would anyone want to do it?" Most of the students enroll because they expect it to be a "how to do it" course. Their expectations are determined by their presuppositions about what marriage is and under what conditions they are going to participate, e.g., meeting the "right person" and then getting married. They simply assume, like most of our culture, that "family" is synonymous with "marriage."

To get them to examine these assumptions, I have them consider the distaste of the early Christians for marriage ("In view of the impending distress it is well for a person to remain as he is" [1 Cor. 7:26]), and the church's support and blessing of arranged marriages. That at least suggests that there might be something more at stake in marriage and the family than "being in love." Some of the reading challenges their romantic notions about marriage, but it has little ultimate effect; they leave the course with much the same attitudes they brought to it.

I have discovered, however, that there are two questions that take them back a bit. First, "What reason would you give why one should be willing to have children?" They say "children are fun," or "as an expression of a couple's love," or "because it is just the thing to do," but they clearly doubt that any of these are an adequate basis for having children. Their often unexpressed doubt seems to me to illustrate the depth of the crisis concerning the family: we lack a moral account of why we commit ourselves to having children.

The other question I raise for which there is no ready answer is "What account of marriage and the family would enable you to tell your wife or husband the truth about each other?" For we all know that we never lie more readily than we do to those who are the closest to us. We tell strangers on a bus or plane things about ourselves that we would never tell those we love, because we fear truth will destroy love. Sometimes this is an adequate description of the relationship, since often what we call love is a tacit agreement on the part of a couple never to challenge one another's self-deceptions. It would indeed require substantive assumptions to exist in a family that has no fear of the truth.

Therefore the problem with appeals to save the family is they continue to assume that we all know what we mean when we say the family is a good thing. The moral issue then appears to be that we are not living up to the standards of what we all know to be good, but that simply fails to confront our inability to describe or evaluate "family." Indeed, I suspect one of the reasons we so extol the value of the family is because we are so unsure of its worth. We attempt to substitute rhetoric for substance and are thus unable to deal with the obvious shortcomings of the institution. In actuality, we must acknowledge that some families are a caldron seething with hate and contempt which have been called love in the supposed interests of the integrity of the unit.

2.   Political Liberalism and the Family

In this respect I think we are a little like Augustus in one of the episodes of Masterpiece Theater's *I, Claudius*. Like many political reformers and radicals since, Augustus was particularly conservative about personal and familial morality. He believed strongly that the traditional Roman family, which literally placed all power in the hands of the patriarch, was the backbone of the state. Thus he was outraged when he discovered that his daughter had entertained half of Rome in her bed, and that her lovers had come from senatorial families.

In a marvelous scene we see Augustus calling his daughter's lovers before him and lecturing them on the depth of their immorality. His concern was not only that they had been willing to sleep with his daughter, but they had betrayed their political duty by failing to begin families of their own. Instead of dallying with his daughter they should be fulfilling their duty as Romans by providing Rome with sons.

Augustus' speech is ironic, because while he no doubt believed everything he was saying, as emperor he was also engaged in policies whose clear result was to decisively weaken the Roman family. Just as he continued to say the Senate ruled while he systematically stripped it of its power, so he continued to believe in the family but also would not allow it to be, as it had been in the past, an independent commonwealth within the state. As Robert Nisbet pointed out, in earlier times families bore responsibility for most independent offenses; but under Augustus individuals were punished (directly by the state) as if they had no family.[3] Thus Augustus subjected his daughter to exile—a penalty pronounced by the state rather than the family. Even more important, Augustus changed inheritance laws so that individuals might own property separate from family membership.

Now, I say we resemble Augustus somewhat because we want to retain the fiction that we hold dear the family, while we adhere to disharmonious convictions and policies that mitigate against the family. In the classic words of Pogo, "We have met the enemy, and he is us." I do not mean to suggest that we are personally responsible, but that we are inheritors of a history which has rendered the family a highly questionable institution.

This is not the place for me to recount this history. Indeed, I have become aware that there is nothing more problematic than historical claims about how the family has changed.[4] Most of us, though, have been influenced by a sociological rendition of what has happened to the family that is useful to recall. In the past the family was large, extended, and patriarchal, but this has been replaced by the nuclear family. This smaller and more democratic family, as a result of growing specialization of social and economic functions, has lost the economic, protective, and educational functions of the traditional family. In the process the family has taken on a more profound and rewarding purpose—namely, it now specializes in emotions.

This new form of family is a correlative of the requirements of industrial society. "Whereas kinship served as the unifying principle of earlier forms of society, the modern social order rests on impersonal, rational, and 'universalistic' forms of solidarity. In a competitive and highly mobile society the extended family has no place. The nuclear family, on the other hand, serves industrial society as a necessary refuge. It provides adults with an escape from the competitive pressures of the market, while at the same time it equips the young with the inner resources to master those pressures."[5] The nuclear family is not characterized by how many people are living under the same roof but by the privileged emotional climate that must be protected from outside intrusion.[6]

This historical account has been challenged by some who insist that the nuclear family was present before the industrial revolution. Aside from whether this particular account is historically or sociologically correct in every detail, it has begun to serve as a norm for our understanding of the family. We use this allegedly descriptive account to justify our assumption that the family should be understood as the paradigm of love and intimacy in our society. Indeed, we tend to see the development of the nuclear family as part of the continuing story of freedom, which represents a break from the necessities of the past.

The power of this narrative is amply illustrated by how it has led us to forget that the family has traditionally not been rooted in contract but in biology—that is, its core function has been to provide human continuity through reproduction and child rearing.[7] As Robert Nisbet reminds us, few people have ever let something as important as the need for future generations rest on anything as fragile as the emotion of love. "Even if we assume that in most places at most times a majority of spouses knew something akin to passionate love, however fleetingly, the great strength of the family has everywhere been consanguineal rather than conjugal. And here, not affection, but duty, obligation, honor, mutual aid, and protection have been the key elements."[8]

Nisbet argues, therefore, that what has weakened the family is not sexual immorality, the revolt of the youth, or women's liberation but the loss of the economic, political, and moral functions of the family. Rather than being accidental, the very moral convictions linked to modern history necessarily had this result. For family kinship has always been an anomaly for the liberal tradition.[9] In liberal thought only if human beings can be separated in a substantial degree from kinship can they be free individuals subject to egalitarian policies of our society. Thus, for example, the Supreme Court recently held in *Planned Parenthood* v. *Danforth* that husbands have no rights if their wives wish an abortion, since "abortion is a purely personal right of the woman, and the status of marriage can place no limitation on personal rights." As Paul Ramsey has observed, in spite of our society's alleged interest in the bond of marriage, that bond is now understood simply as a contract between individuals who remain as atomistic as before marriage.[10]

In the name of freedom we have created "the individual," who now longs for community in the form of "interpersonal interaction." The family is praised, therefore, in Christopher Lasch's marvelous phrase, as a "haven in a heartless world"—the paradigm of "interpersonal relations."[11] Such a concept of the family assumes, moreover, "a radical separation between work and leisure and between public and private life. The emergence of the nuclear family as the principle form of family life reflected the high value modern society attached to privacy, and the glorification of privacy in turn reflected the devaluation of work."[12] Thus, according to Lasch, relations in the family have come to resemble relations in the rest of the society—namely, a relationship between friendly strangers. "Parents refrain from arbitrarily imposing their wishes on the child, thereby making it clear that authority deserves to be regarded as valid only insofar as it conforms to reason. Yet in the family as elsewhere 'universalistic' standards prove on examination to be illusory."[13] And as a result relations in the family too often become nothing less than power struggles between independent principalities.

In an attempt to defuse the destructiveness of this situation for their children, parents tend to undervalue the intensity of family life. By becoming our child's friend we think we can avoid the politics of the family, which are often the dirtiest politics of all. For example, we are aware that when parents make inordinate sacrifices for their children, these sacrifices can be used as blackmail. We assume the way to avoid such strategies is to try to develop a form of life where no one is asked to suffer for anyone else. We treat our children as equals, which, translated, means we place no demands on them.[14] We thus raise our children permissively, because we fear "imposing" our values on them and psychologically damaging them. But we fail to see that permissiveness leads to a different form of social control, wherein the authority of the peer group is substituted for that of the family.

Ironically, this kind of family, which was justified in the name of intimacy, now finds intimacy impossible to sustain. For "in a truly intimate relationship one person makes unique claims upon another, claims for services, affection, respect and attention which can be supplied only by that other person.''[15] By trying to make the relationship between husband and wife, parents and children, impersonal, we try to avoid the demands of intimacy. Ferdinand Mount pointed out, "Intimacy always entails personal authority. The claims of a child for care and love, even if unspoken by child or mother, are just as much a moral authority over his father as the father's claims for filial affection and/or obedience and respect. For authority in this sense does not depend upon inequality nor does it wither away under the beneficent rays of equality. It depends solely upon one person acknowledging another person's right to make claims on him in particular.''[16]

The relationship between liberalism and the family is obviously a complex matter which requires a more nuanced argument than I can develop here. However, in summary, I am suggesting that the "crisis of the family" does not indicate the absence of a moral ethos for the family, but reflects how the family has increasingly been formed by the deepest moral convictions we have about ourselves. Our liberal forefathers assumed that their commitment to the freedom of the individual was consistent with and even supportive of the family. Milton Friedman continues this assumption as he claims that liberals "take freedom of the individual or perhaps the family, as our ultimate goal in judging social arrangements. A society has nothing to say about what an individual does with his freedom: it is not an all-embracing ethic. Indeed, a major aim of the liberal is to leave the ethical problem for the individual to wrestle with.''[17] But as Robert Paul Wolff has stated, from such a perspective

> the ties of blood are merely one source among many of the desires whose satisfaction we seek rationally to maximize. One man enjoys eating, and puts his money into fine food; a second races fast cars, and allocates his resources for carburetors and tune-ups; a third man raises children—his own—and he finds himself possessed of the strong desire that they should be happy and healthy. So he puts his resources into their schooling and food and clothing, and spends his spare time with them. If his desire for his children's welfare is stronger than his taste in fine cars or fine food, then rationality will dictate that he spend more on them than on eating and transportation. But if his desire is not essentially different from those of his fellow citizens, [then] the state has no reason to treat his interest in his children as taking precedence over his neighbor's interest in racing cars or fine food.''[18]

If we accept this as an account of ourselves, the heirs of the liberal tradition, we find ourselves bereft of the moral anchor supplied by those particularistic commitments we used to indicate with the word "family."

3. The Incompetency of Parents

I am aware that many may find all this an exaggeration at best, and at worst useless speculation that has little to do with reality. Perhaps I can make it more concrete by relating it to a phenomenon we all have some experience of today: the utter incompetence parents feel in matters dealing with the rearing of their children. Moreover, I think our feeling of incompetence is a correlative of our moral and political traditions. Thus Christopher Lasch points out that at the same time that the family was being exalted as the last refuge of privacy in a forbidding society, "guardians of public health and morality were insisting that the family could not provide for its own needs without expert intervention."[19]

Lasch argues the even stronger thesis that the family as we know it did not just evolve in response to social and economic factors; it was deliberately transformed by the intervention of planners and policymakers. "Educators and social reformers saw that the family, especially the immigrant family, stood as an obstacle to what they conceived as social progress—in other words, to homogenization and 'Americanization.' The family preserved separatist religious traditions, alien languages and dialects, local lore, and other traditions that retarded the growth of the political community and the national state. Accordingly, reformers sought to remove children from the influence of their families, which they also blamed for exploiting child labor, and to place the young under the benign influence of state and school."[20] Indeed, as Lasch's book goes on to document, a whole scientific tradition in sociology was generated to support this strategy. The family, in this view, continues to be thought of as indispensable for emotional needs, but requires continued help from experts if it is to be healthy.

In substantiation of Lasch's argument, let me call your attention to the recent report by the Carnegie Council on the family, *All Our Children,* authored by Kenneth Keniston.[21] This study represents thousands of man-hours of research, to say nothing of dollars. Moreover, it is bound to exercise a powerful influence on our policy makers as they attempt to respond to the concern that our nation develop a "family policy."

The report begins by pointing out that the family has suffered in America because of the myth of the self-sufficient family. In the nineteenth century, Keniston argues, the idea of self-sufficiency came to apply to families as well as individuals. Americans came to think of the ideal family as one which was "not only independent and self-sustaining but almost barricaded, as if the only way to guard against incursions from the outside was to reduce all contact with the rest of the world to a minimum."[22] The problem is that this ideal became a prevailing myth, and even those who could not make it real in their lives subscribed to it and felt guilty if they failed to meet its standards.

Even more disturbing are the changes that have occurred in the family that make the myth almost impossible to sustain. Three centuries ago, when the family was largely a self-sufficient agricultural unit, the myth was almost a reality. But with the change in economies, work and family became separated. Now the only economic function left to the family is that of consumption, not production. Consequently, the value placed on children has changed entirely, for now children are an economic liability rather than a boon. The report informs us, for example, that having a child and educating him/her through high school at even the most modest levels involves a cost of at least $35,000.

The second major change in the family that has made the self-sufficient myth impossible is the removal of education from the family. The average American child now spends most of the time, not in the presence of his or her family, but in the presence of day-care workers, teachers, and other children. In addition other important family functions, such as the care of the sick and responsibility for health care, have been taken over by others. In summary, the report suggests "at the same time that families have been shorn of many traditional roles with children, new expectations about children's needs have arisen and, along with them, new specialists and institutions to meet the expectations. Part of the change of family functions, which carries with it a new dependence on people and institutions outside the family, rests on the family's needs for forms of help and expert assistance that are creations of the last century."[23]

The only solution is that we recognize that "family self-sufficiency is a false myth, [and] acknowledge that all today's families need help in raising children."[24] We must recognize this not because parents have become selfish, ignorant, or weak, but because they have been dethroned by forces they cannot influence. Keniston sees no possibility or desirability of reversing this trend, for to do so would also involve a turning back to poverty and drudgery, inferior education, and more community interference in what today we consider private.[25] We should rather accept that what it means to be a parent today has changed, since parents no longer have a direct function in regard to their children. Indeed, we should see that the lives parents are leading, and the lives they are preparing their children to live, are so demanding and complex that parents cannot, and should not, have the traditional kind of direct supervision of their children.[26]

The report concludes that the primary function of the family is fulfilling the emotional needs of parents and children. "With work life highly impersonal, ties with neighbors tenuous, and truly intimate out-of-family friendships rare, husbands and wives tend to put all their emotional hopes for fulfillment into their family life. Expectations of sharing, sexual compatibility, and temperamental harmony in marriage have risen as other family functions have diminished."[27] Indeed, the reason divorce is more prevalent today is the greater emphasis placed on emotional satisfaction to be gained from marriage. And when love wanes, what with the presence of schools, doctors, counselors, and social workers to provide support whether the family is intact or not, one loses less by divorce than in earlier times.

Even more important, however, is that parents have a demanding new role: theirs is now the task of choosing, meeting, talking with, and coordinating the experts, the technology, and the institutions that help bring up their children. The specific work involved is familiar to any parent: consultations with teachers, finding good health care, trying to monitor television watching, and so on. "No longer able to do it all themselves, parents today are in some ways like the executives in a large firm—responsible for the smooth coordination of the many people and processes that must work together to produce the final product."[28]

I have no reason to deny the descriptive power of this account of the modern family. Nor do I disagree with some of the policies suggested by the report to upgrade the economic and social well-being of our society. What is significant, however, is that nearly all the proposals suggested are already supported by "liberals" in our society and thought justified with no reference to the family at all. I suspect this is but an indication that our society cannot have a "family policy," as any policy would have to involve some normative understanding of the family, which is impossible in a morally pluralistic society. The best we can do is the Census Bureau definition of the family as "a group of two or more persons related by blood, marriage or adoption and residing together."

Just as Lasch suggested, the Carnegie Report accepts a view of the family that in effect renders parents incompetent to deal with their own children. Moreover it assumes the family is possible only if economic and social conditions are sufficient to prevent hardship. It thus disparages the moral heroism of those who have and care for children under less than fortunate conditions. And finally, it is a sad state indeed when parents are encouraged to think of themselves as managers charged with turning out a "product." I find it unimaginable that anyone could conceive of bearing and raising a child on these terms.

Put more strongly, I find the Carnegie Report to be the closest analogy we have for Augustus in our society. Rather than being a report to save the family, it is in effect a report which, if followed, can only undermine further the moral status of the family. For it reflects a profound fear and distrust of ourselves and our ability to have and raise children. The family defended in the report is the instant family, the family with no past or future, and thus with no moral stake in preserving our past or seeking a better future.

4.   The Family as History and Hope

If my analysis of the moral crisis of the family is even close to being correct, then what we require is a language to help us articulate the experience of the family and the loyalties it represents. Such a language will determine how we understand ourselves and our society, because the family is integral to the entire culture. Such a language must clearly reflect our character as historical beings and denote how our moral lives are based in particular loyalties and relations. If we are to learn to care for others, we must first learn to care for those we find ourselves joined to by accident of birth. Only then will love be understood not simply as attraction for those who are like us, but also as regard and respect for those whom we have not have chosen but to whom we find ourselves tied.

For the most inescapable fact about families, regardless of their different forms and customs, is that we do not choose to be part of them. We do not choose our relatives; they are simply given. Of course we can like some better than others, but even those we do not like are inextricably ours. To be part of a family is to understand what it means to be "stuck with" a history and a people.[29] Thus we even enjoy telling stories about our often less than admirable kin, because such stories help us know what being "stuck with" such a history entails. Unfortunately, we have tended today to understand such storytelling primarily as entertainment (which it surely is), rather than seeing it as a moral affirmation of what it means to be part of a family.

In other words, the family is morally crucial for our existence as the only means we have to bind time. Without the family, and the intergenerational ties involved, we have no way to know what it means to be historic beings. As a result we become determined by, rather than determining, our histories. Set out in the world with no family, without story of and for the self, we will simply be captured by the reigning ideologies of the day.

Put differently, we must recover the moral significance of our willingness to have children.[30] Like it or not, one of the most morally substantive things any of us ever has the opportunity to do is to have children. A child represents our willingness to go on in the face of difficulties, suffering, and the ambiguity of modern life and is thus our claim that we have something worthwhile to pass on. The refusal to have children can be an act of ultimate despair that masks the deepest kind of self-hate and disgust. Fear and rejection of parenthood, the tendency to view the family as nothing more than companionable marriage, and the understanding of marriage as one of a series of nonbinding commitments, are but indications that our society has a growing distrust of our ability to deal with the future.[31]

In this respect, the most telling devaluation of the family in the Carnegie Report is the absence of any indication that the family involves more than those ties necessary to raise children. The complex ties of adult children to adult parents simply do not exist from the perspective of the report. It is as though Social Security has removed all responsibility adult children have for parents and adult parents can now retire to sunny lands, their responsibilities over when their children are "making it on their own." Any sense that the elderly have a responsibility to share their wisdom with their children or that they have a responsibility to lead decent lives in support of their children has been eradicated by convincing the aged that the one benefit of growing old in a society that has no place for them is freedom from all responsibilities.

Ironically, the loss of any moral role for such older parents is a correlative of the loss of any moral task for younger parents. It is not sufficient to welcome children, for we must also be willing to initiate them into what we think is true and good about human existence. For example, I think we should not admire religious or non-religious parents who are afraid to share their values and convictions with their children. It is a false and bad-faith position to think that if we do not teach them values our children will be free to "make up their own minds." What must be said, and said clearly, is that the refusal to ask our children to believe as we believe, to live as we live, to act as we act is a betrayal that derives from moral cowardice. For to ask this of our children requires that we have the courage to ask ourselves to live truthfully.

Only by recovering this kind of moral confidence will parents deserve to reclaim their children from the "experts." In matters moral there are no "experts"; and therefore all parents are charged with forming their children's lives according to what they know best. Rather than "experts," there are moral paradigms, guides for us. The task for parents is to direct their children's attention to those paradigms which provide the most compelling sense of what we can and should be.

In closing, a brief mention of what I think religious faith has to do with marriage and the family. It is not merely that the Judeo-Christian tradition keeps people on the straight and narrow sexual path necessary to sustain marriage. On the contrary, I begin my classes on marriage with the observation that both Christianity and marriage teach us that life is not chiefly about "happiness." Rather, the Hebrew-Christian tradition helps sustain the virtue of hope in a world which rarely provides evidence that such hope is justified. There may be a secular analogue to such hope, but for those of us who identify with Judaism or Christianity, our continuing formation of families witnesses to our belief that the falseness of this world is finally bounded by a more profound truth.

9. The Family: Theological and Ethical Reflections

1. The Social Significance of the Family in Recent History

I think the family, both as we know and experience it and as many want it to be, is in jeopardy. But I think that it is in jeopardy not because the family has lost its significance, but because other institutions have lost their value in our society. Our society has left the individual alone to confront large bureaucracies that have immense power. The family has become for many the last refuge to find personal and social significance in the face of these impersonal institutions.

As Dr. Brigitte Berger suggests in *The Homeless Mind*,[1] the family has become the protective enclave from the harsh reality of economic life. Also with the development of the bourgeois personalistic family, the social institution of childhood has been invested and enshrined as essential to the family. Children become the main rationale for such families; that is, they are seen as ends in themselves, because they reinforce the assumption that the family is a primary institution for sentiment and tenderness in our society.

Please note I am not suggesting, as is so often argued, that the family is in trouble because institutions that once helped keep the family together—i.e., communities and churches—are no longer operating to do this. Rather my point is that with the diminishment of other institutions that claim and carry symbols and practices of personal significance, the family has been broken because it has to carry too great a moral load.

The family as the last haven of trust separating and protecting us from our society is the primary locus for many to find their identity. For our identity is bound up with being able to assume a heroic role—e.g., something as simple as understanding my work as a means of support for my family. Our participation in our families takes on overriding significance because the family is not shaded into other modes of our community life. The family appears as the only remaining "natural" institution capable of commanding complete loyalty, as all other institutions appear as creatures of human will and therefore arbitrary and capricious. As a result our identification with our family stands as much chance of destroying us as sustaining our lives.

When the family is all you have left, then it begins to take on the characteristics of a church. No one has depicted this better than John Updike in his novel *Couples*.[2] For the new "church" is made up of couples that form around artificially created "interests" such as sports, games, parties, or sex—or as Updike suggests, a mixture of all these. We should be careful of criticizing this "church" too quickly, for it does provide a ministry, a way, as one of Updike's characters puts it, "to protect each other from death." However, at the same time such a "church" too easily becomes demonic. For these couples, who must exist without rituals of life and death, the world cannot help but appear uninteresting and boring. All that remains to interest these "enlightened" men and women, who are trying to "break back into paganism," is to eat one another alive. Unfaithfulness becomes the new heroic ethic, since without it they would be left with nothing to do.

Ironically, therefore, the family is threatened today partly because it has no institutions that have the moral status to stand over against it to call into question its demonic tendencies. The first function of the church in relation to the family must, therefore, be to stand as an institution that claims loyalty and significance beyond that of the family. Only when such an institution exists can we have the freedom to take the risk to form and live in families.

2.   The Social Insignificance of the Family in Recent History

What I have to say next may appear to contradict my first point. For now I must say that in spite of the central significance that the family plays for us as a locus for primary relationships, it has also lost most of its actual social significance. Indeed it is my suspicion that exactly part of the reason that we so desperately cling to the family ideologically is that we sense that the family is in deep trouble socially.

As Robert Nisbet pointed out in *Community and Power,* the interpersonal and psychological aspects of familial kinship ties can never rest on personal romance or individual rectitude.[3] The strength of the family traditionally has been its significance as an indispensable social institution rather than a form of interpersonal relationships based on affection and moral probity. Our modern romantic assumption that love is the necessary condition for marriage and the family is profoundly mistaken. Rather, marriage and the family are the necessary conditions for even understanding what love means. Marriage is not sustained by being a fulfilling experience for all involved, but by embodying moral and social purposes that give it a basis in the wider community.

But as Nisbet observes:

In ever enlarging areas of population in modern times, the economic, legal, educational, religious, and recreational functions of the family have declined or diminished. Politically, membership in the family is superfluous; economically, it is regarded by many as an outright hindrance to success. The family, as someone has put it, is now the accident of the worker rather than his essence. His competitive position may be more favorable without it. Our systems of law and education and all the manifold recreational activities of individuals engaged in their pursuit of happiness have come to rest upon, and to be directed to, the individual, not the family. On all sides we continue to celebrate from pulpit and rostrum the indispensability of the family to economy and the state. But, in plain fact, the family is indispensable to neither of these at the present time. The major processes of economy and political administration have become increasingly independent of the symbolism and integrative activities of kinship.[4]

Moreover, the family today is not even seen as the bearer of tradition—whether it be the tradition of a nation, religion, or the family itself. As a result children are not raised or initiated by the family to be worthy of carrying forward the work of their ancestors, but rather they are raised to be able to make "intelligent choices" when they are adults. Perhaps the crassest form of this attitude is exemplified by those parents who raise their children to be able to choose to be "religious or not" when they grow up. To do otherwise is to "impose one's own views" on children, which would be, it is suggested, a violation of their autonomy.

There is, of course, a positive way of understanding the loss of the family's social utility. We are told by some that the loss of the family's legal and economic function has freed the family to flourish as an event of affection and love. The family has progressed from institution to companionship. But as Ortega y Gasset has written, "people do not live together merely to be together. They live together to do something together."[5]

Or again as Nisbet suggests:

To suppose that the present family, or any other group, can perpetually vitalize itself through some indwelling affectional tie, in the absence of concrete, perceived functions, is like supposing that the comradely ties of mutual aid which grow up incidentally in a military unit will long outlast a condition in which war is plainly and irrevocably banished. Applied to the family, the argument suggests that affection and personality cultivation can somehow exist in a social vacuum, unsupported by the determining goals and ideals of economic and political society. But

in hard fact no social group will long survive the disappearance of its
chief reasons for being, and these reasons are not, primarily, biological
but institutional.[6]

While I would not like to make too much of it, I think that this analysis
at least helps partially to explain the plight of women in our society. The basis
of women's liberation is not the oppressive nature of the family, but rather
with the loss of significance of the family the moral status of women is
problematic. The worship of the female as mother in our society is but an
overcompensation for the historical fact that the female has been released
from any clear and indispensable social role within the family. This is in
contrast to the past, for as George Gilder has suggested, the traditional forms
of male dominance were based on men's correct perception of their weakness
in the face of women. Until recently only women have had an indispensable
role in society, whereas everything men can do is clearly secondary.[7] With the
loss of the family the indispensability of women is lost. Women's liberation is
not trying to flee the family, but find a place for women to regain status in the
face of the loss of the family as an indispensable institution of society.

One temptation which this analysis invites is to think we must, if we
want to continue the family, reconstitute the traditional roles of the family or
find new roles for it. Thus some suggest that the family is indispensable for
free democratic societies. And it is certainly true that the character of
societies depends to a large degree on the kind of families they foster. However, I suspect that the relationship between the family and democratic
societies is more ambiguous than many suggest.

In our society the family has been rendered problematic by the attempt to
create the limited state in the name of the freedom of the individual. The
social roles of the family have been sacrificed in the interest of creating an
individualistic economic and political order. This kind of society did not seem
directly inimical to the interest of the family, since the individual could decide
to start a family if he or she so desired. The crucial point, however, is that the
political units were assumed to be, not the state and family, but the state and
the individual.

Ironically it is just such a society that requires the growth of bureaucracy. For when there are no intermediary social units to meet the needs of
society, then you must create administrative units. Moreover, a society of
individuals, in the absence of informal procedures, develops more needs
which require more bureaucracy. It is hard to know what to do once this has
happened for it appears that the only alternative is to call on the bureaucracy to
find ways to enhance the re-emergence of the family. That is somewhat like
asking Ian Smith to solve the problem of race in Southern Africa. In short, I
am suggesting that the rebirth of the family requires more substantive changes
in our society than we currently envision.

In this respect I think we need to state the relation of the family to democratic social orders in a more critical fashion. For it is not clear to me that the function of the family is to produce an individual, that is, a person with an appropriate democratic personality. Indeed it seems to me that it is exactly the individualistic ethos of democracy that has created much of the problem for the family. For the family in such a social order cannot help but appear anomalous. Perhaps I can make this claim clear by considering the moral presuppositions of family.

3. The Moral Presuppositions of Family

The family requires certain kinds of moral presuppositions in order to exist that seem lacking in our society. In particular it often seems that policy makers assume that the sooner wives can be freed from husbands, children from mothers, children from each other, the better off everyone will be. I am unsure what policy makers want, but if this is what they want, I suspect they are but manifesting a deeper problem of our society.

For the moral ideal of our society has been the autonomous, self-sufficient, free person. Autonomy has been taken to mean that we are not and should not be dependent on the past or upon others. To be free means to have no ties. Economically this has been reinforced by a capitalist economy that needs workers who are readily mobile. Politically the development of the autonomous person seemed necessary for democracy, since it is precisely the man without convictions that frees politics from ideological perversions. Democracy is the social order designed to eradicate the true believer in order to create the pragmatic man of compromise.[8]

Contemporary ethical theory with its concentration on the language of rights has embodied this ethic. The important ethical questions are taken to be what we owe one another as strangers rather than friends or kin. Indeed all so-called "special-relations" such as husband-wife, father-daughter, brother-sister are seen as ethically anomalous. For how can you have an obligation to another that was not originally based on a free and informed contractual agreement? And the family, in spite of all the attempts to make it one, is not a contractual social unit.

The family in our society thus appears morally irrational. It is simply part of the necessities of our life that the free person should learn to outgrow. For to be part of a family is to accept a limit that I have not chosen. Of course I can try to explain my commitment to the family, my obligations to parents, brothers and sisters, on grounds that even if I did not choose them I have benefited from them. Therefore, it is not irrational to think that I may owe them something.

However, this kind of argument cannot explain the assumption that there may be obligations to parents even if they are not the best of parents, or that we should continue to care and be concerned about relatives even when they are not our friends. Moreover, it fails to explain why I would for any reason decide to become a parent myself. Any reason I might give for having a child, in the terms of an ethic of autonomy, would appear immoral, on grounds of the use of another as a means for my own satisfaction, or irrational, since a child would only enter the world as a threat to my autonomy.[9]

Equally destructive is the self-fulfillment ethic that often goes hand in hand with the autonomous ideal. We are encouraged to assume that marriage and the family are primarily institutions of personal fulfillment that are necessary for us to be "whole" people. The assumption is that there is someone right for us to marry and that if we look closely enough we will find the right person.

This moral assumption overlooks two crucial aspects to marriage. First, it fails to appreciate the fact that we always marry the wrong person. We never know whom we marry; we just think we do. Or even if we first marry the right person, just give it a while and he or she will change. For marriage, being what it is, means we are not the same person after we have entered it. The primary problem morally is learning how to love and care for this stranger to whom you find yourself married.

Secondly, the self-fulfillment ethic overlooks the power struggle that is part of every relationship. Marriage, even the most intense and loving, does not eradicate this aspect of our lives. Please note I am not suggesting that power is a bad thing which should be eradicated from interpersonal relations such as the family; rather, we need an ethic that trains us to know what kind of relationship we are in. In this respect the ethic of self-fulfillment is a formula for self-deception, since no one rules more tyrannously than those who claim not to rule at all because they only want to love us.[10]

For marriage to be sustained today we need a sense of contributing to a people through having children. Unless marriage has a purpose beyond being together it will certainly be a hell. For it to be saved from being a hell we must have the conviction that the family represents a vocation necessary for a people who have a mission and yet have learned to be patient. Marriage and family require time and energy that could be used to make the world better. To take the time to love one person rather than many, to have these children rather than helping the many in need, requires patience and a sense of the tragic. Indeed such activities remind us of how limited we are, but at least we in the Christian tradition claim that it is only through such limits that we learn what it means to be free.

This does not mean that any one kind of family can be shown to be morally ideal. Every kind of family is capable of producing selfish as well as unselfish people. I remain suspicious about how informative such terms as extended, nuclear, or other such labels are for describing the reality of family life.[11] Rather, all I am trying to suggest is that good communities require the development of an ethos that encourages people to continue to be open to children and to institutions necessary to support and raise them.

4. Morality and the Shape of the Family

In this respect I am less concerned with the question of the shape of the family—whether it is communal, extended, or nuclear—or whether children are or are not in day care. I assume that families find ways to exist, and I am not sure whether one way is right or wrong. Personally I am attracted to more traditional forms of extended families, but I do not assume that there is any great moral issue involved in that preference.

More important to my mind is why we have children at all and how we choose to raise them. I suspect that we have lost any meaningful reason for why we should have children today—that is, any reason that gives us the skill to know how to raise children once we have had them. As a result our children are anomic, not in the sense that they are raised with no rules, but in that they are raised with no moral role that gives them a status in the community.

In a parallel manner the problem of parents is that they represent no role for the community. Children need permanent interaction with someone who cares for them, but equally important is what is expected of the child as a result of such interaction. Too often today the relation between parent and child appears to be a power struggle of contrary wills. The parent's only status against the child is to claim that their views should prevail because they have more experience, knowledge, or responsibility.

Parents are thus left bereft of community roles that make clear that being a parent is not a willful act, but rather an office of a community for the well-being of children. Intimacy and care are indeed important, but equally important is the initiation of children into moral beliefs and institutions which we value. When such beliefs are absent the rightful authority of parents is correctly perceived as a masked authoritarianism.

Morally our children are suffering because we do not have the courage of our convictions. For example: morally I am convinced that Christians are necessarily committed to the ethic of non-resistance. Yet the temptation is for me to teach my son that such an ethic is but one option among others. The reason for my reticence is that such an ethic, in spite of the study and training it represents for me, is simply my opinion. But surely it is a mistake to assume such matters are only opinion. What is missing is the necessary community support that makes it clear to me that not to initiate my son into such an ethic is an act of cowardice. Of course how he is initiated makes all the difference, inasmuch as such an ethic would be betrayed if it were coercively taught. But note that the style of the teaching is not a correlative of a lazy, indifferent ethic of tolerance, but rather of an ethic that assumes that truth needs no power beyond itself.

5.   Christianity and the Family

I want to end by suggesting that one last threat to the family is Christianity itself. I think that we cannot overlook the fact that one of the few clear differences between Christianity and Judaism is the former's entertainment of the idea of singleness as the paradigm way of life for its followers. I cannot take the time to try to defend this exegetically and historically; however, I think it cannot be disputed that Paul and Jesus both tend to say that some people will choose not to get married because of a specific religious mission. Moreover, they seem to imply that this is a good thing.

I think the implications of this have seldom been appreciated. For in a certain sense it breaks the natural necessity of the family. The family is not just something we do because we are in the habit, nor is it something we must do to fulfill a moral purpose. Rather marriage and the family, like the life of singleness, becomes a vocation for the upbuilding of a particular kind of community. Christianity, in a certain sense, thus prepared the way for the romantic view of marriage and the family by setting the institutional form necessary to make marriage voluntary.

The romantic perversion should therefore remind us that if we are to sustain marriage as a Christian institution we will not do it by concentrating on marriage itself. Rather, it will require a community that has a clear sense of itself and its mission and the place of the family within that mission. It may be, however, that for the rethinking of that kind of community we can do no better than consider marriage as our necessary starting point.

Therefore I am ending where I began since again it is clear that the family, in order to be a viable moral enterprise, requires community beyond itself.[12] We see, however, that the special commitments of Christians concerning marriage require an even more substantive community. Yet it is our conviction that the church is formed by a story that gives it the convictions necessary to sustain those called to marry and have children in a world that has been bent by sin and evil. We have the courage to call children into such a world because our hope is not in this world but in a God who has called us to his Kingdom through the work of Christ.

10. Sex in Public: Toward a Christian Ethic of Sex

1. On Speaking Candidly and as a Christian about Sex

Candor is always to be striven for, but it is especially important for any discussion about sex; in particular, the morality of sex. And candor compels me to say that I cannot provide anything like an adequate ethic to deal with sex. This is, no doubt, partly because of my own moral and intellectual limitations. But it also reflects that generally Christians, and in particular Christian ethicists, are unsure what to say or how to respond to our culture's changing sexual mores (if in fact they are changing).[1]

Current reflection about sexual ethics by Christian ethicists is a mess. That may seem an odd state of affairs, for it is generally thought that while the church may often be confused about issues of war or politics, we can surely count on Christians to have a clear view about sex. It has been assumed that the church and her theologians have seldom spoken ambiguously about sex and most of what they have had to say took the form of a negative.[2] "No," you should not have sexual intercourse before marriage. "No," you should not commit adultery. "No," you should not practice contraception. And so on.

Indeed, the proscriptive nature of much of the church's teaching about sex (together with the assumption often associated with such strictures that there is something wrong with sex), seems to me the source of some of the confusion concerning current sexual ethics. By rights, theologians and ethicists should not be able to say enough good about sex. Broad anthropological analysis has shown us that we are fundamentally sexual beings, and that is indeed a good thing. God has created us to be sexual beings and it seems nothing short of Manichaeanism for us to deny that aspect of our lives. But in our rush to show that Christians know that sex can be beautiful, Christian ethicists have often failed to talk candidly about sex. One suspects that if sex can be beautiful, it is as often likely to be messy and/or boring.

Many people are particularly disturbed when they are told that contemporary Christian ethics has little coherent to say about sexual ethics. We live in a cultural situation that is extremely confusing in regard to sex and we rightly feel we need some guidance from somewhere. Whether we are sexually faithful in our marriages or not, we feel at a loss to explain why we live that way rather than another. Thus, some stay faithful because they are fearful of women or men, or lazy, or fear the consequences if found out. If or how sexual fidelity is anchored in our fundamental Christian convictions remains unclear.

Even more disturbing is what appears to be the sheer sexual anarchy characteristic of much of our culture. For example, Paul Ramsey in a recent article cites Dr. Robert Johnson, director of adolescent medicine at the New Jersey College of Medicine, that two of every ten girls in junior and senior high school in New Jersey will get pregnant this year.[3] No matter what one thinks about premarital sexuality, that is a shocking statistic, and we feel we need some ethical guidance on how to deal with such problems.

This is an area that the church and Christian ethicists surely ought to have something to say about, but I think what we should have to say will demand a more thorough rethinking of the nature of Christian life than most who call for a new "sex ethic" anticipate. For it is my thesis that the development of a sexual ethic and practice appropriate to basic Christian convictions must be part of a broader political understanding of the church. Put bluntly, there is no way that the traditional Christian insistence that marriage must be characterized by unitive and procreative ends can be made intelligible unless the political function of marriage in the Christian community is understood. Sexual ethics cannot be separated from political ethics if we are to understand why Christians believe that sexual practices should be determined by how they contribute to the good end of the Christian community.

Methodologically, this means that attempts to base a Christian ethics of sex on natural law—whether natural law be understood as unexceptionable norms or broadly construed anthropological characterizations of human sexuality—must be abandoned. Ironically, the attempt to develop a sexual ethic based on natural law—i.e., the idea that the legitimacy of contraception can be determined by the nature of the act of sex considered in itself—has much in common with the current effort to liberalize sexual ethics through suggestions about what is necessary for the flourishing of human sexuality. The attempt to base an ethic of sex on "nature" results in abstracting sex from those institutions that are necessary to make any ethic of sex intelligible. In contrast, I will try to show that the claim that a sexual ethic derives its form from marriage is a political claim, as it makes sense only in terms of the church's understanding of its mission. Therefore a Christian ethic of sex cannot be an ethic for all people, but only for those who share the purposes of the community gathered by God and the subsequent understanding of marriage.

The thesis that the ethics of sex is a public and political issue seems to be odd or even absurd in our cultural context. We have been taught to understand that sex is private and is determined by two or more people with free consent. It is often assumed that you can do pretty much what you want as long as you do not hurt one another. What we have failed to note is that the claim that sex is a matter of private morality is a political claim dependent upon a liberal political ethos. Any attempt to reclaim an authentic Christian ethic of sex must begin by challenging the assumption that sex is a ''private'' matter.

Because by and large Christians have not lived or understood the political nature of their convictions about marriage and sex, our current sexual ethics is largely made up of inconsistent borrowings from the various options provided by our culture. This is not surprising, as Christians have often had this happen. Indeed, one of our difficulties in articulating what kind of sexual ethic should be characteristic of Christians is our knowledge that too often what has flown the flag of Christian sexual ethics has been a secular ethic baptized by the Christian church in the name of natural law.

Currently there seem to be two main cultural alternatives—realism and romanticism—for us to choose between. These options appear to be fundamentally opposed, but I think on analysis they share some strikingly similar presuppositions. For realism is but chastened romanticism that seeks to ''talk sense'' about sex in order to prevent some of the worst excesses of romanticism. Yet like romanticism, realism continues to underwrite the assumption that sex is a private matter and is subject to public interest only when it has consequences—i.e., teenage pregnancy—that effect the public pocketbook. A brief analysis of realism and romanticism will make evident that they have set the agenda for the current discussion of sexual ethics among Christians.

1.1   Realism

As the term suggests, realism has the virtue of dealing with sex without illusion or cant. Realists often claim to be amoral, but that does not mean the realist vision lacks depth. For the realist simply assumes that it is too late to raise ''moral issues'' about sex, one way or the other. We live in a situation where two out of ten young girls in New Jersey are going to get pregnant this year. The realist may deplore the implications but assumes the situation as a fact and concentrates on the task of information: how to get knowledge and techniques to young people who have become ''sexually active''[4] so some of the consequences of their behavior can be checked.

The realist position is also often coupled with an attempt to help people have a more healthy attitude toward sex. In particular, the realists stress that sex is simply one human activity among others—it can be a profound human expression or it can just be fun—but what is important, no matter how sex be understood, is that it be demystified. The realist thus suggests to young people that they may not be as ready for sex as they think they are, for as the sexually experienced often discover, sex is not easy to keep just fun.

Realism is a position I often find myself tempted to assume. I still remember vividly in my first year of teaching I was asked by a delegation of students from the college's student senate what the "Christian ethical position" should be concerning whether doors could be shut during parietal visitations. Completely taken aback by what seemed to be the triviality of the issue, all I could think to say was I supposed closing the door was better than getting grass stains. My response was meant to be realistic. I assumed that those students who were going to have sex were going to do so whatever rules one thought up about parietals. And like most realists, I thought that the most important thing anyone could do when confronted by such an issue was to speak candidly.

Yet, in spite of the kind of "worldly wisdom" that makes the realist position attractive, it is doomed to failure. What realists fail to recognize is that, in spite of claims to being amoral or at least nonmoralistic, their position in fact presupposes an ethical recommendation. Realists cannot help but assume that the way things are is the ways things ought to be. Therefore, they accept as morally normative the liberal assumption that sexual activity should be determined by what each individual feels is good for him or her.

By accepting such an assumption, moreover, realism fails to provide an adequate response to our other primary cultural alternative, romanticism. For many teenagers get pregnant exactly because of their romantic notion that sex should be a significant gesture denoting the level of commitment between two people. In an ironic way the phenomenon of teenage pregnancy, which no doubt is often the result of ignorance and an absence of proper contraceptive techniques, is the sign of how deeply conservative assumptions about the significance of sex are ingrained in our culture.

1.2   Romanticism

Like realism, "romanticism" is less a coherent position than a general stance about the place of sex and marriage in our lives. The basic assumption of romanticism is that love is the necessary condition for sex and marriage. How love is understood can and often does vary greatly between different versions of romanticism. Yet for all romantics the quality of the interpersonal relation between a couple is the primary issue for considering sexual involvement. Even the arguments which criticize "romanticism" structurally may accept the assumption that the primary issue is the "depth" of commitment between the couple.

Examples of this kind of thinking in our society are almost endless, but by way of illustration let me call your attention to the position of Nena and George O'Neill as developed in their best-selling book, *Open Marriage*.[5] Though I do not think the O'Neills provide a particularly profound version of romanticism, I suspect that they represent broadly shared views and judgments about sex and marriage in our culture.

Theirs is essentially a conservative position, written in the spirit of saving marriage as a worthwhile activity. To save marriage, however, they argue that the meaning of marriage "must be independently forged by a man and a woman who have the freedom to find their own reasons for being, and for being together. Marriage must be based on a new openness—an openness to one's self, an openness to another's self, and openness to the world. Only by writing their own open contract can couples achieve the flexibility they need to grow. Open marriage is expanded monogamy, retaining the fulfilling and rewarding aspects of an intimate in-depth relationship with another, yet eliminating the restrictions we were formerly led to believe were an integral part of monogamy" (41).

Open marriages must necessarily avoid being controlled by presupposed roles denoted by the terms "husband" and "wife." What we do and do not do as husbands and wives should be determined by what we feel as individual human beings, not by some predetermined set of restrictive codes (148). Thus, in an "open marriage, each gives the other the opportunity, the freedom, to pursue those pleasures he or she wishes to, and the time they do spend together is fruitfully and happily spent in catching up on one another's individual activities" (p. 188). Crucial to such a marriage is trust, as only trust provides the possibility for a marriage to be a "dynamic, growing relationship" (224). But it must be an "open trust," in contrast to those forms of trust built on dependability and assured predictability. To have open trust "means believing in your mate's ability and willingness to cherish and respect your honesty and your open communications. Trust is the feeling that no matter what you do or say you are not going to be criticized" (231). "Trust then is freedom, the freedom to assume responsibility for your own self first and then to share that human self in love with your partner in a marriage that places no restrictions upon growth, or limits on fulfillment" (235).

This seems an attractive ideal. After all, who could be against trust? And who would deny the importance of each partner continuing to develop as his or her own person in and outside marriage? For it is surely true that the strength of any marriage is partly judged by the ability of each partner to rejoice in the friendships of the other. Indeed, such friendships can be seen as necessary for the enrichment of any marriage.

Yet, ironically, the O'Neills' account of "open marriage" requires a transformation of the self that makes intimate relationships impossible in or outside of marriage. Many conservative critics of proposals like "open marriage" tend to overlook this element, because all their attention is directed to the sexual implication—namely, that premarital and extramarital sex is not condemned. But that element has long been written into the very structure and nature of romanticism.

What the "conservative" must recognize is that prior to the issue of whether premarital or extramarital sexual intercourse is wrong is the question of character: What kind of people do you want to encourage? Hidden in the question of "What ought we to do?" is always the prior question "What ought we to be?" The most disturbing thing about such proposals as the O'Neills' is the kind of persons they wish us to be. On analysis, the person capable of open marriage turns out to be the self-interested individual presupposed and encouraged by our liberal political structure and our capitalist consumer economy.

Perhaps this is best illustrated by calling attention to the O'Neills' discussion of adultery. Of course, the O'Neills see no reason why adultery should be excluded from open marriage. After all, most people "now recognize sex for what it is: a natural function that should be enjoyed for its own earthy self without hypocrisy" (247). Indeed, extramarital sexual experiences "when they are in the context of a meaningful relationship may be rewarding and beneficial to an open marriage" (254). But the O'Neills do provide a word of caution; they suggest that to have a extramarital affair without first "developing yourself to the point where you are ready, and your mate is ready, for such a step could be detrimental to the possibility of developing a true open marriage" (254).

I have thought a lot about this very interesting suggestion—namely, that we develop ourselves to be ready to engage in an extramarital affair. What could that possibly mean? Would it mean that we each date and then come home and compare notes on our experience to see how it makes the other feel? And what would be the object of such a project? Surely it is nothing less than for us to learn to devalue sexual expression between ourselves in order to justify it with other people.

But even more interesting, such training would also require that we learn to control, if not destroy entirely, that primitive emotion called jealousy. Thus, as I suggested, involved in proposals such as the O'Neills', are extremely profound assumptions about what kind of persons we ought to be. And the O'Neills are quite explicit about this, as they argue that jealousy is but a learned response determined by cultural attitudes dependent on our assumptions about sexually exclusive monogamy. But such possession of another only

> breeds deep-rooted dependencies, infantile and childish emotions, and insecurities. The more insecure you are, the more you will be jealous. Jealousy, says Abraham Maslow, "practically always breeds further rejection and deeper insecurity." And jealousy, like a destructive cancer, breeds more jealousy. It is never, then, a function of love, but of our insecurities and dependencies. It is the fear of a loss of love and it destroys that very love. It is detrimental to and a denial of a loved one's personal identity. Jealousy is a serious impediment, then, to the development of security and identity, and our closed marriage concepts of possession are directly at a fault. (237)

Alas, if only Othello could have had the opportunity to have read *Open Marriage,* the whole messy play could have been avoided.

The irony is that romanticism, which began as an attempt to recapture the power of intimate relation as opposed to the "formal" or institutionalized relationship implied by marriage, now finds itself recommending the development of people who are actually incapable of sustaining intimate relationships. For intimacy depends on the willingness to give of the self, to place oneself in the hands of another, to be vulnerable, even if that means we may be hurt. Contrary to Maslow, jealousy is the emotion required by our willingness to love another at all. Indeed, I suspect that part of the reason the church has always assumed that marriage is a reality that is prior to love is that genuine love is so capable of destruction that we need a structure to sustain us through the pain and the joy of it. At least one reason for sex being limited to marriage, though it is not a reason sufficient to support an intrinsic relation between sex and marriage, is that marriage provides the context for us to have sex, with its often compromising personal conditions, with the confidence that what the other knows about us will not be used to hurt us. For never are we more vulnerable than when we are naked and making the clumsy gestures necessary to "make love."

It is true, of course, that "romanticism" cannot be defeated simply by calling attention to some of the implications inherent in the O'Neills' argument. Indeed, "romanticism" has become far too complex a phenomenon for it to be easily characterized or criticized. I am content at this point simply to suggest that the "romantic" assumption that sexual expression is a "private" matter in fact masks a profound commitment to the understanding of society and self sponsored by political liberalism. Thus, more and more, human relations are understood in contractual terms and the ideal self becomes the person capable of understanding everything and capable of being hurt by nothing.

2.   The Current State of Christian Reflection about Sexual Ethics

I suggested above that current Christian reflection about sexual ethics has been limited to trying to adjudicate between various versions of realism and romanticism in order to establish the "Christian" ethics of sex. What Christian ethicists have been unable to do is provide an account of sexual ethics that is clearly based on an agenda central to the Christian community's own self-understanding. They have been unable to do so because they have failed to see that any discussion of sex must begin with an understanding of how a sexual ethics is rooted in a community's basic political commitments.

As a result sexual ethics, though often very insightful, betrays a fatal abstractness. For example, it is often claimed that it is a mistake to begin reflection about sexual ethics by trying to determine if certain kinds of genital sex are right or wrong. Instead we must begin by recognizing that sexuality is a matter that involves the "whole person," or that "sexuality" so understood must be affirmed as a manifestation of the goodness of God's creation. While all of this is no doubt true, we are not sure how such claims give direction to or help us think better about genital sexual activity. Put bluntly, such analysis does little to help us to answer a teenager who wants to know what is wrong with fooling around before marriage.

The directness of such questions tends to frustrate many ethicists as these questions refer to a specific sort of genital activity. Instead, ethicists prefer to call attention to the importance of the presence of love for wholesome sex. Rather than answering "yes" or "no," we say things like, "the physical expression of one's sexuality with another person ought to be appropriate to the level of loving commitment present in that relationship",[6] or that any one act of "genital sexual expression should be evaluated in regard to motivations, intentions, the nature of the act itself, and the consequences of the act, each of these informed and shaped by love.'"[7] All of which may be true, but is a lot for teenagers in the back seat of a car to remember.

This last comment, while rhetorically clever, is in some ways deeply unfair. For no ethic, not even the most conservative, should be judged by its ability to influence the behavior of teenagers in the back seat of a car. What happens there will often happen irrespective of what "ethic" has been officially taught. Yet I think in a more profound sense people are right to expect ethicists to be concerned about how their "ethic" might be understood or misunderstood for providing guidance about our actual sexual conduct.

"What is wrong with a little fooling around?" is a frustrating and direct question. But such questions are necessary to remind us that often our attempts to provide sophisticated and nuanced accounts of sexuality are misleading and perhaps even corrupting for our children. That is not to say that any ethic of sex should be written from the perspective of only what is good for adolescents or relative to what they are capable of understanding, but I am sure any ethic of sex that does not provide direction for how adolescents should learn to understand and govern their sexual behavior cannot be sufficient.[8] Perhaps one of the crucial tests for any ethics of sex and sexual behavior is that we be able to explain it honestly and straightforwardly to our children.

To provide that kind of account for our children, however, requires that we are able to presuppose a community with the practices and convictions that make such an ethic intelligible. Our children have to see that marriage and having children, and the correlative sexual ethic, are central to the community's political task. For only then can they be offered a vision and an enterprise that might make the disciplining of sex as interesting as its gratification.

2.1   *Recent Roman Catholic Attempts at Sexual Ethics*

Most current attempts at formulating a Christian ethics of sex continue to assume the apolitical nature of sexual practice and ethics. Nowhere is this clearer than in the controversial recent study *Human Sexuality,* commissioned by the Catholic Theological Society of America. The romantic ideal clearly dominates the report, as the authors argue that sexuality must be understood morally as serving

> the development of persons by calling them to constant creativity, that is to full openness to being, to the realization of every potential within the personality, to a continued discovery and expression of authentic self-hood. Procreation is one form of this call to creativity but by no means is it the only reason for sexual expression. Sexuality further serves the development of genuine personhood by calling people to a clearer recognition of their relational nature, of their absolute need to reach out and embrace others to achieve personal fulfillment.[9]

In the light of this "richer" understanding of "sexuality" the authors of the *Report* argue that we should abandon the traditional language of "unitive and procreative" and instead ask whether acts of sexual intercourse are "creative and integrative." "Wholesome human sexuality" is that which should "foster a creative growth toward integration" (86).

The authors of the report find it "woefully inadequate" to evaluate any human sexual behavior "based on an abstract absolute predetermination of any sexual expressions as intrinsically evil and always immoral" (89). The fact that they refuse to find contraception morally unacceptible is not surprising on such grounds, but they also suggest that while it is hard to see how adultery could be good for all involved, the "principle" of "creative growth toward integration" needs also to be applied in these cases (148). Thus, even though some suggest that "co-marital sexual relations"—that is, situations that involve sexual activity with one or more persons beyond the "primary pair bond" with the consent or encouragement of the marriage partner—appear to contradict the "characteristics of wholesome sexual interrelatedness," empirical data "does not as yet warrant any solid conclusions on the effects of such behavior, particularly from the long-range point of view" (149).

On the same grounds the report concludes that no moral theologian has yet succeeded in producing convincing proof why in every case sexual intercourse must be reserved to marriage (158). Yet in no way does this imply an approval of promiscuity, as casual sex "robs human sexuality of its deepest and richest meaning as an expression of intimacy and love" (164). In casual sex the sexual act is separated from the deeper intrapersonal meaning necessary if it is to realize its creative and integrative potential. Yet the report is careful to remind us that on many of these questions we still lack the empirical data to make an informed and objective judgment.

On that criterion one might well argue that it is the moral responsibility of Catholics to experiment with "co-marital sexual relations" in the hopes of generating the appropriate data. Or that some take as their moral mission to find forms of extramarital sexual relations that will help us determine if such relations always rob human sexuality of its "deepest meaning."

In fairness it should be said that the CTSA report is not always so tentative as it states clearly that there is no question that bestiality "renders impossible the realization of the personal meaning of human sexuality" (230). I question, however, if this is consistent with the report's methodology, as such a summary judgment has all the appearance of the biased judgment of city people who have had little experience with country life. At the very least it seems as though the report could have suggested that in these matters, like other forms of sexuality which seem to these writers unusual, we simply need more "data" before we can make a summary judgment.

The difficulty with the *Report*'s recommendations is not just that the criteria "creative and integrative" are so abstract we have no idea what they might exclude, but the *Report* ironically continues to assume, like more conservative sexual ethics of the past, that a sexual ethic can be formulated in abstraction from how it contributes to the upbuilding of the political task of the church. The conservative sexual ethics of the past seemed to be harsher as they not only said "no" more readily, but also seemed to care little for the welfare of persons who were having to live such an ethic. In some ways the conservative was right that a sex ethic was not to be judged by whether it produced integrated persons, but the conservative, as well as the authors of the *Report,* equally fail to understand that the kind of "persons" we should be is a prior question, answered only by the nature of the Christian community.

It is, of course, true that *Human Sexuality* does not represent the general consensus of Catholic attitudes about the morality of sexual conduct. But I suspect what it does accurately represent is the confusion of Catholic thought about sex—not just judgments about particular forms of sexual expression but confusion about where one should even begin thinking about the ethics of sex. For once the connection between sexual intercourse and procreation is broken, and it has been broken in theory and practice for many Catholics, then it is by no means clear what basis you have for maintaining other judgments about the rightness or wrongness of certain forms of sexual expression. No amount of rethinking of natural law will be able to show that every act of sexual intercourse must be procreative; rather, what must be recaptured is that the connection between the unitive and procreative ends of marriage is integral to the Christian understanding of the political significance of marriage.

2.2 *Conservative Accounts of Sexual Ethics*

There are ethicists who continue to argue that sexual expression outside marriage is immoral on grounds of the inseparability of the unitive and procreative ends of marriage. Thus, Paul Ramsey argues that sexual intercourse is an act of love and procreation which is mythically expressed by the necessary creation of Eve to alleviate Adam's aloneness in the garden. "At once Adam's troubled aloneness formed itself into the utterance of his sexuality, and the woman was there not as half of the species with the powers of femaleness in general, but as a unique individual beside whom there were no others. They speak man-woman language. They know even as they are also known; and this was not to wrest some good out of a fallen world, but an improvement that even Paradise needed. . . . The vision inherent in human sexual passion, and in sexual intercourse as an act of love, is the re-creation of Adam and Eve in their marriage."[10] Ramsey argues that this means that both love and conception are the primary ends of the sex act, though this does not mean that every act of sexual intercourse must be open to procreation. But it does mean, "To put radically asunder what God joined together in making love procreative, to procreate without love or to attempt to establish a relation of sexual love beyond the sphere of marriage, means a refusal of the image of God's creation in our time."[11]

Or as William May has recently argued

The marital act is the act of marital coition. This act exhibits or symbolizes the exclusive character of conjugal love both as a communion in being (conjugal love as unitive) and as a life-giving and life-sharing reality (conjugal love as procreative). This is the meaning rooted in the marital act and intelligibly discoverable in it; it is not a meaning arbitrarily imposed upon or given to the act. . . .

The exclusive character of conjugal love as exhibited in the marital act provides the reasons why sexual coition that is non-marital is inherently wicked. Non-marital sexual coition desecrates the meaning that human sexual coition has; that is, it violates its unitive (communion-in-being) and procreative (life-giving) dynamism. Although there may be some tenderness and affection between non-married persons who choose this act, there can be no authentic love in it precisely because it is both an offensive personal touch, even if it is not subjectively experienced as such, and threatens the good of any human person who may come into being as a result of this act.[12]

For those who have desired a nice clear "yes" or "no" answer for the question of whether a little fooling around is wrong, you have it here. Indeed, you not only have a "no," but the description that it is "inherently wicked," though I would suggest you refrain from using the latter description, since it makes such activity far too attractive.

Even though Ramsey's and May's "no" is clear, it is not equally clear that it is convincing. This is not necessarily because there is a stubbornness or immorality in their hearers, but may also be because their hearers simply do not share their presuppositions. As a result their "no" appears arbitrary and authoritarian; it seems to lack any basis in our common experience. For example, many would ask why they assume that sexual intercourse is to be limited only to marriage, especially since both Ramsey and May emphasize the importance of "love" as crucial for morally healthy sex. Yet we know that sex in marriage can often be more "unloving" than sex outside marriage. What is required for such an argument to be intelligible is an account why marriage should be understood as exclusive.[13] It is my contention that such an account requires a recovery of the political function of marriage in the Christian community.

3.   The Public Character of Sex: Marriage as a Heroic Institution

The recovery of a political vision of marriage and appreciation for the public character of sexuality are conceptually and institutionally interdependent. By calling attention to the public context for sexual behavior and ethics I am not simply reasserting the traditional concern that sex should only take place in a publicly recognizable institution, though I certainly think that is important, but I am making the stronger claim that any sex ethic is a political ethic.[14] This is particularly true of Christian marriage. The vision of marriage for Christians requires and calls forth an extraordinary polity for the very reason that Christian marriage is such an extraordinary thing.

William Everett has recently argued that, in spite of what appear to be immense differences between "biologists" and "personalists" concerning sexual ethics, they share more in common than is usually noticed. For both theories are individualistic, since they focus primarily on how persons should deal with their bodies and private actions and thus fail to give adequate attention to the institutional context of sex. In contrast, Everett argues that we must see that sexuality is shaped by humanly created institutions and that this formation works for good as well as for evil. But the question is not whether "the social formation of our sexuality is good or bad, but whether the institutions in which we live are rightly ordered. An ethics of sex must, therefore, be coordinated with an ethic governing the relations among institutions—familial, economic, ecclesial and political."[15]

To illustrate his claim, Everett notes that the development of Christian sexual ethics was not merely a part of the quest for a general social order.

> While Augustine was laying the theological basis for a familist social order, counter-currents were also developing to avoid submerging the Church in that order. As the Church was increasingly drawn into the orbits of the princes, a sexual ethic had to be evolved to separate it from the family-based power of the princes. In the wake of Hildebrand (Gregory VII), celibacy finally became mandatory for clergy in order to separate the Church from the hereditary powers of the princes. Celibacy was as important to the Church's integrity in a familistic social order as constitutional separation of Church and state has become under nationalism. The Augustinian accommodation required a Hildebrandine distance. Celibacy was and is an institutional policy evolved for the sake of the institution. Moreover, this policy had a legitimate purpose—to enable the Church to carry out its mission as a critical and prophetic agent in human affairs. (79)

The church's restraints on various forms of sexual activity were intelligible only to the extent that the church could be a "counter-family" to the princes. But as Everett points out, in our time when family order is no longer the model of societal order or authority, "it becomes very difficult to transfer this self-restraint in order to conform to the demands of other institutions" (79). Indeed, the church's shift to "personalist" accounts of marriage and sexual conduct is an attempt to baptize the transformation of the family occasioned by a capital-intensive economy that needs fewer but better trained workers. The family, having lost its political, social, and economic functions, apart from being a unit of consumption, is only intelligible as the context that provides for "creative integration" through intimate relationship. Thus increasingly the family becomes understood as a voluntary society justified by its ability to contribute to the personal enhancement of each of its members.[16]

Everett is not surprised that such an accommodation has occurred, but he wonders if the correlative understanding of sexuality, as that which functions primarily within the private sphere of emotional and ego-related needs, is sufficient to provide a prophetic perspective on our society. For he claims,

> It is not enough to see the pressures of advertising and bureaucratic life as a natural given, for behind these immediate forces lie the needs of a capital-intensive economy seeking to maintain a high level of consumption for essentially useless products. Our sexual life is shaped by the fundamental workings of this kind of economy. It is not enough, therefore, to invoke [as *Human Sexuality* does] "social responsibility" or "the common good" as a consideration in sexual decisions, without a more critical analysis of the nature of that society and its conception of the good. We need to be able to see how the pursuit of "creative integration" in our bedrooms might depend on the sacrifices of primary-producing nations to the south of us who keep our economy fueled with metals and oil. We need to see how the pleasures and disciplines of mobile individuality are tied to the expressways and housing developments devouring our agricultural land.
>
> The capacity to see those connections is essential to any kind of prophetic or biblical ethic of sex. Not to see the whole is to be victimized by the parts. The CTSA study has comforted those who have adapted to the dominant North American patterns, but it does little to challenge that society or to support those left on the margins. It has met the demands of realistic accommodations but has not gone far enough to provide Christian distance. We have yet to move, in our own time, from Augustine to Hildebrand. (82)

Everett maintains that the development of such a critical ethic awaits an adequate ecclesiology. The ecclesiology of most of the more liberal sexual ethics assumes that the church is a voluntary association which exists for the spiritual enrichment of the individuals comprising it. While admitting that such a voluntaristic theory of church is inextricably bound up with a pluralist social context, Everett doubts that voluntarism can provide the countervailing power we need to counter the tremendous powers which shape and often destroy our lives. "Even granting that God's hand is at work in the dialectic among these massive institutions, can a purely voluntaristic vision of Christian life provide an adequate ecclesiology that relates our sexuality to our society? Is that kind of community enough to protect our fragile psyches from these potent cultural forces? I think not. A sexual ethic which doesn't place the dilemmas of sexuality in this kind of societal context will never reach the Hildebrandine moment'' (83).

I disagree with particular points of Everett's position,[17] but the structure of his argument seems to me to be right. Which ironically means that we cannot expect to begin to develop an adequate Christian sexual ethic without starting with the insistence that sex is a public matter for the Christian community. For our sexual ethic is part and parcel of our political ethic, as our convictions require that we take a critical stance against societies built on no true knowledge of the one true God. How we order and form our lives sexually cannot be separated from the necessity of the church to chart an alternative to our culture's dominant assumptions. Indeed, it is my contention that Christian conviction concerning the place of singleness and the family is perhaps the most important political task of the church in our society.

3.1   Sex and the Church's Mission

The "personalists" are correct that the ethics of sex cannot be determined only in relationship to the institution of marriage, but not for the reason they think. The political nature of the church's sexual ethic is perhaps most clearly illuminated by calling attention to the alternative of singleness as a legitimate form of life among Christians. Indeed, in the strongest possible language the basis and intelligibility of the Christian understanding of marriage only makes sense in relation to the early Church's legitimation for some of "singleness."[18]

This is often forgotten, as the church is prone, for apologetic reasons, to simply underwrite the broad assumption that marriage is a natural and primary institution. Thus most Christians assume that marriage is the first mode of sexual life and that the single therefore must justify his or her mode of life rather than vice versa. But Christian marriage is not a "natural" institution but rather the creation of a people who marry for very definite purposes. The constant institutional reminder of this fact is the assumption of the early Christians that singleness was as legitimate a form of life as marriage.

This is not the place, nor am I competent, to try to analyze the New Testament's texts concerning singleness, marriage, and sexuality. It is worth pointing out, however, that one of the interesting things about the New Testament is that it seems to have so little to say about sex and marriage. And what it does say has a singularly foreign sound for those of us brought up on romantic notions of marriage and sex. We are thus struck by the stark realism of the Pauline recommendations in 1 Corinthians 7 and more than a little embarrassed by the *Haustafeln* passages in Ephesians, Colossians and 1 Peter.[19] As a means to soften these passages, many call attention to 1 Corinthians 13 and Ephesians 5:21–33 to stress that love really is crucial to Christian marriage. Yet this attempt to rescue the New Testament views on marriage and sexuality seem to involve creative forms of eisegesis. I am particularly struck by the supposition that Ephesians 5:22ff can be used to justify the importance of "happy" marriages for Christians. There seems to be nothing in the text itself to suggest that Christ's love and unity with the church implies that unity is without discord.[20]

More important, however, than the interpretation of particular New Testament texts about marriage and sex is the recognition that the church's sexual ethic cannot be determined through examination and collation of individual texts. Of course, the individual texts are significant for helping us understand the early church's sex ethic, but they must be understood in the broader context of the early Christians' understanding of their mission. Ironically, in that respect singleness is a better indication than marriage of the church's self-understanding.

The early church's legitimation of singleness as a form of life symbolized the necessity of the church to grow through witness and conversion. Singleness was legitimate, not because sex was thought to be a particularly questionable activity, but because the mission of the church was such that "between the times" the church required those who were capable of complete service to the Kingdom. And we must remember that the "sacrifice" made by the single is not that of "giving up sex," but the much more significant sacrifice of giving up heirs. There can be no more radical act than this, as it is the clearest institutional expression that one's future is not guaranteed by the family, but by the church. The church, that harbinger of the Kingdom of God, is now the source of our primary loyalty.

And of course such loyalty involves the gravest dangers, as we have recently had tragically displayed at Jonestown. Jones was right that Christianity in some fundamental ways challenges how we "naturally" think about the family. His "solution" to the problem of the family in Christianity reveals the depth of apostasy his peculiar account of Christianity involved,[21] but Jonestown helps us understand what extraordinary assumptions were involved in the early Christians' commitment to marriage and the family. For they too knew they were involved in a revolutionary struggle, yet they continued to sponsor particular commitments and the having of children who were the responsibility of particular parents.

Extraordinary moral commitments are involved in a community that encourages us to form particular attachments which are morally legitimated to override concern for the general welfare of the community. Christians have legitimated such commitments because they believe that the "good" that constitutes the church is served only by our learning to love and serve our neighbors as we find them in our mates and children. The sexual exclusiveness traditionally associated with the Christian understanding of marriage is but a form of the church's commitment to support exclusive relationships.

In this respect there is a certain tension between the church's sponsoring of singleness and marriage as equally valid modes of life. But both singleness and marriage are necessary symbolic institutions for the constitution of the church's life as the historic institution that witnesses to God's Kingdom. Neither can be valid without the other.[22] If singleness is a symbol of the church's confidence in God's power to effect lives for the growth of the church, marriage and procreation is the symbol of the church's understanding that the struggle will be long and arduous. For Christians do not place their hope in their children, but rather their children are a sign of their hope, in spite of the considerable evidence to the contrary, that God has not abandoned this world. Because we have confidence in God, we find the confidence in ourselves to bring new life into this world, even though we cannot be assured that our children will share our mission.[23] For they, too, must be converted if they are to be followers of the way.

From this perspective marriage (as well as the family) stands as one of the central institutions of the political reality of the church, for it is a sign of our faithfulness to God's Kingdom come through the providential ordering of history. By our faithfulness to *one* other, within a community that requires, finally, loyalty to God, we experience and witness to the first fruits of the new creation. Our commitment to exclusive relations witnesses to God's pledge to his people, Israel and the church, that through his exclusive commitment to them, all people will be brought into his Kingdom.

3.2 Marriage as a Heroic Role

Marriage so understood is a heroic task that can be accomplished only by people who have developed the virtues and character necessary for such a task. The development of such virtues and character is a correlative of a narrative that helps us understand that struggle in which we are involved. But it is exactly such a narrative that we have been lacking, or perhaps more accurately, our primary problem is that our experience of marriage has been captured by narratives that have done little for, and have perhaps even perverted, the role of marriage in the Christian community.

Rosemary Haughton argues that the romantic myth has been the primary determinate of our understanding of marriage. Such a myth, though beautiful, is inadequate, as

its importance has depended largely on the general feeling of lack of any but private relevance in domesticity in our culture. If the domestic is the *only* area you can really shape, then a myth which makes sense of that is obviously vital to self-respect and hope. "Private life" is, by definition, something aside from the big issues, the ones that make history, and that is where we have put marriage. We in the West accepted that separation, accepted the irrelevance of marriage as a public fact, and lived marriage as a kind of backyard set apart for private emotional cultivation, using a romantic yardstick to measure our success, even as Christians.[24]

Haughton suggests that this was a disastrous mistake and that is why we must recognize a different myth, or as I would prefer, narrative, to recover the significance of marriage for Christians. Such a myth she finds in the hero—who we must understand is not necessarily a "great leader," but simply one "who realizes the human calling, which is to go out and discover the future, symbolically to find the water of life, rescue the princess and kill the dragon" (136).

I am sure many of us feel that this is surely going too far. It is a rather nice idea to think that our day-to-day struggle to sustain marriage and the family is "heroic," but we know it to be a good deal less than "heroic." Nevertheless, such an objection continues to assume the romantic model of marriage as primary. Haughton, in contrast, seeks to remind us that the reason marriage can be heroic for Christians is because "the couple must dedicate themselves, not simply to each other, but to work together at something greater than themselves, greater than their love, or any love they could ever imagine. The hero requires only goodwill and courage, yet he is, in all the stories, absolutely essential to the salvation of the people. Unless the hero succeeds, the people die. He does not have to be emotionally well-developed; he has only to do what needs to be done" (142). Haughton is not suggesting that such an understanding of marriage will necessarily produce a "better" marriage than the romantic ideal, but rather that the "criteria" of success are simply different. "The point is that the qualities that make people stick out a hard life together, not stopping too much to wonder if they are fulfilled, are the qualities people need if they are to develop the hero in marriage, which is what being married 'in the Lord' is about" (143).[25]

There is one particular quality Haughton finds especially important for the hero: fidelity. The virtue of fidelity is often ignored or attacked by advocates of the romantic model, as romantic love seeks intensity, not continuity. And fidelity seems to contradict the fact that people develop and change, and in doing so it seems unjust that they should remain attached to past commitments.

But from the point of view of the hero myth, fidelity is of the essence. The hero tales always involve endurance, and the determination to complete the quest, however long it takes, however violent the change of fortunes, and however desperate the predicaments in which the quester is involved. To realize this is to discover a quite new rationale for the much criticized demand for sexual exclusiveness and lifelong fidelity in marriage. Extramarital sex may provide new romantic intensity in a life which has lost meaning, but it simply rules out the quest. . . . The emotional alternatives which offer themselves in the course of any marriage (and not all of them are sexual) may appear—and be—more beautiful, more fulfilling, than the commitment to this particular marriage. But it is in this particular marriage, if it is undertaken "in the Lord," that the hero will set out on his (her) quest. (146–147)

But, as I suggested above, such "fidelity" makes sense only if it occurs in a community that has a mission in which marriage serves a central political purpose. And marriage has such a purpose for Christians, as it is a sign that we are a community sustained by hope. Marriage is a sign and source of such hope, "for as long as there are people loving and working together, and bringing up children, there is a chance of new life. To take conscious hold on that life, to realize oneself at the heart of it, for others also, is a tremendously vitalizing spiritual experience" (150).

4.   Practical Implications

"Vitalizing spiritual experience" seems a long way away from answering the query concerning what is wrong with messing around a little before or during marriage. Moreover, there is the added problem that whether the argument above is right or not seems of little relevance to our concrete experience. For the truth of the matter is that few of us had that understanding, if we had any understanding at all, of what we were doing when we got married; nor has our sexual conduct been formed by or lived out in such terms. As a result, most of what has been said may seem but one more idealistic account of marriage and sex that should properly be dismissed by those of us who have to live in this life.

Yet I think my argument, incomplete as it is, at least provides some means of response. It is, of course, true that few of us have been trained to view our marriages in such a manner, but the perspective I have developed should at least help us deal with the fact that even though we may not have known what we were doing when we got married, we find ourselves married. The important issue is how we are to understand what has happened through marriage. Surely it is not just that we have undervalued or overvalued the significance of sex in our lives, but that we have had no sense that such a way of understanding sex may represent a false and perhaps even a destructive alternative.

From the perspective I have tried to develop we can now see why "realism" is insufficient to provide us with ethical guidance about sex. For "realism," as I have argued, turns out to be but a chastened form of romanticism that continues to reflect a culture that insists that sex and marriage have no public function. A true "realism" requires a community that forms our loyalties in such a manner that both the costs and hopes of marriage can be properly held in balance. Only from such a perspective can we reach a more profound sense of the relation of love and marriage, as it is only within such a context that we can begin to understand that the love properly characteristic of marriage is not a correlative of the attractive qualities of our mates. Only a love so formed has the capacity to allow the other freedom to be other without resentment.[26]

I think also the account I have tried to sketch out helps explain aspects of our lives that are simply anomalous given our culture's understanding of marriage and the family. I am thinking of such common matters as our deep commitment to our particular children and their care, or of the extraordinary efforts some couples go through to save their marriages, or why we continue to care about having children at all. To be sure, many are finding that it is possible to train ourselves not to have such "irrational" desires, but there is the lingering feeling that we are poorer for it. And those who continue to care about such commitments are only able to explain them as their own peculiar desires. It's as if they were a matter of taste.

What we forget is that such "peculiar desires" are the product of centuries of Christian insistence and training that the family is central to what the church means in this time between the times. To be sure, the church often forgot its own best insights and justified its practice on grounds that appeared more amenable or "natural" to its cultural context, but it continued to have the advantage of having to deal with the necessity of men and women struggling to figure out what they were doing by being married "in the Lord." Such a "necessity" meant that the church could never forget for long that marriage among Christians involved commitments not readily recognized by the world.

But I think the perspective I have tried to develop does more than simply help us to interpret our past. It also helps us ask the right question for giving direction to our future. For the issue is not whether X or Y form of sexual activity is right or wrong, as if such activity could be separated from a whole way of life. Rather such questions are but shorthand ways of asking what kind of people we should be to be capable of supporting the mission of the church. The question of sexual conduct before marriage is thus a question of what prepares me best for the tasks that the Christian community may ask me to accept—whether the task be single or married.[27]

The issue is not whether someone is chaste in the sense of not engaging in genital activity, but whether we have lived in a manner that allows us to bring a history with us that contributes to the common history we may be called upon to develop with one another. Chastity, we forget, is not a state but a form of the virtue of faithfulness that is necessary for a role in the community.[28] As such, it is as crucial to the married life as it is to the single life.

Of course, we need to remind ourselves again, that is still quite a bit to remember in the back seat of a car. But, as I suggested, there is no "ethic" that in itself can solve all the problems involved in such behavior. Rather, what the young properly demand is an account of life and the initiation into a community that makes intelligible why their interest in sex should be subordinated to other interests.[29] What they, and we, demand is the lure of an adventure that captures the imagination sufficiently that conquest means more than the sexual possession of another. I have tried to suggest that marriage and singleness for Christians should represent just such an adventure, and if it does not, no amount of ethics or rules will be sufficient to correct the situation. But now at least we know where the problem lies.

11. Why Abortion Is a Religious Issue

1. Two Controversial Theses

In this essay I argue that (1) the pro-abortionists have been right to claim that the anti-abortion position[1] presupposes "religious" convictions; and (2) the contention of some anti-abortionists is correct: there is a connection between contraception and abortion. By defending both these controversial theses, I hope to provide a new perspective heretofore unexamined in the public debate on "the abortion issue" and in the more sophisticated philosophical and theological discussions. Because some may find these theses bizarre, let me first explain how they provide a framework for discussion about abortion.

By claiming that abortion is a religious issue I do not mean to suggest, as pro-abortion advocates often assume, it is therefore not subject to public debate or policy.[2] However, the suggestion that religious convictions are integral to moral argument about abortion is meant to force a different perspective than those concerned with the public policy aspects of the problem. Too often the question of the morality or immortality of abortion is limited to those issues that both sides assume are crucial for determining whether and to what extent abortion should or should not be allowed to be public policy within American society. In contrast, my primary concern is what I should think about abortion for my life.[3]

This locus of concern does not imply that the issue of abortion is a "private" matter relative to each agent. It is a commonplace that the "legality" of abortion is an insufficient determiner of one's moral position. Yet my emphasis as to how I should understand abortion goes beyond the claim involved in this commonplace. Contrary to those who argue about public policy, I am less sure than they how properly to understand morally what abortion is and how it "fits" with other convictions I hold. Comprehending "abortion," like other significant moral notions, is dependent upon a set of convictions that require narrative display.[4] Therefore my concern is to articulate the narrative contexts operative for determining the meaning of abortion for Christians, and to explore what those narratives may entail for the character of my community and myself.

Calling attention to the often-overlooked claim that there is a connection between contraception and abortion is also an attempt to show why the "morality" of abortion is primarily a matter of interpretation or understanding. It is by no means clear what an abortion morally involves or why we should think it wrong. For example, traditionally Christians have considered abortion as much a sin of sex as a sin of killing and it is by no means clear that they were wrong to do so. In their concern to find a position concerning abortion that would be compelling for public policy, anti-abortionists have concentrated primarily on abortion as a sin of killing. But it may be, as indeed I hope to show, that the intelligibility of the Christian understanding of abortion does not allow for such a neat separation of issues.

In order to avoid any misunderstanding, let me be quick to add I have no intention of defending the view that every act of sexual intercourse must be open to procreation, or that once you allow contraception, then abortion follows necessarily. Rather, by calling attention to contraception I mean to suggest how certain moral presuppositions about parenting may also be crucial for understanding why Christians have been hesitant to approve of abortion. If that can be shown, the questions shaping the ethical analysis of abortion may well have to be broadened.

In case anyone thinks that this way of beginning is a strategy to circumscribe a position I do not wish to otherwise defend, let me briefly summarize what I believe about abortion. It is my general view that Christians should regard abortion as a morally unhappy practice and should exert every effort to avoid it in their lives. Moreover they should also do all they can to help others avoid it in their lives. However, this does not mean that I think abortions must never occur, as there may well be circumstances when abortions are morally permissable if still morally tragic. It is particularly important, therefore, that the Christian community develop the moral and linguistic skills to discriminate between permissible and impermissible abortions, so that our consciences can be so guided.[5]

Such a stark statement of my view about abortion serves little purpose. As I suggested above, what is important is not that Christians disapprove of abortion but *why* they disapprove and how that is correlative of their deepest convictions.

1.1   Abortion and the "Sacredness of Life"

Before I attempt to argue for my two theses, I want to suggest what is behind my shifting the terms of debate about abortion. It is certainly not just to be different. In fact most of us who are professional "ethicists" are just a bit tired of abortion. Those of us reading, thinking, and writing about this issue have simply become too familiar with it. We know the basic questions—

When does life begin? Is it wrong to take life? Should abortion be against the law? and so on (with the alternative arguments for each position)—so well that it is hard to sustain interest in yet another essay. Despite all the discussion and analysis, little progress has been made toward reaching consensus or agreement about the moral status of abortion. Arguments simply seem to get us nowhere.[6]

One of the reasons, I think, for this lack of progress is that the issues thought to be crucial in determining the "morality" of abortion have been too narrowly circumscribed. Both sides of the controversy have tried to develop arguments that would compel agreement from anyone's point of view in the attempt to determine public policy. For example, since both sides agree that murder is wrong, the issue between them is seen to be whether or not abortion is the unjustified taking of life.

Also, while both sides hold that "life is sacred," or even that there is a "right to life," they cannot seem to agree what implications follow from that language. The pro-abortionists rightly object to being described as "anti-life," as they point out that the slogan prejudges exactly the point at issue— whether the fetus is human life, or if the fetus is life, whether society must accept the injunction that life can *never* be taken. We thus are enmeshed in unending and perhaps, in principle, insoluble debates on when human life or a human being begins and whether the distinction between direct-indirect intention is valid, etc.

While I do not find these issues irrelevant, I want to approach the matter by discussing the reasons why Christians understand abortion as a morally unhappy act. Thus, the preliminary question must be inverted: "What kind of people should we be to welcome children into the world?" Note that the question is *not* "Is the fetus a human being with a right to life?" but "How should a Christian regard and care for the fetus as a child?"

Some, especially the pro-abortionists, are bound to object that this statement of the problem appears to prejudge the issue. Surely, it can be pointed out, it can only make sense to ask whether the fetus is a child after it has been determined that the fetus deserves the status of "human being." Yet I am suggesting that the question of whether X or Y is or is not a human being may well be a secondary question to whether X or Y is a child. At the very least, our attention to the matter reminds us how abstract and unreal it is to ask if X or Y is a "human being" or "person."[7] In other aspects of our lives we rarely raise that question to determine our behavior toward another. Surely it must be a highly theory-laden account of human behavior that has convinced us that there is some crucial moral significance in determining if the fetus can or cannot be considered a "human being."

My appeal for a transition in our thinking is analogous to a current debate in philosophical theology. Most assume that prior to "How should I

pray to God?'' is the question, ''Does God exist?'' While it appears intelligible, in fact, the latter question makes little sense apart from some account
of God that is worthy of worship and prayer. Similarly, I am trying to
suggest that in spite of its apparent force, whether the fetus is a human
being has little moral sense apart from ''Is the fetus a child?'' or better ''What
kind of people should we be to welcome children into the world?'' To ask such
questions, however, does not mean all abortions are morally impermissible,
though it does probably mean that abortion as a practice cannot be regarded as
morally indifferent.

1.2   Abortion and Ordinary Discourse

Apart from these considerations, my beginning discussion, by positing
the opposing theses, attempts to embody the language people actually employ
when regarding abortion. For I am impressed that in spite of the hundreds of
articles published defending or opposed to abortion, the way people decide to
have or not to have an abortion rarely seems to involve the issues discussed in
those articles. People contemplating abortion do not ask if the fetus has a right
to life, or when does life begin, or even if abortion is right or wrong. Rather,
the decision seems to turn primarily on the quality of the relationship (or lack
of relationship) between the couple.

I have no hard evidence for this contention. The best I can do is to call
your attention to Linda Bird Francke's extremely interesting book *The
Ambivalence of Abortion*.[8] The primary thrust of Francke's book is to dispel the
anti-abortionist claim that abortion has become a matter that women now take
lightly and as a matter of routine. The book powerfully demonstrates that
abortion is seldom undertaken in a morally insensitive manner; for even the
most committed pro-abortionist, abortion in actual practice continues to
produce ''ambivalence.''

The anti-abortionists might well reply that they are less than impressed
with such evidence, as ''ambivalence'' is hardly sufficient to indicate the
moral seriousness of abortion. Yet I think such a response fails to do justice to
the genuine moral agony of the women and men on whom Francke reports.

More importantly, to read her book from that perspective fails to appreciate the moral argument against abortion to which the book witnesses
almost in spite of itself. Few of the women Francke describes claim they are
doing a good thing by having an abortion. Rather they say they are acting out
of ''necessity.'' Strange as it may seem, they seldom claim to have aborted a
fetus—they abort a ''child'' or a ''baby.'' Thus one of her respondents says,

> If my parents were dead, then I'd have had the baby. But they're here to
> remind me of guilt and lay on their disapproval. I had my second

abortion after I'd been living with a guy for two years. I missed a couple of pills and got knocked up. I must have done it on purpose. I really believe that. I love children, you know. I've been a mother's helper since I was thirteen and spent a whole year as a governess. I was old-fashioned enough with this guy to want to have his baby, but not admitting it to myself. I was really half-assed. He was very sensitive. He sort of wanted to have the baby too, but then he said I better have the abortion. So I did.[9]

The fact that this woman soon felt disgust for her partner and left him aptly illustrates Francke's general observation that the most critical factor in the decision to abort was the relationship with the male partner. Indeed she says that in her research almost every relationship between single people broke up either before or after the abortion. Thus

if the pregnancy is a result of a one-night stand or a meaningless relationship, the decision is easier. But when it is a result of an ongoing relationship, the emotional issues become myriad. The relationship suddenly reaches a crisis point and can seesaw wildly. Some women are stunned when their partners bolt and run in panic. Others are resentful that their partners support the abortion decision, feeling this represents a lack of commitment. Forced to evaluate the quality of their relationship, other couples split up because the fact of pregnancy and abortion is too weighty for them to handle. Many couples, on the other hand, become closer in facing such an agonizing decision together.[10]

It should not be surprising, of course, that abortion, like any major decision a couple must make, surfaces tensions in a marriage or a relationship that are usually repressed. Yet there seems something peculiar about abortion, as it seems to ask for a vote of confidence in one another and in the relationship like few other decisions. Thus another of Francke's respondents said,

I think abortion is best for both my husband and me. I'd like to get a little bit of something someday. I had to quit high school in the eleventh grade, and I don't know how to do anything. The problem is deep down I want to keep the baby. I realize it's not the smart thing to do. The abortion will give us more of a chance to get something. But I think about the baby all the time, about my little girl. That's what I had always hoped it would be if I would have had it. If it had been born, what would she have looked like? I just guess I feel bad that when my next one comes along that I would have had another one that I loved. I come in tomorrow. I'm going to go through with it. I hope I feel better than I do today. I love the baby. I love my husband. I just think it would be better for him if I had the abortion. I'll get over it. I'm sure there'll be a lot of times when I think about it, but we got so many problems now.

So many. I know I can have another baby someday. But it's this one I love now. I just love her so much.[11]

Abortion is often defended as the necessary condition for the freedom of women from male oppression. Yet if we are to believe the testimony of Francke's witnesses, abortion often is the coercive method men use to free themselves from responsibility to women.[12] But even more ironic, for many women, rather than a declaration of independence, abortion is a subtle vote of no-confidence in their ability to determine their destiny. As one man (who generally approved of abortion) put it, "This new breed of women has got it all wrong when they decide not to have children. What these intelligent women owe the world is not just what they do or are—they owe the world a legacy to pass on."[13] And the unwillingness to pass on such a legacy may be a sign of the profoundest self-hate.

I am aware that these passages from Francke's book cannot or should not determine whether abortion is morally acceptable or not. However, they at least suggest that calling attention to the relationship between contraception and abortion may not seem as crazy as it first appears, if the relationship between a man and a woman is one of the crucial factors in the decision to have an abortion. Nor is it absurd to suggest that such a decision might well involve religious assumptions if, as it seems, abortion involves our deepest attitudes of confidence in ourselves, others, and our world.

Of course some philosophers or theologians may well argue that all this is beside the point. While Francke's interviews are psychologically or biographically interesting, they have almost nothing to tell us about the morality or immorality of abortion. Indeed, at best all that her book demonstrates is that most people, even those getting abortions, do not understand morally what they are doing. The interviews simply represent philosophically confused positions and attitudes which could be corrected by any moderately good introductory course in philosophy.

Nevertheless, the language used by Francke's respondents is much closer morally to the heart of the matter than the arguments about the status of the fetus made by ethicists. And I think this can be shown philosophically, as arguments concerning our obligation to the fetus often depend on assumptions about the kind of responsibilities we have as parents. Thus I will first defend my second thesis, concerning the relation between contraception and abortion, and then, on the basis of that relation, I will suggest in what manner abortion is properly a religious matter.

2.   Sex, Abortion, and Parental Responsibility

In order to explore the connection between contraception and abortion I am going to concentrate on the arguments made by Dr. Susan Nicholson in

Abortion and the Roman Catholic Church.[14] Nicholson begins by pointing out that in the past Roman Catholic condemnation of abortion and contraception was linked by the assumption that both were sexual sins. This assumption was based on the claim that there is or ought to be a link between sexual activity and procreation to the extent that procreative intent is morally required for intercourse. Thus contraception was condemned as homicide and abortion was understood to be as much a sin of lust as murder. Dr. Nicholson substantiates her case by quoting the eleventh-century *Decretum* of Buchard, "If someone to satisfy his lust or in deliberate hatred does something to a man or women so that no children be born of him or her, or gives them to drink, so that he cannot generate or she conceive, let it be held as homicide."[15]

Dr. Nicholson includes this position only for sake of completeness, since she regards as deeply flawed the condemnation of abortion as a sexual sin. She contends that the absolute linking of sexual activity to procreation is not only internally inconsistent, without plausible rationale, and injurious to human love, but it actually conflicts with the other value found in Catholic condemnation of abortion—the protection of fetal life. Thus, "a moral theology which recognizes the positive contribution of erotic love to human existence, while seeking to protect fetal life, might *discourage* potentially procreative sex except where accompanied by an intent or at least a willingness to procreate, while *encouraging* sexual activity incapable of procreating. The Catholic Church has proclaimed almost the exact opposite, and has thus created an unconscionable tension between erotic love and the protection of fetal life."[16]

Secondly, Dr. Nicholson argues that even if the Catholic view of sex were defensible, it could not be legitimately promoted as a basis for restrictive abortion legislation. There can be no justification for imposing on the rest of society the Catholic requirement that sex be procreatively linked. Abortion as a frustration of procreation is not a legitimate subject for legislation, but abortion as the killing of a human being surely is. Therefore, Dr. Nicholson chooses to ignore the argument concerning abortion as a sexual sin in favor of concentrating on what she takes to be the central issue, the sin of killing.

Yet ironically, as we shall see, Nicholson's own argument for the legitimacy of abortion explicitly involves assumptions about the relationship between sex and procreation. To be sure it is not the same kind of connection that Roman Catholics have assumed because of their position that every act of sexual intercourse must be open to procreation, but rather involves assumptions about the kind of responsibility that should be prerequisite for voluntary sexual intercourse. But that is all I wish to establish since I, no more than Dr. Nicholson, want to argue that every act of sexual intercourse must have a procreative intention. Like her I assume that sexual intercourse can and should have a place in human relationship that is intrinsic to the activity itself. To accept this, however, does not mean that the Catholics have been wrong to maintain, in principle, that there is a relationship between contraception and abortion.

Before trying to show how Nicholson's own argument turns on an understanding of the relation of sex and abortion, I should confront a possible objection to my use of her argument. Nicholson's argument gives the Catholics everything they want—the conceptus is full human life and should be protected accordingly—and yet she wants to show that on their own grounds Catholics have to allow for a greater range of permissible abortion than they are officially willing to accede to.[17]

By accepting the Catholic claims concerning the status of the fetus, Nicholson seems to have already conceded what the pro-abortionist thinks I must show. And to a certain extent that is correct. Yet it is not my intention to provide grounds to convince others that the fetus is "fully human," but rather to show why the issue of abortion cannot and should not turn on the status of the fetus considered in itself. Dr. Nicholson's carefully developed argument thus helps us understand how a negative judgment about abortion requires display by a whole set of convictions and practices of a community.

2.1   Rape and the Justification of Abortion

Unlike many, Nicholson rightly sees that the moral analysis of abortion requires carefully controlled analogical arguments.[18] She thus tries to show that if it is permissible in some situations to kill innocent post-natal human beings, it cannot be wrong in similar circumstances to kill fetuses. In her view the Roman Catholic understanding of abortion mistakenly confers greater protection upon fetal life in cases of life-threatening pregnancies and pregnancies resulting from rape than it requires be extended to human life in other circumstances.[19] In order to demonstrate this she considers Judith Jarvis Thomson's now famous defense of abortion based on the analogy of the "unconscious violinist." Thomson's case is meant to provide a close parallel to certain kinds of pregnancies, particularly those resulting from rape:

> You wake up in the morning and find yourself back to back in bed with an unconscious violinist. A famous unconscious violinist. He has been found to have a fatal kidney ailment, and the Society of Music Lovers has canvassed all the available medical records and found that you alone have the right blood type to help. They have therefore kidnapped you, and last night the violinist's circulatory system was plugged into yours, so that your kidneys can be used to extract poisons from his blood as well as your own. The director of the hospital now tells you, "Look, we're sorry the Society of Music Lovers did this to you—we would

never have permitted it if we had known. But still, they did it, and the violinist now is plugged into you. To unplug you would be to kill him. But never mind, it's only for nine months. By then he will have recovered from his ailment, and can safely be unplugged from you.[20]

Thomson places what Nicholson takes to be the Roman Catholic argument against abortion in the mouth of a hospital director: "All persons have a right to life, and violinists are persons. Granted you have a right to decide what happens in and to your body, but a person's right to life outweighs your right to decide what happens in and to your body."[21] Thomson's assumption is that most people, including Catholics, will be outraged at the hospital director's attitude. And given the close analogy between this case and pregnancy resulting from rape, it is therefore inconsistent to allow yourself to be disconnected from the violinist without letting pregnant rape victims have an abortion.

The one disanalogy[22] between the two cases, however, is that there is a genetic relationship between the rape victim and the fetus unlike that between ourselves and the violinist. Nicholson argues that such a relationship makes no moral difference, however, since it would be permissible for a woman to terminate the life support of a blastocyst conceived *in vitro* from her ovum and involuntarily implanted in her. The genetic relationship might conceivably influence the woman to want to continue the pregnancy, but it certainly would not obligate her to do so.

Nicholson takes Thomson's argument to have shown decisively that it is morally permissable to abort a fetus resulting from rape even on the premise that the fetus is a human being. The Roman Catholic denial of this means that Catholics treat fetal life as *more* sacred than postnatal life on the assumption that "the fetus has a parasitical relationship to a woman's body."[23] However, there may be grounds for the Catholic attitude about this matter other than that such a "parasitical" relationship exists.

Nicholson suggests that Thomson's position involves a contradiction, since if a woman is permitted to abort a fetus resulting from rape, she cannot have a parental relationship to the fetus; yet after a child resulting from rape is born, the woman to whom it is genetically related is defined as the child's mother. Thus we describe a woman as having a maternal relationship to a child born after rape, but not to an unborn child.

In order to remove this apparent contradiction, Nicholson calls our attention to how our society assumes parental relationships are acquired. Namely we are unwilling to assign "the duties of parenthood to a person who has neither (1) voluntarily participated in the event(s) producing the child in question, nor (2) voluntarily contracted to perform those duties (adoption), nor (3) had an opportunity, prior to the assignment of such duties, to transfer them to another party. That a woman can be maternally related to a *born,* but not an *unborn*, child resulting from rape is due to the fact that she normally has the option of releasing the *born* child for adoption.''[24]

The point is, according to Nicholson, parental responsibility is not thrust on people, but related to the performance of, or failure to perform certain acts. ''Thus a person has some control over whether or not s/he becomes parentally obligated to another human being. Parental duties are normally associated with voluntary sexual acts.''[25] At most, then, the responsibility of a woman carrying a child resulting from rape is not that of a parent to a child, but the general duty to assist another human being in distress. But the latter responsibility is much less stringent than the former.

While we may think parents have a duty to risk their lives to aid their child (for example, to rescue a child from a burning house), we think no such general duty exists for one stranger to aid another. We may, for example, think we have a duty to feed an infant abandoned at our door for awhile, but that duty is not the same as would be involved in asking a rape victim to provide bodily life-support. The latter involves an invasion of one's body, while the former does not. ''One may be morally required to feed another, simply because the other is a human being in distress. However, this general obligation to provide minimal assistance to another human being in distress does not require that one be host/ess in a parasitical physical relationship.''[26]

Nicholson, therefore, suggests it is morally inexact to describe a rape victim's intention in seeking an abortion as ''killing the fetus.'' Rather, what they seek, analogous to Thomson's violinist care, is a way to cease providing bodily life-support. It just happens in our present state of technology the means is the removal of the fetus, and where the fetus is non-viable, this results in fetal death. In the future, if an artificial uterus were developed, it might be possible to save fetuses resulting from rape without imposing parental responsibilities on the rape victim.

Thomson extends her argument to all cases of a woman pregnant despite contraception, saying that if parents

> have taken all reasonable precautions against having a child, they do not simply by virtue of their biological relationship to the child who comes into existence have a special responsibility for it. They may wish to assume responsibility for it, or they may not wish to. And I am suggesting that if assuming responsibility for it would require large sacrifices, then they may refuse. A Good Samaritan would not refuse—or anyway, a Splendid Samaritan, if the sacrifices that had to be made were enormous. But then so would a Good Samaritan assume responsibility for that violinist. . . .[27]

In contrast, however, Nicholson argues that a woman does have ''a parental duty to administer to the needs of a human being conceived through her voluntary intercourse. One foreseeable need, obviously, is for bodily life-support at the fetal stage. Thus, on the assumption that the fetus is a human being, motherhood involves a duty to provide fetal life-support. Contraception merely reduces the likelihood that sexual intercourse will give rise to a new human being requiring bodily life-support. The raped woman, on the other hand, does not voluntarily participate in the act producing a new human being. Consequently, she has no parental duty prior to the child's birth.''[28]

2.2   Contraception, Parenthood, and Abortion

But then it must be asked why Nicholson assumes that parental duties normally accrue with voluntary sexual acts.[29] From Thomson's perspective that must surely appear as absurd as Nicholson finds the Roman Catholic assumption that a raped woman has become a mother. Why is the ''voluntariness'' of sexual intercourse a more rational indication of the assumption of parental roles than the genetic relationship?

Such an assertion seems particularly problematic if we further question the conditions necessary to make sexual intercourse ''voluntary.'' How ''voluntary'' is sex for a unattractive adolescent girl who feels her acceptance by others depends on her ability to attract boys? Or how ''voluntary'' are those many acts of sexual intercourse within marriage that too often are but subtle bribes or threats against the other? Or why should anyone be held to living out the consequences of the act of sexual intercourse even if it was voluntarily and even, at the time, procreatively intended? Circumstances change and we allow people to change with them. People make many supposed completely free decisions and later are not held responsible for them.

Nicholson seems to mean by ''voluntary'' any act not rape, yet with some understanding (how much is not clear) of the connection between sexual intercourse and pregnancy. Surely that definition is insufficient to serve as a necessary condition for all the responsibilities of being parents for a couple who thus happen to get pregnant. (Nicholson is not entirely clear about this, as she does not say if the responsibilities that accrue require the willingness to raise the child or simply to have it; if it is the former, then she has, in a particularly glaring sexist oversight, paid insufficient attention to the responsibility of the male for the child.)

That such questions can be asked are but a credit to the strength of Nicholson's position, for by directing our attention to parental responsibilities she has put the moral question in the right context. Moreover she has reintroduced the issue of sexual responsibility as crucial to her own consideration of abortion, for her position requires an account of what moral expectations should be present in forming our sexual activity if we are engaged in that activity in a manner that does not exclude the life that may result.

Moreover, I think she has made the Roman Catholic position at the same time less and more attractive. It is less attractive insofar as it depends on "sanctity of life" or "right to life" language. Such phrases, ironically, are attempts to develop an ethic for protecting the fetus as though the relationship between fetus and parent were that of a stranger to a stranger. But that is exactly what the fetus is not—it is a child which may only later become a stranger to and for its parents. On such an assumption the Roman Catholic attitude concerning the status of the fetus resulting from rape makes sense, in that such a being is protected not because life is inherently sacred, but because of its role essential to our vocation—namely as parents to a child. Crucial, of course, is the kind of community and correlative understanding of "parenthood" that would encourage such attribution of responsibility.[30]

Nicholson's resort to the language of "parasite," which is clearly not justified or required by the main lines of her argument, may indicate that she feels at a loss how to discriminate the kind of parental responsibility associated with rape from that inherent in other forms of sexual intercourse. "Parasite" is rhetoric in search of an argument. In contrast, the Catholic position asserts that the presence of the fetus is sufficient to determine parental responsibility.

In truth, neither position has been satisfactorily argued. What is required is a normative account of parenthood correlative to the ends of a community. We live in a culture where there is no such normative account or even any community that might be able to guide us in articulating such an account. As a result the best we can do is make arbitrary claims about the importance of genetics or voluntary commitment as necessary conditions for parenthood.[31]

Put differently, the force of Nicholson's argument is to make us reconsider, in a more serious way than most seem willing, the status of extramarital sexual intercourse. For if Nicholson is right to contend that "voluntary" sexual intercourse, even when engaged in for pleasure, involves a commitment to receive children that may result, then we must again ask if our accepting attitude toward sex as recreation[32] or self-fulfillment is morally sufficient. At least it is useful to remind ourselves that the traditional limitation of sexual intercourse to marriage was not a puritanical desire to prevent pleasure, though at times it may have been used for that, but rather an attempt to mark off institutionally those contexts for sexual intercourse so that if pregnancy resulted a child would be welcomed into a home.

It is not sufficient to ask what kind of attitudes we have and how we can make them consistent with our willingness to have children if an accident occurs. Rather, the question should be what kind of attitude should we have toward the having of children and what kind of sexual behavior is most appropriate to that attitude. Because the issue of contraception raised that question (and to be sure the form the prohibition of contraception took meant the question was often obscured), it was and is essentially related to the question of abortion. Finally, our willingness to have children and form our lives in a way appropriate to their care will determine both attitudes and practices regarding sexual behavior and abortion.

It is particularly important, moreover, that the problem understood in this manner not be interpreted in the individualistic terms of most discussions of sex in our society. The issue is not what "individuals" decide, but what a community encourages. For example, many parents, including Catholics, encourage their unmarried daughters to get an abortion rather than "ruin" their lives by a public acknowledgement of an out-of-wedlock pregnancy. Ironically, such an attitude assumes that individual sexual conduct is more significant than a community's willingness to receive its children. There are probably very good reasons for a woman in such circumstances not to raise her child, but there may be substantial reasons for the community to encourage her to have the child so as to see that it is properly raised.

3.   Religious Convictions and Abortion

Even though I have tried to show that our convictions about the place of children in our lives forge a connection between contraception and abortion, I have not tried to argue for any particular understanding of our willingness to have children or what that might mean for how we form our sexual behavior and our attitudes toward abortion. Now, however, let me consider how certain religious convictions should be central for how Christians understand their obligation to have children and how those convictions form the necessary background for their attitude about abortion.

For most people and for most times, having children was regarded as a "natural" fact. That is, it has been assumed to be an activity that requires little thought or understanding. It is simply something that everyone "wants to do." The question of why we should "want to do" such a thing never comes up. In most cases, it is appropriate that the question never come up, as we are carried along by the sheer vitality of life in a manner that makes the question of "why" seem almost obscene.

But often hidden in the vitality are corrupt and corrupting attitudes toward children and ourselves. Unwillingness to expose our attitudes to critical analysis magnifies the power of our false convictions. There are some things that we prefer not to examine for fear of what we might find or for fear there is nothing to discover. We must face the fact that culturally we are simply not sure what it is we are doing when we have children.[33] We continue to depend on the "habit," but we are no longer sure what does or should inform the "habit" and give it direction. This is not an entirely bad thing: it helps us see, contrary to our first assumption, that having children is not after all a "natural" occurrence. Rather, having children is one of the most morally charged things any community of people does, as nothing else says more about who they are and what they think life is about.

In particular, a community's willingness to encourage children is a sign of its confidence in itself and its people. For children are a community's sign to the future that life, in spite of its hardship and tedium, is worthwhile. Also, children are symbols of our hope—please note that they are not the object of our hope—which sustains us in our day-to-day existence. Life may be hard, but it can be lived. Indeed, it can be lived with zest and interest to the extent that we have the confidence to introduce others to it.

More profoundly, children signal a community's confidence because they are bound to change our society and their existence fortells inevitable challenge. Our stories and traditions are never inherited unchanged. Indeed, the very power and truth of a tradition depends on its adaptation by each new generation. Thus, children represent a community's confidence that its tradition is not without merit and is strong enough to meet the challenge of a new generation.

What then, do these rhetorical flourishes have to do with abortion and, in particular, religious convictions? Put simply, they indicate the background beliefs that make intelligible why abortion is generally a morally objectionable act. When institutionalized and regarded as morally acceptable or at least morally indifferent by society, abortion is an indication that a society is afraid of itself and its children.

3.1 The Christian and Children

The Christian attitude toward children and the family is often identified with our society's ideology about the importance of the family. Thus Christianity is recommended as a "good thing" because it is alleged to keep the family together, and Christians are supposed to be especially loving when it comes to children. Such a view of the relation of Christianity to the family, however, is a lie that fails to do justice to the basic documents of the faith and to our fundamental convictions.

For example, what was remarkable about the early church is not what it said about the family and children, but that it said so little. Most of what it did say about marriage and the family was not exactly complimentary. This negative attitude has often been taken to be a sign that Christians fear or dislike sex, but far more is at stake. What the early church did was establish a community whose understanding of its mission was such that singleness was of equal status with marriage. As a result, the church challenged the natural necessity of marriage, thus making marriage a vocation as serious as single-ness.

As a vocation, marriage was understood to have a peculiar service to the community—namely, it served a symbolic function denoting God's loyalty to his people and as such was the appropriate context for reception of new life. And remember, Christians were not called to have children assured that their children were going to be lovely people, nice folk to be with. We forget that the early Christians had deep convictions about the reality and force of sin and they saw no reason why their children were to be exempt from that reality. Nor could they even assume that their children would be Christian, since they knew also that one must be called in order to be a member of the church. Rather, these people were called to marriage and to having children as their obligation. For their children were their pledge to be a community formed by the conviction that, in spite of evidence to the contrary, God rules this world.

Therefore, for Christians, having children or getting married is not a "natural" event but one freighted with the deepest moral and religious sig-nificance. Their attitude toward abortion is but an aspect of their conviction that they must be people who are ever ready to welcome children into the world. To be such a people is in a certain sense to "be out of control," for children often have a way of being born when we "are not ready for them." Yet for Christians, to "be in control" to the extent that new life is excluded from their world, is an indication that we are in fact controlled by powers other than the God we know as the mover of the sun and the stars.

3.2   The Non-Christian and Children

It may be objected that the most established so far is that Christian attitudes about abortion involve religious convictions, but that by no means shows that all anti-abortion positions presuppose such assumptions. Of course that is true, but my case is a little stronger than such an objection suggests. For if I am right that the issue of the morality of abortion gains its intelligibility in relation to assumptions about parenting, then the case I have developed at least suggests that both pro- and anti-abortionists may well have attitudes that are functionally equivalent to the Christian. I am not anxious to call such attitudes religious, but I do want to claim that there are matters involved that we Christians think are central to our understanding of the religious life.

Put differently, I am not suggesting that only Christians have good reasons for having children. Rather I have tried to suggest the narrative context that makes the activity of having children intelligible to Christians and why abortion is thus understood in a negative light. I do not know why people who are not Christians have children, nor do I think there is any reason to investigate and make summary judgment about that. What I think I have shown, however, is that their attitudes toward parenting are crucial for determining their understanding of abortion. Or even more strongly, that their attitudes about abortion may be crucial in determining their understanding of what it means to be a parent. Such issues draw on our profoundest assumptions about what makes life worthwhile.

One of Francke's respondents who had had two previous abortions asked what I take to be the crucial question. She says, "I don't think for many women abortion is as blithe an experience as women are led to believe. I know I'm not totally unique, but how many women going into it know what to expect? I have no moral handle on abortion—none at all. I've never been able to work it out. Is there a right and a wrong? I don't know what to tell my own children."[34] For how do we tell our children what we are doing and still make them glad that they are our children?

12. Abortion: Why the Arguments Fail

1. Have the Arguments Failed?

   Essays on the morality of abortion, whether they be anti or pro, have begun to take on a ritualistic form. Each side knows the arguments and counterarguments well, but they continue to go through the motions. Neither side seems to have much hope of convincing the other, but just as in some rituals we continue to repeat words and actions though we no longer know why, in like manner we continue to repeat arguments about why abortion is right, wrong, or indifferent. It is almost as though we assume that the repetition of the arguments will magically break the moral and political impasse concerning the status of abortion in our society.

   The intractability of the debate frustrates us and our frustration gives way to shrillness. Having tried to develop good philosophical, theological, legal, and social arguments we find our opponents still unconvinced. In the heat of political exchange, both sides resort to rhetoric designed to make their opponents appear stupid or immoral. Thus we are besieged by slogans affirming the "right to life" or that every woman has the "right over her body"; or it seems we must choose between being "pro-life" or "pro-choice." Some, concluding that there is no hope of conducting the public debate in a manner befitting the moral nuances of the abortion issue, have withdrawn from the field of battle.

   Yet before anyone beats too hasty a retreat it is worth considering why the arguments seem to have failed and why we have been left with little alternative to the oversimplifications of the public debate. There may be a moral lesson to be learned from the intractable character of the debate that is as important as the morality of abortion itself. And I suspect it offers a particularly important lesson for Christians. It is my contention that Christian opposition to abortion on demand has failed because, by attempting to meet the moral challenge within the limits of public polity, we have failed to exhibit our deepest convictions that make our rejection of abortion intelligible. We have failed then in our first political task because we accepted uncritically an account of "the moral question of abortion" determined by a politics foreign to the polity appropriate to Christian convictions. We have not understood, as Christians, how easily we have presumed that the presuppositions of our "liberal" cultural ethos are "Christian." As a result, our temptation has been to blame the intractability of the abortion controversy on what appears to us as the moral blindness or immorality of pro-abortionists. We fail to see how much of the problem lies in the way we share with the pro-abortion advocates the moral presumptions of our culture.

As Christians we have assumed that we were morally and politically required to express our opposition to abortion in terms acceptable in a pluralist society. To be sure, we did this with depth of conviction, as we assumed those terms were the ones which should inform our understanding of the moral injustice involved in abortion. Hence we could claim that our opposition to abortion was not based on our special theological convictions, but rather founded on the profoundest presumptions of Western culture. All agree murder is wrong; all agree life is sacred; all agree that each individual deserves the protection of law; such surely are the hallmarks of our civilization.

Yet we discovered that not every one agrees about when human life begins. This, we have supposed, is the point of dispute. And no matter how earnestly we tried to document genetically that human life begins at conception, we found many accepting Justice Blackmun's claim that the unborn are not "persons in the whole sense."[1] Philosophically we are told that our assumption that the fetus has moral status confuses the moral sense of being "human" or a "person" with the genetic,[2] and that we have to understand how the intelligibility of the notion of being a human or of being a person is anchored in our civilization's deepest moral values.[3]

Indeed even as strong an anti-abortion advocate as John Noonan has recently suggested that the issue of when human life begins is part of the public controversy that cannot be settled. "It depends on assumptions and judgments about what human beings are and about what human beings should do for one another. These convictions and conclusions are not easily reached by argument. They rest on particular perspectives that are bound to the whole personality and can shift only with a reorientation of the person."[4] But if that is true, then surely we Christians have already lost the battle by letting the enemy determine the terrain on which the battle must be fought.

If the issue is limited to the determination of when human life begins, we cannot prevail, given the moral presuppositions of our culture. When the debate is so limited, it has already been uncritically shaped by the political considerations of our culture, the "moral" has already been determined by the "political," and the very convictions that make us Christian simply never come up. Indeed we have made a virtue of this, since some allege that appeals to religious convictions invalidate our views for the formulation of public policy.[5] As a result the Christian prohibition of abortion appears as an irrational prejudice of religious people who cannot argue it on a secular, rational basis.

But if Noonan is right that the convictions about human life rest on a perspective that is bound up with the "whole personality," then it seems that we Christians must make clear what we take such a "personality" to involve. For the Christian prohibition of abortion is a correlative to being a particular kind of people with a particular set and configuration of virtues. Yet we have tried to form our moral arguments against abortion within the moral framework of a liberal culture, as though the issue could be abstracted from the kind of people we should be. How the moral description and evaluation of abortion depends on more profound assumptions about the kind of people we ought to be was thus not even recognized by ourselves, much less by those who do not share our convictions. As a result Christian arguments about abortion have failed. They have not merely failed to convince, but have failed to suggest the kind of "reorientation" necessary if we are to be the kind of people and society that make abortion unthinkable.

Of course it may be objected that the arguments have not failed. The fact that not everyone agrees that abortion is immoral and the failure to pass a constitutional amendment are of themselves no indication that the anti-abortion arguments have been invalid. Even at the political level there is still good reason to think that all is not lost, for there are political and legal strategies that are just beginning to have an effect on reversing our society's current abortion stance.[6] Yet even if such strategies succeed, our success may still be a form of failure if we "win" without changing the presuppositions of the debate.

To understand why this is the case it is necessary to look more generally at the obstacle to moral agreement in our society. Only from such a perspective can we appreciate why the Christian stance concerning abortion may be a far more fundamental challenge to our society's moral presuppositions than even the most radical anti-abortionists have considered.

2.   Abortion in a Liberal Society

According to Alasdair MacIntyre there is nothing peculiar about the failure of our society to reach a moral consensus concerning the appropriate manner to deal with abortion. Indeed the very character of debate in a liberal, secular, pluralist culture like ours shows that there is no rational method for resolving most significant matters of moral dispute. Any rational method for resolving moral disagreements requires a shared tradition that embodies assumptions about the nature of man and our true end.[7] But it is exactly the presumption of liberalism that a just society can be sustained by freeing the individual from all tradition.[8]

MacIntyre illustrates his argument by calling attention to three different positions concerning abortion:

> A: Everybody has certain rights over their own person, including their own body. It follows from the nature of these rights that at the stage when the embryo is essentially part of the mother's body, the mother has a right to make her uncoerced decision on whether she will have an abortion or not. Therefore each pregnant woman ought to decide and ought to be allowed to decide for herself what she will do in the light of her own moral views.
>
> B: I cannot, if I will to be alive, consistently will that my mother should have had an abortion when she was pregnant with me, except if it had been certain that the embryo was dead or gravely damaged. But if I cannot consistently will this in my own case, how can I consistently deny to others the right to life I claim for myself? I would break the so-called Golden Rule unless I denied that a mother has in general a right to abortion. I am not of course thereby committed to the view that abortion ought to be legally prohibited.
>
> C. Murder is wrong, prohibited by natural and divine law. Murder is the taking of innocent life. An embryo is an identifiable individual, differing from a new-born infant only in being at an earlier stage on the long road to adult capacities. If infanticide is murder, as it is, then abortion is murder. So abortion is not only morally wrong, but ought to be legally prohibited.[9]

MacIntyre suggests the interesting thing about these arguments is that each of the protagonists reaches his conclusion by valid forms of inferences, yet there is no agreement about which premises are the right starting points. And in our culture there is no generally agreed upon procedure for weighing the merits of the rival premises. Each of the above positions represents fragments of moral systems that exist in uneasy relation to one another. Thus position A, premised as "an understanding of rights which owes something to Locke and something to Jefferson is counterposed to a universalibility argument whose debt is first to Kant and then to the gospels and both to an appeal to the moral law as conceived by Hooker, More, and Aquinas."[10]

The fact that these are "fragments" of past moral positions is particularly important. For as fragments they have been torn from the social and intellectual contexts in which they gained their original intelligibility and from which they derive such force and validity as they continue to possess. But since they now exist *only* as fragments, we do not know how to weigh one set of premises against another. We do not know what validity to grant to each in isolation from those presuppositions that sustained their original intelligibility.

To understand the roots of our dilemma, MacIntyre argues that we must look to the moral presuppositions on which our society was founded. For in spite of the appeal to self-evident truths about equality and rights to life, liberty, and the pursuit of happiness, there was the attempt to provide some cogent philosophical basis for these "truths." The difficulty, however, begins when appeals such as Jefferson's to Aristotle and Locke fail to acknowledge these to be mutually antagonistic positions. We are thus a society that may be in the unhappy position of being founded upon a moral contradiction.

The contradiction, in its most dramatic form, involves the impossibility of reconciling classical and modern views of man. Thus as MacIntyre points out:

> the central preoccupation of both ancient and medieval communities was characteristically: how may men together realize the true human good? The central preoccupation of modern men is and has been characteristically: how may we prevent men interfering with each other as each of us goes about our own concerns? The classical view begins with the community of the *polis* and with the individual viewed as having no moral identity apart from the communities of kinship and citizenship; the modern view begins with the concept of a collection of individuals and the problem of how out of and by individuals social institutions can be constructed.[11]

The attempt to answer the last question has been the primary preoccupation of social theorists since the seventeenth century, and their answers to it are not always coherent with one another.

In the face of this disagreement the political consensus has been that the most nearly just social arrangement is one which requires no commitment to any good except the protection of each individual to pursue his or her interests fairly. Thus John Rawls describes the way we ought to envisage the terms of an original contract between individuals on which a just society can be founded as one where they "do not share a conception of the good by reference to which the fruition of their powers or even the satisfaction of their desires can be evaluated. They do not have an agreed criterion of perfection that can be used as a principle for choosing between institutions. To acknowledge any such standard would be, in effect, to accept a principle that might lead to a lesser religious or other liberty."[12]

Such a view can no longer provide a place for the classical perspective's insistence on the development of virtuous people. From the classical perspective judgments about virtues and goods are interdependent, since the good is known only by observing how a virtuous man embodies it. But in the absence of any shared conception of the good, judgments about virtues and judgments about goods are logically independent of one another. Thus it becomes a political necessity, anchored in our society's profoundest moral convictions, that an issue such as abortion be considered on grounds independent of the kind of persons we would like to encourage in our society. The morality of the "act" of abortion must be considered separately from the "agent," for to take the character of the agent into account offends the basic moral and political consensus of our society.

We should be hesitant to criticize the moral achievement of political liberalism too quickly. By making the moral purpose of government the securing of the equal right of all individuals to pursue their happiness as they understand it, liberalism was able to secure political peace in a morally pluralistic and fragmentary society. Its deepest advantage is to remove from the political arena all issues that might be too deeply divisive of the citizenry.[13] The ideal of liberalism is thus to make government neutral on the very subjects that matter most to people, precisely *because* they matter most.

Of course our society has never acted with complete consistency on the principle of neutrality. Thus, we ended slavery, and polygamy was outlawed. And, more recently, the modern welfare function of the state appears to require that certain beliefs about what is good for people be the basis of public policy. But it can still be claimed that the state leaves to individuals and groups the power to determine what private vision of happiness to pursue. "Hence governmental programs to assure full employment, to guarantee equal opportunity to enter the professions, to give everyone as much education as he wants, etc., imply no communal understanding of the good which is to be imposed on all. These programs aim only at establishing the conditions that enable everyone to pursue his own good as he understands it."[14]

One of the ironies, however, is that the liberal state so conceived has worked only because its citizens continued to assume that the classical conception still held some validity for the regulation of their lives. Thus even though the virtues could not be encouraged as a "public" matter, they were still thought important as a private concern and of indirect benefit for our public life. Religion and the family institutions appropriate for the training of virtue were encouraged on the assumption they were necessary to sustain a polity based on the overriding status of the individual.

Thus, as Francis Canavan has argued,

> Liberal democracy has worked as well as it has and as long as it has because it has been able to trade on something that it did not create and which it tends on the whole to undermine. That is the moral tradition that prevailed among the greater part of the people. It is not necessary to pretend that most Americans in the past kept the Ten Commandments,

certainly not that they kept them all the time. It is enough that by and large Americans agreed that there were Ten Commandments and that in principle they ought to be kept. The pluralist solution of withdrawing certain areas of life from legal control worked precisely because American pluralism was not all that pronounced. In consequence, many important areas of life were not withdrawn from the reach of law and public policy and were governed by a quasi-official public ethos.[15]

But in our day the moral consensus has disintegrated in a number of significant respects: we no longer have agreement on the value of human life, or on such basic social institutions as marriage and the family, or for that matter on the meaning of being human.

At this point, it is doubtful whether the typical response of the liberal pluralist society is any longer adequate, that is, to take the dangerously controversial matters out of politics and relegate them to the conscience of individuals. For this way of eliminating controversy in fact does much more. Intentionally or not, it contributes to a reshaping of basic social institutions and a revision of the moral beliefs of multitudes of individuals beyond those directly concerned. It turns into a process by which one ethos, with its reflection in law and public policy, is replaced by another. Liberal pluralism then becomes a sort of confidence game in which, in the guise of showing respect for individual rights, we are in reality asked to consent to a new kind of society based on a new set of beliefs and values.[16]

Perhaps this is nowhere better seen than in the phenomenon that Noonan has called the "masks" of liberty. By masks he means the linguistic conventions that are developing to redescribe the object and means of injustice.[17] Language such as child, baby, and killing have to be avoided, for if such language is used it will require a break with the moral culture we assume we wish to preserve.[18] "If all that has happened may fairly be described as 'termination of a pregnancy' with 'fetal wastage' the outcome, abortion may be accepted without break with the larger moral culture. If, however, such a description is a mask, if the life of an unborn child is being taken, it is difficult to reconcile the acceptance of abortion with the overarching prohibition against the taking of life."[19]

Thus we attempt to change our language so our commitment to greater individual liberty concerning abortion will not contradict our traditional views about what kind of people we should be to deserve to be free. The reason that our arguments concerning abortion are bound to fail is that we cannot resolve the morally antithetical traditions that form our society and our Christian ambitions for ourselves. Attempting to resolve the issue as though the act of abortion could be separated from our conviction about character has been a futile attempt to settle a substantive moral issue on "objective" or procedural grounds acceptable to a liberal culture.

Thus Justice Blackmun's opinion, while no doubt out of harmony with the majority of opinion concerning abortion in America, may actually be in accordance with our deepest views if we apply them more consistently. An indication, perhaps, that we are better off as a people if we fail to think and act consistently! For the underlying presupposition of *Rose* v. *Wade* is consistent liberalism in assuming that the only entity with political standing is the individual. And individuals are understood to consist of characteristics sufficient to make him or her a "person." Of course, as Noonan points out, a liberalism so consistently applied also challenges some of our presumptions about the family,[20] but that may be but another price we have to pay in order to be "free."

Noonan has located the paradox of Justice Blackmun's opinion:

> To invalidate the state abortion statutes it was necessary for him not only to ignore the unborn child but to recognize a liberty anterior to the state in the carrier of the child. The invocation of liberty which was the very heart of his opinion was the invocation of a standard superior to enacted law. His radical use of "higher law" was only disguised by his claim that something in the Constitution supplied the standard by which the state laws on abortion were invalid. The ultimate basis of his decision was nothing in the Constitution but rather his readings of the natural law liberties of an individual.[21]

Blackmun has based his opinion on the most cherished moral presumption of our society: freedom of the individual.[22] Ironically, in the absence of a tradition, the ideal of a society constituted by individuals free of all tradition remains the sole moral basis we have for settling issues of moral significance.

3.   Christians and Abortion: The Philosophical Issues

I showed above how in attempting to form their arguments against abortion in a manner that could be translated into public policy, Christians have accepted the moral limits imposed by our liberal heritage. As a result the reasons that Christians qua Christians should oppose abortion have not become a matter of public record. It should be noted that this was not just a strategic policy, but it also witnesses to our standing conviction of a profound commonality between Christianity and liberalism. Christians have assumed that the liberal commitment to the individual carried with it the prohibition of abortion. Yet what they have found is that the "individual" whom liberalism has an interest in protecting does not, either conceptually or normatively (though perhaps legally), necessarily include the fetus.

Such a discovery is shocking in itself; worse, it seems to leave Christians without further appeal. For we must admit that the fact and way abortion became a matter of moral controversy caught us by surprise and unprepared. We were prepared to argue about whether certain kinds of abortion might or might not be legally prohibited or permitted, but that we would be required to argue whether abortion as an institution is moral, amoral, or immoral was simply unthinkable. As Christians we knew generally that we were against abortion, but we were not clear why. We assumed it surely had to do with our prohibition against the taking of life, and we assumed that that was surely all that needed to be said.

There is nothing unusual about the Christian failure to know why abortion is to be prohibited. Most significant moral prohibitions do not need to be constantly justified or rethought. They are simply part and parcel of the way we are. When asked why we do or do not engage in a particular form of activity we often find that it makes perfectly good sense to say "Christians just do or do not do that kind of thing." And we think that we have given a moral reason. But it is moral because it appeals to "what we are," to what kind of people we think we should be; yet liberalism wishes to exclude such contentions from moral consideration in the interest of securing cooperation in a morally pluralistic society. Liberalism seeks a philosophical account of morality that can ground the rightness or wrongness of particular actions or behavior in a "theory" divorced from any substantive commitments about what kind of people we are or should be—except perhaps to the extent that we should be rational or fair.[23] However, as Stuart Hampshire has argued, such theories falsify the way in which moral injunctions function, such as those about life-taking, sexual relations, relations between parents and children, truth-telling. The meaning and unity between such injunctions cannot be easily inferred from the axioms of a theory. Rather,

> taken together, a full set of such injunctions, prohibiting types of conduct in types of circumstance, describes in rough and indeterminate outline, an attainable and recognisable way of life, aspired to, respected and admired: or at least the minimum general features of a respectworthy way of life. And a way of life is not identified and characterized by one distinct purpose, such as in the increase of general happiness, or even by a set of such distinct purposes. The connection between the injunctions, the connection upon which a reasonable man reflects, is to be found in the coherence of a single way of life, distinguished by the characteristic virtues and vices recognized within it.[24]

Of course ways of life are complicated matters marked out by many details of style and manner. Moreover the "connectedness" of any set of injunctions often has the character, not of "rational" necessity, but rather of a "reasonableness" that derives from the history of a community's moral experience and wisdom. Such a community may well have prohibitions that have an almost absolute character, such as the Christian prohibition of abortion, but such prohibitions need not be categorical, in the Kantian sense, nor based on principles of rationality. Rather they are judgments of unconditioned necessity,

> in the sense that they imply that what must be done is not necessary because it is a means to some independently valued end, but because the action is a necessary part of a way of life and ideal of conduct. The necessity resides in the nature of the action itself, as specified in the fully explicit moral judgment. The principal and proximate grounds for claiming that the action must, or must not, be performed are to be found in the characterization of the action offered within the prescription; and if the argument is pressed further, first a virtue or vice, and then a whole way of life will have to be described.[25]

But I am suggesting that this is exactly what we as Christians failed to do when it came to explaining why abortion is to be avoided. We failed to show, for ourselves or others, why abortion is an affront to our most basic convictions about what makes life meaningful and worthwhile. We tried to argue in terms of the "facts" or on the basis of "principles" and thus failed to make intelligible why such "facts" or "principles" were relevant in the first place. We have spent our time arguing abstractly about when human life does or does not begin.[26] As a result, we have failed to challenge the basic presuppositions that force the debate to hinge on such abstractions.

Hampshire suggests that the best means to avoid the kind of abstract thinking encouraged by moral theories given birth by liberalism is to tell stories. For

> telling stories, with the facts taken from experience and not filtered and at second hand, imposes some principles of selection. In telling the story one has to select the facts and probabilities which, taken together, constitute the situation confronting the agent. Gradually, and by accumulation of examples, belief that the features of the particular case, indefinite in number, are not easily divided into the morally relevant and morally irrelevant will be underlined by the mere process of storytelling. One cannot establish conclusively by argument in general terms the general conclusion that the morally relevant features of situations encountered cannot be circumscribed. One can only appeal to actual examples and call the mind back to personal experience, which will probably include occasions when the particular circumstances of the case modified what would have been the expected and principled deci-

sions, and for reasons which do not themselves enter into any recognized principle.[27]

In a like manner I am suggesting that if Christians are to make their moral and political convictions concerning abortion intelligible we must show how the meaning and prohibition of abortion is correlative to the stories of God and his people that form our basic conviction. We must indicate why it is that the Christian way of life forms people in a manner that makes abortion unthinkable. Ironically it is only when we have done this that we will have the basis for suggesting why the fetus should be regarded as but another of God's children.

For as Roger Wertheimer has shown, arguments concerning the status of the fetus's humanity are not factual arguments at all, but actually moral claims requiring the training of imagination and perception. Wertheimer suggests that the argument over the status of the fetus is a

> paradigm of what Wittgenstein had in mind when he spoke of the possibility of two people agreeing on the application of a rule for a long period, and then, suddenly and quite inexplicably, diverging in what they call going on in the same way. This possibility led him to insist that linguistic communication presupposes not only agreement in definitions, but also agreement in judgments, in what he called forms of life—something that seems lacking in the case at hand (i.e., the fetus). Apparently, the conclusion to draw is that it is not true that the fetus is a human being, but it is not false either. Without agreement in judgments, without a common response to the pertinent data, the assertion that the fetus is a human being cannot be assigned a genuine truth value.[28]

Wertheimer suggests that there seems to be no "natural" response, no clear forms of life, which provide the basis for why the fetus should be regarded one way rather than another. Thus failure to respect the fetus is not analogous to failure to respect blacks or Jews, since we share forms of life, common responses, with them that make the denial of their humanity unintelligible. Thus the forms of life that lead some to believe and treat blacks and Jews as less than human can be shown to be perverse by appeal to obvious factual counterclaims based on our common experiences.

Wertheimer may be right that the case for respect for blacks and Jews is more immediately obvious than the case for the fetus, but I hope to show that the Christian form of life provides powerful reasons why the fetus should be regarded with respect and care. Moreover such respect is as profoundly "natural" as our current belief that blacks and Jews have moral status. What we must understand is that all "natural" relations are "historical" insofar as the natural is but what we have come to accept as "second nature."[29] The recognition of blacks and Jews was no less dependent on a history than the recognition of the status of the fetus. Both are the result of the experience of communities which are formed by substantive convictions of the significance of being open to new life. Because such an "openness" has become so "natural," and often so perverted, we have forgotten what profound moral commitments support and are embodied in the simple and everyday desire and expectation of new life that appears among us through and after pregnancy. Such a desire is obviously not peculiar to Christians, but by attending more directly to the Christian form of life I hope to show why and how the Christian desire for children makes it imperative that the fetus be regarded with respect and care.

4.   Christians and Abortion: The Narrative Context

If my analysis has been correct we should now have a better hold on why arguments concerning abortion have failed in our society. At one level I have tried to show they must fail given the moral presuppositions and language offered by our liberal ethos. But I have also tried to suggest that failure at this level is but an indication of a deeper failure for Christians. Christians have failed their social order by accepting too easily the terms of argument concerning abortion offered by our society. If we are to serve our society well, and on our own terms, our first task must be to address ourselves by articulating for Christians why abortion can never be regarded as morally indifferent for us. Only by doing this can we witness to our society what kind of people and what kind of society is required if abortion is to be excluded.

Such a suggestion may sound extremely odd, since it seems to ask that we reinvent the wheel. Surely that is not the case, for both anti- and pro-abortion advocates know that, rightly or wrongly, Christians have had their minds made up about abortion from the beginning. It is certainly true that Christians, drawing on their Jewish roots, have condemned abortion from earliest days.[30] Yet this condemnation does not come from nowhere; it is a correlative of a way of life that must be constantly renewed and rethought. The task of each new generation of Christians is to rediscover that way of life and why prohibitions such as that against abortion are critical reminders of what kind of life it is that they are called to lead. The Christian way of life, though often lived simply, is no simple matter but involves a complex set of convictions that are constantly being reinterpreted as our understanding of one aspect of the tradition illuminates another. What we must do is show how this process makes a difference for our understanding of the prohibition of abortion.

It is important, furthermore, to distinguish my argument in this respect from those who make the often unfair criticism that the church must rethink its position on abortion because it allows the taking of life in other contexts. Though I do not wish to deny that Christians have often been inconsistent, especially in practice, about the protection and taking of life, there is nothing conceptually inconsistent about the prohibition of abortion as the unjust taking of life and the permissibility of just war and capital punishment. My call for the church to rethink her understanding of abortion involves the more fundamental concern that the church understand why abortion is incompatible with a community whose constitution is nothing less than the story of God's promise to mankind through the calling of Israel and the life of Jesus.

Such a discussion must be both theological and political. One cannot be separated from the other. Our beliefs about God are political, as they form the kind of community that makes the prohibition of abortion intelligible. But the discussion is also political, as it must be done in such a manner that Christians listen and learn from one another concerning their different understanding of what is at stake in abortion. Only by proceeding in this way can we be a paradigm, and perhaps even a witness, to our society of what a genuine moral discussion might look like.

I do not mean to imply that such discussion has been missing entirely in recent Christian history. Yet I think it is fair to say that we have not paid sufficient attention to how Christians as Christians should think about abortion.[31] Indeed I suspect many are not even sure what a call for this kind of discussion entails. Therefore I will try to suggest the kind of theological concerns that any discussion of abortion by Christians should involve.

To begin with, the first question is not, "Why do Christians think abortion is wrong?" To begin there already presupposes that we know and understand what abortion is. Rather, if we are to understand why Christians assume that by naming abortion they have already said something significant, we have to begin still a step back. We have to ask what it is about the kind of community, and corresponding world, that Christians create that makes them single out abortion in such a way as to exclude it.

For we must remember that "abortion" is not a description of a particular kind of behavior; rather it is a word that teaches us to see a singular kind of behavior from a particular community's moral perspective. The removal of the fetus from the mother's uterus before term can be called an "interruption of pregnancy," the child can be called "fetal matter," and the mother can be called a "patient." But from the Christian perspective, to see the situation in that way changes the self and the community in a decisive way. The Christian insistence on the term "abortion" is a way to remind them that what happens in the removal of the fetus from the mother in order to destroy it strikes at the heart of their community. From this perspective the attempt of Christians to be a community where the term "abortion" remains morally intelligible is a political act.

In this respect the pro-abortionists have always been at a disadvantage.[32] For they have had to carry out the argument in a language created by the moral presuppositions of the Jewish and Christian communities. "Abortion" still carries the connotation that this is not a good thing. Thus to be "pro-abortion" seems to put one in an embarrassing position of recommending a less than good thing. It is not without reason, therefore, that pro-abortion advocates seek to redescribe both the object and act of abortion. We must remind them, however, that by doing so they not only change the description of the act, they also change themselves.

Christians insist on the significance of such a change by refusing to live in a world devoid of abortion as a moral description—a world which admittedly may, as a result, involve deep tragedy. There can be no doubt that the insistence that unjust termination of pregnancy be called "abortion" has to do with our respect for life, but that is surely too simple. Jews and Christians are taught to respect life, not as an end in itself, but as a gift created by God. Thus life is respected because all life serves God in its way. Respect for human life is but a form of our respect for all life.

But note that just as no particular life can claim highest value, except as it exists for the love and service of God, neither can human life be thought to have absolute value. The Christian prohibition against taking life rests not on the assumption that human life has overriding value, but on the conviction that it is not ours to take. The Christian prohibition of abortion derives not from any assumption of the inherent value of life, but rather from the understanding that as God's creatures we have no basis to claim sovereignty over life.

And we cannot forget that this creator is also our redeemer. The life that lies in the womb is also a life that has come under the lordship of Jesus Christ. As Karl Barth has said,

> this child is a man for whose life the Son of God has died, for whose unavoidable part in the guilt of all humanity and future individual guilt He has already paid the price. The true light of the world shines already in the darkness of the mother's womb. And yet they want to kill him deliberately because certain reasons which have nothing to do with the child himself favor the view that he had better not be born! Is there any emergency which can justify this? It must surely be clear to us that until the question is put in all its gravity a serious discussion of the problem cannot even begin, let alone lead to serious results.[33]

The temptation, in this secular age, is to ignore this kind of rhetorical flourish on the assumption that all it really amounts to is that Christians also believe in the value or sacredness of life. But from the perspective of Christian convictions about life as the locus of God's creating and redeeming purpose, claims of life's "value" or "sacredness" are but empty abstractions. The value of life is God's value and our commitment to protect it is a form of our worship of God as a good creator and a trustworthy redeemer. Our question is not "When does life begin?" but "Who is its true sovereign?" The creation and meaningfulness of the term "abortion"[3] gain intelligibility from our conviction that God, not man, is creator and redeemer, and thus, the Lord of life. The Christian respect for life is first of all a statement, not about life, but about God.[34]

Yet the way of life of Christians involves more than the conviction of God's creating and redeeming purposes. We also believe that God has created and called us to be a people whose task it is to manifest and witness to his providential care of our existence. Thus to be a Christian is not just to hold certain beliefs, but it is to be part of a historic community that has the task of maintaining faithful continuity with our forebears. To be a Christian is to be part of a people who live through memory, since we only know how to face and create our future by striving to be as faithful and courageous as our forebears. The necessity of memory for our continued existence is but a form of our worship of our God, who wills to be known through the lives of his followers.

Christians are thus a people who have an immense stake in history. We look neither to escape nor to transcend history. Rather we are determined to live within history, hopefully living faithful to the memory of our founder. There is no conviction, therefore, more significant for Christians than our insistence on having children. For children are our anchors in history, our pledge and witness that the Lord we serve is the Lord, not only of our community, but of all history. The family is, therefore, symbolically central for the meaning of the existence of the Christian people.

From a Christian perspective children represent our continuing commitment to live as a historic people.[35] In the Christian community children are, for those who are called to be married, a duty. For the vocation of marriage in part derives its intelligibility from a couple's willingness to be open to new life. Indeed that is part of the test of the validity of their unity as one worthy to be called "love" in the Christian sense. It must necessarily be open to creation of another.

The Christian community's openness to new life and our conviction of the sovereignty of God over that life are but two sides of the same conviction. Christians believe that we have the time in this existence to care for new life, especially as such life is dependent and vulnerable, because it is not our task to rule this world or to "make our mark on history." We can thus take the time to live in history as God's people who have nothing more important to do than to have and care for children. For it is the Christian claim that knowledge and love of God is fostered by service to the neighbor, especially the most helpless, as in fact that is where we find the kind of Kingdom our God would have us serve.

It is the Christian belief, nurtured by the command of Jesus, that we must learn to love one another, that we become more nearly what we were meant to be through the recognition and love of those we did not "choose" to love. Children, the weak, the ill, the dispossessed provide a particularly intense occasion for such love, as they are beings we cannot control. We must love them for what they are rather than what we want or wish them to be, and as a result we discover that we are capable of love. The existence of such love is not unique or limited to Christians. Indeed that is why we have the confidence that our Christian convictions on these matters might ring true even for those who do not share our convictions. The difference between the Christian and the non-Christian is only that what is a possibility for the non-Christian is a duty for the Christian.

But the Christian duty to welcome new life is a joyful duty, as it derives from our very being as God's people. Moreover correlative to the language of duty is the language of gift. Because children are a duty they can also be regarded as gift, for duty teaches us to accept and welcome a child into the world, not as something that is "ours," but as a gift which comes from another.[36] As a result Christians need not resort to destructive and self-deceiving claims about the qualities they need to have, or the conditions of the world necessary to have children. Perhaps more worrisome than the moral implications of the claim "no unwanted child ought ever to be born," are the ominous assumptions about what is required for one to "want" to have a child.

Christians are thus trained to be the kind of people who are ready to receive and welcome children into the world. For they see children as a sign of the trustworthiness of God's creation and his unwillingness to abandon the world to the powers of darkness. The Christian prohibition of abortion is but the negative side of their positive commitment to welcome new life into their community: life that they know must challenge and perhaps even change their own interpretation of their tradition, but also life without which the tradition has no means to grow.

It is, of course, true that children will often be conceived and born under less than ideal conditions, but the church lives as a community which assumes that we live in an age which is always dangerous. That we live in such a time is all the more reason we must be the kind of community that can receive children into our midst. Just as we need to be virtuous, not because virtue pays but because we cannot afford to be without virtue where it does not pay, so we must learn how to be people open to new life. We can neither protect them from that suffering nor deny them the joy of participating in the adventure of God's Kingdom.

For Christians, therefore, there can be no question of whether the fetus is or is not a "human being." That way of putting the matter is far too abstract and formal. Rather, because of the kind of community we are, we see in the fetus nothing less than God's continuing creation that is destined in hope to be another citizen of his Kingdom. The question of when human life begins is of little interest to such a people, since their hope is that life will and does continue to begin time after time.[37]

This is the form of life that brings significance to our interaction with the fetus. Our history is the basis for our "natural" sympathies, which have been trained to look forward to the joy and challenge of new life. Wertheimer may well be right that there is no corresponding "natural" welcome for life in our society that would make intelligible the recognition of the fetus as having moral status. Yet I suspect that the expectation of parents, and in particular of women, for the birth of their children remains a powerful form of life that continues to exert a force on everyone. Such an "expectation," however, in the absence of more substantive convictions about parenting, too easily becomes a destructive necessity that distorts the experience of being a parent and a child. Particularly repugnant is the assumption that women are thus primarily defined by the role of "mother," for then we forget that the role of being a parent, even for the childless, is a responsibility for everyone in the Christian community.

Nor should it be thought that the Christian commitment to welcome new life into the world stems from a sentimental fondness for babies. Rather, for Christians the having of children is one of their most significant political acts. From the world's perspective the birth of a child represents but another drain on our material and psychological resources. Children, after all, take up much of our energy that could be spent on making the world a better place and our society more just. But from the Christian perspective the birth of a child represents nothing less than our commitment that God will not have this world "bettered" by destroying life. That is why there is no more profound political act for Christians than taking the time for children. It is but an indication that God, not man, rules this existence, and we have been graciously invited to have a part in God's adventure and his Kingdom through the simple action of having children.

5. Christians and Abortion: The Immediate Political Task

To some it may seem that I have argued Christians right out of the current controversy, for my argument has made appeal to religious convictions that are inadmissable in the court of our public ethos. But it has certainly not been my intention to make it implausible for Christians to continue to work in the public arena for the protection of all children; nor do I think that this implication follows from the position I have developed. Of course, Christians should prefer to live in societies that provide protection for children. And

Christians should certainly wish to encourage those "natural" sentiments that would provide a basis for having and protecting children.

Moreover Christians must be concerned to develop forms of care and support, the absence of which seem to make abortion such a necessity in our society. In particular Christians should, in their own communities, make clear that the role of parent is one we all share. Thus the woman who is pregnant and carrying the child need not be the one to raise it. We must be a people who stand ready to receive and care for any child, not just as if it were one of ours, but because in fact each is one of ours.

But as Christians we must not confuse our political and moral strategies designed to get the best possible care for children in our society with the substance of our convictions. Nor should we hide the latter in the interest of securing the former. For when that is done we abandon our society to its own limits. And then our arguments fall silent in the most regrettable manner, for we forget that our most fundamental political task is to be and to point to that truth which we believe to be the necessary basis for any life-enhancing and just society.

In particular, I think that we will be wise as Christians to state our opposition to abortion in a manner that makes clear our broader concerns for the kind of people we ought to be to welcome children into the world. Therefore, rather than concentrating our energies on whether the fetus is or is not a "person," we would be better advised by example and then argument to make clear why we should hope it is a child. We must show that such a hope involves more than just the question of the status of the fetus, but indeed is the very reason why being a part of God's creation is such an extraordinary and interesting adventure.

Notes

1: A STORY-FORMED COMMUNITY

1. The idea for using theses in this manner I got not from Luther but Peter Berger in his book *Pyramids of Sacrifice* (New York: Anchor Books, 1976).

2. Thus John Howard Yoder argues that "the triumph of the right is assured not by the might that comes to aid of the right, which is of course the justification of the use of violence and other kinds of power in every human conflict; the triumph of the right, although it is assured, is sure because of the power of the resurrection and not because of the inherently greater strength of the good guys. The relationship between the obedience of God's people and the triumph of God's cause is not a relationship of cause and effect but one of cross and resurrection." *The Politics of Jesus* (Grand Rapids, Mich.: Eerdmans, 1972), p. 238.

3. For at least a beginning defense of the significance of narrative for moral rationality see my *Truthfulness and Tragedy: Further Investigations in Christian Ethics* (Notre Dame, Ind.: University of Notre Dame Press, 1977).

4. Richard Adams, *Watership Down* (New York: Avon Books, 1972). All page references to *Watership Down* will be made in the text.

5. Robert Paul Wolff has pointed out how each form of society has a corresponding virtue in his *The Poverty of Liberalism* (Boston: Beacon Press, 1968), p. 123.

6. Alasdair MacIntyre, "Epistemological Crisis, Dramatic Narrative, and the Philosophy of Science," *Monist,* 60/4 (October, 1977), pp. 460–461. The general debt this paper owes to MacIntyre's work will be obvious to those familiar with his position. I have relied on MacIntyre's occasional essays; however, his *After Virtue* (Notre Dame, Ind.: University of Notre Dame Press, 1981) will soon be published. There MacIntyre systematically develops his position in a powerful and compelling manner.

7. See, for example, Simone Weil's powerful reflections on this theme in her *The Iliad or The Poems of Force* (Wallingford, Pa.: Pendle Hill Pamphlet, 1964).

8. Langdon Gilkey provides an insightful analysis of fate in his *Reaping the Whirlwind* (New York: Seabury Press, 1976), pp. 49–50.

9. Our culture has unfortunately confused the moral significance of gift giving by assuming that what is important is giving rather than receiving. As a result we have failed to pay adequate attention to the difficulty of knowing how to receive a gift. For nothing is harder than knowing how to simply accept a gift and be thankful for it. We fear the power of the gift-giver and want to do something in return so we will not be in debt. Pipkin's gift was the ability to accept gifts without assuming that he owed anyone anything in return, and also not to feel resentment that he was the one that had to receive the gifts. Of course, Pipkin's ability to receive gifts depended on his community sense that they would not have it otherwise.

For further reflections on this theme, particularly as it challenges how the commitment to equality can too easily be used to deny the importance of diversity for a good polity, see my "Community and Diversity: The Tyranny of Normality," in *National Apostolate for the Mentally Retarded Quarterly,* 8/2 (Summer 1977), pp. 20–22.

10. One of the most persistent problems with the liberal understanding of society is how to account for and legitimate authority. As John Rawls says clearly, it is the primary purpose of liberalism to make "society a cooperative venture for mutual advantage." *A Theory of Justice* (Cambridge, Mass.: Harvard University Press, 1971), p. 4. In other words, it is the intention to supplant the need for leadership with procedural rules of fair play. The continued phenomenon of leadership in society thus can only appear to the liberal as due to the incomplete institutionalization of liberal principles. Robert Nozick is, perhaps, a clearer example of the tendency of liberalism to assume that some kind of invisible-hand explanation of state power and authority is possible. See his *Anarchy, State, and Utopia* (New York: Basic Books, 1968), pp. 10–25.

A correlate of the liberal attempt to avoid providing an account of legitimate authority is their assumption that society can be construed as a voluntary venture. It is the function of liberal theory to convince us that we can choose our own story, that we are free from the past, that our participation in society is "voluntary." There is perhaps no better metaphor for this than Rawls' utilization of the "original position," where we are explicitly stripped of all history in an effort to have us assume the "moral point of view." Even though one can appreciate the powerful moral motivation behind Rawls' method, he fails to give an adequate account of how our social order is as much our fate as it is our destiny. As a result, liberalism can become self-deceptive, as it gives us the illusion that freedom is more a status than a task. See, for example, Richard Sennett's insightful analysis of the deceptions involved when "autonomy" is claimed to replace "authority" in his *Authority* (New York: Knopf, 1980), pp. 84–121.

11. It is important to point out that the stories of El-ahrairah are not only told, but told at the right time. Thus, for example, the story of the "Trial of El-ahrairah," which involves El-ahrairah's use of other animals, is told as they are beginning to develop Watership Down, i.e., just before Hazel's care of Kehaar, the wounded gull. Adams seems to be suggesting that good communities not only know how to tell truthful stories truthfully, but also when to tell them.

12. Contemporary political and ethical theory seems to ignore entirely the nature and social signficiance of friendship and other special relations such as the family. As a result we are left devoid of any language that can help articulate the significance of friendship and the family for our personal and political existence.

13. Alasdair MacIntyre has argued that our culture lacks a moral scheme which might provide "a vision" of man's true end, of the relation of his empirical nature to his essential nature. "It is a tacit assumption of secular, liberal, pluralist culture, of the culture of modernity, that to a rational man no such vision is now available, because we can have no rationally defensible concept of man's true end or of an essential human nature. Consequently, what we inherit from the varied and different strands of our past is a collection of fragments, of moral premises detached from the contexts in which they were once at home, survivals now available for independent moral assertion from a variety of moral points of view. It is this that makes moral argument appear to consist merely of the clash of bare assertion and counterassertion, marked by what is only the appearance of argument, so that nonrational persuasion seems to be the only way for an agent to resolve the issues in his own mind." "How Virtues Become Vices," *Evaluation and Explanation in the Biomedical Sciences,* edited by H. T.

Engelhardt and Stuart Spicker (Boston: Reidel Publishing, 1974), p. 100. See also MacIntyre's, "An Essay Prepared for the National Commission for the Protection of Human Subjects of Biomedical and Behavior Research on the Subject of How to Identify Ethical Principles," *The Belmont Report* (Washington, D.C.: DHEW Publications, 1978), article 10, pp. 1-20, 41. From this perspective the commitment of liberal political and ethical theory to the autonomy of the individual is not so much a rational necessity as it is the only practical alternative. The problem with such a strategy, however, is that it only leads us further away from confronting our situation, as we fail to see the narratives that in fact constitue our "autonomy."

14. For one of the few attempts to provide a philosophically adequate account of luck, see Bernard Williams, "Moral Luck," *Aristotelian Society Supplementary Volume* 50 (1976), pp. 114-135. Williams makes an important distinction between luck that is intrinsic to my project and luck that is extrinsic, but points out that knowing how to make such a distinction in respect to our own lives is extremely difficult. He also rightly criticizes Rawls' claim that the guiding principle of a rational individual is to act so that he need never blame himself for how things turn out. For such a view "implicitly ignores the obvious fact that what one does and the sort of life one leads condition one's later desires and judgments: the standpoint of that retrospective judge who will be my later self will be the product of my earlier choices," pp. 130-131. In other words, Rawls fails to see that my "autonomy" depends exactly on my being able to accept responsibility for what I have not, strictly speaking, "done."

15. It may be that the popularity of *Watership Down* denotes a change of consciousness in our culture. For it was just a few years ago that the Kennedy administration represented the "can do" mentality of our society. If we have a problem, then it is bound to be solvable by well-trained people using the amazing technology developed by our scientists. However, since then we have found ourselves brought to a halt by our lack of oil, our solutions seem to cause as many problems as they solve, and ecologically we are damned if we do and damned if we do not. In other words, it may be that we identify with rabbits because we suddenly feel that like them we do not have control of our world. But even more disturbing we do not know how to get control of our world, nor are we sure how to live in such a world.

16. I suspect the continual return of natural law is best explained as an indication that our "nature" seldom tells us what we ought to do but often tells us what we are doing is inappropriate. Thus natural law is primarily a test, as the "principles" of natural law are means to sensitize us to ways our nature can and may be distorted. The traditional claim that the Christian life is in harmony with natural law is a promissory note that Christian existence stands ready to be challenged by "nature." It has been a mistake, however, to assume Christian ethics can therefore begin on the basis of clearly articulated "principles" of natural law. For the "principles" of natural law are only known through the articulation of a positive tradition.

17. *Watership Down* is obviously not a book that women liberationists will find very satisfactory. However it is at least worth observing that Hyzenthlay's affirmation of being a doe made her the freest of the rabbits at Efrafa. For every society corrupts us by tempting us to identify with the ends of the society in order to do good as a means for personal aggrandizement. Those who are the "outs" in a society often have the best perspective to appreciate the coercive aspects of a social order, since they are not easily tempted to accept the stated idealizations of their society.

2: JESUS: THE STORY OF THE KINGDOM

1. Alasdair MacIntyre, *Difficulties in Christian Belief* (New York: Philosophical Library, 1959), p. 118. I am not suggesting that the truthfulness of Christianity or any

other faith depends only on exemplary lives, but rather whatever the rationale for religious truth claims, they are inseparable from such lives. Individual challenges to the coherence of religious belief will need to be dealt with individually. It is often thought that the truthfulness of religious belief is dependent on one's being able to provide a foundational account of truth; in contrast I am suggesting that the truthfulness of religious convictions needs no "foundation" that is separable from the claims themselves. Even though this is an issue of religious epistemology, it has christological implications, since foundationalist accounts always tend to make Jesus' particularity accidental to the meaning of the "Christ-event." For positions similar to the one I am suggesting, see Diogenes Allen, "Motives, Rationales, and Religious Beliefs," *American Philosophical Quarterly,* 3/2 (April 1966), pp. 1–17, and James McClendon and James Smith, *Understanding Religious Convictions* (Notre Dame, Ind.: University of Notre Dame Press, 1975).

2. St. Athanasius, *The Incarnation of the Word of God* (New York: Macmillan, 1946), p. 96.

3. See, for example, George Hutson Williams, "Christology and Church-State Relations in the Fourth Century," *Church History,* 20/3 and 4 (September 1951, December 1951), pp. 3–33; 3–26.

4. It is instructive, for example, that most christologies are written with almost no concern for the social form of Jesus' work or the sociological situation of the church. At best authors may include a last chapter on the "social-ethical implications." Without denying much valuable work is thereby done, it is my contention that to so structure one's christology is to distort the kind of messiah Jesus was. I have in mind such significant and sophisticated presentations as those of Pannenberg, Rahner, Kasper, and Barth. A recent notable exception is Jon Sobrino's, *Christology at the Crossroads* (Maryknoll, N.Y.: Orbis Books, 1978). I am in deep sympathy with Sobrino's intention, especially as he locates discipleship as a central christological motive. Moreover, unlike much of "liberation theology," he carefully controls the meaning of "liberation" by insisting that its meaning be christologically controlled. (I continue to doubt, however, if "liberation" should be the central metaphor to describe Christian life and existence, especially in the light of Sobrino's sensitive discussion of the place of suffering in the Christian life.) I am also sympathetic with his emphasis on the "historical Jesus," though I am doubtful whether his thesis that Jesus' understanding of the Kingdom changed at the middle of his career can be historically established. Moreover, Sobrino seems to fail to appreciate that the demand to recover a "historical Jesus" separate from the Gospels is a historical abstraction. Sobrino rightly emphasizes, however, that classical christological formulations, including claims about "incarnation," must come at the end, not at the beginning, of our christological reflection.

5. John Howard Yoder, *The Politics of Jesus* (Grand Rapids, Mich.: Eerdmans, 1972), pp. 15–19. My indebtness to Yoder's position throughout should be evident.

6. Ernst Troeltsch, *The Social Teaching of the Christian Churches* (New York: Macmillan, 1931), p. 50. Bill Garrett and Max Stackhouse have pointed out to me that Troeltsch can be interpreted in a manner more sympathetic to my thesis. That may well be, but I remain convinced that Troeltsch, though critical of some forms of "church type," remained committed to a liberal version of a "church type" strategy.

7. Troeltsch, pp. 39–40.

8. Yoder, pp. 16–19.

9. For example, Duane Friesen documents that Troeltsch's own understanding of the church-world problem was Lutheran, and his typology was thus biased, since it made the social ethic of the church type appear to be the only viable alternative. "Normative Factors in Troeltsch's Typology of Religious Association," *Journal of*

Religious Ethics, 3/2 (Fall 1975), pp. 271–283. H. R. Niebuhr's famous typology, developed in *Christ and Culture* (New York: Harper, 1951), is more adequate, but in spite of Niebuhr's attempt not to favor one type over the other, his general preference for the "Christ Transforming Culture" type seems evident.

10. Richard McCormick, "Christianity and Morality," *Catholic Mind,* 75 (October 1977), p. 18.

11. McCormick, p. 28. One would like to have a fuller discussion from McCormick about what the christological implications are for the claim that Jesus is normative only because he experienced what it means to be *human* in the fullest manner. Where, for example, did McCormick find out what it means to be human? If that is determined on grounds prior to Jesus, then is Jesus simply the best example we have of such an experience? If so, then why prefer Jesus to Moses or Buddha? To be fair, McCormick is not alone in his failure as an ethicist to develop the christological implications of his position, for that is generally the case.

12. Philip Wogaman, *A Christian Method of Moral Judgment* (Philadelphia: Westminster Press, 1976), p. 185.

13. Ibid., p. 193. By "extrinsic forms of motivation" I assume Wogaman means violence.

14. Ibid., p. 104.

15. The work of Reinhold Niebuhr and Paul Ramsey are particularly interesting from this perspective. Niebuhr was of course explicit about the irrelevancy of Jesus for social ethics except as he provided an indiscriminate norm that stands in judgment over all social activity. In spite of his criticism of the social gospel, much of Niebuhr's christology continued in the vein of treating Jesus not as the redeemer but as the perfect example or teacher of love. Ramsey seems to be trying to develop a more "orthodox" christology, though his emphasis on love as the essence of Jesus' teaching may continue to separate the teacher from the teaching. Thus at least early in his career Ramsey was willing to justify picking and choosing among Jesus' "teachings." In *Basic Christian Ethics* (New York: Scribner's, 1950) he argues that "the radical content of Jesus' strenuous sayings depends, it seems, on his apocalyptic expectation. As a consequence they cannot be translated from their mother tongue without danger of serious loss of meaning. We cannot, for example, recommend non-resistence or returning good for evil as obvious to the degree in which anger or impure thoughts or even anxiety may be discouraged among men and sabbath observances set aside. Therefore, non-resistance has frequently first been turned into non-violent resistance, and this then generalized to fit perhaps any age or circumstance. Jesus' original teaching about non-resistance seems in contrast to suit only an apocalyptic perspective," p. 35. In the absence of such a perspective Ramsey concludes that such a teaching cannot be literally followed.

16. I am sympathetic with José Segundo's claim that every theology is political, and that is especially true of "academic theology's" pretentious assumption that it is not "political." I am less sure than Segundo that it is easy to characterize "academic theology," but he is certainly correct that much of the theology done in our universities ignores its tie with the political status-quo. Such theology is surely in "bad-faith" when it tries to defeat "liberation theology" by accusing it of politicizing theology. Given that, however, I find Segundo's general position misleading if not perverse. By turning everything into ideology, even if by the latter you only mean a system that serves as a necessary backdrop of any human action, Segundo makes the question of truth irrelevant. And by denying the question of truth we also make Jesus irrelevant. He fails to see that it is not sufficient to claim that every theology is political, but more important is the question of the kind of politics required by the Gospel. For the political power of the Gospel is exactly its ability to provide the critical skills necessary to free

us from those ideologies that would claim our lives. José Segundo, *Liberation of Theology* (Maryknoll, N.Y.: Orbis Books, 1976).

17. Yoder, p. 106.

18. Nils Dahl argues that we cannot draw a sharp distinction between the Gospel message and the recollection of the apostles, as that is a distinction that early Christianity did not know. "On the contrary, for the evangelists—and we dare add, for the apostles themselves—it was precisely the encounter of the apostles with the resurrected Christ that revived their recollection of his earthly life." *Jesus in the Memory of the Early Church* (Minneapolis: Augsburg, 1976), p. 27. Leander Keck has developed a powerful argument that there is a stronger continuity between the "historical Jesus" and the "faith of the disciples" than the Bultmann school assumed. See his *A Future for the Historical Jesus* (Nashville: Abingdon Press, 1971).

19. Yoder, p. 107. Julian Hartt contends "The distinction between faith in Jesus Christ and the faith Jesus Christ himself held, is theologically unreal and Christianly unimportant. Even if historical scholarship were able to uncover the 'faith' Jesus Christ held in the same sense in which the historian might be able to tell us what faith Abraham Lincoln held, we would have in that alone an insufficient reason, if a reason at all, for making the distinction here rejected." *A Christian Critique of American Culture* (New York: Harper and Row, 1967), p. 181.

20. Keck, p. 19.

21. Wolfhart Pannenberg, *Jesus—God and Man* (Philadephia: Westminster Press, 1968), pp. 164–165.

22. Keck, p. 127.

23. Walter Kasper, *Jesus the Christ* (New York: Paulist Press, 1977), p. 238.

24. See, for example, James McClendon's *Biography as Theology* (Nashville: Abingdon Press, 1974), pp. 127–128. The problem with the doctrine of the "incarnation" is that it too often becomes an object in itself rather than directing us to the kind of life necessary to appreciate what it means to say that Jesus' life is the revelation of God.

25. Though my general christological approach is closer to those that want to do christology from "below," I generally find the contrast between christology from "above" or "below" less than helpful. See, for example, Peter Hodgson's criticism of that way of conceiving the issue in *Jesus—Word and Presence* (Philadelphia: Fortress Press, 1971), pp. 60–71. He says, "What is needed is a way of avoiding the supernaturalism and docetism of the Logos-flesh christology, of overcoming the subjectivistic bias of a self-transcending anthropology, and of moving beyond the impasse of the doctrine of the two natures entirely, while at the same time holding radically to the historical man Jesus as the criterion of christology," p. 71.

26. Pannenberg, p. 47.

27. Those that are usually identified with a "low christology," often appear more tolerant. For by placing Jesus' significance in his moral teaching or his personality it seems what is important is whether someone exemplifies the morality rather than learn to follow Jesus. However, what many fail to notice is when Jesus is primarily treated as the perfect example or teacher of morality he turns out to be remarkably anti-Semitic. For then it must be shown that the Jews were somehow morally deficient, if not degenerate, to reject the obvious moral superiority of Jesus. Nowhere can this be more clearly seen than in Kant's portrayal of the Jews. He thus claims that in contrast to the Christian commitment to universal morality, "Judaism is really not a religion at all but merely a union of a number of people who, since they belonged to a particular stock, formed themselves into a commonwealth under purely political laws, and not into a church; nay, it was intended to be merely an earthly state so that, were it possibly

to be dismembered through adverse circumstances, there would still remain to it the political faith in its eventual reestablishment." *Religion Within the Limits of Reason Alone* (New York: Harper Torchbooks, 1960), p. 116. The "liberal" condemnation of the Jews is often attributed to ignorance of Judaism, but I am suggesting that it is structurally built into their position. The liberals' failure to appreciate the particularity of Jesus is a correlative of their assumption of the backwardness of the Jews. Ironically enough, and given proper qualifications, Kant's characterization of the Jews above is very close to my view of what the church, and its corresponding christology, should entail. Central to my position is the assumption that Jesus' significance can only be appreciated by recognizing the continued significance of Judaism.

28. Walter Rauschenbusch, *Theology of the Social Gospel* (Nashville: Abingdon Press, 1917), pp. 146–187. I think there are other aspects of Rauschenbusch's position, however, that qualify his more explicit christological claims in a manner not too unlike the position I am trying to develop.

29. James Gustafson, *Christ and the Moral Life* (New York: Harper and Row, 1968), p. 183.

30. Hans Frei, *The Identity of Jesus Christ* (Philadelphia: Fortress Press, 1975), p. 65.

31. Frei, p. 59.

32. George Hendry, *The Gospel of the Incarnation* (London: SCM Press, 1959), p. 31.

33. Kasper, p. 17.

34. From this perspective I am sympathetic with Kasper's criticism of Rahner's christology. He rightly observes that Rahner takes too little notice of the fact that the true reality of "history implies a determination of the transcendental conditions affecting the possibility of understanding. It is a determination which is not derivable from and not wholly conceivable in terms of those conditions," pp. 48–52.

35. Warren Groff, *Christ the Hope of the Future* (Grand Rapids, Mich.: Eerdmans, 1971), p. 47.

36. Pannenberg, p. 205.

37. In some ways the position I am defending has close affinities with Abelard's "subjective" theory of the atonement, but I hope to avoid some of the legitimate criticisms of that theory by emphasizing the moral context and meaning of the way Jesus affects us.

38. Frei rightly argues that "if the Gospel story is to function religiously in a way that is at once historical and christological, the central focus will have to be on the history-like narration of the final sequence, rather than on Jesus' sayings in the preaching pericopes. . . . Jesus' individual identity comes to focus directly in the passion-resurrection narrative rather than in the account and teaching in his earlier ministry. It is in this final and climatic sequence that the storied Jesus is most of all himself, and there—unlike those earlier points at which we can get to his individual identity only ambiguously—we are confronted with him directly as an unsubstitutable individual who is what he does and undergoes and is manifested directly as who he is," pp. 141–142.

39. Kasper, p. 81.

40. Karl Barth, *Church Dogmatics* II/2 (Edinburgh: T. and T. Clark, 1957), p. 177.

41. Origen, "Commentary on Matthew," in *Ante-Nicene Fathers* (New York: Scribner's, 1926), p. 498.

42. Hartt, pp. 166–167.

43. Hartt, p. 198. Jesus is the son of God, therefore, to the extent he is the agent of the Kingdom. The quandary of how to account for the unity of his person in the traditional very God-very man formulas is less a problem from this perspective. Jesus' Sonship rests on his perfect obedience to the cross and his divinity is thus the form of his humanity.

44. The influence of some of the work in sociology of religion and knowledge is beginning to have a fruitful effect on the kind of work that is done in New Testament ethics. For example, even though John Gager's *Kingdom and Community* (Englewood Cliffs, N.J.: Prentice-Hall, 1975), implicitly seems to have a destructive intent, his methodology makes clear that "despite protests to the contrary, the churches from the very beginning presented Rome with a serious problem. Christians were constantly amazed to find themselves cast as enemies of the Roman Order, but in retrospect we must admit that it was the Romans who had the more realistic insight," pp. 27–28. Or as Leander Keck observes, pursuing the "concern for the ethos of early Christians, and the relation of the NT to it, would recast the study of early Christian ethics and theology. NT ethics would no longer be confined to any analysis of the ways in which the dialectic of indicative and imperative becomes concrete, nor would it be presented as a series of attempts to apply principles to situations or to spell out the Christian ideal. Once the ethos of Christians came into view, it would become clear that NT ethics was sweated out of the interaction between the ethos and the gospel, an interaction which in turn helped to produce an ongoing ethos." "On the Ethos of Early Christians," *Journal of American Academy of Religion,* 43/3 (September 1974), p. 451. For an excellent review of some of the recent work on early Christianity's social background, see Gager's review of Grant, Malherbe, and Theissen in *Religious Studies Review,* 5/3 (July 1979), pp. 174–180.

45. Keck, *A Future for the Historical Jesus,* p. 245.

46. Walter Rauschenbusch, *The Righteousness of the Kingdom* (Nashville: Abingdon Press, rpt. 1968), pp. 92–93.

47. Kasper, p. 102. Kasper makes some very interesting suggestions how various aspects of Jesus' life implicitly rest on assumption of his authority as the messiah. His kind of approach has much to commend it as it avoids the concern with Jesus' consciousness and instead concentrates on his life. The historical and philosophical difficulties connected with the question of the messianic consciousness make that way of asking the question fruitless. Rather it is better to ask Did this man teach and act with authority?

48. Frei, p. 159. Put differently, Peter had not learned, indeed, could not have yet learned at this point, that "Christ" cannot be separated from Jesus. For the kind of "Lord" Jesus is, is revealed finally only on the cross, thus making it impossible to separate the meaning of being "the anointed one" from his life. Too often the attempt to substantiate who Jesus was by trying to find the meaning of the various titles in the Gospel fails to acknowledge that the titles are given new meaning from the narrative. As Sobrino suggests, "The theological importance of the name 'Jesus Christ,' then, is that the two words are brought together. The abstract term cannot be separated from the concrete name. Isolated from the proper name, the term 'Christ' is an abstract honorific into which people can project all sorts of ideas and yearnings. It could become the basis for *some* new religion, in the pejorative sense of that term. But the term loses its abstract air if it is linked with the proper name 'Jesus,' " p. 285.

49. Yoder, p. 61.

50. Ibid., p. 101. See also my "Ethics and Ascetical Theology" *Anglican Theological Review,* 61/1 (January 1979), pp. 87–98.

51. Ibid., p. 132.

52. The way the early Christians put this was simply that with Jesus a new "aeon" had begun. Such an "aeon" is not simply a "worldview" but requires that a social world be created in accordance with the new social relations envisaged. Elsewhere I have tried to suggest the Christian story teaches us to see the world differently, but such seeing requires a community if such a vision is to be sustained. See my *Vision and Virtue* (Notre Dame, Ind.: Fides, 1974).

53. Anthony Burgess has recently put this well as he points out "the technique of loving others has to be learned, like any other technique. The practice of love is, we may say, ludic; it has to be approached like a game. It is necessary first to learn to love oneself, which is difficult; love of others will follow more easily then, however. The serious practitioners of the game, or *ludus amoris,* will find it useful to form themselves into small groups, or 'churches,' and meet at set intervals for mutual encouragement and inspiration." "Love and Sin in 1985," *New York Times Book Review,* August 13, 1978, p. 3.

54. For a further development of this point, see my "Politics of Charity," in *Truthfulness and Tragedy* (Notre Dame, Ind.: University of Notre Dame Press, 1977), pp. 132–143.

55. I have not explicitly tried to suggest how the resurrection is an integral aspect of Jesus' story, though it certainly is. As Frei suggests, the gospels seem to be saying something like this: "Our argument is that to grasp what this identity, Jesus of Nazareth (which has been made directly accessible to us), is is to believe that he has been, in fact, raised from the dead. Someone may reply that in that case the most perfectly depicted character and most nearly lifelike fictional identity ought always in fact to have lived a factual historical life. We answer that the argument holds good only in this one and absolutely unique case, where the described entity (who or what he is, i.e., Jesus Christ, the presence of God) is totally identical with his factual existence. He *is* the resurrection and the life. How can he be conceived as not resurrected?" pp. 145-146. It is, of course, true that the only Jesus the gospel writers know is the resurrected Christ, but that does not mean that their depiction of his life is thereby distorted. For example, see Nils Dahl's *Jesus in the Memory of the Early Church,* pp. 11–29.

56. For an account of the powers, see Yoder, pp. 135–162. Richard Mouw also bases his account of a Christian social ethic on this theme. See his *Politics and the Biblical Drama* (Grand Rapids, Mich.: Eerdmans, 1976), pp. 85–116. Mouw's criticisms of Yoder are interesting, but I think fail to challenge the primary point that the powers can only be brought back to their true nature by refusing to acknowledge their false claims of authority.

57. I still find Rauschenbusch's account of the forces that put Jesus to death—religious bigotry, graft and political power, corruption of justice, mob spirit and action, militarism, racial sin in class contempt—one of the most compelling accounts of the kind of powers Jesus exposed and redeemed. According to Rauschenbusch theology "has made a fundamental mistake in treating the atonement as something distinct, and making the life of Jesus a mere staging for his death, a matter almost negligible in the work of salvation." *Theology of the Social Gospel,* p. 260. It is necessary to keep the two connected; otherwise we fail to see how Jesus' life provided the grounds for solidarity necessary to overcome those powers that conspired to put him to death.

58. For example, see Shubert Ogden's review of Jon Sobrino, *Christology at the Crossroads: A Latin American Approach,* in *Perkins Journal,* 31/4 (Summer 1978), pp. 47-49.

59. Dahl, *Jesus in the Memory of the Early Church,* p. 171. Keck maintains "that probing the ethos of religious communities with respect to the functions of traditions and texts could help us see that the NT is not simply a compilation of the literary justifications for the (diverse) Christian ethos, but a series of trenchant critiques of that ethos as well. I also suspect that no small part of the ethos was the habit of being willing to submit to judgment by its own prophets and traditions, and those of sister churches and their leaders (e.g., Ignatius)." "On the Ethos of Early Christians," p. 450.

3: THE MORAL AUTHORITY OF SCRIPTURE

1. Joseph Blenkinsopp, *Prophecy and Canon* (Notre Dame, Ind.: University of Notre Dame Press, 1977), p. 152.

2. John Howard Yoder, "Radical Reformation Ethics in Ecumenical Perspective," *Journal of Ecumenical Studies,* Fall 1978, p. 657. I think it is no accident that the best recent book that utilizes scripture for ethics is Yoder's *The Politics of Jesus* (Grand Rapids, Mich.: Eerdmans, 1972). Yoder was able to see the New Testament with fresh eyes because he came from a separated community with the physical and intellectual space and time to appreciate the radical demands in scripture.

3. David Kelsey, *The Uses of Scriptures in Recent Theology* (Philadelphia: Fortress Press, 1975), pp. 208–209.

4. Ibid., pp. 185–192. Kelsey observes, "the translation picture wrongly assumes that 'meaning' has only one meaning. By suggesting that theological proposals express the same 'meaning' as the biblical texts that authorize them, it obliges one to assume that the texts do have some sort of meaning. What the translation picture obscures, however, is that 'meaning' may be used here in two different senses. That is, it obscures the possible conceptual discontinuity between text and proposal," p. 190. See also James Barr, *The Bible in the Modern World* (New York: Harper and Row, 1973), p. 141.

5. Erich Auerbach, *Mimesis* (Princeton, N.J.: Princeton University Press, 1968), p. 48. This is, of course, the quote as well as the theme which dominates Hans Frei's *The Eclipse of Biblical Narrative* (New Haven, Conn.: Yale University Press, 1974), p. 3. That Frei's analysis is crucial for the argument of this essay is obvious. Frei, even more than Barth, has helped me see that the problem is not in our scriptures but in ourselves.

6. James Gustafson, "Christian Ethics" in *Religion,* ed. Paul Ramsey (Englewood Cliffs, N.J.: Prentice-Hall, 1965), p. 337. See also Gustafson, *Christian Ethics and the Community* (Philadelphia: Pilgrim Press, 1971) for an excellent overview of recent attempts to use the scripture ethically. For Gustafson's own more constructive proposals, see his *Theology and Christian Ethics* (Philadelphia: Pilgrim Press, 1974), pp. 121–159. Bruce Birch and Larry Rasmussen provide an equally helpful account in their *Bible and Ethics in the Christian Life* (Minneapolis: Augsburg, 1976), pp. 45–78.

7. Brevard Childs, *Biblical Theology in Crisis* (Philadelphia: Westminster Press, 1970), p. 124.

8. This is, of course, the problem that Childs is struggling with in his *Introduction to the Old Testament as Scripture* (Philadelphia: Fortress, 1979). I think he is right to suggest that the crucial issue resides in how we understand the significance and function of the canon, but I think that Childs fails to adequately indicate the interdependence of canon and community. Therefore his sense of the status of the text

appears too unmediated. However, he rightly suggests that "the fixing of a canon of scripture implies that the witness to Israel's experience with God lies not in recovering such historical processes, but is testified in the effect on the biblical text itself. Scripture bears witness to God's activity in history on Israel's behalf, but history per se is not a medium of revelation which is commensurate with a canon," p. 76. For a very helpful analysis of the differences between the Bible as scripture and as text, see Kelsey, pp. 198-201.

9. It is important not only that theologians know text, but it is equally important how and where they learn the text. It is my hunch that part of the reason for the misuse of the scripture in matters dealing with morality is that the text was isolated from a liturgical context. There is certainly nothing intrinsically wrong with individuals reading and studying scripture, but such reading must be guided by the use of the scripture through the liturgies of the church. For the shape of the liturgy over a whole year prevents any one part of scripture from being given undue emphasis in relation to the narrative line of scripture. The liturgy, in every performance and over a whole year, rightly contextualizes individual passages when we cannot read the whole. As Aidan Kavanagh has recently observed, "the liturgy is scripture's home rather than its stepchild, and the Hebrew and Christian bibles were the church's first liturgical books." *The Shape of Baptism: The Rite of Christian Initiation* (New York: Pueblo Publishing Co., 1978), p. xiii.

10. Even more damaging in this respect than the subsequent ethical concentration of a limited range of "biblical concepts" is the underwriting of destructive prejudices of the scripture scholars. For example, Joseph Blenkinsopp has documented the often implicit anti-Semitism involved in portrayals of the history of Israel, so that the second temple period was invariably interpreted as a time of "decline." See his "The Period of the Second Commonwealth in the Theology of the Old Testament," forthcoming from Paulist Press, New York. E. P. Sanders has exposed the equally distorting interpretation of Paul by Protestants who tended to read back into Paul's relation to Judaism the issues of the relation of Protestantism to Catholicism. See his *Paul and Palestinian Judaism* (Philadelphia: Fortress Press, 1977).

11. See, for example, James Barr's criticism of "biblical theology" in his *The Bible in the Modern World,* pp. 135-136. Kelsey's critique of the "biblical concept" approach to scripture is equally devastating. *The Uses of Scripture in Recent Theology,* pp. 25-29.

12. Childs, *Biblical Theology in Crisis,* p. 130. For a particularly egregious example of the failure to appreciate the significance of the question of how "ethics" should be understood as well as the claim that the New Testament ethic must be judged by its adequacy for negotiating the "modern world," see Jack Sanders, *Ethics in the New Testament* (Philadelphia: Fortress Press, 1975). For a critique of Sanders, see my "A Failure in Communication: Ethics and the Early Church," *Interpretation,* 32/2 (April 1978), pp. 196-200.

13. Gustafson, *Theology and Christian Ethics,* pp. 122-123.

14. Birch and Rasmussen, p. 185. Birch and Rasmussen's book has the virtue of being the most methodologically aware of how different conceptions of ethics will determine not only what and how one identifies descriptively the "ethics in the scripture," but also the continuing status of that ethic for use today.

15. Gustafson has drawn and analyzed the distinction between "revealed morality" and "revealed reality" in *Theology and Christian Ethics,* pp. 129-138 and in *Christian Ethics and the Community*, pp. 48-51. He notes that the Bible as revealed morality can be understood in terms of law, ideals, analogies, and as a pattern of interpretation.

16. For example, Paul Ramsey maintains that the conception of justice in the Bible is radically different from all others because it consists in the principle: "To each according to the measure of his real need, not because of anything human reason can discern inherent in the needy, but because his need alone is the measure of God's righteousness toward him." *Basic Christian Ethics* (New York: Scribner's, 1950), pp. 13–14. Ramsey is a classical example of an ethicist exploiting the assumption that biblical theology is primarily a matter of locating the central "biblical" concepts. Thus Ramsey stresses the centrality of love and covenant on the assumption that by doing so his ethic is thereby "biblical."

17. Barr, *The Bible in the Modern World*, p. 122.

18. For what remains a very useful discussion of these issues, see John Knox, *The Ethics of Jesus in the Teaching of the Church* (Nashville: Abingdon Press, 1961). As noted this issue involves the still controversial question of eschatology and ethics in the New Testament. In that respect it is still worth anyone's time to read Amos Wilder, *Eschatology and Ethics in the Teaching of Jesus* (New York: Harper and Row, 1939) and Hans Windisch, *The Meaning of the Sermon on the Mount* (Philadelphia: Westminster Press, 1949).

19. Victor Paul Furnish in his *Theology and Ethics in Paul* (Nashville: Abingdon, 1968) and *The Love Command in the New Testament* (Nashville: Abingdon, 1972) has emphasized both these themes with great effect.

20. See, for example, Robert Tannehill's *Dying and Rising wtih Christ* (Berlin: Verlag Alfred Topelmann, 1967), pp. 80–83, for substantiation of this point.

21. Furnish resorts to this means of expression simply because he has no other conceptual or moral means to articulate the way Paul's ethics is but an extension of his theology. For an effective critique of Furnish's method in this respect, see Gil Meilander, "Does Gift Imply Task?: Some Ethical Reflections" (unpublished paper read to Ethics Section of the AAR, 1979).

22. James Gustafson, "Introduction" to H. R. Niebuhr's *The Responsible Self* (New York: Harper and Row, 1963), p. 23. For an extensive analysis of H. R. Niebuhr's use of scripture, see Ben Jordan, "The Use of Scripture in the Ethics of H. R. Niebuhr" (diss., Emory University, 1974).

23. Gustafson, *Christian Ethics and the Community*, pp. 50–51.

24. See, for example, Gustafson's attempt to illuminate the Cambodian invasion through the use of scriptural analogies in *Theology and Christian Ethics*, pp. 138–145.

25. Kelsey, p. 97.

26. Those familiar with the work of Yves Simon will recognize how dependent this account of authority is on his work. In particular, see his *Philosophy of Democratic Government* (Chicago: University of Chicago Press, 1951), pp. 1–71, 144–194. See also Clarke Cochran's very helpful "Authority and Community: The Contributions of Carl Friedrich, Yves Simon, and Michael Polanyi," *American Political Science Review*, 71/2 (June 1977), pp. 546–558.

27. J. P. Mackey, *Tradition and Change in the Church* (Dayton, Ohio: Pflaum Press, 1968), p. x. Ironically Catholic theologians at Tübingen were among the first to realize the importance of this for understanding the significance of scripture. It is a tragedy that they were silenced before they were appreciated. See James Burtchaell's *Catholic Theories of Biblical Inspiration Since 1810* (Cambridge: Cambridge University Press, 1969).

28. Mackey, pp. 42–43. Those familiar with Kuhn's analysis of the development and change in science will see that many of the issues discussed and debated about his account are relevant here. Indeed I suspect a very interesting comparison could be drawn between the breakdown and reinterpretation of traditions in the Bible and those

in science. That Kuhn's work might be relevant to such an analysis should not be surprising, for I suspect that Kuhn's interpretation of science gains its inspiration from politics. For an attempt to develop this suggestion, see Richard Vernon, "Politics as Metaphor: Cardinal Newman and Professor Kuhn," *The Review of Politics,* 41/4 (October 1979), pp. 513–535.

29. James Barr, *Old and New Interpretation* (New York: Harper and Row, 1966), p. 190. However Barr goes on to remind us that "this positive evaluation of the 'tradition,' i.e., of the body of previous decisions and interpretations, of customs and accepted methods, nevertheless should not conceal from us the fact that this tradition can constitute the chief agency for the damaging and distorting of the meaning of the Bible." He notes, however, that this cannot be corrected by the possession of "pure" theological presuppositions, but rather the "primary ethical problem in interpretation will very often, perhaps always, lie *within* the Church," p. 191. That is why the church must always remember that the Bible belongs to the world and not the church only. "When the Church addresses the world on the basis of the Bible, it invites people to look for themselves and see if these things are not so. The possibility that people may do this looking for themselves carries with it a consequence on the more scholarly level: non-Christian interpretation of the Bible is a possibility, indeed it is more, it is a reality," p. 191.

30. "What is needed is more awareness of how religious texts live by reinterpretation. The very mechanics of creative interpretation in the religious realm requires that we understand the Bible, not as a philosophical text expressing certain ideas, but as scripture, inspired and authoritative and consequently capable of assuming new meanings. This understanding leads to the puzzling insight that in the living religious traditions continuity is affirmed and achieved by discontinuity. Authority is affirmed and relevance asserted by reinterpretation." Krister Stendahl, "Biblical Studies in the University," in *The Study of Religion in Colleges and Universities,* ed. P. Ramsey and J. Wilson (Princeton, N.J.: Princeton University Press, 1970), pp. 30–31.

31. See, for example, Jon Gunnemann's extremely interesting interpretation of revolutions in terms of Kuhn's understanding of a paradigm shift in his *The Moral Meaning of Revolution* (New Haven, Conn.: Yale University Press, 1979).

32. Simon, pp. 29–30.

33. Ibid., p. 33. In his *A General Theory of Authority* (Notre Dame: University of Notre Dame Press, rpt. 1980), Simon points out that the "need for authority and the problem of the need for a distinct governing personnel have often been confused: it is already clear that they are distinct and that the argumentation which establishes the need for authority, even in a society made of ideally enlightened and well-intentioned persons, leaves open the question of whether some communities may be provided with all the authority they need without there being among them any distinct group of governing persons," p. 49. So to claim scripture as authority does not preclude the necessity of distinct officers and others in the church exercising authority. But again as Simon reminds us, "when an issue is one of action, not of truth, the person in authority has the character of a leader; but when the issue is one of truth, not of action, the person in authority has the character of a witness. Indeed, a witness may also be a leader and, in the capacity of leader, exercise command. But in the mere witness, and universally in the witness as such, authority does not involve, in any sense or degree, the power to give orders and to demand obedience. We would say that an event, for some time considered doubtful, finally has been established by the authority of sound and numerous witnesses. We would go so far as to say that yielding to their testimony is a duty and a matter of honesty. The authority of the mere witness is nothing else than

truthfulness as expressed by signs which make it recognizable in varying degrees of assurance,'' p. 84. In this respect the authority of scripture is surely that of a witness which, however, tests the authority of any who would lead in the church. For the development of this idea of authority in relation to the papacy, see my and Robert Wilken's "Protestants and the Pope," *Commonweal,* 107/3 (February 15, 1980), pp. 80–85.

34. Cochran observes that the modern attack "on tradition as such, however, is fundamentally an attack on history. It is at bottom an attempt to escape history and the necessarily historical (and therefore limited) existence of man. Tradition is what makes historical existence bearable by giving some meaning and perspective to the distance between the given and the demanded. Political theorists can do little, perhaps, directly to respond to the practical crisis of authority. Yet ideas have consequences, and the practical crisis of authority has roots in the undernourished soil of our theoretical understanding of authority, tradition, knowledge, and community," p. 557. The church, however, not only has the opportunity to enrich "ideas" but to provide the positive experience of tradition and community.

35. Barr, *The Bible in the Modern World,* p. 147.

36. Of course it is true, as Barr observes, that tradition comes before scripture, as well as following after it. *Bible in The Modern World,* p. 127. However as Kelsey has observed the concepts of "tradition" and "scripture" are not on a logical par. " 'Tradition' is used to name, not something the church uses, but something the church *is,* insofar as her reality lies in a set of events and practices that can be construed as a single activity. 'Scripture' is used to name, not something the church is, but something she must *use,* according to some concepts of 'church,' to preserve her self-identity," p. 96.

37. Blenkinsopp, *Prophecy and Canon,* p. 94. For a fascinating study of the problem of authority in Paul, see John Schutz, *Paul and the Anatomy of Apostolic Authority* (Cambridge: Cambridge University Press, 1975). Schutz's primary thesis is that "Jesus' death brings life to the Christian, but not without Jesus' life. So Paul's death is also Paul's life, his weakness, his power; and this weakness or suffering alone can stand for the union of the two, just as the cross stands for Christ's death and new life. The work of Christ is the work of God and cannot be taken from God's hand. But the appropriation puts Paul into the life of the communities alongside of the gospel, itself power and weakness. This is how the authority of the apostle is to be understood. In Paul's whole apostolic life one sees the manifestations of God's same act which one sees in the gospel itself," p. 246.

38. Kelsey, pp. 14–15. Elsewhere Kelsey suggests "To call a text or set of texts 'scripture' is not only to say that their use in certain ways in the church's life is essential to the preservation of her identity, and therefore to say that they are 'authoritative' over that life, it is also to ascribe some sort of wholeness to the text or set of texts. However, there is an irreducible variety of kinds of wholeness that may be ascribed to the texts. Thus 'scripture' turns out to be, not one concept, but a set of different concepts that bear one another some family resemblances. All uses of 'scripture' are dialectically related to uses of the concept of 'church' and entail ascribing authoritativeness and wholeness to the texts called 'scripture'; this much all uses of 'scripture' share. But in the actual practice of appealing to scripture in the course of doing theology, there turns out to be an irreducible logical diversity of ways the texts are concretely contrued as 'whole,' '' pp. 100–101. Later I will suggest that the kind of "wholeness" that is most appropriate to the scripture is that of a story.

39. Kelsey, pp. 37ff.

40. Ibid., p. 94.

41. Ibid., p. 101.

42. It is important to note that ascriptions of "wholeness" to the canon are not identical with claims about the "unity" of the canon. Kelsey, p. 106. See also Barr's very useful discussion of the problem of the "unity" of scripture, *The Bible in the Modern World,* pp. 98ff.

43. Kelsey, p. 160.

44. Ibid., p. 205.

45. Reynolds Price, *A Palpable God: Thirty Stories Translated from the Bible: With an Essay on the Origins and Life of Narrative* (New York: Atheneum, 1978), p. 14. Of course as Price himself would emphasize such a story is indeed complex—so complex it requires the many narrative lines of scripture for us to understand what the existence of such a God entails.

46. Barr, *The Bible in the Modern World,* pp. 117–118.

47. Ibid., p. 118. For an extremely interesting account of the concept of a "classic" and its importance for Christian theology, see David Tracy, "Theological Classics in Contemporary Theology," *Theology Digest,* 25/4 (Winter 1977), pp. 347–355.

48. Barr, *The Bible in the Modern World,* p. 147. See also, Barr, *Old and New in Interpretation,* pp. 21ff and his "Story and History in Biblical Theology," *Journal of Religion,* 56/1 (January 1976), pp. 1–17. In the latter Barr suggests that the narrative form of the Old Testament better merits the title of story rather than history, though much of it illumines as well as recounts history. I cannot here try to deal with what Frei calls the "history-like" quality of the biblical narrative and the questions thereby raised about the "accuracy" of scripture. However I think Frei is exactly right to challenge the assumption that the "real" meaning of the text resides in how accurately or inaccurately the writers report occurrences. For an extremely fruitful discussion of these issues, see Julian Hartt's chapter "Story as the Art of Historical Truth," in his *Theological Method and Imagination* (New York: Seabury Press, 1977), and James Coughenour, "Karl Barth and the Gospel Story: A Lesson in Reading the Biblical Narrative," *Andover Newton Quarterly,* 20 (1979), pp. 97–110.

49. Kelsey interprets Barth in this manner, p. 39ff.

50. Kelsey, p. 45.

51. Ibid., p. 48.

52. From this perspective the most important question about how to tell the story in the scripture still involves how to understand the connections between the two testaments. And it is important to note that this is not just a matter of studying the text but, as I have argued, continues to be a political issue of the nature of the Christian community as well as Judaism. As Blenkinsopp has suggested, "In view of the break between Christianity and Judaism towards the end of the Second Commonwealth— profoundly tragic in its consequences as it has been—the two faiths must necessarily address a critique to each other, and such a critique will necessarily inform any attempt to give a theological account of the classical texts to which both bodies appeal. Is it inconceivable that such mutual testing be carried out in dialogue and co-operation? And, from the Christian side, what would an Old Testament theology look like which at least envisioned such a situation by taking Judaism with absolute theological seriousness?" "The Period of the Second Commonwealth in the Theology of the Old Testament," p. 29. In his *Discerning the Way* (New York: Seabury, 1980), Paul Van Buren rightly argues that the relationship between the Hebrew scriptures and the Apostolic Writings is "unavoidably a question of the relationship between the Jewish

people and the Gentile church,'' p. 139. I am in deep sympathy with Van Buren's attempt to take seriously the fact that the God Christians worship is Israel's God.

53. Blenkinsopp, *Prophecy and Canon,* pp. 78–79.

54. Charles Talbert has suggested that though the early Christians agreed that God was present in Jesus for our salvation, they differed about how that presence was manifest in Jesus. As a result the Gospel was preached and written down in different ways—some concentrated on the miracles, some morality, some knowledge of the future. But what is important is that the ''canonical gospels appear to be attempts to avoid the reductionism of seeing the presence of God in Jesus in only one way and attempts to set forth a comprehensive and balanced understanding of both the divine presence and the discipleship it evokes.'' ''The Gospel and the Gospels,'' *Interpretation,* 33/4 (October 1979), pp. 351–362. As Talbert has shown elsewhere, what was crucial about the Gospels is not their genre, but the kind of discipleship they assumed appropriate to the character of Jesus. See his *What is a Gospel: The Genre of the Canonical Gospels* (Philadelphia: Fortress Press, 1977).

55. This is a statement by Fiver from Richard Adams' *Watership Down* (New York: Avon Books, 1972), p. 124.

56. Blenkinsopp suggests that ''the prophetic canon found a place alongside Torah as a compromise or way of maintaining a balance between law and prophecy, institution and charisma, the claims of the past and those of the future. Such an inclusive canon, which contained within itself both the seeds of tension and the means of overcoming it, corresponds to something important in the makeup of Judaism and Christianity. Both faiths can test the truth of the proposition that a theocratic institution which excludes prophecy and the millenarian hope leaves itself open to assimilation, while prophecy left to itself tends of its nature toward disunity and sectarianism. It is the fate of prophecy to be always necessary and never sufficient.'' *Prophecy and Canon,* p. 116. However, as I have tried to suggest, without a prophetic community there is no chance that the moral force of the scripture story can be intelligible.

57. On the political presuppositions of forgiveness, see Hadden Willmer, ''The Politics of Forgiveness,'' *The Furrow*, April 1979, and my ''Forgiveness and Political Community,'' *Worldview,* 23/1–2 (January–February 1980), pp. 15–16.

58. In his otherwise admirable *The First Followers of Jesus* (London: SCM Press, 1977), Gerd Theissen suggests ''in the New Testament for the first time the revolutionary—and healthy—insight that to take any human ethical requirement seriously will demonstrate its inadequacy, that ethics without forgiveness is a perversion, and that there is more to morality than morality, if it is to remain human. This recognition certainly points far beyond the particular historical context in which it came into being. But at one time it was a contribution towards overcoming a deep-rooted crisis in Judaism. The identity of Judaism could not be achieved by rival intensifications of the demands of the Torah, each of which sought to outbid the others; the only answer was the recognition of divine grace. In the last resort, solidarity between men could not be achieved by an intensification of norms; this could only heighten latent and open aggressiveness. What was needed was a new relationship to all norms: putting trust and freedom from anxiety before demands of any kind,'' p. 107. Not only does this accept a far too restricted sense of ''morality,'' but more damaging is the assumption that forgiveness was absent prior to the coming of Jesus and the church. I have tried to suggest that the ability of Israel to reinterpret her traditions presumed a profound experience and understanding of forgiveness. Theissen's argument in this respect still betrays the Protestant reading of Paul that has recently been challenged by E. P. Sanders in his *Paul and Palestinian Judaism.* Sanders

rather decisively shows that for Paul the problem with Judaism was not the law, but that it is not Christianity—that is, a new community based on the work and person of Jesus, p. 552.

59. If this is the case, it is but another indication that ethics at best is only bad poetry—that is, it seeks to help us see what we see every day but fail to see rightly. Put differently, ethics is an attempt to help us feel the oddness of the everyday. If ethicists had talent, they might be poets, but in the absence of talent, they try to make their clanking conceptual and discursive chains do the work of art.

60. Yoder, *The Politics of Jesus*, p. 178.

4: THE CHURCH AND LIBERAL DEMOCRACY

1. For an anthology that helps clarify many of the issues surrounding claims about "secularity," see *Secularization and the Protestant Prospect*, ed. James Childress and David Harned (Philadelphia: Westminster Press, 1970). Too often discussions about religion and secularity are attempts, explicitly or implicitly, to make summary judgments, positive or negative, about our culture. I doubt that any one description, whether it be claims about secularity or that this is a post-modern culture, has the power to describe the diverse activities that make up our culture or any other. What we require are discriminating criteria that will let us get a descriptive as well as normative hold on those aspects of our society of particular importance to Christians.

2. Nor do I intend to enter the debate concerning the existence, meaning, or status of civil religion in America. Robert Bellah is, of course, the primary focus of this debate. See his *Beyond Belief: Essays on Religion in a Post-Traditional World* (New York: Harper and Row, 1970) and *The Broken Covenant, American Civil Religion in Time of Trial* (New York: Seabury, 1975). Equally if not more important is the work of Sidney Mead, for in many ways Mead has argued more forcefully for the significance of a "religion of the republic." See his *The Lively Experiment* (New York: Harper and Row, 1963) and *The Nation with the Soul of a Church* (New York: Harper and Row, 1975). Nor should H. R. Niebuhr's *The Kingdom of God in America* (New York: Harper, 1937) be overlooked.

3. Some, of course, would question this understanding of "secular" on grounds that a secular society finally in fact, if not as a matter of policy, is biased against religion per se. Whether that is the case remains to be seen. It is certainly true that our country's toleration of "religious" symbols at our state ceremonies may, on a strict enforcement of the Constitution, be illegitimate.

4. John Courtney Murray bases his defense of democracy primarily on God's sovereignty and Reinhold Niebuhr places the emphasis on sin. There is much to be said for both accounts and neither is exclusive of the other. The primary difference between Niebuhr and Murray is not that Murray had a more optimistic view of man, but that Murray presupposed the necessity of the existence of the church to remind the state of its limits. In a peculiar way Niebuhr was more profoundly an American theologian, as America was his primary community. See Murray's *We Hold These Truths* (New York: Sheed and Ward, 1960) and Niebuhr, *The Children of Light and the Children of Darkness* (New York: Scribner's, 1944).

5. The popularity of the image of "transformation" in Christian social ethics has had the unfortunate effect of oversimplifying the description of social change and the church's relation to it. For it is assumed that H. R. Niebuhr's "type" or "image" of

transformation is clearly normative for Christian social ethics, irrespective of the kind of society in which Christians find themselves. As a result the "image" of transformation is too quickly accepted as entailing a strategy of involvement. What we fail to notice is that Niebuhr's account of the types failed to deal with a crucial problem—namely how to discriminate between different kinds of cultures and different aspects of any culture for what might be transformed and what might be accepted. Niebuhr's uncritical use of the word "culture" allowed him to load his case too simply against the "Christ against Culture" type and to present the "Christ transforming Culture" type in a far too uncritical light. It is not my intention to challenge the heuristic value of Niebuhr's typology, but to remind us that the account of types is not a sufficient argument for a particular social ethic. H. R. Niebuhr, *Christ and Culture* (New York: Harper and Row, 1956).

6. See, for example, *Reinhold Niebuhr on Politics*, ed. Harry Davis and Robert Good (New York: Scribner's, 1960), pp. 70–130.

7. There is no inherent reason that liberalism or secularism should exclude a concern for the development of citizen virtues. I suspect that the past association of "morality" with "religion" accounts for the lack of emphasis on the development of virtuous people. For virtue, like religion, is relegated to the "private" sphere in order to make sure that the "freedom of the individual" is properly safeguarded. For a fascinating account of how these issues were formed in the Renaissance see Quentin Skinner's *The Foundation of Modern Political Thought,* I (Cambridge: Cambridge University Press, 1978), pp. 45, 92–101, 228–236.

8. The distinction between church and world is a complex one. Even though in some Christian texts "world" simply means those who reject Christ and is thus understood in a negative light, the world is also recognized elsewhere as God's creation. Moreover Christian judgment of the world is always self-referential, as we can never forget that the world is not "out there" but in us. The church must be separated from the world, for without separation we have no way to make discriminating judgments about the negative and positive aspects of the world. But the necessity of separation cannot blind us to the significance of the world for the church. For the church also learns what it should be from the world. The church's task is not to destroy or deny the world, or even to make it Christian, but to be a witness in the world of God's Kingdom.

9. One of the difficulties of American society and government is that rather than being a people prior to the state, as is true for most European countries, we had to found a state in order to try to make ourselves a people. Therefore where many societies can provide the mechanism for a strong government, knowing that social custom can still act as a limit on government, the United States had to resort to legal means to substitute for the lack of custom. We morally justified our legal arrangements by claiming they were necessary to protect, not society, but the individual from government. Thus the only two entities recognized in our polity became the state and the individual. As a result more traditional political theory that makes the state one agency among others for the protection of the common good of a society, and not just individuals, simply does not apply to America.

In some ways our situation is even more complex, as America was originally a society profoundly underwritten by Protestant presupposition—America was the great experiment in constructive Protestantism. Exactly because our founders, irrespective of their own personal religiosity, could presuppose such a society, they thought all they needed to provide was a framework, a constitution, for our society to work. But as we lost the social presuppositions supplied by Protestantism or as they were increasingly replaced by Enlightenment assumptions, the framework became what it was never meant to be—an end in itself.

10. Solzhenitsyn, address at Harvard University; *Harvard Gazette,* June 1978, p. 2.

11. Indeed one of the problems with America is the divorce of political consideration from culture. One of the signs of this is the association of politics with issues of power rather than symbols. In such a polity symbolic acts are reduced to issues of maintaining or projecting an "image" rather than the articulation of our profoundest loyalties. Lincoln was one of the few American presidents who appreciated the symbolic role of the political.

12. As George Will has suggested, "Men and women are biological facts. Ladies and gentlemen—citizens—are social artifacts, works of political art. They carry the culture that is sustained by wise laws, and traditions of civility. At the end of the day we are right to judge a society by the character of the people it produces. That is why statecraft is inevitably soulcraft." *The Pursuit of Happiness and Other Sobering Thoughts* (New York: Harper and Row, 1978), p. 3.

It is important to note that neither Will nor Solzhenitsyn argues (nor do I) that it is the function of the state to *make* people good, but rather to direct them to the good. Politics as a moral art does not entail the presumption that the state is a possessor of the good, but rather that the good is to be found in a reality profounder than the state. In the absence of such a good the temptation is for the state to try to create a cause that can serve as a substitute. Thus it is profoundly and chillingly true that there is nothing wrong with America that a good war could not cure.

13. Jimmy Carter promised us a government as good as the American people and it may be unfortunately true that is what we have. This does not mean that the American people are particularly bad, as they certainly are not. As many have pointed out, the American people continue to be extraordinarily generous and kind. The difficulty is that we simply do not have any way to understand the political significance of such virtues. Politically we seem caught in a system that reinforces our assumption that our political task is to pursue our self-interests aggressively and fairly. In contrast, George Will argues that "politics should be citizens expressing themselves as a people, a community of shared values, rather than as merely a collection of competing private interests inhabiting the same country. Instead, politics has become a facet of the disease for which it would be part of the cure. The disease is an anarchy of self-interestedness, and unwillingness, perhaps by now an inability, to think of the public interest, the common good. This disease of anti-public-spiritedness is not a candidate's disease. It is a social disease." *The Pursuit of Happiness and Other Sobering Thoughts,* p. 192. Will is one of the few American conservatives who seems to understand that conservatism in America is a radical position vis-à-vis our liberal heritage.

14. Solzhenitsyn, p. 1. Though often condemned for being too competitive, competition is one of our most important moral endeavors. For all societies need to provide a sense of participation in an adventure. Insofar as many feel they lack such an adventure, all that is left is beating the next person. Thus the dominance of the comparative mode in American life—we must be the first this or the best of that. It is very hard for us simply to be different and to enjoy that fact as an end in itself.

15. "Talk of the Town," *New Yorker,* May 23, 1977, pp. 24–25.

16. Solzhenitsyn, p. 3.

17. Ibid.

18. However I am in profound disagreement with Solzhenitsyn's more positive proposals as well as his understanding of the international situation. His hatred of communism and reliance on the "will of the West" to oppose communism gives far too uncritical support to some of the more reactionary political positions in our country. His profound commitment to Orthodoxy, I am afraid, remains still far too tied to Russia and Russian nationalism. For a good critique of Solzhenitsyn's thought on this point, see Andrei Sinyavsky, "Solzhenitsyn and Russian Nationalism," *New York Review of Books*, 26/18 (November 22, 1979), pp. 3–6. For an interesting critique of Solzhenitsyn's inability to understand the moral status of pluralism, see Martin Marty, "On Hearing Solzhenitsyn in Context," *World Literature Today*, Autumn 1979, pp. 578–584. However, also see John Garvey's "In Defense of Solzhenitsyn," *Commonweal*, 105/17 (September 1, 1978), pp. 553–555.

19. For example, C. B. Macpherson suggests that liberal democracy can mean simply the democracy of a capitalist market society (no matter how modified that society appears to be by the rise of the welfare state), or it can mean a society striving to ensure that all its members are equally free to realize their capabilities. *The Life and Times of Liberal Democracy* (Oxford: Oxford University Press, 1977), p. 1. It has, of course, been the thrust of Macpherson's work to show that liberalism as a political institution was transformed and perverted by capitalism and that now our task is to save liberalism from the perversion. For a critique of liberalism, and in particular Rawls, similar to my own, see George Parkin Grant, *English-Speaking Justice* (Sackville, New Brunswick: Mount Allison University Press, 1974). Grant makes the interesting point that Rawls' theory of justice is abstracted from any consideration of the facts of war and imperialism, pp. 44ff. I am grateful to Paul Ramsey for calling Grant's work to my attention.

A criticism of the following account of liberalism is that I take far too seriously philosophical theories of liberalism—i.e., Rawls, Nozick—and fail to pay appropriate attention to the historical experience of liberalism. For accounts of the latter one should not look to the philosophers but the work of cultural and social historians. Such work shows the American experience often provided a richer sense of history and the common good than the philosophical accounts of liberalism could give expression to. There is much to commend such a strategy, but it is my contention that it is no longer viable. For liberalism has become a self-fulfilling prophecy such that now theories of liberalism are not only descriptively powerful but shape our dominant public policies. Of course, much still occurs in our society that is not explicable from the point of view of liberalism and denotes fragments of other political moralities that have been present in American life and thought.

20. I am not suggesting that the Constitution was the product of an explicit political theory in some deductive manner. Certainly the American form of society and government, like most governments and societies, was as much the product of historical accidents as theory. But our history has increasingly been interpreted and formed through liberal political philosophy. As Louis Hartz has argued in his now classic study, *The Liberal Tradition in America* (New York: Harcourt, Brace, and Company, 1955), even though life in the Puritan colonies and the South was in some ways deeply antagonistic to liberalism, liberalism became our dominant political tradition because we had no other tradition to which we might appeal. In the absence of any feudal experience, Americans simply have, in Hartz's phrase, a "natural liberalism" which they ironically dogmatically adhere to and defend.

21. Macpherson rightly observes that liberalism has "always meant freeing the individual from the outdated restraints of old established institutions." *The Life and*

Times of Liberal Democracy, p. 21. This has had a peculiar effect on the form of our political theory, as it tends to be excessively removed from the actual process of our government and society. The latter are treated by political science and history, which often putatively claim to have no normative interests.

22. William Hixson, "Liberal Legacy, Radical Critique," *Commonweal,* 105/20 (October 13, 1978), p. 649. Thus Americans' paradoxical attitude toward politicians. They want only people of integrity to run for office, but they make them subject to a polity that defines the essence of the political as compromise and a willingness to subject one's own convictions to the interests of one's constituency. Perhaps that is one of the ways we have for devaluing the realm of the political—namely, we have created a system where only the morally compromised can be political actors.

23. Hixson, p. 649.

24. Alasdair MacIntyre argues further that the "lack of shared moral beliefs in our political culture—which in eighteenth century terms is part, although only part, of our lack of virtue—is a great threat and possibly even the great threat to our liberties. I shall argue toward the conclusion by suggesting that the consequence of a lack of shared moral beliefs tends to be *either* that government acts without the proper assent of the people to its actions, because lack of shared moral beliefs prevents the occurrence of the kind of political dialogue which would enable the people to understand the proposed acts of government *or* the government connives at the creation of false simulacra of moral consensus, moods either of public hysteria or of public fatigue, which happily are transitory, but which while they last deceive both the government and many of those over whom they rule. And when government fails because its policies lack proper support or because that support derives from false simulacra the temptation to government to act in covert and clandestine ways sometimes becomes overwhelming." "Power and Virtue in the American Republic" (unpublished manuscript), pp. 8–9.

25. Richard Titmuss, *The Gift Relationship* (New York: Random House, 1972).

26. Of course, in many ways there is nothing more human, as it seems to be our nature to deny that our security may rest in the hands of another. Thus it is a characteristic of human society to turn all gift relationships into exchanges. For example, it is very hard for us not to think of gifts as "putting us in debt" and thus at a disadvantage. We, therefore, quickly try to give something in return so that we will not be another's "debt."

27. Kenneth Arrow, "Gifts and Exchanges," *Philosophy and Public Affairs,* 1/4 (Summer 1972), p. 355. The power of the economic model is perhaps no better exemplified than in Arrow's assumption that "altruistic" behavior is a "scarce resource." Moreover, he seems to be right to claim that once you have established a system that works on the presumption of self-interest, it becomes a disvalue for anyone to act "ethically," since such behavior is not predictable. Thus we have the odd state of affairs where a morally altruistic person must act self-interestedly, for not to do so is to act "selfishly."

28. For a critique of "rights" language in relation to children, see my "Rights, Duties, and Experimentation on Children: A Critical Response to Worsfold and Bartholome," *Research Involving Children: Appendix* (Washington, D.C.: National Commission for Protection of Human Subjects of Biomedical and Behavioral Research Publication, No [OS] 77-0005, 1977), article 5, pp. 1–24.

29. For a spirited argument against this view, see Paul Ramsey, *Ethics at the Edges of Life* (New Haven, Conn.: Yale University Press, 1978), pp. 3–18.

30. Milton Friedman, *Capitalism and Freedom* (Chicago: University of Chicago Press, 1962), p. 12.

31. This is also the great dilemma of the ''neo-conservatives.'' As Peter Steinfels points out, ''The institutions they wish to conserve are to no small extent the institutions that have made the task of conservation so necessary and so difficult.'' *The Neoconservatives* (New York: Simon and Schuster, 1979), p. 103. Particularly illuminating is Steinfels' analysis of Daniel Bell's work, for Bell's understanding of the ''Cultural Contradictions of Capitalism'' clearly makes him the most interesting of those loosely identified as neo-conservatives. Michael Walzer, in a review of Steinfels' book, points out, ''What made liberalism endurable for all these years was the fact that the individualism it generated was always imperfect, tempered by older restraints and loyalties, by stable patterns of local, ethnic, religious, or class relationships. An untempered liberalism would be unendurable. That is the crisis the neoconservatives evoke: the triumph of liberalism over its historical restraints. And that is a triumph they both endorse and lament. . . . Neoconservatives are nervous liberals, and what they are nervous about is liberalism. They despair of liberation, but they are liberals still, with whatever longing for older values.'' ''Nervous Liberals,'' *New York Review of Books,* 26/15 (October 11, 1979), p. 6.

32. C. B. Macpherson, *The Real World of Democracy* (Oxford: Oxford University Press, 1972), p. 54. Many who seek to secure a more equitable distribution of goods in our society often fail to see that a ''justice'' so secured may well only reinforce a more fundamental unjust view of ourselves. The problem with American egalitarianism, as Michael Walzer has argued, is that egalitarians fail to see that different goods should be distributed to different people for different reasons. We have tried to avoid articulating or institutionalizing the criteria for such differences by making the ability to make money the common denominator for everyone, the assumption being that if everyone has a basic minimum of money, then the distribution of their other talents will take care of itself. But such a system is inherently unjust, since many have no talent for making money. As Walzer suggests, ''Equality requires a diversity of principles, which mirrors the diversity both of mankind and of social goods,'' but as a society we seem to have no way of embodying such diversity in our public policies, for the recognition of diversity seems to result in injustice and envy. ''In Defense of Equality,'' *Dissent*, 20/4 (Fall 1973), pp. 399–408. To avoid envy a society must have a sense of those offices and tasks that receive special favor because of the service they perform for the existence of the community as a whole.

33. Macpherson, *The Real World of Democracy*, p. 62. Though I am in deep agreement with much of Macpherson's analysis of the dilemma of contemporary liberalism, I am unconvinced by his claim that technology has now freed us from scarcity to the extent that we can now throw off our dependence on the market. Rather, I suspect, as his own analysis suggests, that we can only free ourselves from the coercion of the market when we are morally trained not to think of ourselves as deserving whatever we desire, or perhaps more accurately, when we learn to desire the right things rightly.

34. This criticism may appear unfair to Rawls, as his own criticism of ideal observer theory and utilitarianism rests on those theories' tendencies to conflate into one, thereby eradicating their individual histories. Rawls' strategy, in contrast, is to try to provide an account of justice that will allow for the development of an appreciation for individual differences without envy. However, his attempt requires him to resort to the device of the original position that seems to entail exactly the loss of individuality

he was trying to avoid. *A Theory of Justice* (Cambridge, Mass.: Harvard University Press, 1972), pp. 184–192. Thus Robert Paul Wolff has argued that "Rawls conceives of the moral point of view as an atemporal vantage from which, like Lucretius gazing down upon the plain of battle, we contemplate all time and all space equanimously and isotropically. But human existence is not accidentally temporal; it is essentially temporal. What makes it a matter of justice how a subgroup chooses for the whole society is the fact that in principle that entire group *could* be included in the choosing. What makes it seem a matter of justice how parents choose for their children is the human fact that generations overlap, so that the children, the parents, and the grandparents must live for a time in the same world. What makes it manifestly *not* a matter of justice how this generation chooses for a generation far in the future is the certainty that they cannot share the same world, and hence could not even in principle gather together to share the act of choice. The veil of ignorance creates a choice situation in which the *essential* characteristics of human existence are set aside along with accidents of individual variations. What results, it seems to me, is not a moral point of view, but a nonhuman point of view from the perspective of which moral questions are not clarified but warped and distorted." *Understanding Rawls* (Princeton, N.J.: Princeton University Press, 1977), p. 97.

35. Some have argued, for example, that our American experience, especially as it is understood in terms of the theological notion of covenant, must be taken seriously as an important moment in God's history. Thus Richard Neuhaus' *Time Toward Home: The American Experiment as Revelation* (New York: Seabury, 1975), pp. 46–67. I do not have the space to deal adequately with the challenge of this position. However, without denying the power and profundity often associated with such attempts to understand theologically the American experience, I am often left wondering if they have anything to do with reality.

For a particularly provocative account of the political implications of covenant, see Robin Lovin, "Covenantal Relationships and Political Legitimacy," *The Journal of Religion,* 60/1 (January 1980), pp. 1–16. Lovin argues convincingly that political community interpreted in terms of covenant, in contrast to the contractarian tradition, has the advantage of not treating "the power of the state as some extraordinary menace, to be restrained from infecting the more creative institutions of family and culture. Like all other powers, the state must act in accordance with duty, but it also shares with other powers a creative role in establishing relationships of communication and obligation." Moreover, covenant reminds us that freedom emerges precisely at the point "that it is possible to speak meaningfully about duty as a reminder that covenantal freedom always contains an element of mutuality," pp. 9–10. Lovin also rightly suggests that equality understood covenantally is not, in the first instance, distributive, but rather that it is necessary to insure political participation. What Lovin does not do, however, is to provide an account of whether covenant is really an operative ideal in our polity or, even more important, what is the nature, status, and task of the church for such a polity. Also needing justification is the implicit assumption that the notion of "covenant" adequately sums up the "biblical" understanding of God.

36. Such a recognition would require white Americans to claim the history of slavery as their history, rather than simply an unfortunate event that can now be forgotten. In effect we are trying to say to the American black community that now that blacks have allegedly the same opportunities as whites, slavery can be forgotten, for after all what is a little slavery between friends. In the face of what cannot be changed, we often think the only thing we can do is forget, but when we forget we lose our own history. What is required is forgiveness, but for forgiveness to work politically we

must be the kind of people capable of making another people's history our own. For a remarkable account of the significance of forgiveness as an integral aspect of any political process, see Haddon Willmer, "The Politics of Forgiveness—A New Dynamic," *The Furrow*, 30/4 (April 19, 1979), pp. 207–218; see also my "The Necessity of Forgiveness," *Worldview*, 23/1-2 (January–February 1980), pp. 15–16. See also H. R. Niebuhr's provocative account of the necessity of shared history for community in *The Meaning of Revelation* (New York: Macmillan, 1960), pp. 114–132.

37. The claim that the first social task of the church is to be herself is not "sectarian" if by that is meant a retreat or withdrawal from the world. Indeed, I am in some respects deeply sympathetic with the social strategy that Max Stackhouse has called "conciliar denominationalism"—that is, the combination of the free church tradition with a concern for the wider social order. However, as Stackhouse denotes, this strategy seems to entail two conflicting motifs: sectarianism and Christendom. Thus, a figure such as Rauschenbush "saw the necessity of the select body of believers anticipating the Kingdom in the word and deed in good sectarian fashion, and of taking the world seriously on its own terms, as did all visions of Christendom." "The Continuing Importance of Walter Rauschenbush: Editor's Introduction," in Walter Rauschenbush's *The Righteousness of the Kingdom*, edited and introduced by Max Stackhouse (Nashville: Abingdon Press, 1968), p. 23. What advocates of this stance often overlooked, however, in their enthusiasm for liberal society was that such a society made the internal discipline necessary to sustain a free church as an independent and socially significant presence appear arbitrary and coercive. Moreover, they failed to see that the kind of "constitutional" democracy of the free church was radically transformed when translated into the language of liberalism. Thus Rauschenbush too readily assumed that his understanding of messianic theocracy could be institutionalized through the increasing democratization of institutions. And he failed to understand that a Christian social order that would "make bad men do good things" is antithetical to the moral presuppositions of a liberal society. The enthusiasm for the American experiment has been one of the primary sources for the failure of Christian social ethicists to appreciate the difficulty of making analogies between church (and Kingdom) and our society work. As H. R. Niebuhr has observed, Protestantism was hard put to provide principles for human construction, given the old societies in which it was born. In many ways one of the most healthy aspects of Protestantism was it was always forced to live in a world it had not or could not make. But with America the situation changed, as here Protestantism could finally turn from protest to construction and America, in fact, became, as I suggested above, an experiment in constructive Protestantism. See Niebuhr, *The Kingdom of God in America* (New York: Harper Brothers, 1937), pp. 28-44. Therefore Christian social ethicists in America have never been clear what the primary object of their work should be—the church or America— since attention to the latter seemed to be the immediate task of the church.

38. To be sure, many of those active in the founding and development of American democracy assumed that the limits imposed on government were not based on the sovereignty of man, but because all government was subject to the Kingdom of God. See H. R. Niebuhr, *The Kingdom of God in America*, pp. 75-87. However, the Enlightenment assumption of the sovereignty of man has increasingly become the more prominent, as a "government under God" simply makes no sense in a pluralist society.

39. This does not mean that Christians live in a night in which all "cats and/or nations are grey," (Barth). To be sure the church has a stake in developing relative

criteria to distinguish between more nearly just and unjust, more violent and less violent, freer and coercive states. Nor would I deny that in many ways pluralist societies, such as America, provide a unique opportunity for the church. It is not pluralism itself that causes the problem but the theories of pluralism that we must reject.

40. A. D. Lindsay has rightly argued that the key to democracy is discussion, but discussion can only be effective when we have genuinely different points of view. That is why equality is not only compatible with but demands differences. Perhaps the most significant thing the church can do for any society is to be a community capable of sustaining the kind of discussion necessary for the formation of good and truthful arguments and lives. See A. D. Lindsay, *The Modern Democratic State* (Oxford: Oxford University Press, 1962), pp. 249–286.

41. John Howard Yoder, "The Christian Case for Democracy," *Journal of Religious Ethics,* 5 (Fall 1977), p. 220.

42. This does not mean, however, that the church expects little from society as a way of enhancing the moral role of the church. On the contrary the church wants whatever society in which it finds itself to live up to its highest aspirations. Even though this paper has been primarily negative, my primary intentions are positive. For it is my central contention that the church will serve our social order best when it is able to form a people who have something to offer our social order. I have tried to suggest that that "something" is nothing less than the virtues and trust necessary to sustain a polity capable of maintaining a rich pluralism of differences.

5: THE CHURCH IN A DIVIDED WORLD

1. For an extremely useful comparison of Catholic and Protestant ethics see James Gustafson, *Protestant and Roman Catholic Ethics* (Chicago: University of Chicago Press, 1978).

2. H. R. Niebuhr, *The Purpose of the Church and Its Ministry* (New York: Harper and Row, 1956), p. 26.

3. Too often we forget that enormous moral presuppositions are involved in the assumption that a history of the "world" is possible. For the very attempt to execute such a history is frustrated by the lack of a clear or coherent subject—i.e., a world. Conceptually and empirically, the concept of "world" is elusive, but it makes theological sense if we remember that our existence is eschatologically formed.

4. Frank Kermode, *The Genesis of Secrecy: On the Interpretation of Narrative* (Cambridge, Mass.: Harvard University Press, 1979).

5. For insightful development of this theme see Thomas Ogletree, "Hospitality to the Stranger: Reflections on the Role of the 'Other' in Moral Experience," *American Society of Christian Ethics: Selected Papers,* ed. Max Stackhouse (Waterloo: Council on the Study of Religion, 1977), pp. 16–40; and Enda McDonagh, *Gift and Call* (St. Meinrad, Ind.: Abbey Press, 1975). For a marvelous analysis of the general importance of hospitality for Christians see Rowan Greer, "Hospitality in the First Five Centuries of the Church," *Monastic Studies,* 10 (Easter, 1974), pp. 29–48.

6. John Howard Yoder, "The Basis of Barth's Social Ethics," paper for Karl Barth Society of America (unpublished), p. 11.

7. Ibid.

8. Samuel Johnson reminds us that "There is nothing more dreadful to an author than neglect, compared with which reproach, hatred, and opposition, are names of happiness; yet this worst, this meanest fate every man who dares to write has reason to

fear." *The Rambler*, ed. N. J. Bates and Albrecht Strauss (New Haven, Conn.: Yale University Press, 1969), p. 13. I am therefore particularly grateful to those that have taken the time to criticize my work, for as Johnson suggests, it is better than being ignored. Even more important, I need the criticism even when it is unfriendly. I have understood my task to offer a different way to think about the moral life. Too often, however, I remain caught in the language and concepts of what I have called elsewhere, the "standard account." Thus it seems I must choose between an ethics of obligation or virtue, or between teleological or deontological modes of justification. As a result, I fail to make the explanatory power of my position intelligible. Critiques such as Wes Robbins', therefore, help me understand how much I have to do. See, for example, his "On the Role of Vision in Morality," *Journal of American Academy of Religion*, 45/2 (Supplement, June 1977), pp. 623-642; and my "Learning to See Red Wheelbarrows: On Vision and Relativism," *Journal of American Academy of Religion*, 45/2 (Supplement, June 1977), pp. 643-655. In his latest essay Dr. Robbins repeats some of the arguments and assertions of his previous essay, which indicated his deep adherence to what I have called the "standard account." Cf. J. Robbins, "Narrative, Morality, and Religion," *Journal of Religious Ethics* 8/1 (Spring 1980); and my *Truthfulness and Tragedy* (Notre Dame, Ind.: University of Notre Dame Press, 1977), pp. 15-39. I assume this means he found my response to his first essay to be less than adequate. But just as he continues to stand by his first arguments, so I continue to stand by my response. That such is the case does not necessarily indicate we are equally hardheaded, but how deeply we disagree about what ethics is about.

9. Robbins, "Narrative, Morality, and Religion," p. 174.

10. Thomas Ogletree, "Character and Narrative: Stanley Hauerwas' Studies of the Christian Life," *Religious Studies Review,* 6/1 (January 1980), p. 27. I am particularly indebted to Dr. Ogletree, as he has provided the internal criticism that has helped me see where I have been less than clear.

11. Kermode, pp. 76-77. Wesley Kort provides a helpful analysis of the elements of narrative—atmosphere, character, plot, and tone—in his *Narrative Elements and Religious Meaning* (Philadelphia: Fortress Press, 1975). He argues that it is mistaken "to assert in an a priori way that one of the elements of narrative always will be dominant. While startling advances can be made in narrative theory by emphasizing one of narrative's elements in this way, the insights thereby gained are eventually offset by the confusion which results when such an emphasis encounters a discussion which presumes or argues that one of the other elements is always and necessarily primarily in a fiction," p. 43.

12. As John Gardner has recently suggested, "The medium of literary art is not language but language plus the writer's experience and imagination and, above all, the whole of the literary tradition he knows. Just as the writer comes to discoveries by studying the accidental implications of what he's said, he comes to discoveries by trying to say what he wants to say without violating the form or combination of forms to which he's committed." *On Moral Fiction* (New York: Basic Books, 1978), p. 124. For a similar account applied to art see E. H. Gombrick's, *Art and Illusion* (New York: Pantheon Books, 1960).

13. In his review of Kermode's *The Genesis of Secrecy,* E. D. Hirsch may be correct that Kermode's understanding of the significance of institutions for controlling interpretation of texts is not sufficient to prevent radical relativism of interpretation. Indeed I suspect that Kermode's thesis works as well as it does exactly because of the text he makes central to his book—namely Mark. For Mark has a community of interpretation that few texts have ever mustered. But I think it equally unlikely that

Hirsch's suggestion that the only alternative is to stay with the "author norm" as primary will be successful—though it may be more appropriate to certain kinds of literature. What I suspect these hermeneutical disputes reveal is that they cannot be resolved without returning to more fundamental questions about how matters of truth and falsity can be asked about traditions and how traditions are necessary to ask questions of truth and falsity. See E. D. Hirsch, "Carnal Knowledge: Review of Kermode's *The Genesis of Secrecy,*" *New York Review of Books,* 26/10 (June 14, 1979), pp. 8–10.

14. For example, James Johnson argues that "a religious community defines its own identity in terms of its memory of what is significant from its history: while its doctrines, scriptures and institutional forms provide unconscious remembrances of its past, its systematic theology, ethics, liturgical innovations, and scriptural interpretation exemplify its conscious remembering activity. Speaking of the community as a whole, what is kept in these ways is significant for the identity of that community; when it is no longer perceived as significant, it is forgotten. As for the individual, his identification with such a community is closer or more remote according to how closely his own perceptions of what is significant agree with what the community takes to be definitive for its own existence. His own significant history—that is, his memory of what is significant out of a past that includes, in some way, the past of the religious community in question—overlaps but is never identical with that of the community as a whole. The degree of identification with the community's significant history is, by another name, the matter of faithfulness to a tradition. My argument is that a religious ethicist does not properly understand either his own significant history or his task as a religious ethicist if he does not consciously attempt to take account of what is remembered (in both senses) as significant in his religious community. Since what is significant for the moral self is not only what is remembered as such by choice (i.e., consciously), but also that which impresses itself upon the self as significant, the problem of religious identity becomes crucial for the moral self." "On Keeping Faith: The Use of History for Religious Ethics," *Journal of Religious Ethics,* 7/1 (Spring 1979), p. 105.

15. Van Harvey suggests just "because politics has finally to do with the formation of our culture it is impossible to completely bracket the moral appraisal of policies. So, also, it is because the vocation of scholarship ultimately informs the spiritual substance of our culture that moral appraisal in historical reasoning cannot be completely eliminated. Historiography is a truth-telling profession. Clifford would have argued, as important as the shipbuilding profession. The corrosion of the sense of entitlement to speak in the one is ultimately as destructive of the general good as in the other. The morality of believing arises most obviously and acutely, I have argued, when the ethos of a role-specific mode of inquiry is violated; that is, in situations in which we are usually dealing with matters of evidential belief. It would seem, therefore, an entirely different matter, as William James saw, when we are dealing with beliefs that are not evidential or where there is no accepted repertoire of procedures for their assessment and adjudication." "The Ethics of Belief Reconsidered," *Journal of Religion,* 59/4 (October 1979), p. 420. As a general description Harvey is no doubt right, though I think that we are not devoid of means of assessment of religious convictions as he suggests—and certainly not in a manner that makes religious convictions fare badly when compared to the means of assessment used in history.

16. Robbins, "Narrative, Morality, and Religion." Of course not all narratives claim normative status in the sense they lay a claim on our lives. Thus I can question if a certain account of the founding of the Massachusetts Bay Colony by the Puritans is

true without thinking that anything hangs on that for how I live my life. What I cannot remain indifferent to, however, is whether the story that formed the Puritans' lives is true or not, as it is one account of what it means to be Christian. How well the Puritans "narrated" that story for themselves and for us must, by their own reckoning, be tested by the classical narration—i.e., the scripture.

17. Gene Outka, "Character, Vision, and Narrative," *Religious Studies Review,* 6/2 (April 1980), pp. 116–118. I have made no attempt in this essay to answer the more significant issues Outka raises in his fine essay. I think the reader will find some of the points made here about tragedy and in the discussion of virtue in the next two chapters will help clarify some of the issues he raises about my position in those respects. And the book as a whole will, I hope, make clearer my understanding of the status of a "natural" morality. But the primary issue Outka raises—namely, that there is a tension between my stress on agency and sociality, or at another level between character, vision, and narrative—cannot be easily answered. I think Outka is right that a tension does exist between these emphases in my position and I remain unsure how to adequately resolve that tension. But I think that set of issues is a problem not only for my work, but for any adequate account of the moral life, since it seems both sides of the tension need to be affirmed. It is my hunch that these issues cannot be resolved in principle, but rather turn on the kind of agency that is made possible through the way particular narratives teach us to see and be. Put differently, we can never remove our dependency, but we can integrate our dependency into a more determinative character. A more detailed discussion of these matters must be left for another time. Needless to say, I am indebted to Outka for raising these issues so sharply.

18. Johnson suggests ("On Keeping Faith: The Use of History for Religious Ethics So Frustrating," *Hastings Center Report,* 9/4 (August 1979), pp. 21–22. critique of the "standard account," as the utilitarians present just as much a problem. I think he is completely right and I regret that I was unclear, as I certainly assumed in my description and critique of the standard account in *Truthfulness and Tragedy* that utilitarians were functionally the same as the Kantians in their disregard for history or the moral agent. Indeed, it is my own view that utilitarians and Kant at a formal level share more in common than they disagree upon; both seek for a single principle by which the variety of moral principles and virtues can be ordered.

19. For example, Alasdair MacIntyre has recently pointed out that the debate between the deontologists and consequentialists actually involves three major areas of disagreement: (1) the concepts of causality, predictability, and intentionality, and the relationship of consciousness to the world; (2) the concepts of law, evil, emotion, and the integrity of the self; and (3) the relationship of individual identity to social identity and subsequent questions of the relation of ethics to politics. Attempts to resolve these issues in terms of deontological or consequential alternatives is not only a gross oversimplification, but more profoundly masks the fact that we now live in a culture in which it is not possible to provide a systematic, consistent, and interrelated vision satisfactory for resolution of these issues. "Why Is the Search for the Foundation of Ethics So Frustrating," *Hastings Center Report,* 9/4 (August 1979), pp. 21–22.

20. Alasdair MacIntyre, "Theology, Ethics, and the Ethics of Medicine and Health Care," *Journal of Medicine and Philosophy,* 4/4 (Winter 1980), p. 437.

21. Robbins, "Narrative, Morality, and Religion," p. 165.

22. Ogletree, "Character and Narrative," p. 27.

23. William Frankena, "Conversation with Carney and Hauerwas," *Journal of Religious Ethics,* 3/1 (Spring 1975), pp. 45–62.

24. Alasdair MacIntyre, "Can Medicine Dispense with a Theological Perspective

on Human Nature,'' in *Knowledge, Value, and Belief,* II, ed. H. Engelhardt and D. Callahan, (Hastings-on-Hudson, N.Y.: Hastings Center Publication, 1977), pp. 33–34.

25. Ibid., p. 34.

26. Ibid.

27. For an interpretation of Kant along the same lines see Hans Frei, *The Eclipse of Biblical Narrative* (New Haven, Conn.: Yale University Press, 1974), pp. 263–264.

28. MacIntyre, ''Can Medicine Dispense with a Theological Perspective on Human Nature?'' pp. 40–41.

29. Ibid., p. 40.

30. For example, Robbins suggests that benevolence and justice are usually thought of and stated in propositions that have no particularly narrative characteristics. ''Moral continuity,'' he argues, ''would then be a matter of the continued acceptance and application of these propositions. And the settled tendency to live and to act in these terms would constitute, at least in part, possession of the characteristics of benevolence and justice. The point is that the recognition of the importance of the continuity of selfhood and of character to moral life is, in and of itself, in no way incompatible with a pure non-narrative theory of moral rationality.'' ''Narrative, Morality, and Religion,'' p. 168. For a similar position see Frankena's ''mixed deontological theory of obligation'' in his *Ethics* (Englewood Cliffs, N.J.: Prentice-Hall, 1963), pp. 43–52. What Robbins (and Frankena) ignore, however, is how their advocacy of benevolence and justice continues to trade on a narrative tradition, which they disavow but which is necessary to make their own commitments intelligible.

31. Hauerwas, ''Learning to see Red Wheelbarrows: On Vision and Relativism,'' pp. 643–655. Indeed, Charles Reynolds has suggested that to even call my position ''relativist'' is misleading. He may well be right about this, but the term still seems useful as a contrast to many of the dominant paradigms in ethics today.

32. Gilbert Harman, ''Moral Relativism Defended,'' *Philosophical Review,* 84 (1975), pp. 3–22. See also Alasdair MacIntyre's dicussion of relativism in his *Short History of Ethics* (New York: Macmillan Co., 1966), pp. 95ff.

33. Harman has more recently argued that his conception of morality is closer to that of politics. Thus he maintains ''moral argument can involve not only argument over the consequences of basic demands but also bargaining over the basic demands themselves. Morality is therefore continuous with politics. Furthermore, a person may belong to a number of different groups with different moralities which sometimes have conflicting implications. When that happens, a person must decide which side he or she is on.'' ''Relativistic Ethics: Morality as Politics,'' *Midwest Studies in Philosophy,* III (Morris, Minn.: University of Minnesota Press, 1978), p. 120. Though I think Harman is largely right about this, his conception of ''politics'' is too determined by liberal political experience and theory. Morality as politics is not just bargaining between different sets of convictions within ourselves or between groups but the process of discovery required by communities who seek to know and reflect the good and the true.

34. Harman, ''Moral Relativism Defended,'' pp. 17ff.

35. Bernard Williams, ''The Truth in Relativism,'' *Aristotelian Society: Supplementary Volume,* 52 (1978), pp. 216–217. See also Williams' discussion of relativism in his *Morality: An Introduction to Ethics* (New York: Harper Torchbooks, 1972), pp. 20–39. For an interesting critique of Williams, see Philippa Foot, ''Moral Relativism,'' *Lindley Lecture* (Lawrence: University of Kansas, 1979), pp. 3–19. Though I think Foot's criticism misses the mark, I am in essential agreement with her

suggestion that the problem of relativism is that there are some concepts—the value of human life, happiness—which we do not understand well, and thus cannot employ competently in argument, but which are essential to genuine discussion of the merits of different moral systems. Interestingly, this seems to me to be very close to the point Williams is trying to make.

36. Williams, "The Truth in Relativism," p. 222.

37. Williams explicitly borrows the distinction between real and notional assent from Newman's *Grammar of Assent*. This use of Newman strikes me as particularly inspired, as I suspect some of the crucial issues connected with religious belief and moral behavior might be best discussed in the terms suggested by Newman. For example, I suspect that many of our deepest moral quandaries are bound up with our only holding notionally what we should know by a real assent. Or again I suspect that many of the problems of moral development could be clarified by paying close attention to Newman's suggestions about the kind of movement necessary to move from notional to real assent.

38. This is an extremely complex point that I cannot treat as fully as it deserves. The claim I would have no idea what it would mean to be a medieval Samurai—or a woman, or a black, or my father—is an exaggeration. I might read all I could about the Samurai, begin to walk and dress like a Samurai, act in a courtly way, and so on. To that extent I could not only have an idea what it was like to be a Samurai, but I might even become a Samurai. But there are two decisive reasons I could not really be a Samurai. First, I would never reach the point where I could forget that I was *acting* like a Samurai—a consciousness that Samurai never had, since they *were* Samurai. Second, I cannot be a Samurai because I am already something else and can become such only by illusion or self-deception. We are historic beings such that when we attempt to forget our history we pervert our nature. Of course we are capable of change and growth, indeed any adeqaute understanding of Christian conversion entails the possibility of extraordinary change and growth, but change and growth, even for Christians is no less historical and community dependent. I am indebted to Dr. David Solomon for forcing me to see the significance of these issues.

39. Williams, "The Truth in Relativism," p. 226.

40. I am particularly grateful to Dr. Terry Tilley's, "The Radical Pluralism of Stanley Hauerwas" (unpublished manuscript) for helping me see this more clearly.

41. John Barbour, "Narrative Tragedy or a Critique of Virtue: *The Princess Casamassima, Nostromo, and All the King's Men*" (University of Chicago: dissertation proposal, 1979, unpublished).

42. Ibid., pp. 8–9. The theological implications of this understanding of tragedy are as significant as they are obscure. Certainly I cannot try to develop this aspect of the problem here. However, I am very sympathetic with suggestions made by Donald MacKinnon in various of his writings that the story of Jesus must be read as a tragedy. For example, MacKinnon observes that many have maintained that there is no place for tragedy in the Judaeo-Christian worldview. "But is this in fact true of the Gospels as we have them? . . . There is a sense in which Christianity demands to be presented as the tragedy of Jesus, of the one who, for intentions that the believer must judge of supreme significance, abdicated any responsibility that his influence might have conferred on him to arrest the movement of his people towards the final catastrophe of A.D. 70. The Christian believes that in Christ's Passion he finds at once the judgment and the redemption of the world; it is a desperately human occasion fraught not with a great, but with an ultimate significance. But it is also failure; and that not in the language of devotion, but in that of literal fact. It is in the figure of Judas Iscariot that

the failure of Jesus is focused, and the tragic quality of his mission becomes plain, 'Good were it for this man if he had not been born.' Yet through his agency the Son of Man goes his appointed way, and of his own choice; for in a few hours' time, he will say: 'Thy will, not mine, be done.' There is no solution here of the problem of the moral evil; there is nothing moreover which the Easter faith somehow obliterates. For it is to his own, and not to the world, that the risen Christ shows himself; and even those who accept as factual the record of the empty tomb admit that in itself that emptiness is no more than a sign pointing.'' ''Theology and Tragedy,'' *Religious Studies,* 2/1 (1967), pp. 168–169. See also MacKinnon's *Borderlands of Theology and Other Essays,* edited and introduced by George Roberts and Donovan Smucker (London: Lutterworth Press, 1968), pp. 97–104.

43. Stanley Cavell, *Must We Mean What We Say?* (Cambridge: Cambridge University Press, 1969), pp. 349–350. See also his more recent, *The Claim of Reason* (Oxford: Clarendon Press, 1979); also of some interest is my ''Reflections on Suffering, Death, and Medicine,'' *Ethics in Science and Medicine,* 6/4 (December 1979), pp. 229–237.

44. Robbins, ''Narrative, Morality, and Religion,'' p. 173.

45. Thus Johnson rightly argues that ''It is one of the sad ironies of history that [the] origin of the just war tradition has been so badly remembered as to turn it inside out; rather than a sign of a reluctance to justify violence for Christians, the tradition has come to be regarded, and not only by pacifists, as an attempt to declare the need to justify Christian resort to violence a non-question, a question that has already been answered. This is a perversion of memory because it represents a failure to keep faith with those before us in the Christian community who wrestled deeply and conscientiously with the issues at stake and produced this highly restrictive response. An attempt to recollect again, in and for the Christian community, what this original just war question was about leads to the somewhat startling discovery that pacifist and non-pacifist just war Christians have something profoundly in common: a searching distrust of violence.'' ''On Keeping Faith: The Use of History for Religious Ethics,'' p. 113.

46. In this respect, I suspect that we still have much to learn from Augustine, at least as he is interpreted by R. A. Markus in his extraordinary book *Saeculum: History and Society in the Theology of St. Augustine* (Cambridge, Mass.: Cambridge University Press, 1970). Markus points out that Augustine had to find a way between Eusebius, who sought to baptize the Roman Empire as Christian, and the Donatist. Markus argues in this respect that Augustine was much closer to the Donatist than is often realized, as he says that Christians can never be at home in the world. As a result, Augustine provides an interesting alternative for us, Markus suggests, as ''It is really only very recently that Christians have widely begun to see the present as an opportunity to break the fetters of the past; to recognize that if the world in which they, as Christians, are 'at home' collapses, the response should not be an attempt to create or to find another world in which the Church may thus find itself 'at home,' but rather a determination to enter into the much more ambiguous relation with the world which Christian eschatological hope demands,'' pp. 165–166.

6: THE VIRTUES AND OUR COMMUNITIES

1. Werner Jaeger's *Paideia,* I–III (Oxford: Basil Blackwell, 1939), still remains the classical treatment of the meaning of *arete* in Greek culture. (See particularly I, pp.

3–14.) For a brief account, see C. B. Kerferd, "Arete," *Encyclopedia of Philosophy,* I, ed. Paul Edwards (New York: Free Press, 1967), pp. 147–148.

2. Thomas Aquinas, *Summa Theologica,* I–II, 55, 1, trans. Fathers of the English Dominican Province (Chicago: Encyclopaedia Britannica, 1952).

3. Aristotle, *Nicomachean Ethics,* trans. Martin Ostwald (Indianapolis: Bobbs-Merrill Co., 1962), 1106b35–37.

4. Aquinas, *Summa Theologica,* I–II, 59, 1–2.

5. Immanuel Kant, *The Doctrine of Virtue,* trans. Mary Gregor (New York: Harper Torchbooks, 1964), p. 380. Whether Kant should even be grouped among those attempting to develop a theory of virtue is a matter of controversy. He certainly thought an examination of duties was prior to any account of the virtues, though that does not necessarily mean he thought the virtues unimportant. Missing in Kant's analysis is any sense in which the virtues are rooted in the self through habit. But even that must be qualified if one understands Kant's project as attempting to suggest the conditions necessary for the development of the "person of virtue" rather than the virtues. Yet Kant's manner of construing those conditions proved to be so stringent it is hard to see how the more "phenomenal" aspects of the self are in any manner integral to a "person of virtue." Any analysis of Kant from this perspective would have to deal with his extremely confusing account of the "dispositions." The effect of Kant's position, however, is to make one virtue—namely, conscientiousness—the necessary, if not sufficient, virtue for the moral life.

6. James Wallace, *Virtues and Vices* (Ithaca, N.Y.: Cornell University Press, 1978), p. 37. Wallace places the emphasis on "generally" as he tries to establish and ground the individual virtues by calling attention to those traits that are necessary for any group of people to live a life characteristic of human beings. In a similar vein Philippa Foot suggests "that virtues are in general beneficial characteristics, and indeed one that a human being needs to have for his own sake and that of his fellows." *Virtues and Vices and Other Essays in Moral Philosophy* (Berkeley: University of California Press, 1976), p. 3.

7. Donald Evans, *Struggle and Fulfillment* (New York: Collins, 1979), p. 14.

8. The novels of Jane Austen are studies in the difficulty of distinguishing persons of character from those who simply exhibit virtues of a polite society. It was Austen's great insight that "the person of character" is not necessarily at odds with societal manners but often the person for whom manners are a second nature. Convention may well stifle moral growth, but it may also be in some ages and for some people in any age the condition necessary for becoming virtuous. Yet that very condition also often makes it difficult to distinguish a person of character from those who are but observers of convention.

9. Aristotle and Aquinas both maintained that only those virtues acquired in a manner befitting a person of virtue can be said to "be" virtuous. Aristotle, *Nicomachean Ethics,* 1105a30–1105b8. According to Aquinas, an "imperfect virtue" is but an "inclination in us to do some kind of good deed," whereas a "perfect moral virtue is a habit that inclines us to do a good deed well." Perfect virtue requires all virtues to be connected, since all can be had only with prudence. One cannot have prudence unless one has all the other moral virtues, "since prudence is right reason about things to be done, and the starting-point of reason is the end of the thing to be done, to which end man is rightly disposed by moral virtue." Thus we cannot become virtuous by doing good deeds in regard to just one matter but not in regard to another; "for instance, [a person] will indeed acquire a certain habit of restraining anger; but this habit will lack the nature of virtue, through the absence of prudence, which is wanting in matters of

concupiscence. In the same way, natural inclinations fail to have the complete character of virtue if prudence is lacking." *Summa Theologica*, I–II, 65, 1. Thus, for example, someone may be "naturally" temperate, but such a natural inclination cannot be a virtue unless it has been formed and made my own through my character.

10. Contemporary philosophical ethics bases the ability to claim our action as our own on the "autonomy" of the self. My rebuttal, which follows, requires that the self be formed by a tradition (and its correlative virtues) that is sufficient to interpret our behavior truthfully.

11. A skill in its most basic sense is simply an acquired ability to do something well. It is interesting that the obsolete definition of skill is that of understanding or judgment as well as the reason or ground for doing something. Of course, not all skills are virtues, but I suspect that we would have no way to learn the virtues if we did not also have the experience of acquiring skills in other aspects of our lives. Learning to read intelligently will not make one kind, but kindness certainly includes many of the subtle discriminations involved in learning to read well. I suspect it would be an extremely rewarding project to analyze different kinds of non-moral skills for their analogies and disanalogies to particular moral virtues. Some have begun to provide an account of "ability" and "repertoires" as part of contemporary action theory. For example, see Lawrence Davis, *Theory of Action* (Englewood Cliffs, N.J.: 1979), pp. 42–56. Davis' analysis is in many ways very informative but it suffers from the general tendency of action theory to isolate and abstract "action" from the narrative contexts that make an action intelligible.

12. Wallace suggests that one can lose a skill, but we cannot forget how to be courageous or controlled. See Wallace, *Virtue and Vices*, pp. 44–45. He may be right, but the issue is more complicated. We may well forget how to be courageous under certain conditions if we have not been confronted by those conditions for a long time, just as someone who was once a great batter may no longer be able to hit a ball. Yet there are some skills which, if done long enough, may never be forgotten, such as driving a nail. I suspect the more pronounced distinction between the kind of skills engaged by virtue and that of the crafts is that acquiring a skill such as driving a nail is not required of everyone, whereas we feel that we can fault an agent who does not possess a virtue expected of everyone in our society. Yet again that is a complex matter, since someone with a virtue such as courage may not have learned the kind of behavior it may entail in all aspects of their lives. Thus someone physically courageous may not have learned how to be intellectually courageous.

13. That is the reason that initiation into a craft involves studying under a master. Learning how to do something well finally requires absorbing the nuances that simply cannot be taught formally, but only by watching and imitating how the master performs all tasks. That is why a craft is so similar to art and also why craft apprenticeships resemble joining a profession. One of the current difficulties of the crafts is that many have gradually been reduced to technique, since there are no longer masters to train others to lay brick or cut cornices. Thus buildings are increasingly designed so that construction of them can be accomplished without the need for master craftsmen; likewise, morality is increasingly understood in a manner that makes it more a matter of technique than art.

14. Frithjof Bergmann, *On Being Free* (Notre Dame, Ind.: University of Notre Dame Press, 1977), p. 65.

15. Integrity is a puzzling moral notion alluding to convictions about things one cannot or will not do, even though one does not necessarily demand the same convictions of others. Most societies probably have some sense of those things all persons

are excluded from doing if they are to claim integrity, but the mere adherence to such regulations is by no means sufficient to constitute integrity. Even though integrity is personal in this special sense, one's own integrity is not a peculiarity relative to individual circumstance. Rather, good societies are ones that encourage integrity—as well as the differences between people involved—as the means to enrich the community's tradition and life. Kantian accounts try to free integrity from any such tradition by positing a universal and timeless rational order as the necessary condition for integrity. Such an order has the ironic effect of discounting individual integrity, since by definition such moral convictions must "belong" to anyone. In this respect our sense of integrity continues to trade on the more traditional sense of honor, but our society may not provide sufficient moral basis to sustain even the less substantive sense of integrity.

16. See, for example, the work of James Gustafson, Alasdair MacIntyre, Elizabeth Anscombe, Stuart Hampshire, Philippa Foot, and the works cited earlier.

17. Peter Geach alleges that philosophy has overlooked the virtues in his *The Virtues* (Cambridge: Cambridge University Press, 1977). Geach's own analysis of the virtues proves disappointing, however, as he makes no attempt to suggest how the virtues form the self. As a result the virtues are depicted as recommended traits rather than characteristics of a person of virtue.

18. For example, Alasdair MacIntyre has argued that much of the work in contemporary English and American moral philosophy is more a symptom than a cure for the disease it takes as its object to eradicate. MacIntyre attributes this partly to the modern ethicist's failure "to understand either himself or morality historically; and in so failing he condemns himself to handling systematically rival positions without the context of systematic thought that was and is required even to define the nature of such rivalries, let alone decide between the contending positions." "Why Is the Search for the Foundations of Ethics So Frustrating?" *Hastings Center Report,* 9/4 (August 1979), p. 20.

19. Lawrence C. Becker, "The Neglect of Virtue," *Ethics,* 85/2 (January 1975), p. 111.

20. Ibid.

21. William Frankena, *Ethics* (Englewood Cliffs, N.J.: Prentice-Hall, 1973), p. 66.

22. Ibid., p. 65. For what in many ways is a more satisfactory account than Frankena's of the priority of "law" over virtue, see Alan Donagan, *The Theory of Morality* (Chicago: University of Chicago Press, 1977). Though Donagan supplies a much more adequate moral psychology and theory of action than Frankena, his distinction between first order and second order principles results in making virtue secondary to an ethics of law.

23. Frankena, p. 67. For a more extended treatment of my understanding and criticism of Frankena's position, see my "Obligation and Virtue Once More" and Frankena's response, "Conversation with Carney and Hauerwas" in *Journal of Religious Ethics,* 3/1 (1975), pp. 27–67. My essay can also be found in my *Truthfulness and Tragedy* (Notre Dame, Ind.: University of Notre Dame Press, 1977), pp. 40–56. The unresolved nature of our exchange on this issue probably results from radically different conceptions of the nature of ethical reflection. The debate does not, therefore, concern the interdependence of obligation and virtue, but whether a "theory" of obligation or of virtue is necessary at all.

24. R. M. Hare, "Utilitarianism," *Encyclopedia of Bioethics,* ed. Warren Reich (New York: The Free Press, 1978), p. 425. Bernard Williams has suggested that the

utilitarian cannot give an account of integrity exactly because from a utilitarian point of view we are morally required to consider our own commitments as no more significant than anyone else's. See his "A Critique of Utilitarianism" in *Utilitarianism: For and Against* (Cambridge: Cambridge University Press, 1973), p. 116.

25. This is an extremely complex matter, however; we are often unsure how to describe the meaning of our behavior even for ourselves. Thus the idea that our deeds reveal our character or our character determines our conduct involve matters which cannot be resolved in principle. For example, we may even mislead ourselves when, in thinking we are acting out of self-interest, in fact we are really charitable. The appropriate description cannot succinctly be determined by what we consciously thought we were doing at the time, but finally must fit within a narrative context appropriate to an entire life.

26. Becker, "The Neglect of Virtue," p. 112.

27. Alan Montefiore, "Self-Reality, Self-Respect, and Respect for Others," *Midwest Studies in Philosophy,* III (Morris: University of Minnesota, 1978), p. 201. Self-esteem and the ability to respect the differences of others are obviously closely related but insufficiently analyzed. The Kantian tradition suggests that only as we recognize and rule our lives in accordance with internal law do we have the basis for respecting others. Such an account is inadequate, as it asks us to respect others not as they represent a history separate from mine, but insofar as they are rational like me. The very differences necessary for self-esteem and mutual respect of others are thereby rendered morally irrelevant in the interest of securing a sound basis for respect. One of the deepest moral issues for any community is how to preserve the necessary differences between individuals without injustice and envy corrupting all grounds for moral cooperation.

28. For an account of self-deception, see my *Truthfulness and Tragedy,* pp. 82–100.

29. Not only do such theories fail to account for the significance of virtue, but they equally ignore the problem of definition and interpretation of moral behavior. It is almost as if they assumed that a description (such as that of abortion) is simply there to be seen rather than the creation of a particular community's experiences and history. See, for example, my *Vision and Virtue* (South Bend, Ind.: Fides/Claretian, 1974), pp. 11–29, 127–165.

30. Becker, "The Neglect of Virtue," p. 113. Perhaps these ambiguities explain why those who wrestle with descriptions of the moral life in the language of virtue have frequently been attracted to the psychoanalytic process as a paradigm of moral reflection.

31. See, for example, W. B. Gallie's analysis of Kant's commitment to peace in *Philosophers of Peace and War* (Cambridge: Cambridge University Press, 1978), pp. 8–36.

32. Ed Long in his "The Social Roles of the Moral Self," in *Private and Public Ethics,* ed. Donald Jones (New York: Edwin Mellen Press, 1978), argues that virtues necessarily imply public and social commitment (pp. 158–179); see also the essays in *Public and Private Morality,* ed. Stuart Hampshire (Cambridge: Cambridge University Press, 1978).

33. Wallace, in his *Virtue and Vices,* tries to have it both ways. Thus he argues that the virtues are commitments to forms of behavior that we as a community reasonably require of one another, but his description of community is a highly formal account of those kinds of behavior we require of one another in order to secure minimal societal cooperation. Thus conscientiousness becomes the central moral virtue because it is the characteristic we can require of anyone on rational grounds, pp. 90–127.

34. Plato, *The Republic,* trans. F. D. Cornford (New York: Oxford, 1964), pp. 119–144.

35. See, for example, Aquinas' extremely artificial attempt to justify why these are cardinal virtues, *Summa Theologica,* I–II, 61.

36. Thus Geach simply asserts that "there is a sufficiency of theoretical and practical consensus between men, for people of diverse opinions to cooperate in building houses and roads and railways and hospitals, running universities, and so on. And on the basis of this consensus we can see the need of the four cardinal virtues to men: these virtues are needed for any large-scale worthy enterprise, just as health and sanity are needed. We need prudence or practical wisdom for any large-scale planning. We need justice to secure cooperation and mutual trust among men, without which our lives would be nasty, brutish, and short. We need temperance in order not to be deflected from our long-term and large-scale goals by seeking short-term satisfactions. And we need courage in order to persevere in face of setbacks, weariness, difficulties, and dangers." *The Virtues,* p. 16. Yet even if Geach is right in this, he does not show why he should stop with just these four. Surely kindness, humility, caring, and so on can be seen as equally important on these grounds.

37. Aristotle, *Nicomachean Ethics,* 1103a23–25. I have made no attempt to develop Aristotle's extremely subtle account of the kind of habit characteristic of the virtues. However, see my *Character and the Christian Life* (San Antonio: Trinity University Press, 1975), pp. 45–60.

38. Though Aristotle has often been criticized in this respect, I suspect any account of virtue involves some depiction of what it means to be noble.

39. Augustine, "On the Morals of the Catholic Church," in *Christian Ethics: Sources of the Living Tradition,* ed. Waldo Beach and H. R. Niebuhr (New York: Ronald Press Company, 1955), p. 112. See also H. R. Niebuhr, "Reflections on Faith, Hope and Love," *Journal of Religious Ethics,* 2/1 (1974), p. 152.

40. Augustine, p. 115.

41. I have not indicated the nature of Stoic thought on the virtues as it has less interest for the issues I am concerned with here. For the Stoics were writing primarily an ethic for the training of public officials. Their account of the virtues therefore consists largely in grouping under the names of the virtues certain public duties. Aquinas followed their example in the II–II of his *Summa,* and it was that aspect of his work that became central for later Roman Catholic ethics. Thus the language of the virtues remained, though they were interpreted primarily as duties to be performed.

42. Aquinas, *Summa Theologica,* I–II, 69, 4. Justice is quite different from the other virtues since it does not form a passion so much as form a relation. But that raises the interesting question of how a relation can be subject to virtue. In the same way Aristotle said friendship is a virtue. See, for example, Philippa Foot's interesting remarks on this in her *Virtues and Vices,* pp. 9–11.

43. Aquinas, *Summa Theologica,* I–II, 60, 4.

44. It may be, however, that virtues such as courage and temperance are integral to all attempts to reason rightly, but the stress must be on the "rightly." It is not as if reason *simpliciter* requires courage, but any account of rationality that is normative implies courage.

45. Thus Geach argues that "there can be no virtue in courage, in the facing of sudden danger or endurance of affliction, if the cause for which this is done is worthless or positively vicious." *The Virtues,* p. 160. Determining whether the cause is worthless or vicious requires testing by example. Indeed the issue is more complex, as often we cannot determine beforehand if the cause be worthless, and thus

there may be no way to prevent our virtues from serving and even giving moral stature to a less-than-worthy moral cause. It is simply part of the tragedy of the moral life that nothing guarantees that we can avoid such complicity. The opposite side of this question is whether a bad man can have integrity. I suspect if integrity is interpreted in terms of Kantian "conscientiousness," there is nothing that prevents a bad man from having integrity. But if integrity is used in the fuller sense of indicating a person of virtue, then a bad man cannot have integrity.

46. Thus Wallace justifiably argues "it is obvious that living well, living fully, flourishing for a human being is different from living well for other kinds of creatures. The most striking difference between human life and all other kinds is that human life is characterized by activities that are possible only in a community with elaborate conventions. The point I wish to stress is that living a life informed by convention is natural for human beings in much the way that perception, nutrition, growth, and reproduction are natural." *Virtues and Vices,* p. 34.

47. Mary Midgley, *Beast and Man: The Roots of Human Nature* (Ithaca, N.Y.: Cornell University Press, 1978), p. 207.

48. Yet Aquinas insisted also that prudence could not operate without the other virtues. Moreover, Aquinas' understanding of prudence is extremely rich, involving memory, open-mindedness, and clear-sighted vision. For discussion of this, see Josef Pieper, *The Four Cardinal Virtues* (Notre Dame, Ind.: University of Notre Dame Press, 1966), pp. 3–42.

49. Williams, *Morality: An Introduction to Ethics* (New York: Harper Torchbooks, 1972), pp. 65–66.

50. Our "nature" is often associated with the passions partly because they seem to be simply "given." Thus some suggest that it is our passions that make us akin to the animal world. But our passions are as "unnatural" as our "reason" and as natural as our reason. Far from being alien to us, and precisely because they are human passions, they make us what we are. Aristotle and Aquinas seem to have had a firm hold on that point.

51. Aquinas, *Summa Theologica,* I-II, 59, 2. Aquinas' manner of putting the matter is that moral virtue "does not exclude the passions, but is consistent with them." It is unfortunate that one of the richest aspects of Aquinas' thought, namely his extended analysis of the passions, has consistently been ignored. See *Summa Theologica,* I-II, 22–48.

52. "If by passions we understand any movement of the sensitive appetite, it is plain that moral virtues, which are about the passions as about their proper matter, cannot be without the passions. The reason for this is that otherwise it would follow that moral virtue makes the sensitive appetite altogether useless, and it is not the function of virtue to deprive the powers subordinate to reason of their proper activities, but to make them execute the commands of reason by exercising their proper acts." *Summa Theologica,* I-II, 59, 5. Attempts to read from our natural inclinations normative judgments are doomed to failure as positive recommendations, but I suspect that our "passions" or our "nature" may well indicate that we are doing something wrong.

53. Robert Solomon, *The Passions* (Garden City, N.Y.: Anchor, 1976), pp. 15, 187. Solomon rightly suggests the "control of my anger is not (as the concepts of 'suppression' and 'repression' suggest) the containment of an invading force from the mysterious depths 'within' me. The anger is my own as well as the control; the 'suppression' is but part of the structure which I am imposing upon the world through my anger. To think otherwise is to view my anger as not mine," pp. 170–171. It would

be very useful to compare Solomon's analysis of the passions with Evans' account of the attitudes in his *Struggle and Fulfillment*. For Evans suggests that our attitudes are more basic than our beliefs, in contrast to Solomon's claim that our emotions are judgments inseparable from our beliefs. See Evans, pp. 12–13, and Solomon, pp. 186–193. My emphasis on the historical nature of the self obviously makes me more sympathetic to Solomon on this issue. However, there may be a deeper agreement between Evans and Solomon, as Evans' analysis of the centrality of trust for human flourishing bears close resemblances to Solomon's claim that "self-esteem is the ultimate goal of every passion," p. 97.

54. Solomon, *The Passions*, p. xvii. Though I find Solomon's analysis of the passions compelling, I think his attempt to ground morality in the passions is but the other side of the Kantian attempt to ground morality in reason. Both seek to avoid a particular society's history as the locus of moral development and reflection. Evans' very insightful account of the attitude-virtues necessary for human fulfillment strikes me as but another form, admittedly one that is more amenable to my own perspective than the Kantian, of our longing for a universal morality.

For an account of the passions very similar to my own analysis, see Don Saliers' marvelous book, *The Soul in Paraphrase: Prayer and Religious Affections* (New York: Seabury, 1980).

55. Dr. Patricia Jung in her Vanderbilt dissertation, "The Embodied Nature of Character: A Study in Theological Ethics" (1979) has criticized my account of character for being "one-sidedly intellectualistic" and for failing to provide an appropriate account of the "embodied nature of the moral agent." In particular, she attributes my failure to account for our passions and desires to my reliance on the model of agency developed in contemporary analytical philosophy and action theory. I think there is a good deal that is right about this criticism, but I am unconvinced Dr. Jung's use of Ricoeur is more helpful for developing a fuller account of how the passions form and are formed through our character. It is my suspicion that something like Jonathan Edwards' account of the "affections" may provide one of the fruitful ways to think further about how the "involuntary" is embodied in the "voluntary." Part of our difficulty in this respect is our loss of Aristotle's and Aquinas' richer sense of habit.

56. Geach, *The Virtues*, p. 17.

57. MacIntyre has developed this theme in a number of his recent articles. For the fullest account, see his *A Short History of Ethics* (New York: Macmillan, 1966) and his *After Virtue* (Notre Dame, Ind.: University of Notre Dame Press, 1981).

58. That is why all genuine forms of non-violence require such extraordinary forms of training in virtue. Only those who are people of power can risk denying themselves the protections most· of us feel we need if we are to survive psychologically and physically. Moreover, the non-violent need not only to be virtuous but to participate in a community that provides them with the moral resources for living non-violently. For the disadvantages correlative to living non-violently can quickly generate self-hate if we are not sustained by a more substantive community that is able to remind us what we are about.

59. Lionel Trilling, *Sincerity and Authenticity* (Cambridge, Mass.: Harvard University Press, 1972), p. 12.

60. David Little, "Duties of Station vs. Duties of Conscience: Are There Two Moralities?" in *Private and Public Ethics*, ed. Donald Jones, p. 138. Little's article is an excellent criticism of Reinhold Niebuhr's argument that there is a sharp distinction between the morality of groups and individuals.

61. Little, p. 141. Little is not strictly talking about conscience in this respect, but

conscientiousness. He rightly argues that we assume there are public tests for determining whether someone has been conscientious, which is a clear indication that conscientiousness is an art that is learned in communication with others (p. 146). Wallace, who also makes conscientiousness the central virtue, insists that it is a composite virtue that includes honesty, fairness, truthfulness, and being a person of one's word. *Virtue and Vices,* p. 90. However it is useful to contrast those virtues Little assumes central to being conscientious with Wallace, as Little's are substantive in contrast with the more procedural nature of Wallace's list. The latter is what MacIntyre has called secondary virtues because "their existence in a moral scheme of things as virtues is secondary to, is if you like parasitic upon, the notion of another primary set of virtues which are directly related to the goals which men pursue as the ends of their life. The secondary virtues do not assist us in identifying which ends we should pursue." MacIntyre goes on to suggest that the best our society can do is to make secondary virtues primary. *Secularization and Moral Change* (London: Oxford University Press, 1967), p. 24.

62. See, for example, Thomas Shaffer and Hauerwas, "Hope Faces Power: Thomas More and the King of England," *Soundings,* 61/4 (Winter 1978), pp. 456–479.

63. That is why appeals to "autonomy" are so unsatisfactory as a basis for why we should be willing to resign from certain tasks and roles rather than cooperate with what we take to be morally doubtful enterprises. See, for example, Edward Weisband and Thomas Franck's account of autonomy in their otherwise fine book, *Resignation in Protest* (New York: Grossman Publishers, 1975), pp. 181–192. For a more satisfying account of what is morally involved in acts of resignation, see James Childress, "Appeals to Conscience," *Ethics* 89/4 (July 1979), pp. 315–335.

64. It may seem odd to consider cynicism a virtue at all, but it is certainly one form of disposing our intellectual skills. Moreover, the cynic is formed by profound moral convictions about the nature and centrality of living truthfully and without illusion. For a more complete analysis of honor, see my "Truth and Honor: The University and Church in a Democratic Age," *Proceedings of the James Hector Seminar* (Winston-Salem: Wake Forest University Press, 1976), pp. 35–58.

65. There is a close resemblance between patience and suffering, but as Kierkegaard suggests, patience differs from courage as it voluntarily accepts unavoidable suffering. See his *Purity of Heart Is to Will One Thing,* trans. Douglas Steere (New York: Harper Torchlights, 1948), p. 173. For a more extended analysis of suffering, see my "Reflections on Suffering, Death, and Medicine," *Ethics in Science and Medicine,* 6 (1979), pp. 1–9.

66. It may seem odd to some that I have chosen to stress hope and patience rather than love as virtues central to the Christian life. In doing so I certainly do not mean to deny the significance of love for Christian life and community. However, it is my view that the concentration on love as the most important if not single virtue of the Christian life has often resulted in distortion of Christian existence. For when love is separated from hope and patience, the eschatological and political aspects of Christian existence can be overlooked.

7: CHARACTER, NARRATIVE, AND GROWTH IN CHRISTIAN LIFE

1. It is not clear what a theory of "moral development" is meant to do. Is it an attempt to describe how moral development *does* occur? Or is the object to indicate how moral development *should* occur? In much of the recent literature these two issues

are confused. The assumption seems to be if you can learn how development occurs you will be better able to suggest how it ought to occur, but that by no means follows. Descriptive "stages" do not in themselves indicate what *ought* to be the case.

2. I have no doubt that there must be some correlation between cognitive development and moral development. But I am less sure that there is or can be any one account sufficient to describe this relationship, since what is meant by "moral" will necessarily differ between cultural contexts. Empirical cross-cultural correlations cannot resolve the issue, for they presuppose exactly the conceptual point at issue—namely, the assumption that "moral" is a univocal term.

3. James Fowler argues that Kohlberg and his colleagues have "not attended to the differences between constitutive-knowing in which the identity of worth of the person is not directly at stake and constitutive-knowing in which it is. This has meant that Kohlberg has avoided developing a theory of the moral self, or character, or of conscience. Strictly speaking, his stages describe a succession of integrated structurers of moral logic. He has given very little attention to the fact that we 'build' our selves through choices and moral (self-defining) commitments. His theory, for understandable theoretical and historical-practical reasons, has not explicated the dynamics of the inner dialogue in moral choice between actual and possible selves." "Faith and the Structuring of Meaning," *Toward Moral and Religious Maturity,* ed. James Fowler (New York: Silver Burdett Co., 1980), pp. 60–61. Even though I think Fowler is right about this, Kohlberg, like Kant, can and does give an account of moral character. The difficulty is that such accounts lack what we think is crucial for having character—our personal history. Later I will try to show why this is the case.

4. It must not be forgotten, however, that Christians have developed spiritual writings and disciplines that provide means to make their lives conform more perfectly with their language. Their practice was often better than they knew how to say.

5. Kohlberg simply assumes, for example, that faith denotes our most general attitude toward the world—it is how we answer the question of "the meaning of life." "Faith" is thus understood to be a general epistemological category that categorizes a necessary stance anyone must take vis-à-vis the world. In fairness to Kohlberg it must be admitted that modern theology has often described "faith" in this manner, but such an understanding of faith can do little to advance our understanding of how Christian convictions work and require moral growth. For what Christians are concerned with is not that all people need to assume an ultimate stance toward the universe, but that Christians learn to be faithful to the way of God revealed in the death and resurrection of Christ. Faith is not an epistemological category, but a way of talking about the kind of faithfulness required of worshipers of the God of Israel. For Kohlberg's understanding of "faith," see his "Education, Moral Development and Faith," *Journal of Moral Education,* 4/1 (1974), pp. 5–16.

6. For a critique of the concept of autonomy, see Gerald Dworkin, "Moral Autonomy," in *Morals, Science and Sociality,* ed. Engelhardt and Callahan (Hastings-on-Hudson, N.Y.: Hastings Center, 1978), pp. 156–170. Dworkin rightly argues that "it is only through a more adequate understanding of notions such as tradition, authority, commitment, and loyalty, and of the forms of human community in which these have their roots, that we shall be able to develop a conception of autonomy free from paradox and worthy of admiration," p. 170. But the whole force of the modern concept of autonomy has been to make the individual "a law unto himself" and thus free from history. See Kant, *Foundations of the Metaphysics of Morals* (New York: Liberal Arts Press, 1959), p. 65.

7. For an exposition of this point, see James McClendon's *Biography as Theology*

(Nashville: Abingdon Press, 1974). In stark contrast to McClendon, Kant argued that imitation of another, even God or Jesus, would be pathological except as the other is a representative of the moral law known through reason. Thus Kant says, "The living faith in the archetype of humanity well-pleasing to God (in the Son of God) is bound up, in itself, with a moral idea of reason so far as this serves us not only as a guide-line but also as an incentive; hence, it matters not whether I start with it as a rational faith, or with the principle of a good course of life. In contrast, the faith in the self-same archetype in its (phenomenal) appearance (faith in the God-Man), as an empirical (historical) faith, is not interchangeable with the principle of the good course of life (which must be wholly rational), and it would be quite a different matter to wish to start with such a faith (which must base the existence of such a person on historical evidence) and to deduce the good course of life from it. To this extent, there would be a contradiction between the two propositions above. And yet, in the appearance of the God-Man (on earth), it is not that in him which strikes the senses and can be known through experience, but rather the archetype, lying in our reason, that we attribute to him (since, so far as his example can be known, he is found to conform thereto), which is really the object of saving faith, and such a faith does not differ from the principle of a course of life well-pleasing to God." *Religion Within the Limits of Reason Alone,* trans. Theodore Green (New York: Harper Torchbooks, 1960), pp. 109-110. Of course, it was Kant's hope that "in the end religion will gradually be freed from all empirical determining grounds and from all statutes which rest on history and which through the agency of ecclesiastical faith provisionally unite men for the requirements of the good; and thus at last the pure religion of reason will rule over all, 'so that God may be all in all,' " p. 112.

It is extremely instructive to note the contrast in style between Kant's way of doing ethics and works dealing with the spiritual life. For the latter, the use of examples is crucial, as they invite the reader to imaginatively take the stance of another as the necessary condition for the examination of their own life. Thus, for example, in William Law's *A Serious Call to Devout and Holy Life* (New York: Paulist Press, 1978), characters are created and discussed with almost the same detail as a novelist. Indeed, it may be for that reason that the novel remains our most distinctive and powerful form of moral instruction.

8. I suspect that there are extremely significant theoretical reasons why this is the case which reach to the very heart of what morality is about. For if Aristotle is right that ethics deals with those matters that can be otherwise (*Nicomachean Ethics,* trans. Martin Ostwald [Indianapolis: Bobbs-Merrill, 1962], 1904b10–1095a10), then ethics must deal with particular and contingent events and relations. Because Aristotle posited a "final good," it is often overlooked that he maintained that "the good cannot be something universal, common to all cases, and single, for it it were, it would not be applicable in all categories but only in one" (*Ethics,* 1096a26). Or again: "The problem of the good, too, presents a similar kind of irregularity, because in many cases good things bring harmful results. There are instances of men ruined by wealth, and others by courage" (*Ethics,* 1094b16). To learn to be "moral," therefore, necessarily requires a guide, since there are no universal standards that are sufficient to insure our "morality."

9. At least one curiosity concerning the current enthusiasm among Christians for "moral development" is the complete lack of any sense of sin associated with the process of moral development. From the Christian perspective, growth necessarily entails a heightened sense of sinfulness. For only as we are more nearly faithful do we learn the extent of our unfaithfulness. Put differently, "sin" is not a natural category,

that is, another way of talking about a failure of "moral development" or immoral behavior, but rather a theological claim about the depth of the self's estrangement from God. That is why we are not just "found" to be sinners, but that we must be "made" to be sinners.

10. That such is the case is not surprising, as most communities are not called upon to articulate the conceptual linkages between what they "believe" and what they do. Such "linkages" are forged through the traditions and customs of a people developed from the interaction of their convictions and experiences. Once such "linkage" is broken, no amount of "conceptual clarification" can restore the "naturalness" of the relationship. Indeed, the development of "ethics" as a distinct discipline that takes as its task the establishment of the "foundation" of morality may in fact denote that something decisive has happened to a community's moral convictions that no "foundation" can rectify.

11. For a fuller discussion of this distinction, see my "Ethics and Ascetical Theology," *Anglican Theological Review,* 61/1 (January 1979), pp. 87–98.

12. For a more complete analysis of the idea of character, see my *Character and the Christian Life* (San Antonio: Trinity University Press, 1975). There I described "character" as "the qualification or determination of our self-agency, formed by our having certain intentions rather than others," p. 115. However no one-sentence description can do justice to the complexity of a concept such as character. Indeed, it is my hope that this essay, through the development of the idea of narrative, will supplement the insufficiency of my analysis in *Character and the Christian Life* of how character is acquired and the necessary condition for us to be able to "step back" from our engagements.

13. For an analysis of the relation of narrative and self-deception as well as a more general account of the nature of narrative, see my *Truthfulness and Tragedy: Further Investigations into Christian Ethics* (Notre Dame, Ind.: University of Notre Dame Press, 1977), pp. 82–100, 15–39.

14. For more detailed critiques of moral philosophy from this perspective, see my *Vision and Virtue* (South Bend, Ind.: Fides/Claretian, 1974) and *Truthfulness and Tragedy*. In particular, I criticize recent moral philosophy's assumption that the primary moral question is "What should I do?" rather than "What should I be?" From my perspective the former question masks a deep despair about the possibility of moral growth, as it accepts us as we are. The only sign of hope such a view entertains is that we can free ourselves from who we are by making moral decisions from "the moral point of view." Yet the material content of the "moral point of view" assumes the description of the "situation" does not require reference to the self for how the description should be made. In contrast, the question "What should I be?" demands we live hopeful lives, as it holds out the possibility that we are never "captured" by our history, because a truer account of our self, that is, a truer narrative, can provide the means to grow so that we are not determined by past descriptions of "situations." Our freedom comes not in choice but through interpretation.

Interestingly, almost all ethical theory since Kant assumes that the moral life is lived primarily prospectively—i.e., our freedom comes only as each new "choice" gives us a new possibility. But as we look back on our "choices," they seldom seem to be something we "chose," for we often feel we would have done differently had we "known what we now know." In contrast I assume that ethics must be concerned with retrospective judgments, as we seek the means to make what we have "done" and what has happened to us our own. Moral "principles" cannot do that; what is required is a narrative that gives us the ability to be what we are and yet go on.

15. Kohlberg's Kantian commitments are commendably explicit, and like most Kantians he seems to assume that there really exist no other moral alternatives. He thus argues that morality must be "autonomous," that is, independent of any community or tradition, and "formal." Yet, like many Kantians he wants to claim that this "formal" understanding of morality provides substantive and material implications for actual moral behavior—i.e., his concern for justice. Yet in fact it remains to be shown that purely formal accounts of morality can generate the kind of commitment to justice Kohlberg desires. In particular, see Kohlberg's "From Is to Ought: How to Commit the Naturalistic Fallacy and Get Away With It in the Study of Moral Development," *Cognitive Development and Epistemology,* ed. T. Mischel (New York: Academic Press, 1971), pp. 215–218. For a perspective on Kant very similar to mine, see Alasdair MacIntyre, *A Short History of Ethics* (New York: Macmillan, 1966), pp. 190–199. MacIntyre helps make clear that the Kantian program is not as free from history as it claims but rather is a moral philosophy written to meet the needs of liberal societies. In other words, we should not be surprised to get the kind of theory of moral development we find in Kohlberg, as it is an attempt to secure "moral" behavior in a society of strangers. It is questionable, however, whether such a "morality" is sufficient to produce good people. Martin Luther King, whom Kohlberg admires, would never have been produced nor would he have been effective if all we had was Kohlberg's sense of "justice." Rather Martin Luther King's vision was formed by the language of black Christianity, which gave him the power to seek a "justice" that can come only through the means of "non-resistance." See, for example, McClendon's account of King in *Biography as Theology,* pp. 65–86.

Ralph Potter has documented Kohlberg's impoverished sense of justice in his "Justice and Beyond in Moral Education," *Andover Newton Quarterly,* 19/3 (January 1979), pp. 145–155. He suggests that Kohlberg's difficulty involves an attempt to define a program of moral education which can be undertaken within what are assumed to be constitutionally defined limitations of the content suitably treated in public schools. Thus he quotes Kohlberg's claim that the "moral development approach restricts value education to that which is moral or, more specifically, to justice. This is for two reasons. First, it is not clear that the whole realm of personal, political, and religious values is a realm which is non-relative, i.e., in which there are universals and a direction of development. Second, it is not clear that the public school has a right or mandate to develop values in general. In our view, value education in the public schools should be restricted to that which the public school has the right and mandate to develop: an awareness of justice, or of the rights of others in our Constitutional system," p. 149. That seems to be a nice confirmation of MacIntyre's argument and also explains the current enthusiasm for Kohlberg's work among educators, for it allows them to discuss "moral issues" in the classroom, seemingly without substantive moral commitments. The ideological bias of the assumption that a "formal" account of morality is "neutral" vis-à-vis actual moral convictions is overlooked, as it is exactly the ideology necessary to sustain a society that shares no goods in common.

16. For an extremely interesting account that treats "childhood" as an integral moral project, see David Norton, *Personal Destinies: A Philosophy of Ethical Individualism* (Princeton, N.J.: Princeton University Press, 1976), pp. 170–178. Kohlberg, unfortunately, never analyzes or defends his assumption that the metaphor of stages is appropriate to describe the process of moral development. One of the reasons for this, I suspect, is that he has not noticed that it is, in fact, a "metaphor."

One of the anomalies of Kohlberg's commitment to Kant is that Kant was very clear that the development of virtue could not be learned or come through "stages."

Thus in *Religion Within the Limits of Reason Alone,* Kant says, "The ancient moral philosophers, who pretty well exhausted all that can be said about virtue, have not left untouched the two questions mentioned above. The first they expressed thus: Must virtue be learned? (Is man by nature indifferent as regards virtue and vice?) The second they put thus: Is there more than one virtue (so that man might be virtuous in some respects, in others vicious)? Both questions were answered by them, with rigoristic precision, in the negative, and rightly so; for they were considering virtue *as such,* as it is in the idea of reason (that which man ought to be). If, however, we wish to pass moral judgment on this moral being, man *as he appears,* i.e., such as experience reveals him to us, we can answer both questions in the affirmative; for in this case we judge him not according to the standard of pure reason (at a divine tribunal) but by an empirical standard (before a human judge)," p. 20.

From Kant's perspective, Kohlberg's attempt to provide a naturalistic account of "autonomy" is a category mistake, since autonomy must be free from all "natural" causes. Kohlberg's interests are, oddly enough, Aristotelian in inspiration, but I think his attempt to express them through Kantian categories has prevented him from having the conceptual tools for a fuller account of moral development.

17. For a more detailed argument concerning this point, see *Truthfulness and Tragedy,* pp. 15–39.

18. For example, Aquinas maintains the more excellent a man is the graver his sin, *Summa Theologica,* trans. Fathers of the English Dominican Province (Chicago: Encyclopaedia Britannica, 1952), I-II, 73, 10. Other references to the *Summa* will appear in the text.

19. See for example Herbert Fingarette's analysis in his *Self-Deception* (New York: Humanities Press, 1969), p. 140. See also *Truthfulness and Tragedy,* pp. 82–100.

20. Kohlberg, "Education for Justice: A Modern Statement of the Platonic View," in *Moral Education,* ed. Nancy and Theodore Sizer, (Cambridge, Mass.: Harvard University Press, 1970), p. 59. In an interesting manner Kohlberg rightly seems to see that there is a deep connection between Plato and Kant, as each in quite different ways tries to provide a "foundation" for "morality" that makes the acquisition of "habits" secondary. Aristotle's insistence that "morality" must begin with habits simply assumes that there is no "foundation" for "morality" abstracted from historic communities.

21. Kohlberg, "From Is to Ought," pp. 226–227. Kohlberg's criticism in this respect seems a bit odd, since his own commitment to a formal account of morality entails that a moral theory is not required to adjudicate between various accounts of "honesty." Kohlberg assumes far too easily that the "individuation" of "moral" situations is unproblematic. If he delved more deeply into this kind of issue he might be less sure that he holds a "nonrelative" moral theory. Moreover, in this criticism he fails to distinguish or confuses the issue of the individuation of the virtues with the suggestion that virtues and vices are arbitrary categories of public praise or blame.

22. Indeed, the whole problem of how the various virtues are individuated remains still largely unexamined. It seems that there is a general agreement that honesty, justice, courage, temperance should be recognized as essential, but the fact that such "agreement" exists tends to mask the fact that there is little consensus about what "honesty" should entail. For an extremely interesting analysis of this kind of problem, see Alasdair MacIntyre, "How Virtues Become Vices: Medicine and Social Context," in *Evaluation and Explanation in the Biomedical Sciences,* ed. Engelhardt and Spicker (Boston: Reidel, 1975), pp. 97–121. MacIntyre argues that truthfulness, justice, and

courage are virtues that are necessary parts of any social structure, but that these "central invariant virtues" are never adequate to constitute "a morality." He holds that "to constitute a morality adequate to guide a human life we need a scheme of the virtues which depends in part on further beliefs, beliefs about the true nature of man and his true end," p. 104. In the absence of such a "scheme" MacIntyre argues that once the traditional virtues are no longer pursued for themselves they in effect become vices.

For an interesting example of the different transformations of meaning of one virtue, see Helen North's analysis of temperance in Greek and Roman society, "Temperance and the Canon of the Cardinal Virtues," *Dictionary of the History of Ideas*, IV (New York: Scribner's, 1973), pp. 365-378.

23. All references to Aristotle's *Ethics* will appear in the text.

24. It is well known that Aristotle thought "ethics" to be primarily a branch of politics, since "becoming good" ultimately depended on the existence of good polities. Yet Aristotle was by no means ready to despair at the possibility of producing morally decent people if such a polity did not exist. Thus he says, "with a few exceptions, Sparta is the only state in which the lawgiver seems to have paid attention to upbringing and pursuits. In most states such matters are utterly neglected, and each man lives as he pleases, 'dealing out law to his children and his wife' as the Cyclopes do. Now, the best thing would be to make the correct care of these matters a common concern. But if the community neglects them, it would seem to be incumbent upon every man to help his children and friends attain virtue. This he will be capable of doing, or at least intend to do" (*Ethics* 1180a 26-31). Friendship thus becomes the crucial relationship for Aristotle, since, in the absence of good polities, it provides the context necessary for the training of virtue. It is certainly not too farfetched to suggest that Aristotle's description of his social situation is not that different from our own. The ethics of "autonomy" is an attempt to secure the objectivity of "morality" by basing "morality" in "rationality" abstracted from primary relations. Perhaps a more fruitful strategy is for us to try to recover the centrality of friendship for the moral life.

25. Kohlberg, "Education for Justice," p. 59. For Aristotle, practical wisdom is not necessary just to know the good, but to "become just, noble, and good" (*Ethics*, 1143b 29). For a more complete account of Aristotle's understanding of practical wisdom and choice, see my *Character and the Christian Life*, pp. 56-61. R. S. Peters has argued in a very similar fashion in his critique of Kohlberg. See Peters' "Moral Development: A Plea for Pluralism," *Cognitive Development and Epistomology* (New York: Academic Press, 1971).

Needless to say, I am in agreement with Peters' critique. In particular, I think Peters is right that Kohlberg has failed to appreciate the "rational" character of Aristotelian "habits." Moreover, as he suggests, Kohlberg's failure to deal with the class of virtues involving "self-control" is a serious deficiency. I suspect, however, that Kohlberg has not felt compelled to respond to Peters' criticism because he thinks "virtues of self-control" remains too vague. In a sense, he is correct about that, as obviously more is needed than "virtues of self-control"—namely, the self requires a narrative that suggests what kind and how self-control is to function within our project.

26. There are actually two circles in Aristotle: (1) that only by acting justly can we become just, but to act justly seems to require that we be just, and (2) that in order for practical reason to desire and choose the right things rightly it must first be formed by the virtues, but the latter require the right use of right reason to be formed well. The two circles are obviously interrelated, but it is not easy to say how. Aristotle seems to have felt that the first circle, which he was quite aware of, was not vicious, since if a

person was taught to do the right things and to think about what they were doing, they would simply become people of character. The circularity of Aristotle's account of the virtues is but an indication that he rightly understood that morality needs no "foundations." Rather he assumed we are already morally engaged—the task of ethics being to help us understand and refine our engagement. Ethics for Aristotle is, therefore, an activity that is meant to remind us and draw out the implications that our nature is an activity.

27. I cannot develop it here, but I suspect it is no accident that Aristotle treats the virtue of courage immediately after his analysis of voluntary activity. For to act "voluntarily" is but a way of indicating that a man of practical wisdom must act in a manner that he is "in possession of himself." To act in such a manner requires more than "knowledge," for we must have the "courage" to face the world as it is, not as we want it to be. Courage and self-control involve more than restraining the passions, for they require the kind of self-knowledge that enables man to face reality and renounce delusion. Because he may have been assuming something like this, Aristotle may have thought that the exercise of practical reason in certain aspects of our lives necessarily would have an effect on the self, so that the other virtues would be formed accordingly.

28. Aristotle's claim that all men have a "natural" desire for happiness can easily be misleading for interpreting his thought. For the "end" of happiness is not simply given, but rather the "happy life is a life in conformity with virtue" (*Ethics,* 1099b27). Moreover, it must be the kind of "happiness" that encompasses a complete span of life (*Ethics,* 1177b25). Therefore the "end" is not simply given, but correlative of the kind of persons we ought to be as people of virtue or character.

29. Of course, what is tricky about this is that how much the "initiative" resides in us is a correlative of the kind of "character" we have. So "freedom" for Aristotle is not a status prior to our acquisition of character, but is exactly dependent on our having become virtuous. It was Kant's great project to make morality dependent on freedom, in order that we might be held responsible for our "morality." In contrast, Aristotle (and I) assumed that our ability to hold ourselves responsible for our "character" is context-dependent on the kind of narratives into which we have been initiated.

30. To try to analyze Aristotle's theory of moral weakness would simply take us too far afield of this point. However, it would provide a fascinating way to attack the issue of "moral development." It is interesting that Aquinas does not discuss the issue of moral weakness in the *Summa.*

31. Peters' account of different kinds of habits and virtues strikes me as very promising in this respect, pp. 257–262.

32. It is interesting that though Aquinas argues that the virtues must be connected, sins cannot be. Thus the "goods, to which the sinner's intention is directed when departing from reason, are of various kinds, having no mutual connection; in fact, they are sometimes contrary to one another. Since, therefore, vices and sins take their species from that to which they turn, it is evident that, in respect of that which completes a sin's species, sins are not connected with one another. For sin does not consist in passing from the many to the one, as is the case with virtues, which are connected, but rather in forsaking the one for the many" (*Summa Theologica* I–II, 73, 1).

33. Stuart Hampshire, *Two Theories of Morality* (Oxford: Oxford University Press, 1977), p. 44.

34. Ibid., pp. 17–18.

35. Kohlberg, "Moral Stages and Moralization," in *Moral Development and*

Behavior, ed. by Thomas Lickona (New York: Holt, Rinehart and Winston, 1976), p. 52. At least part of the difference between my position and Kohlberg's involves my attempt to show through the idea of character that "personality" can be more than a "psychological" category.

36. Kohlberg, "From Is to Ought," p. 185. I suspect that there is much to be said for Kohlberg's contention that moral growth occurs though the cognitive dissonance occasioned through our role conflicts. Exercises that help us to anticipate and rehearse such conflicts, moreover, may well help us to moral maturity. But such "growth" cannot simply be a question of being better able to justify our decisions from a "universal" perspective. For the subject of growth is the self, which is obviously more than the sum of principles to which we adhere.

37. Of course, it is equally true that every "binding" requires a "loosing," as we cannot and should not be bound to everything in our past. It may even be true that some of us inherit a history so destructive we may rightly wonder how we could ever be bound to it. Yet my freedom from such a history cannot come by having "no history" but by acquiring a narrative that helps me have a stance toward my past without resentment. For resentment would continue to bind me to the destructive, since the self would still be essentially defined by my assumption that I am primarily a creature of injustice. I suspect that one of the reasons growth in the Christian life is described as conversion is that it requires us to learn to live without resentment. And to be able to live in that manner requires us to learn that our life, including the destructive past, is nothing less than gift. I wish to thank Mr. Michael Duffy for helping me formulate this point.

38. I am particularly grateful to James McClendon for suggesting this way of putting the matter.

39. For example, see Enda McDonagh's suggestion that "threat" is always the necessary other side of a "gift." *Gift and Call* (St. Meinrad, Ind.: Abbey Press, 1975), pp. 36–39. That such is the case makes Aristotle's understanding of the centrality of courage for moral wisdom all the more compelling.

40. Law, *A Serious Call to a Devout and Holy Life,* p. 55. There is an unjustified intellectualistic bias in much of the literature dealing with moral development. The assumption seems to be that the more "self-conscious" we are of our "values" and principles, the better chance we have for moral growth. While I suspect any significant tradition must develop some who are "self-conscious," it is by no means clear that all need to be such. We must remember that the Gospel does not require us to be self-conscious as our first order of business. Rather it requires us to be faithful.

8: THE MORAL VALUE OF THE FAMILY

1. Tamara Hareven, "Family Time and Historical Time," *Daedalus,* 106/2 (Spring 1977), p. 58.

2. For a critique of the idea of the "rights of children," see my "Rights, Duties, and Experimentation," *Research Involving Children: Appendix* (Washington, D.C.: DHEW Publication 77-0005, 1977), article 5, pp. 1–24. Charles Fried, to his credit, has been one of the few ethicists to even deal with the issue of the status of the family. But the best he can do is suggest that "the right to *form* one's *child's* values, one's child's life plan and the right to lavish attention on that child are the extensions of the basic right not to be interfered with in doing these things for oneself." Children are thus moral entities only as they are extensions of adult life plans. See his *Right and*

Wrong (Cambridge, Mass.: Harvard University Press, 1978), p. 152. Roger Wertheimer confirms this point in his "Philosophy on Humanity," in Manier, Liu and Solomon, eds., *Abortion: New Directions for Policy Studies* (Notre Dame, Ind.: University of Notre Dame Press, 1977). He says, "Probably the least discussed and most badly treated matter in the literature of moral philosophy is the one that matters most in most people's lives: familial relationships. That's not surprising since that literature lacks a theory that could say much about those matters that would be both interesting and true. The familiar philosophical models for understanding or justifying the special regard we accord familial relations are inadequate to the task. That regard must be treated as a phenomenon of rationality, for we don't take imprinting quite as well as ducks do, and neither do we have the mechanisms by which lost lambs are reunited with their mothers. Our natural family has a hold on us whoever brings us up, and we find out who our real relations are by being *told*.... But neither are our relatives like ordinary benefactors, business partners, or friends; the special regard goes beyond reciprocity, love, or likeness—as often as not, those things are lacking, and even when present they can't explain the special regard for natural parents as opposed to adopted, foster, or stepparents. Let us admit that a family forms a small (exogamous) caste system. It can be understood and justified in terms of the special role the family has in determining an individual's identity. We identify with our relations, not (and not just) because we are akin to them but because we are kin to them. I, personally, am largely unmoved by the fact that the human race has got itself to the moon or that blacks dominate in my favorite sports, but I can't imagine what it would be like to be immune to pride or embarrassment at the achievements and antics of those in my immediate family," p. 136.

3. Robert Nisbet, *Tradition and Revolt* (New York: Vintage Books, 1970), pp. 203–224.

4. This is partly due to the newness of social history as a discipline. The attempt to depict the history of the family requires historians to utilize data that is extremely hard to control. For example, see Lawrence Stone's discussions of this in his *The Family, Sex, and Marriage in England, 1500–1800.* (New York: Harper Colophon Books, 1979), pp. 21–36. It is obviously too early to know how well Stone's groundbreaking research and argument will hold up, but his work has clearly set the standard for further research. For a review of the literature in this much neglected field see Christopher Lasch's, "The Family and History," *New York Review of Books,* 22/8 (November 13, 1975), pp. 33–38.

5. Lasch, p. 33.

6. Edward Shorter, *The Making of the Modern Family* (New York: Basic Books, 1977), p. 205.

7. Alice Rossi, "A Biosocial Perspective on Parenting," *Daedalus,* 106/2 (Spring 1977), p. 2.

8. Robert Nisbet, *Twilight of Authority* (New York: Oxford University Press, 1975), p. 257.

9. For example John Rawls notes that "even in a well-ordered society that satisfies the two principles of justice, the family may be a barrier to equal chances between individuals. For as I have defined it, the second principle only requires equal life prospects in all sectors of society for those similarly endowed and motivated. If there are variations among families in the same sector in how they shape the child's aspirations, then while fair equality of opportunity may obtain between sectors, equal chances between individuals will not. This possibility raises the questions as to how far the notion of equality of opportunity can be carried." *A Theory of Justice* (Cambridge,

Mass.: Harvard University Press, 1971), p. 301. Robert Nozick makes the interesting observation that radicals have always had an ambiguous relationship to the family, as it is not appropriate to enforce across wider society the love and care within a family, where such relationships are voluntarily undertaken. Nozick must surely have an odd sense of "voluntary," since the family is anything but "voluntary." Nozick, commenting on Rawls' difference principle, notes it is inappropriate as a governing principle for a family: no family should devote its resources to maximizing the position of the least well off and least talented child while holding back the more talented. But of course that is just what happens in many families that are regarded as important moral examples for us all. See his *Anarchy, State and Utopia* (New York: Basic Books, 1974), pp. 167–168.

10. Paul Ramsey, *Ethics on the Edges of Life* (New Haven, Conn.: Yale University Press, 1978), p. 9.

11. Christopher Lasch, *Haven in a Heartless World* (New York: Basic Books, 1977), pp. 6–7.

12. Ibid., p. 174.

13. Ibid., p. 141.

14. Ferdinand Mount, "The Dilution of Fraternity," *Encounter,* October 1976, p. 30.

15. Ibid.

16. Ibid., p. 20.

17. Milton Friedman, *Capitalism and Freedom* (Chicago: University of Chicago Press, 1962), p. 12.

18. Robert Paul Wolff, "Nobody Here But Us Persons" in *Women and Philosophy,* ed. Gould and Wartofsky (New York: Putnam, 1976), p. 132.

19. Lasch, *Haven in a Heartless World,* p. 12

20. Ibid., p. 13. For an analysis in many ways similar to Lasch's, but documenting what ways this development took a different form in France, see Jacques Donzelot, *The Policy of Families.* (New York: Pantheon Books, 1979). Donzelot notes that through philanthropy France made the transition from a government of families to a government through the family, pp. 82–95. See, for example, Lasch's review of Donzelot, "Life in the Therapeutic State," *New York Review of Books,* 27/10 (June 12, 1980), pp. 24–32.

21. Kenneth Keniston, *All Our Children: The American Family Under Pressure* (New York: Harcourt Brace Jovanovich, 1977).

22. Ibid., p. 11.

23. Ibid., p. 17.

24. Ibid., p. 22.

25. Ibid.

26. Ibid., p. 13.

27. Ibid., p. 17.

28. Ibid.

29. Lionel Trilling has suggested that "The disfavour into which narrative history has fallen with historians is reflected in its virtual extirpation from the curriculum of our schools and its demotion in the curriculum of our colleges. It bears upon the extreme attenuation of the authority of literary culture, upon the growing indifference to its traditional pedagogy; the hero, the exemplary figure, does not exist without a sharp and positive beginning; the hero is his history from his significant birth to his significant death. And perhaps the low status of narration can be thought to have a connection with revisions of the child's relation to the family—traditionally the family

has been a narrative institution; it was the past and it had a tale to tell of how things began, including the child himself; and it had counsel to give.'' *Sincerity and Authenticity* (Cambridge, Mass.: Harvard University Press, 1972), p. 139.

30. See my ''Having and Learning to Care for Retarded Children,'' in *Truthfulness and Tragedy* (Notre Dame, Ind.: University of Notre Dame Press, 1977), pp. 157–164. For a profound statement about this see Michael Rossman, ''Where Are Our Children: A Requiem for the Unborn,'' *Mother Jones,* May 1978, pp. 57–62; and Mary Catherine Bateson, ''Caring for Children, Caring for the Earth,'' *Christianity and Crisis,* 40/5 (March 31, 1980), pp. 67–70.

31. Lasch, *Haven in a Heartless World,* p. 139.

9: THE FAMILY

1. Peter Berger, Brigitte Berger, Hansfried Kellner, *The Homeless Mind* (New York: Vintage Books, 1973), pp. 191–195.

2. John Updike, *Couples* (New York: Knopf, 1968).

3. Robert Nisbet, *Community and Power* (New York: Galaxy Books, 1962), p. 59. This book was originally published as *The Quest for Community* (1953).

4. Ibid., p. 60.

5. Quoted in ibid., p. 61.

6. Ibid.

7. George Gilder, *Sexual Suicide* (New York: Bantam Books, 1975), p. 98. As Margaret Mead observed many years ago, the central issue of every society is what to do with their males. I do not share the criticism Gilder makes of women's liberation on the basis of this point.

8. See, for example, Robert Paul Wolff's account of how pluralistic democratic theory has attempted to combine liberal individualistic views of man with the social conception of the self as articulated by the sociological tradition. *The Poverty of Liberalism* (Boston: Beacon Press, 1968), pp. 138–150.

9. For example see my ''Having and Learning to Care for Retarded Children'' in my *Truthfulness and Tragedy* (Notre Dame, Ind.: University of Notre Dame Press, 1977), pp. 147–156.

10. Christopher Lasch thus argues, ''A society that fears it has no future is not likely to give much attention to the needs of the next generation, and the ever-present sense of historical discontinuity, the blight of our society, falls with particularly devastating effect on the family. Whereas parents formerly sought to live vicariously through their offspring, now they tend to resent them as intrusions and to envy their youth. Formerly the young sought to escape the smothering embrace of the older generation, but for the last several decades they have been more likely to complain of emotional neglect. The modern parent's attempt to make children feel loved and wanted does not conceal an underlying coolness—the remoteness of those who have little to pass on to the next generation and who in any case give priority to their own right to self-fulfillment. The combination of emotional detachment with attempts to convince a child of his favored position in the family is a good prescription for a narcissistic personality structure.'' ''Narcissist America,'' *New York Review of Books,* 231/115 (September 30, 1976), p. 12.

11. These types too often tend to become ideologies to support one type of family at the expense of others. Indeed it seems to me that it was exactly seizing one type as normative—i.e., the nuclear—that was behind the misleading conclusion of the Moynihan Report on black families.

12. "No act in life seems more private, more intimate, than the decision by two people to get married, particularly in this age when we celebrate the distance we have come since the times of arranged marriages. It is true, of course, that people 'select' their own mates now, whatever that may mean. But there are other ways to arrange marriages than becoming a formal partner to the contract—spoken and unspoken encouragements that pass among families and friends beforehand, as well as a million other hints and suggestions that become a part of the marriage scene afterward. While we do not know very much about those subtle chemistries, it is clear enough that marriage, too, is something of a community affair. It is validated by the community, witnessed by the community, commemorated by the community, and every married couple in the world knows something about the pressures exerted on the union by interests outside of it. In one sense, then, a marriage between two persons lies in a kind of gravitational field. The human particles who form the union are held together by interpersonal charges passing between them, but they are also held together by all the other magnetic forces passing through the larger field; and when the outer currents and tensions lose their force, the particles find that the inner charge, the interpersonal bond, begins to fade as well. Wholly devoted husbands and wives were to discover on Buffalo Creek that they did not know how to care for each other or to work together as a team or even to carry on satisfactory conversations when the community was no longer there to provide the context and set the cadence." Kai T. Erikson, *Everything in Its Path: Destruction of Community in the Buffalo Creek Flood* (New York: Simon and Schuster, 1976), pp. 218–219.

10: SEX IN PUBLIC

1. Indeed, I suspect that the "crisis" concerning sexual behavior in our society is not what people are actually doing or not doing, but that we have no way to explain to ourselves or to others why it is that we are doing one thing rather than another. Thus, people simply do not know why they do or do not have sexual intercourse before marriage, or even more disturbing, why they should or should not get married at all, or why they should or should not have children. In the absence of any such accounts, pragmatic considerations, which are often filled with wisdom and much good sense, rule the day. However, pragmatic reflection is not sufficient to guide our lives in a manner that helps us have a sense of worth necessary to sustain our own and our community's moral projects.

2. For an excellent brief historical overview of the historical development of sexual ethics see Margaret Farley, "Sexual Ethics," *Encyclopedia of Bioethics,* 4 (New York: Free Press, 1978), pp. 1575–1589.

3. Paul Ramsey, "Do You Know Where Your Children Are?" *Theology Today,* 36/1 (April 1979), pp. 10–21.

4. Of course the very phrase "sexually active" already embodies realist assumptions, since it tries to describe what many assume is a serious moral issue in morally neutral language. Of course, the "realist" may be right that such language is more appropriate because it avoids the "moralistic" language of the past, but it must be recognized that this kind of language-transforming proposal assumes substantive moral presuppositions.

5. Nena and George O'Neill, *Open Marriage* (New York: Avon Press, 1972). Page references will be given in the text.

6. James Nelson, *Embodiment* (Minneapolis: Augsburg, 1978), p. 127. Like the

O'Neills, Nelson does not believe that the question of infidelity in marriage can be limited to the issue of adultery, but rather is the rupture of the bonds of "faithfulness, honesty, trust, and commitment between the spouses." He therefore thinks we must remain open to the possibility that people can be maritally faithful without being sexually exclusive. My difficulty with such arguments is how you would ever have any basis to know if you are in fact "faithful" or not. It is certainly the case that often married people harm one another in more profound ways than by having sex with someone else. But it is also the case that sexual fidelity may be the way we learn to be faithful in other aspects of our lives together. I am aware that some couples may have sustained impressive marriages without the commitment to sexual fidelity, but that is not the issue. The issue is what kind of marriage Christians want to encourage as essential to the purposes of their community.

7. Nelson, p. 127. Again the difficulty with such "criteria" is that one has no idea what would count for or against whether certain forms of activity should be considered "shaped by love."

8. I owe this point to Anne Harley Hauerwas.

9. Anthony Kosnik, et al. *Human Sexuality* (New York: Paulist Press, 1977), p. 85. It should be noted that though their report was published by the Catholic Theological Society of America the board of that society took pains to make clear this action implied neither approval or disapproval of the report. Page references will be given in the text.

10. Paul Ramsey, "One Flesh" (Bramcote, Nottingham: Grove Booklet on Ethics, 8, 1977), p. 5.

11. Ibid., p. 15. Ramsey rightly rejects the Roman Catholic attempt to talk of "primary" and "secondary," as such ranking suggests in misleading fashion that unitive and procreative can be separated in a marriage.

12. William May, "Conjugal Love," *Proceedings of the Catholic Theological Society of America,* 33 (1978), pp. 139-140. The difference between May's and Ramsey's positions would be interesting to explore. May seems to want to maintain the traditional position that every act of sexual intercourse must be open to procreation, whereas Ramsey is arguing that a marriage must be open to procreation. What May fails to show is why the requirement that every act of sexual intercourse be open to procreation follows from or is implied by the permanent and exclusive character of Christian marriage. It makes conceptual sense to claim that the permanent character of Christian marriage is a necessary context for sexual expression, but it does not follow that therefore every act of sexual intercourse must be open to procreation. Indeed, I have sympathy with the traditional claim that the goods of marriage (which are not the same thing as the ends of marriage) are permanence, fidelity, and procreation, but I fail to understand why some assume that the relationship between these "goods" requires that every act of sexual intercourse be open to procreation. That argument seems to require a physical account of "natural law" that is inconsistent with the theological claims necessary to make Christian marriage intelligible in the first place. For there is surely no justification for monogamy apart from the special theological convictions of Christians about the symbolic role of marriage vis-à-vis the nature of the church.

One of the ironies of current thinking about sexual ethics, especially among those who want to defend more conservative forms of sexual behavior, is the glorification of the sexual act. They tell us that this is an act unlike any other and because of its special significance, it must therefore be limited to marriage. I have no wish to deny that sex can have significance for marriage and in marriage, but that significance is not inherent in the act itself. More mundane behavior, such as holding hands, can often be more intimate and significant as an expression of love than sex. The heightening of the importance of the act of sex in order to limit it to marriage, or at least to significant "interpersonal relationships," can only lead to a distortion of the act itself. We quite properly would sometimes prefer to read a book.

13. For example, Daniel Maguire has suggested that marriage is "the ultimate form of friendship achievable by sexually attracted persons." "*Human Sexuality:* The Book and the Epiphenomenon," *Proceedings of the Catholic Theological Society of America,* 33 (1978), p. 63. Many would find such a claim unobjectionable, but I think the assumption that marriage is a "kind" of friendship calls for a good deal more analysis than it usually receives. At the very least it can be observed that friends change and grow apart, but married people are supposed to stay married no matter how they change. Of course Maguire may well respond that is the reason he calls marriage the "ultimate" form of friendship, but I am not sure that is very helpful. For I suspect that such an understanding of marriage cannot help but underwrite some form of a romantic conception of marriage that assumes marriage is an intelligible institution apart from any willingness of the couple to be open to children. The meaning of marriage is thus separated from any relationship to "family" on the supposition that the quality of relationship between the couple is more important than the moral significance of the family as the essential place for having and rearing children.

14. For a more extensive analysis of this point see my "Sex and Politics: Bertrand Russell and 'Human Sexuality,'" *Christian Century,* 95/14 (April 19, 1978), pp. 417–422. The church's traditional condemnation of "secret marriages" involves substantive assumptions that can be too easily overlooked. For the significance of maintaining that sex should occur in publicly sanctioned contexts (which might well include "engagements") suggests that we should not trust our declaration of love unless we are willing to commit ourselves publicly. For there is surely no area where we are more liable to self-deception than in those contexts where love is mixed with sexual desire. Of course, there is nothing wrong with love or sexual desire except that we may often confuse the two. The problem with the suggestion that sexual expression should be relative to the level of loving commitment is that it is simply too hard to test the latter. I would suggest instead that the form and extent of our sexual expression is best correlated to the extent we are willing to intermix our finances. It may sound terribly unromantic, but I am convinced that one of the best tests of "love" is the extent a couple are willing to share a common economic destiny. As John Howard Yoder has suggested, "The ethical question is not whether the sex-with-true-love is by definition sinful, but whether true love can be honest, can be true love if it dodges the honest outward expressions which are its normal social form. . . . Therefore what is questionable about 'pre-marital sex' is not that it is sex, nor that it is pre-marital, but that the maintenance of secrecy, the avoidance of legality, the postponement of common residence and finances, the withholding of public pledge, constitute both a handicap for the marriage's success and *prima facie* evidence that the love is not true. This is not sex-without-marriage but marriage without honesty. It is not that the hasty youngsters sin against backward cultural mores while fulfilling themselves and consummating their own love: it is that they sin against themselves, their lives and their marriage, by depriving their love of the social consummative, the orderly cohabitative, the fresh air, without which it is stunted or amputated." "When Is a Marriage Not a Marriage" (unpulished manuscript), p. 12.

15. Willian Everett, "Between Augustine and Hildebrand: A Critical Response to *Human Sexuality,*" *Proceedings of the Catholic Theological Society of America,* 33 (1978), p. 78. All other page references in the text. It would be a mistake to charac-

terize the kind of arguments advanced by May and Ramsey as "biologist," as neither makes appeal to the "natural purpose" of the act of sexual intercourse to substantiate his argument. It is, of course, true that some arguments, particularly those concerned with contraception, are properly described as "biological." Having said this, however, it must be conceded that what Ramsey means, or at least the status of his "ontological" account of sexuality, is far from clear.

16. See, for example, Christopher Lasch's account of the effect of liberalism on the family in his *Haven in a Heartless World* (New York: Basic Books, 1977).

17. In particular I think that Everett is incorrect in implying that the only way that the church challenged the empire was through celibacy. It is extremely important to recognize that the kind of family that the church started to create from the beginning was a means to gain a critical edge against its wider society.

Moreover even though Everett is right to suggest that no church, not even "the Catholic church, in our current pluralist context can provide a total ritual environment in which people grow up with their sexual activities already integrated into the symbolism of Church and family" (p. 83), I suspect a more normative form of sectarianism will be required if we have any hope of articulating and institutionalizing a form of sexual life appropriate to Christians.

18. I am using the locution "singleness" rather than celibacy, as it is by no means clear that they are the same. Celibacy denotes a life-long vocation, while "singleness" may be a form of life assumed for awhile without excluding the possibility of marriage. While both may be sexually celibate, the rationale for their celibacy is not necessarily of the same order. For an extremely insightful article on singleness that criticizes the church's limitation of the category to the religious, see Mary Jo Weaver, "Singleness and the Family," *Commonweal,* October 26, 1979, pp. 588–591.

19. For an extremely interesting interpretation of the *Haustafeln,* see John Howard Yoder, *The Politics of Jesus* (Grand Rapids, Mich.: Eerdmans, 1972), pp. 163–192.

20. Many interpret Ephesians 5:21–33 to mean that marriage is a paradigm of the unity of Christ and his church, but in the passage itself the analogy works the other way, as the relationship between Christ and his church is the paradigm for marriage.

21. For a fuller development of this point see my "Self-Sacrifice as Demonic: A Theological Response to Jonestown," *Violence and Religious Commitment in the Seventies,* ed. by Ken Levi (forthcoming).

22. Donald Goergen argues this well in his *The Sexual Celibate* (New York: Seabury Press, 1975), p. 107.

23. It must be remembered that for Christians parenting is not simply a biological role, but an office in a community which everyone in the church shares to some extent. That biological parents bear a particular responsibility for the rearing of children is but one of the ways Christians are reminded how deeply we are anchored in "nature" and it manifests the church's stake in exclusive commitments.

24. Rosemary Haughton, "Marriage: An Old, New Fairy Tale," in *A Curious Tradition: Marriage Among Christians,* ed. James Burtchaell, C.S.C. (Notre Dame, Ind.: Ave Maria Press, 1977), p. 136. All other page references in the text.

25. Traditionally all that marrying "in the Lord" meant was simply that Christians should marry other Christians. See, for example, the discussion by E. Schillebeeckx in his *Marriage: Secular Reality and Saving Mystery* (London: Sheed and Ward, 1956), pp. 192–202. Schillebeeckx rightly emphasizes that the early Christians did not think they were "spiritualizing" marriage, but rather that their Christian commitment gave marriage a new intentionality. Thus Christian marriage did not happen in spite of the human institution of marriage, but in it. That does not mean that

Christian marriage can be justified because it involves some special magic that insures domestic bliss and happiness. Rather Christian marriage is justified because it is what Christians are called to do for the building up of the community of the faithful.

26. Christians have far too readily underwritten the romantic assumption that people "fall" into love and then get married. We would be much better advised to suggest that love does not create marriage; rather marriage provides a good training ground to teach us what love involves. Indeed one of the assumptions that Christians should challenge is the general belief that love is an intrinsic aspect of "natural" marriage. There is simply no good reason to think that, as many cultures provide very acceptable forms of marriage without requiring the couple to "love" one another. The relation between love and marriage is not necessarily peculiar to Christians, though I suspect the kind of love characteristic of Christian marriage has distinctive aspects. Moreover I think we should be hesitant to identify this distinctiveness with "self-sacrifice," as no marriage can long survive as a truthful relation built on "self-sacrifice." Rather the distinctiveness of love between Christians must rest on the fact that they share a commitment in common that provides the basis not to fear the truth about themselves or their relation.

It has been suggested to me that my positing of Hauerwas' Law "You always marry the wrong person," though meant to challenge romanticism, presupposes romanticism. That may be, but the deeper intent of the "law" is to suggest that marriage among Christians requires an account that allows us to form a life together where fidelity and love are required without assuming "common interests." We learn to love the other not because they are like us but because they are not. See, for example, my "Love and Marriage," *The Cresset,* 40/8 (June 1977), pp. 20–21.

27. There are many roles in the church, but the roles of singleness and marriage are particularly fundamental, since they derive immediately from what the community is about. Thus "singleness" is not first justified because of the requirements of certain tasks or functions, but because it is symbolically crucial to the church's understanding of itself as an eschatological community.

28. Goergen, pp. 98–99.

29. I suspect that part of the current difficulty of developing a sexual ethic for young people is the absence of any other signs and rituals for becoming an adult. Thus sexual experimentation and/or involvement become the signs in the youth subculture that one has "grown up." Of course rituals of initiation into adulthood only make sense when being an adult involves special privileges and responsibilities because of the tasks it requires.

11: WHY ABORTION IS A RELIGIOUS ISSUE

1. It is not my intention to argue that all anti-abortion positions presuppose religious claims, but it is my own view that the strongest arguments against abortion involve religious presuppositions. Moreover, I suspect that most anti-abortion arguments are parasitic on religious convictions, but that is a topic for another paper. However, as Philip Devine has recently suggested, "Any moral argument, including mine, takes as its starting point a set of intuitions, and a determined defender of forms of killing against which I have argued can regard my intuitions as religious responses. The difficulty is our lack of criterion for distinguishing religious from secular norms. Perhaps prohibitions on bribery are religious ones, for example: the practice is forbidden in the Torah (Deuteronomy 16:19) and is consistent with at least the minimum

conditions of social life. In any event, it is necessary to face the following questions: Why should we care so much about infants? Why should the status of those who are not able to bargain for their rights not be a matter of the convenience of those who are able to do so? Why should we object to the use of small children in cancer research, if their parents consent and any damaged subjects are painlessly killed?'' *The Ethics of Homicide* (Ithaca, N.Y.: Cornell University Press, 1978), pp. 207–208.

2. Devine provides a very nuanced account of how a religiously based judgment is not thereby excluded from constitutional and/or legal expression. As he suggests, ''Although the precise way in which religion bears on morality, and morality on politics and law, is a matter requiring considerable discussion, it is safe to say that someone who resolves not to let his religious beliefs influence his moral ones, or his moral beliefs influence his political ones, either is willfully perverse or does not know what it is to hold a moral or a religious conviction. And there are limits to how far one can go in accommodating those whose beliefs are different from one's own without wholly compromising one's adherence to one's positions.'' *The Ethics of Homicide,* pp. 205–206.

3. My previous reflections on abortion are in *Vision and Virtue: Essays in Christian Ethical Reflection* (South Bend, Ind.: Fides/Claretian, 1974), pp. 127–165.

4. For my methodological presuppositions see my *Truthfulness and Tragedy: Further Investigations in Christian Ethics* (Notre Dame, Ind.: University of Notre Dame Press, 1977), pp. 15–39. Influenced by Kovesi's account of ''moral notions,'' I emphasized in *Vision and Virtue* that ''abortion'' is a category requiring a set of practices to be intelligible. However I did not develop the conceptual strategy to make clear how those practices were narrative-dependent.

5. Indeed, that is what I take much of the casuistry about abortion in the Christian tradition to have been doing. Such casuistry makes sense when it is serving a community that shares a common viewpoint on these matters. When such shared presuppositions are no longer present, no amount of casuistry can force agreement. And that is exactly the problem with so much of the reflection on abortion—namely, it attempts argument in the absence of the presuppositions that undergird the argument. For an excellent treatment of the Church's reflection on abortion, see John Connery, *Abortion: The Development of the Roman Catholic Perspective* (Chicago: Loyola University Press, 1977).

6. Alasdair MacIntrye has argued that this is not accidental for ''it is impossible in our culture to find a systematic way of using such words as 'ethical' and 'moral' which does not already embody not merely a particular morality, but a particular contentious morality which is at war with its rivals. [And] because disagreements among moral philosophers parallel and reflect the disagreements among moral agents themselves—moral philosophers turn out to be merely the most articulate and systematic examples of moral agents—philosophy cannot as of now resolve these rivalries in any logically compelling way.'' ''How to Identify Ethical Principles,'' *The Belmont Report: Ethical Principles and Guidelines for the Protection of Human Subjects of Research* (Washington, D.C.: DHEW Publication No. (OS) 78-0013), article 10, p. 3.

7. For discussion of these presuppositions, see ''Must a Patient Be a Person to Be a Patient, Or, My Uncle Charlie Is Not Much of a Person But He Is Still My Uncle Charlie,'' in *Truthfulness and Tragedy,* pp. 127–131; and Joseph Margolis, ''Human Life: Its Worth and Bringing It to an End,'' in *Infanticide and the Value of Life,* ed. Marvin Kohl (New York: Prometheus Books, 1975), p. 183.

8. Linda Bird Francke, *The Ambivalence of Abortion* (New York: Random House, 1978).

9. Ibid., p. 61. Another respondent says, "My feeling at that time was not one of shame, but of sadness. I tried not to think of the fetus as a baby, but I did. I wanted it over as quickly as possible emotionally. Mostly I wanted the option of divorcing my husband. That was the prime reason for the abortion. He never realized it at that time and still doesn't. We've been married sixteen years, and we've had a difficult time," p. 107.

10. Ibid., p. 47.

11. Ibid., p. 95.

12. Ibid., p. 81.

13. Ibid., p. 133. Or as a Jewish couple responded to their son and daughter-in-law's decision to have an abortion, "It's a special thing, you know, a grandchild. It's continuity. And if you have a strong family, which we do, then it's the first dividend. It's more than loss of family continuity, too. Jews are being screwed out of existence. Who uses birth control? Who gets all these abortions? We're being physically wiped out," p. 20.

14. Susan Nicholson, *Abortion and the Roman Catholic Church* (Knoxville, Tenn.: Religious Ethics, Inc., 1978).

15. Ibid., p. 7. Dr. Nicholson's account is almost completely dependent on John T. Noonan's *Contraception: A History of the Treatment by the Catholic Theologian* (Cambridge, Mass.: Harvard University Press, 1966). I think it fair to say that Noonan's account of the relations between contraception and abortion should be read as a supplement to Nicholson's summary; otherwise the complexity of the relation can be lost.

16. Nicholson, p. 11.

17. Nicholson's critique of the way the principle of double effect has been traditionally stated and Germain Grisez's revision of it seems to me to be largely correct. (Cf. Germain Grisez, *Abortion, the Myths, the Realities, and the Arguments* [New York: Corpus Books, 1970]). However, for a recent defense of double effect that does not seem to involve the difficulties of those theories dependent on analogy with self-defense, see Devine, *The Ethics of Homicide,* pp. 106–133. I find it curious, in the light of Nicholson's trenchant criticism of double effect, that she continues to assume that the distinction between ordinary and extraordinary is valid. It may be that she simply accepts the distinction in order to show that Roman Catholics have failed to apply it consistently to abortion, but it is a distinction that has at least as many, if not more, problems than double effect.

18. For a similar point, see *Vision and Virtue* pp. 20–29 and 154.

19. Nicholson, p. 49.

20. Ibid., p. 50. Thomson's justly famous article, "A Defense of Abortion," appeared in *Philosophy and Public Affairs,* 1971, pp. 47–66.

21. Nicholson, p. 50.

22. Nicholson argues effectively that while it may be correct to describe aborting as "killing" and disconnecting the violinist as "letting die," no moral importance hangs on this, since the distinction between acting and refraining does not carry any immediate moral implications. Ibid., pp. 53–54.

23. Ibid., p. 53.

24. Ibid., pp. 54–55.

25. Ibid., p. 55.

26. Ibid., p. 57. Later Nicholson uses this argument to defend therapeutic abortion to save the life of the mother on grounds that even parents are not duty-bound to assist their child at the expense of their own life (p. 64). Even though I am in agreement with

Dr. Nicholson's conclusion, I am less sure than she that we have such a clear idea of what is and is not required of parents in respect to care of their children. Indeed, that seems exactly the point at issue.

27. Thomson, p. 65, quoted in Nicholson, pp. 58–59.

28. Nicholson, p. 59.

29. Ibid., p. 55.

30. It does not follow from this, however, that the church must thereby prohibit all abortions following rape. Rather, Christian women might at least consider bearing such a child; correspondingly, if she does so choose, the church must provide the sufficient support.

31. For a more extended argument concerning this point, see my "Rights, Duties, and Experimentation on Children: A Critical Response to Worsfold and Bartholome," *Research Involving Children: Appendix* (Washington, D.C.: DHEW Publication, No. [OS] 77-00005, 1977), article 5, pp. 1–24; and my "Theological Reflections on *In Vitro* Fertilization," *Research Involving Human In Vitro Fertilization and Embryo Transfer: Report of Ethics Advisory Board of Department of Health, Education, and Welfare* (Washington, D.C.: HEW Publication, 1979), article 5, pp. 1–20.

32. There is no way that the problem of teenage pregnancy can be separated from the issue of sexual conduct. Indeed, one of the great problems seems to be the refusal of parents to recognize that their daughters are "sexually active." As Francke points out, "instead of dealing with her problems maturely and encouraging her to use contraception, they pretend this is a one-time accident. In contrast, Dr. Lonnie Myers, midwestern chairman of Sex Education Counselors and Therapists, believes that parents should start talking about contraception to their children when they are as young as four years old. 'We insist on the absolute integrity of our children's development, yet we distort matters of sex,' says Myers. 'Most sex is recreational, but we continue to tell kids it's something mommies and daddies do only when they love each other and want a baby. That's lying!' " *The Ambivalence of Abortion*, p. 211. Without question Dr. Myers is correct that we need a more honest and realistic approach to discussing sex with children, but his claim that most sex is "recreational" is as illusory as the claim that most sex is an expression of "love" or to have babies. The question is not how sex is or is not used, but how it ought to be formed to embody those forms of life we most care about.

33. For an argument against the whole idea that we "choose" to have children, see my "Having and Learning to Care for Retarded Children," *Truthfulness and Tragedy*, pp. 147–156. The articles in note 31 above are also relevant.

34. Francke, p. 108. One of the often overlooked consequences of abortion is how it implicitly requires us to try to be too "perfect" as parents. For if children are aborted because we are not ready for them, the assumption is that there is a time when we will be "ready" and be able to do everything "right." That kind of compulsiveness for perfection can only rob parenting of the joy that comes from the sheer contingencies of our children.

12: ABORTION: WHY THE ARGUMENTS FAIL

1. Roe v. Wade, 410 U.S. 113.

2. For example see Mary Anne Warren, "On the Moral and Legal Status of Abortion," in *Contemporary Issues in Bioethics*, ed. I. Beauchamp and L. Walters (Encino: Dickenson Publishing Co., 1978), pp. 222–225. Warren's argument in this

respect is common in current philosophical literature. Perhaps the most celebrated form of it is Michael Tooley's article, "Abortion and Infanticide," in *The Rights and Wrongs of Abortion*, ed. M. Cohen, T. Nagel, and T. Scanlon (Princeton, N.J.: Princeton University Press, 1974), pp. 52–84.

3. Thus Warren argues that "the moral community consists of all and only *people*, rather than all and only human beings," and the characteristics of the former she takes to be consciousness, reasoning, self-motivated activity, the capacity to communicate whatever the means, and presence of self-concepts, pp. 223–224. For an extremely interesting article dealing with the ambiguity of deciding whether a class of beings are human see Edmund Pincoffs, "Membership Decisions and the Limits of Moral Obligation," in *Abortion: New Directions for Policy Studies*, ed. E. Manier, W. Liu, and D. Solomon (Notre Dame, Ind.: University of Notre Dame Press, 1977), pp. 31–49. I have argued elsewhere against the significance of "person" as a moral ascription, but it is hard to deny its significance in a society such as ours. For the idea of "person" embodies our attempt to recognize that everyone has a moral status prior to any role they might assume. It therefore represents the profound egalitarian commitment of our culture. The difficulty, of course, is that the notion of being a "person" seems to carry with it psychological implications that simply exclude certain beings from being treated with respect. See my *Truthfulness and Tragedy* (Notre Dame, Ind.: University of Notre Dame Press, 1977), pp. 127–132, 157–163.

4. John Noonan *A Private Choice: Abortion in America in the Seventies* (New York: The Free Press, 1979), pp. 2–3. In his earlier essay, "An Almost Absolute Value in History," Noonan had argued that conception is the decisive moment of humanization because "at conception the being receives the genetic code. It is this genetic information which determines his characteristics, which is the biological carrier of the possibility of human wisdom, which makes him a self-evolving being. A being with a human genetic code is man." In John T. Noonan, ed., *The Morality of Abortion* (Cambridge, Mass.: Harvard University Press, 1970), pp. 1–59. Noonan obviously no longer regards such empirical claims as decisive for establishing the moral status of the fetus, though they may certainly be sufficient for claiming that the fetus is a human being. Underlying the issue of the relation between the moral and descriptive status of the fetus may be the larger assumption that the distinction between facts and values, or better, how values include factual claims, makes sense. Thus the claim that the anti-abortionist is confusing a "moral" claim with a "factual" claim may involve the unwarranted assumption that such "facts" are not moral.

5. Thus Roger Wertheimer suggests that the anti-abortionist "realizes that, unless he uses religious premises, premises inadmissible in the court of common morality, he has no way of categorically condemning the killing of a fetus except by arguing that a fetus is a person." "Understanding the Abortion Argument," in *The Rights and Wrongs of Abortion*, p. 37. But, as we shall see, the assumption that there is a common morality with an agreed upon content can hardly be accepted in our society. Moreover, I hope to show that theological convictions play quite a different role than Wertheimer and many others seem to assume. For there is no theological means to determine when life begins. Indeed, a Christian understanding of the morality of abortion should make such a question irrelevant.

6. Noonan has made a strong case, for example, for a constitutional amendment that would not prohibit states from protecting unborn life if it is the will of their legislatures. Such an amendment would at least provide the possibility of a more refined moral debate on this issue in our society. Moreover it might result in laws that

do not have the negative effect on other institutions, such as the family, that the current abortion ruling seems to involve. See Noonan, *A Private Choice,* pp. 178–188.

7. Alasdair MacIntyre, "How Virtues Become Vices," in *Evaluation and Explanation in Biomedical Sciences,* ed. Engelhardt and Spicker (Dordrecht: Reidel: 1974), p. 104.

8. Ironically the anti-traditional stance of liberalism results in self-deception, since liberalism is only intelligible in the light of its history. It is, of course, true that liberalism is an extremely complex phenomenon that is not easily characterized even by the most sophisticated forms of political theory. I associate liberalism, however, with the political philosophy of Rawls and Nozick, the political science of Dahl, and the economics of neo-capitalism. There often appear to be deep disagreements between the advocates of liberalism in America, but such disagreements are finally arguments between brothers.

9. Alasdair MacIntyre, "How to Identify Ethical Principles," *The Belmont Report: Ethical Principles and Guidelines for the Protection of Human Subjects of Research,* I (Washington, D.C.: DHEW Publication No. (OS) 78-0013, 1978), article 10, pp. 9–10. For an extremely able development of this argument, see Philip Devine, *The Ethics of Homicide* (Ithaca, N.Y.: Cornell University Press, 1978). Devine argues "that acts of homicide are prima facie seriously wrong because they are acts of homicide, and not for any supposedly more fundamental reason, such as that they tend to produce disutility or are unjust or unkind, and that this prima facie wrongness cannot be overridden by merely utilitarian considerations," p. 11. He correctly refuses to try to give a further theoretical account for why unjustified homicide is wrong, since such an account necessarily has the effect of qualifying the prohibition.

10. MacIntyre, "How to Identify Ethical Principles," p. 10. Garry Wills' recent study of Jefferson certainly requires a reconsideration of Jefferson's position vis-à-vis Locke. Wills makes clear that Jefferson's position owes more to the communitarian strains of the Scottish Common Sense philosophers, such as Hutcheson, than had been suspected. An indication of the power of Locke and the general liberal-contractarian tradition in America is that, in spite of what Jefferson's own views might have been, they were simply interpreted through the eyes of Locke. See Garry Wills, *Inventing America: Jefferson's Declaration of Independence* (Garden City, N.Y.: Doubleday, 1978).

11. MacIntyre, "How to Identify Ethical Principles," p. 22. This change in perspective also makes clear why so many attempt to form all moral arguments in the language of "right." "Rights" become our way to protect ourselves from one another.

12. John Rawls, *A Theory of Justice* (Cambridge, Mass.: Harvard University Press, 1971), p. 327. One of the difficulties with Rawls' assumption that the meaning of justice can be separated from a conception of the good is that he ends up endorsing an understanding of the good to which he would object on other grounds. For, in spite of Rawls' richer view of the relation of individual and community in the last sections of *A Theory of Justice,* methodologically his position does not exclude the economic man enshrined in liberal theory.

13. Francis Canavan, "The Dilemma of Liberal Pluralism," *The Human Life Review* 5/3 (Summer 1979), p. 7. The social and political experience of the American people has often contained more profound moral commitments than our commitment to liberal ideology could express. As a result we have often been unable to give some of our most significant achievements political standing.

14. Ibid., p. 9.

15. Ibid., p. 14.

16. Ibid., p. 15.

17. Noonan, *A Private Choice*, pp. 153-169.

18. It is interesting, however, that women undergoing abortion often continue to describe the fetus as a baby or child. See, for example, Linda Bird Francke, *The Ambivalence of Abortion* (New York: Random House, 1978).

19. Noonan, *A Private Choice*, p. 175. Warren's attempt to deny that her arguments imply infanticide are interesting in this respect. She says that it would be wrong to kill a new-born infant, "because even if its parents do not want it and would not suffer from its destruction, there are other people who would like to have it, and would in all probability, be deprived of a great deal of pleasure by its destruction. Thus, infanticide is wrong for reasons analogous to those which make it wrong to wantonly destroy natural resources, or great works of art. Secondly, most people, at least in this country, value infants and would much prefer that they be preserved, even if foster parents are not immediately available," p. 227. Warren seems to feel no difficulty in making the prohibition against infanticide depend on whether someone might want a child. Moreover she is rigorously consistent and clear that if an "unwanted or defective infant is born into a society which cannot afford and/or is not willing to care for it, then its destruction is permissible," p. 227. It does not seem to occur to her that we ought to be the kind of society, no matter what our material appetites, that is able to receive children, even retarded children, into our midst. Her argument is a clear example, therefore, of the assumption that the rightness or wrongness of acts can be abstracted from the kind of people we ought to be.

20. Noonan, *A Private Choice*, pp. 90-96.

21. Ibid., p. 17.

22. The abortion decisions of the current Supreme Court can in some ways be interpreted as further extensions of the arguments of the laissez faire capitalist, only now they are being applied to issues of personal morality. Just as those earlier decisions that enshrined for a time such views as the law of the land regarding the regulation of business distorted the law, so do these recent decisions. Indeed there has always been an uneasy tension between our legal tradition and the ideology of liberalism. It may well be, however, that as liberalism has become an increasingly self-fulling prophecy in so many other aspects of our life, so it will ultimately transform our legal tradition.

23. It is my contention that current ethical theory involves an attempt to write about "morality" in a manner required by a liberal society. The very assumption that "ethics" can be a "discipline" separate from political theory and economics seems to me to be an indication of the power of liberalism over our imagination. Such moral philosophies attempt to provide highly formal accounts of the conditions of moral argument and judgment separate from the beliefs of actual agents. One cannot help but admire their attempt to find a way to make moral argument work between people who share no common values, but they fail to see that such accounts too easily become ideologies for the status quo.

24. Stuart Hampshire, "Morality and Pessimism," in *Public and Private Morality* ed. Hamphire (Cambridge: Cambridge University Press, 1978), p. 11.

25. Ibid., p. 13.

26. Ironically, Christians have often tried to construct their arguments by using moral theories, especially the more deontological theories, that make rationality the basis for any moral claim. Though these theories often provide powerful accounts for

why everyone deserves a minimum of respect, by their very structure they exclude the fetus from their account.

27. Stuart Hampshire, "Public and Private Morality," in *Public and Private Morality*, pp. 38–39.

28. Wertheimer, p. 42. See Wertheimer's fine article, "Philosophy on Humanity," in *Abortion: New Directions for Policy Studies* (Notre Dame: University of Notre Dame Press, 1977), pp. 117–136.

29. I suspect that Wertheimer would not deny this point as he is not using "nature" in a theory-laden sense but simply means by it "what is common." Thus whereas we have many everyday experiences with blacks, we do not "bump into" the fetus in the same manner. Yet as I will argue below, there are powerful forms of life which are unintelligible apart from the existence of the fetus.

30. See for example John Connery's excellent history of moral reflection on the subject, *Abortion: The Development of the Roman Catholic Perspective* (Chicago: Loyola University Press, 1977).

31. In a sense, Christian discussion of abortion has been too "ethical" and insufficiently theological. In effect we became the victim of our own highly refined casuistry on the subject and failed to rethink the theological context that made the casuistry intelligible in the first place. Thus consideration of whether certain acts of abortion might be permissible were abstracted from the community's narrative that made the prohibition of abortion intelligible. No community can or should avoid casuistical reflection, but it should always remember that the function of casuistry is to help the community save its language and judgments from distortion through analogical comparisons. And control of the analogies ultimately depends on paradigms rooted in the community's experience as interpreted through its central narratives.

32. There is a broader issue involved here, which can only be mentioned. For just as liberalism has often "worked" only because it could continue to count on forms of life that it did not support and even worked against, so current ethical theory has often seemed intelligible because it continued to be able to rely on moral language and descriptions for which it can give little basis. Thus contemporary ethical theory tends to concentrate on questions of decision and justification and avoids issues of how we learn to see and describe our experience morally.

33. Karl Barth, *Church Dogmatics*, III/4, trans. MacKay, et al. (Edinburgh: T. and T. Clark, 1961), p. 416.

34. There is nothing about this claim that requires that all abortions are to be prohibited. Indeed, when abortions may be permitted will depend on the experience and discussion of a community formed by the conviction of God's sovereignty over life. The broad theological claims I am developing here cannot determine concrete cases, though they can determine how abortion as a practice can and should be understood and evaluated.

35. In his *The Culture of Narcissism* (New York: Norton, 1978), Christopher Lasch suggests that a people's sense of historical time and their attitudes toward children are closely interrelated. Thus "the narcissistic personality reflects among other things a drastic shift in our sense of historical time. Narcissism emerges as the typical form of character structure in a society that has lost interest in the future. Psychiatrists who tell parents not to live through their offspring; married couples who postpone or reject parenthood, often for good practical reasons; social reformers who urge zero population growth, all testify to a pervasive uneasiness about reproduction—to widespread doubts, indeed, about whether our society should reproduce itself at all. Under these conditions, the thought of our eventual suppression and

death becomes utterly insupportable and gives rise to attempts to abolish old age and to extend life indefinitely. When men find themselves incapable of taking an interest in earthly life after their own death, they wish for eternal youth; for the same reason they no longer care to reproduce themselves. When the prospect of being superseded becomes intolerable, parenthood itself, which guarantees that it will happen, appears almost as a form of self-destruction,'' p. 211.

36. For a fuller presentation of this theme see my *Truthfulness and Tragedy*, pp. 147–156.

37. The issue of when life begins will of course come up in considering hard cases. Connery, for example, provides a good overview of the history of such reflection in his book. Yet just as hard cases make bad law, so hard cases can distort our moral reflection if, in the process of our reflection on them, we forget the more positive commitments that make the casuistry intelligible. It is noteworthy, however, as Connery makes clear, that the question of when life begins has always been a side issue for Christian casuistry. Rather, the concern has been whether the taking of the life of the fetus under particular circumstances is analogous to other situations where it is unavoidable or permissible that life be taken.

Index

293